KPI MEGA LIBRARY

17,000 KEY PERFORMANCE INDICATORS

RACHAD BAROUDI PhD

ISBN: 1451551665
ISBN-13: 9781451551662

Scotts Valley, California
The United States of America

DEDICATIONS

To My Family…

- My father's encouragement and care since my childhood has given me the motivation to complete my studies.

- My Mother's simple belief in me and my abilities are the pearls she has worn with humility all her life.

- No book of this size can be completed without disruption of ones normal family routine. The key here was the support, sacrifice, and love of my wife.

PREFACE

The purpose of this book is to give the reader a quick and effective access to the most appropriate Key Performance Indicator (KPI). The 17,000 KPIs are categorized in a logical and alphabetical order.

Today, many organizations are spending a lot of funds on building their strategic planning and performance management capabilities. One of the challenges that currently exists, is the difficulty of knowing what KPIs are used in similar situations. The main objective of this book is to let the reader know what KPIs are available for measuring performance of a specific industry, sector, and functional area.

The background colors have the following meanings throughout the book for simplification and easier reference:

Section	Chapter	Group	KPI
A. Organization	Industry	Function	KPI Description
B. Government	Sector	Function	KPI Description
C. International	Topic	Source	KPI Description

This book is divided into three sections. There are 89 Chapters, 761 Functions, 114 Sources, and 17,000 Key Performance Indicators. The book contents are grouped based on the following categories:

Section	Chapter	Group	KPI
A. Organization	32	317	6,600
B. Government	33	444	8,600
C. International	24	114	1,800
Total	89	875	17,000

The listed KPIs are for public and private institutions. Government agencies' internal KPIs related to in-house processes, human resources, and other organizational activities could also be found under "Organization" section (A).

TABLE OF CONTENTS

A. ORGANIZATION KPIs

TABLE OF CONTENTS

A. ORGANIZATION KPIs

TABLE OF CONTENTS

A. ORGANIZATION KPIs

TABLE OF CONTENTS

A. ORGANIZATION KPIs

TABLE OF CONTENTS

A. ORGANIZATION KPIs

TABLE OF CONTENTS

A. ORGANIZATION KPIs

TABLE OF CONTENTS

B. GOVERNMENT KPIs

TABLE OF CONTENTS

B. GOVERNMENT KPIs

TABLE OF CONTENTS

B. GOVERNMENT KPIs

TABLE OF CONTENTS

B. GOVERNMENT KPIs

TABLE OF CONTENTS

B. GOVERNMENT KPIs

TABLE OF CONTENTS

B. GOVERNMENT KPIs

TABLE OF CONTENTS

B. GOVERNMENT KPIs

TABLE OF CONTENTS

C. INTERNATIONAL KPIs

TABLE OF CONTENTS

C. INTERNATIONAL KPIs

TABLE OF CONTENTS

C. INTERNATIONAL KPIs

SECTION A

ORGANIZATION

6600 Key Performance Indicators

ORGANIZATION CHAPTERS
(1 to 32)

1. Agriculture

Farming

of culverts installed

# of drains constructed

# of drains de-silted

# of dryers

# of farm roads graveled

# of lots bund leveling completed

# of nurseries for seedling production

% access to buy farm land

% availability of resources

% land utilization rate

% management structures and systems are up to standards

% of drainage works completed

% of farm roads upgraded

Milling efficiency rate

Irrigation & Drainage

% efficiency of water use

% of estimated soil moisture

Irrigation return interval

Irrigation scheduling coefficient

Rate of applied volume of water

Ratio of water charges collected / operation and maintenance expenses

Ratio of water charges collected / water charges due

Ratio of water charges due / operation and maintenance expenses

Productivity & Efficiency

of crop development programs

# of demonstration plots

# of hybrid varieties planted

# of permits / licenses on hand

# of total area of land cultivated

# of total land irrigated

# of total quantity of fertilizers, chemicals and other agro-inputs

% increase in production

% of crop extension projects completed satisfactory

% of weather impact on production

Total volume of production potential

Standards & Compliance

% air emissions compliance

% air quality compliance

% of transportation system and logistics are in compliance

% of waste discharge compliance

% prescribed burning compliance

Quality and timely policy advice

1. Agriculture

Volume of wastewater discharge

2. Banking & Investment

Banking

# of brokered deposits

# of changes in loan classifications

# of early pay-off loans

# of large changes in large-balance deposit accounts

# of other Securities

# of past due loans

% adjusted return on assets

% annual equivalent rate

% capital adequacy ratio

% efficiency ratio

% financial self-sufficiency

% gross debt service ratio

% of subprime mortgages

% of total value of subprime mortgages

% operating self-sufficiency

% portfolio at risk

% portfolio yield

% total debt service ratio

Adjusted net operation income as % of average assets

Adjusted operating income

Advances to deposit ratio (ADR)

Agricultural loans

Agricultural loans yield

Applicable income taxes

Assets growth rate

Assets per domestic office

Available-for-sale securities

Average assets during quarter

Average assets per employee

Average earning assets/average assets

Average interest-bearing funds/ average assets

Average personnel expense per employee

Average sum deposited in new deposit accounts

Average value of past due loans

Brokered deposits maturing < 1 year to brokered deposits

Brokered deposits to deposits

Capital adequacy ratio (CAR)

Cash dividends declared

Cash dividends to net income

Commercial & industrial loans yield

2. Banking & Investment

Commercial loans

Common & preferred capital

Core capital ratio

Core deposits

Credit card yield

Current tax equivalent adjustment

Demand deposits

Deposit service charges

Deposits in foreign offices

Domestic banking offices (#)

Earnings coverage of net loss

Efficiency ratio

Estimated tax benefit

Federal funds purchased & repos ratio

Federal funds purchased & resales

Federal funds sold & resales ratio

Federal funds sold and resales

Federal home loan bank borrowing maturing over 1 year

Federal home loan bank borrowing maturing under 1 year

Fiduciary activities

Foreign branches (#)

Foreign office deposits ratio

Foreign securities

Goodwill impairment

Gross loans (average balance)

Gross margin on managed assets

Held-to-maturity securities

Income from lease financing

Income on loans & leases

Individual loans

Individual loans yield

Insurance commissions and fees

Interest and fee on loans

Interest expense as % of average assets

Interest expense/average assets

Interest income (TE) as % of average assets

Interest income (TE)/average assets

Interest on all other deposits

Interest on deposits in foreign offices

Interest on due from banks

Interest on federal funds purchased & repos

Interest on federal funds sold/resales

Interest on mortgages & leases

Interest on subordinated notes & debentures

2. Banking & Investment

Interest on time deposit over $100M

Interest on trading liabilities and other borrowings

Interest-bearing bank balances

Interest-bearing bank balances ratio

Interest-bearing funds ratio

Investment banking, advisory income

Loan & lease allowance net losses

Loan & lease allowance to loans & leases not held for sale

Loan & lease allowance to total loans & lease

Loan and lease allowance

Loan and lease net gain/loss

Loans and leases in foreign offices

Loans held for sale

Loans in foreign offices yield

Loans not held for sale

Money market deposit accounts

Mortgage backed securities

Mortgage backed securities ratio

Municipal securities

Net extraordinary Items

Net income

Net income adjusted sub S as % of average assets

Net income as % of average assets

Net interest income

Net interest income (TE) (% of average earning assets)

Net Interest income (TE) as % of average assets

Net interest margin

Net international income

Net loan charge-offs

Net loans & leases growth rate

Net loans & leases to assets

Net loans & leases to core deposits

Net loans & leases to deposits

Net loans and leases

Net loans, leases & standby letters of credit to assets

Net loss to average loan & leases

Net new money

Net non core funding dependence

Net non core funding dependence as % of average assets

Net operating income

Net operating income as % of average assets

Net servicing fees

Net short term liabilities to assets

Non interest expense

2. Banking & Investment
Non interest income
Non interest-bearing cash and due from banks
Noncurrent loans & leases to gross loans and lease
Non-interest expense as % of average assets
Non-interest income as % of average assets
Non-Investment ORE
Occupancy expense
Occupancy expense as % average assets
Officer, shareholder loans (#)
Officer, shareholder loans ($)
Other borrowed money ratio
Other borrowing maturing over 1 year
Other borrowing maturing under 1 year
Other intangible amortization
Other interest income
Other loans and leases in domestic offices
Other net gains/losses
Other non interest income
Other operating expense
Other operating expenses as % of average assets
Other real estate owned
Other savings deposits ratio
Other securities ratio
Other tax equivalent adjustments
Overhead less non-interest income as % of average assets
Personnel expense
Personnel expense as % of average assets
Premises, fixed assets and capitalized leases
Pretax net operating income
Pretax net operating income (TE) as % of average assets
Pretax operating income
Pretax operating income (TE) as % of average assets
Provision for loan/lease losses
Provision—loan/lease losses as % of average assets
Ratio of active depositor to dormant depositor
Real estate loans
Real estate loans yield
Realized G/L avail. for sale sec.
Realized G/L Hld to maturity sec.
Realized gain/loss secs as % of average assets
Retain earns to average total equity
Retained earnings
Short term assets to short term liabilities
Short term non core funding growth rate

2. Banking & Investment

Subordinated notes & debentures

Subordinated notes & debentures ratios

Tax exempt

Tax-exempt securities income

Tier 1 capital

Tier one capital growth rate

Tier one leverage capital as % of average assets

Time deposit of $100M or more ratio

Time deposits of $100M or more

Time deposits ratio

Time deposits under $100 thousand

Total acceptances & other liabilities

Total acceptances and other assets

Total deposits

Total earning assets

Total interest expense

Total interest income

Total interest-bearing deposits ratio

Total investments

Total liabilities & capital

Total liabilities (including mortgages)

Total loans & lease yield

Total loans or loans in domestic offices yield

Total non interest income

Total of un-invested funds

Total overhead expense

Total overhead expense as % of average assets

Total quantity of new deposit accounts

Total sum deposited in new deposit accounts

Total value of past due loans

Trading account assets

Trading account income

Trading, venture capital, securitization income

Transaction accounts yield

U.S. treasury and agency securities

UBPR liabilities

UBPR non interest income & expenses

UBPR other income/expense ratios

UBPR yield or cost ratios

Unearned income

US treasury & agency (excluding MBS) ratio

Investment

of investments exceeding 5% of net assets

# of new investment proposals

2. Banking & Investment

of venture capital deals

% of investment proposals worth setting up a meeting with

Annual equivalent rate

Average delivery cost

Average size of venture capital deal

Average total return to investors

Capacity utilization

Contingency %

Cost by sale

Customer lifetime value

Growth against market

Internal rate of return

Investment in unconsolidated subsidiaries

Investment Interest income

Management fees as % of fund size

Market value of fund

Net present value (NPV)

Net short term liabilities to assets

New product development rate

Order processing cost

Profit/(loss) retained

Ratio of members and pensioners

Return on capital

ROI on invested venture capital

Short term assets to short term liabilities

Short term investments growth rate

Short term investments to short term non core funding

Total invested venture capital

Total investment securities (book) ratio

Total investment securities ratio

Un-invested funds

3. Communication & PR

Communication Training

of conference sponsorships

# of course completions

# of courses developed

# of meetings attended

# of workshops

Community Investment

of employee volunteering

# of mandatory social contributions

3. Communication & PR
Index community score
Total community contribution
Total voluntary social contributions

Features & Services
# of commercial initiatives
# of new features/services
% of new of features/services
Total management costs

Fundraising
donation to delivery time
of charitable gifts
% appeal coverage
% assessment accuracy
% donation transportation cost efficiency
% donors financial efficiency
% improved alliances in the community
% of appeal coverage
% of items delivered
% of volunteers working more than x hours
Average cost per gift
Average donation
Average gift amount
Average gift per donor
Cost per dollar raised
Donation-to-delivery time
Donor assessment accuracy
Participation %

Newsletters
# of email subscribers
# of newsletters issued on time
# of hard copy subscribers
# of newsletters published

Webinars
# of attendees
# of messages received/responded to
# of pre/post survey taken
# of webinars

4. Compliance

Business Control
# of analysis of compliance rules
# of data items
% interaction between process owners and compliance officers

4. Compliance
% of distributed operations
% of quantifications of the effort required
% of risk based audit assignments
% of specification and documentation compliance
% of working space maintenance
Total investment in compliance software

Business Operations

# of approval of orders
# of task identified for audit
% correct flow of activities/transactions
% flexibility achieved
Objectivity index
Quality of advice index
Role of officers
Total audit cost / year

Business Practice

# of agreement on terms and usage
# of discovery of hidden dependencies
% adherence to corporate policy
% inconsistencies and redundancies margin
% of clear roles and performance
% of process ownership
Average time to do one audit

Business Processes

# of process improvement activities
% of outsourcing
% of quality of service initiatives
% of time assessment done on all processes
Average time to remediation and/or mitigation of control deficiencies
Business process enrichment and analysis

Compliance Support

# of fraud detection
% of security measured followed as per rules
Average run time

Policies & Procedures

# of obligations
# of permissions
# of prohibitions
# of violations
% flow of activities in normal channels
% of data management according to policy
% of policy compliance
% of process relevant application data
% of resource management according to policies

4. Compliance
% of temporal constraints, resources and requirements needed

5. Construction

Client Satisfaction

% achievement of business committed
% achievement of customer-requested date
% client satisfaction on product
% client satisfaction on service
% of quality standards not met
Average process time

Improve Efficiency

earned man-hours
of critical constraints
# of techniques improved
time to rectify defects
% complexity of core process (affecting delivery)
% cost predictability
% of economical efficiency
% of just-in-time delivery
% of lean production met
Average project workface flow
Flow production
Quick employee startup to guaranteed 100% quality
Quick setup & changeover for 100% quality
Total lost time accounting

Project Build

application average cycle time
built area
caseload
of appliances
# of bath accessories
# of cabinets/counters
# of contingency plans
# of drawings & specifications
# of drywall/tape/texture
# of electrical and trim fixtures
# of exterior doors & garage doors
# of fireplace/stove/insert
# of flat concrete/aprons/patios/sidewalks
# of floor coverings
# of foundation/structural slab-on-grade
# of frame lumber/trusses
# of gutters/downspouts/storm water
# of heating/ventilation/air conditioning

5. Construction

of interior doors/trim/hardware

# of plumbing and trim fixtures

# of siding/exterior Trim

# of site access and street culvert / driveway

# of superintendence on the ground

# of windows/skylights/solar tubes

% material requirements met and secured from source

% of excavation/backfill/grade done

% of material flow to facilitate project

% of roofing/flashing/ventilation done

% of weatherization/fire stuffing/insulation completed

Paint interior/wall coverings

Receivables turnover

Space of landscaping needed

Total receivables

Total space of paint/stain exterior

Project Costs

% reductions in cost from increased plan reliability

Actual construction hours vs. Planned construction hours

Actual construction time

Average cost of employment

Average time for predictability design

Average time spent directly delivering output

Cost of decks/porches/veranda

Cost of electrical service

Cost of fire sprinkler

Cost of goods sold (COGS)

Cost of labor

Cost of materials

Cost of well

Critical path scheduling

Gas or oil costs

Gross profit

Net profit from project

Payables turnover

Sales tax

Septic costs

Square meter price

Total cost of clean-up/recycle/landfill

Total cost of permits & special fees from department of building

Total cost to repair

Work intensity (man hours per m2)

Quality Monitoring

building performance index

5. Construction

of construction drawing and specification review
# of design consistency and constructability analysis
# of forensic defect evaluation
# of on-site inspections/Standard of care
# of remediation and repair recommendations
# of remediation of defects after handing over
# of root cause analysis done
% daylight factor
% of defects entered in the handing-over protocol
% of relevant building code and industry standard compliance
Average time to rectify defects in maintenance period

6. Consulting Services

Budget & Revenue

% chargeable ratio
% consultants generating revenue
% consulting hours generating revenue
% of consultants generating revenue
% of consulting hours that generate revenue
% of profitable projects
% of work chargeability
% realization rate
Average hourly fee
Bill rate
Net profit per project
Training ROI

Legal Service

legal dispute cycle time
legal staff per billion revenue
% correspondence service level
% of cases lost
% total legal Spending as a percentage of revenue
Average cost per lawyer hour
Average cost to litigate a lawsuit
Average response time on request for legal opinion
Average time to prepare patent claims

Service Delivery

completion to billings
of coaching to sub-contractors
% consultant client retention
% consultant retention by client
% consultant utilization rate
% of time sheets in need of correction/validation
% realization of delivery

6. Consulting Services
Annual billable utilization %
Average length of assignments
Backlog of commissioned projects

7. Contracting

Administration

# of credit notes per month
# of targeted value-added activities identified in advance
% of invoice contains all information required to enable prompt payment
% of invoices presented in a timely manner to allow on-time payment
% of reports in relation to the product/service
% realization of cost-reduction targets
% success rate in bringing value added ideas
Quotations requests are turned around within x days

Monitor Implementation

# of backlog items
# of unapproved change-order
% liquidity
% margin variance
Committed cost
Schedule variance

Organization & Management

% of scheduling accuracy & efficiency
% of supervision for total workforce
Average construction time
Efficiency of supervisor to oversee
Efficiency of supervisor to provide direction

Procurement

# of units of stock to offer a reliable service
% of cost breakdown given when requested
% of delivery to made within the agreed time
% of product/service is competitively priced against market rates
% of quantity supplied matches the quantity ordered
% of supporting documentation received within x days
% of time in line with agreed SLA turnaround
Current lead time compares favorably with previous lead time
Total volume of offers discounts

Service Quality

# of days average notice before delays
# of planned "downtime" of the system required
# of targeted cost-reduction activities identified in advance (per year)
# of unplanned "downtime" of the system required
% of acceptable quality of technical information/support provided by contractor for goods supplied

7. Contracting

% of compliance with agreed lead times for repairing the product or restoring service

% of contractor provide notification of any supply problems for orders placed with X days

% of contractors proactive in managing its relationship with final customer

% of product is user-friendly when in use

% of product/service meet the agreed, documented standards

% of product/service to have been reliable /durable

% of resource dedicated to monitoring contractor performance

% of timely attendance on site in response to initial fault report

Subcontractor Performance

of alterations carried out

# of electrical work carried out

# of improvements by specialists

# of mechanical work carried out

# of onsite repairs and installations

# of site demolition

% of plumbing work carried out

8. Customer Service

Call Centre

average call handling time

average speed of answer

of abandoned calls

# of call management operator activities

# of call transfers

# of calls answered within ten seconds

# of complaints cleared up to the satisfaction of the customer within 3 days

# of complaints received

# of contacts per agent

# of hours of 1 on 1 coaching time/agent

# of hours of agent time available for service

# of hours of agent time available for telephone service

# of one call resolutions

# of queries dealt with and cleared up within 1 day

# of unique callers

service calls to travel time

% agent adherence to schedule

% agent utilization

% answer accuracy

% answered calls within automatic call distribution system

% call abandon rate

% completion call rate

% consistency of agent answers

8. Customer Service

% customer calls answered in the first minute

% first contact resolution rate

% lead conversion rate

% of accurate referral when redirect to the correct service

% of agent time spent in direct service

% of all calls abandoned

% of all services calls answered in one minute

% of blocked calls

% of call agent's work time spent speaking to callers

% of callers who attempt and successfully access service

% of calls answered within set timeframe

% of calls presented that get into the system

% of calls that reach an agent

% of calls which are abandoned while in queue

% of cross-sell/up-sell opportunities

% of customers that are satisfied

% of email inquiries responded within 24 hours

% of e-mails answered in one day

% of failure to pass caller data

% of first call resolution

% of lost calls

% of misrouted calls

% of phone calls adherence to script

Abandon rate of incoming phone calls

Agent adherence to schedule %

Agent attendance %

Agent utilization rate

Agents FTEs as % of total call center FTEs

Answered calls per hour

Answering % within 10 seconds

Average # of calls to resolve issue/problem

Average # of times call agents are monitored

Average abandonment time

Average call length

Average cost per call

Average delay while in queue before connecting to an agent

Average hold time of calls

Average quality of call

Average queue time of incoming phone calls

Average revenue per call

Average speed of answer

Average talk time of phone calls

Average time a customer spends with a service agent

Average wait time

8. Customer Service

Average waiting time for a customer to reach a service agent
Average wrap-up time
Call volume
Callbacks made - % to peers
Contact frequency
Cost per minute of handle time
Phone occupancy rate
Total calling time
Total calls received
Total training days delivered to agents
Zero-out or bail rate

Customer Satisfaction

of complaints concerning phone channel
# of complaints per 1,000 pre-paid customers per month
# of complaints per 100 bills per month
# of customer claims
# of customer complaints
# of customer complaints after 1 week of service
# of customer service policy document
# of customers lost
# of footfall counts
# of negative feedbacks from customers
# of user opinions to improve service
% customer invoice accuracy rate
% customer responsiveness
% customer retention
% customer satisfaction
% customer service performance against standard
% customer survey results
% delivered in full to customer
% delivery in full and on time
% of car park usage
% of correct documentation
% of customer claims
% of customer orders delivered in full
% of customer orders delivered on time
% of customers lost
% of office cleanliness
% of order entry accuracy
% of orders delivered on time
% of product damage
% of product returns
% of trained technical experts and certified
% of visitor feeling safe

8. Customer Service

% of visitor postcode data available

Average # of products in customer baskets

Average lead time for all orders

Average response time

Average time spent on customer relations

Average waiting time for check out

Customer satisfaction rating

Customer-loyalty index

Net promoter score

Response rate

Retail crime perception

Satisfied customer index

Mail Centre

of applications completed and sent

# of applications received

# of applications/mail in process

# of applications/pieces opened

% applications / mail in processing

% applications completed

% applications/ pieces opened

Mail Service Quality

of hours of agent time available for mail service

# of service complaints

% of application/transaction errors

% of mail client satisfaction level

% of mail completed within target processing time

% of response accuracy

Average cost per application / mail

Average cycle time

Pass through ratio

Marketing & Sales

of advertising standards complaints

# of customers with post-paid / pre-paid breakdown

# of on-time deliveries

# of product returns

# of sales complaints

# of service awards

% disconnect with overall / post-paid / pre-paid breakdown

% of blended overall / post-paid / pre-paid breakdown

% price comparisons to competition

% usage of electronic links for customer orders

% usage of electronic links for fund transfer

Average # of times the phone rings

Minutes of use with overall / post-paid / pre-paid breakdown

8. Customer Service

Non-voice services as a % of overall revenue

Stakeholder Satisfaction

% distributors satisfaction

% export agents satisfaction

Customer satisfaction index

Stakeholders satisfaction index

Suppliers satisfaction index

Walk-In Service

# of total visitors entering the office

# of visitors who are serviced at agent stations

% of answer accuracy

% of customers use self-service computers

% of first visit resolution

% of visitors receiving agent service to total visitors

Average cost per service

Average time to transaction complete

Average wait time in person

Critical error rate

9. Education

Administration

# of institutional research

% satisfaction with the timeliness and accuracy of reports requested

% users' perceptions of quality of service

Average admissions application response timing

Average admissions telephone response timing

Average printing services reduction of pre-press time

Average time for printing services bulk mail

Average time for registrar's office grade posting

Registrar's office clearing transcript average time

Assessment

# of assessment plan

# of development programs offered to students

# of external program review

# of library usage by teachers and principals

# of student scoring 4 or higher on CST assessments, disaggregated by all subgroups

# of students demonstrating their understanding in a variety of ways

# of students enrolling in 8th grade algebra and reduction in support classes in core areas

# of students grades 4, 7, 9 taking the writing assessment

# of students participating in Algebra performance assessment- grade 8

# of students participating in common ELA, Mathematics, History, and Science assessments

9. Education

of students participating in K-7 mathematics with a focus on Algebra readiness

# of students participating in mathematics performance assessment

# of students reflecting on their own learning and needs based on common assessment results

# of teachers and principals attending professional assessment

# of teachers participating in Algebra performance assessment

# of teachers participating in mathematics performance assessment

# of teachers receiving professional development for writing assessment

# of teachers results-oriented cycles of inquiry

# of teachers using critical information from common assessment results to inform instruction

# of teachers using multiple sources to assess student achievement

# of writing and mathematics assessments developed

# of writing and mathematics assessments scored and reported to teacher, students, and parents

% increase in applications of scholarships

% of ICT user satisfaction rate

% of student diversity

% of student satisfaction

% of student scoring 4 or higher on CST assessments, disaggregated by all subgroups

% of students enrolling in 8th grade algebra and reduction in support classes in core areas

% support for the educational needs of multicultural students

Higher satisfaction responses by ES, MS, & HS teachers and principals of common assessment program

Rating of the institution and its programs by external evaluators

Ratings of the institution and its programs by external audiences

Ratio of nationally accredited programs to programs eligible for national accreditation

Reports of program changes made as the result of internal or external reviews

Career Services

of employer surveyed

# of employers recruiting interns

% employer evaluation of students

% employer satisfaction

% of academic students employed within six months of graduation

% of career interest testing

% of graduates employed in their field of study

% of graduates from undergraduate programs who within six months of graduation are employed

% of graduates from undergraduate programs who within six months of graduation are enrolled in further study

9. Education

% of graduates were satisfied with the usefulness of their education

% of graduates working within six months of leaving school

% of participation in career days

% of students counseled

% of students entering employment

% of technical students employed within six months of graduation

Average graduate starting salary

Average rating of student on the adequacy of career counseling

Completion rates for graduate survey

Employment rate of graduates in chosen field as their primary post-graduation goal

Graduate employment rate

Graduate placement rate

Disability Services

% faculty perceptions of disability services

% of disabled student satisfaction with range and quality of assistance offered

% of student perception that academic success was enhanced with disability services assistance

Engagement & Partnership

of alliances or participation to a joint academic program or consortium

# of community education programs provided as a % of # of departments

# of cooperative proposals involving other educational institutions, businesses, communities, and government entities

# of off-shore partnerships

# of on-shore partnerships

% national accreditation

% of full time faculty and staff actively engaged in community service activities

% use of multidisciplinary teams for educational projects, programs, and courses

Responsiveness index to regional labor market demand

Total earned income internationally

Enrolment

of methods in recruiting students

# of methods of maximizing funding for students

# of new student recruitment

# of student headcount by college of attendance

# of student headcount by college of registration

# of student transfers

# of students recruited

# of students recruited from local high-schools

# of students recruited from outside the country

% apparent (gross) intake rate

% change of full-time students admitted in the fall term semester

9. Education
% delivering admissions information to prospective students
% of growth in student enrolments
% of part time students
% of students are disabled
% of students from low participation neighborhoods
% of students from minority ethnic groups
% of students recruited from local high-schools
% of students recruited from outside the country
% participation in specialization area
% student acceptance rate
% students in a preferred student group targeted for enrollment
Ratio of first-preference applicants
Student acceptance ratio (# of students/# of people applying in a program)
Turnaround time required to process admissions applicants
Turnaround time required to process financial aid applicants

Facilities & Equipment

# of accessible computer terminals per student
# of facilities services work order response
% addition of new equipment and services
% expenditure on utility costs
% of buildings in poor condition
% of time that network servers were kept online
% safety record for employees and users of campus facilities
% satisfaction with cleanliness and comfort
Amount spent on facilities investment
Annual expenditure on IT as a % of # of students
Average overall rating of adequacy of facilities and equipment in a survey of faculty
Average response time for technical assistance
Internet bandwidth per user
Ratio of operation and maintenance of physical building over total budget
Total amount of deferred maintenance
Total expenditure on repairs and maintenance

Faculty & Staff

# of absenteeism / days per staff
# of accrued leave entitlements
# of books published
# of conferences/presentations given
# of courses given by full time professors to candidates of honor degrees
# of faculty and staff of diverse backgrounds
# of faculty holding teaching diplomas
# of faculty publications, performances, presentations to professional groups, and similar scholarly activities
# of full time professors

9. Education
# of minorities faculty or staff employment
# of outcomes to assess faculty and staff development
# of patents received
# of research projects
# of research projects completed
# of research proposals written
# of special recognition/honors received by faculty and staff
# of work cover claims
% of academic staff participating in professional development activities during the past year
% of academic staff with a doctorate
% of classified staff indicate they feel they are recognized and valued by faculty and technical staff
% of faculty and staff of diverse backgrounds
% of faculty and staff using blackboard
% of faculty engaged in inter-disciplinary programs
% of faculty engaged in research
% of faculty holding teaching diplomas
% of faculty leaving the institution in the past year for reasons other than age retirement
% of faculty with verified doctoral qualifications
% of instructional staff with terminal degrees
% of minorities faculty or staff employment
% of participants apply trained skills in their teaching
% of participation in ICT training
% of senior assignments accomplished as a part of a capstone experience
% of teaching faculty participating in professional development activities during the past year
% participation in staff development
% responses of faculty, staff, and students to a biannual climate survey
% results of students for admission tests
% retention rate
% student reports of out-of-class interactions with faculty
Alumni rating of the pedagogy
Attrition rate
Average # of papers published
Average international years of staff experience
Professor to students ratio
Ratio of student/full time professors
Satisfaction rate for staff
Staff perception rate
Student-faculty ratio

Financial
# of external audit of the organization and its programs

9. Education

of sources of recurring income

% discount on tuition fees

% market share in the industry for a program

% market share of leading competitors for a program

% of average faculty and staff salaries compared to benchmark institutions or other appropriate comparators

% of budget devoted to development and support of faculty and staff

% of budget devoted to instruction and instructional services

% of budget devoted to instruction and instructional support services

% of university revenue available for strategic initiatives

Academic activity cost per student

Amount given by alumni

Amount of contingency fund

Amount of funding overall

Amount of unallocated unrestricted budget reserve

Amount spend on research

Amount spend on student services

Amount spent on per-student funding

Average cost of course

Average cost of program

Average expenses for students/learners

Average full time professor annual salary

Cost per graduate

Deferred maintenance base budget

Distribution of recurrent expenditure

Distribution of recurring costs per student

Distribution of service costs per program or course

Earned income by division

Financial yield per division

Grant Income by division

Human resources expenses

Institutional/organizational income

Net revenue of students/learners

Professional fees rate of academic personnel

Professional fees rate of service staff

Ratio of # of graduate to undergraduate students

Ratio of dollars spent on strategic initiatives over total institutional dollars

Total current fund expenditures adjusted divided by # of registered students

Total earned income

Total equipment and technology expenses

Total expenses coverage (excess deficit of current fund revenues)

Total expenses per period

Total operating expenditure per student

Total paid professional fees

9. Education
Total private contributions to university
Total recurrent cost per student
Total recurrent costs
Total revenues from grants and gifts
Total royalties obtained for programs, courses
Total tuition and fee revenues (minus scholarships and fellowships)
Working capital ratio

Financial Aid
# of regional school student scholarships
% effectiveness in distribution of financial aid and scholarships
% effectiveness in sharing information on financial payments and aid
% student satisfaction
Average time required for students to complete financial transactions
Total regional grant-funded commencing students

International Learning
# of international students
# of students studying abroad
% of students in multi-cultural immersion experiences
% of students studying abroad

Library
# of book titles held in the library as a % of # of students
# of catalogue records created
# of cataloguing backlogs
# of children attending educational sessions
# of digital images created
# of document supplied
# of electronic materials
# of exhibition loans to other institutions
# of items acquired
# of items supplied/consulted remotely and on site
# of monographs
# of newspaper issues
# of pages of digitized material viewed over the web
# of patent specifications
# of periodical subscriptions as a % of # of programs offered
# of searches of the Library's online catalogue
# of serial titles
# of visitors to the library's 'learning' website
# of visitors to the library's on site and virtual exhibitions
# of visits to reading rooms
# of Web site subscriptions as a % of # of programs offered
% if reading rooms availability within 15 minutes
% of children attending educational sessions from inner city schools
% of legal deposit material acquired

9. Education
% of material delivered electronically
% of material held onsite
% of published output available in perpetuity: acquired by the library via purchase, donation and exchange
% of published output available in perpetuity: all 'research level' monographs acquired by the library
% of published output available in perpetuity: current 'research level' serial titles published worldwide
% of published output available in perpetuity: via purchase, donation and exchange
% of remote users who are 'completely satisfied' with the document supply service
% of visitors rating the quality of their visit as either 'excellent' or 'good'
Amount of library collection
Average # of issues per borrower
Average rating of students on adequacy of library services
Average time taken to satisfy book requests
Borrowers as a % of the resident population
Library user satisfaction rate
Monograph lending fulfillment rate
Rating the services and facilities they used as either 'excellent' or 'good'
Reading room user satisfaction rate
Total library expenditure

Participation

# of pupils
% kids not in education, employment or training
% kids with no formal learning being undertaken
% of 16 - 18 year olds in learning
% of participation in education of # year olds
% young people progressing to higher education at age 19
% young people progressing to higher education at age 20

Public Relations

# of reviewed publications for clarity and comprehensiveness
% attendance at open house events in relation to # of inquiries
% increases in revenues from contribution campaigns
% of delivering accurate and timely information to students
% of satisfaction with campus facilities by community visitors using facilities
% positive community views of the college
Average response time to student inquiries

Quality Assurance

# of institutional audit
# of subject health reviews
% achievement rates (# achieving qualification / # completers)
% colleges learning lessons good or better
% of courses in which student evaluations were conducted during the year

9. Education
% of programs in which there was independent verification of standards of student achievement
% of programs in which there was independent verification within the institution of standards of student achievement
% student retention rate
% success rates (# achieving qualification / # starts)
Average rating of the overall quality of student program

Registrar

# of services provided to faculty in distributing academic calendar, course, and grading information
% processing procedures and staffing patterns
% timeliness of information given to students

Research

# of citations in refereed journals in the previous year per full time faculty member
# of full time faculty with at least one refereed publication during the previous year
# of papers or reports presented at academic conferences during the past year per full time faculty member
# of publications in refereed journals in the previous year per full time faculty member
# of research active academic staff
# of research competitive grants
# of research higher degree completions
# of total operating funds spent on research
% academic staff with a Doctorate
% higher degree research load
% of funding for research
% of staff deemed to be research active
Research income from external sources in the past year as a % of # of full time faculty members
Total research income
Value of knowledge transfer grant
Value of research grants
Weighted research publications

Retention

% of FT students who achieve an award
% of FT students who progressed
% of student engagement - academic challenge
% of student engagement - active & collaborative learning
% of student engagement - student effort
% of student engagement - student-faculty interaction
% of student engagement - support for learners
% of student repeating a period of study
% of students are going for further study

9. Education

Course completion rate

FT Fall-to-Fall persistence rate

Student Achievement

\# A points per student

\# of degrees and certificates awarded

\# of student entries

\# of subjects

% A points per subject entry

% achieving Level 1 at age 16

% achieving level 2 at age 16

% achieving level 3 at age 19

% graduation rate

% of fall students who transfer to a senior institution

% student repetition rate

Advanced value added colleges

Advanced value added schools

FT 3-year graduation rate

Module completion rate

Student progression ratio

Undergraduate retention rate

Student Body

\# of active graduate students

\# of international student

\# of merit scholars of freshman class

\# of responses to student questionnaire

\# of students who participate in orientation program

% international students

% of student satisfied

Average ACT score of freshman class

Average high-school rank of freshman class

Male / female student ratio

Student / staff ratio

Student / teacher ratio

Student Learning

\# of courses offered on learning portal

\# of curriculum and syllabus analysis done

\# of degrees granted

\# of experiential learning

\# of external reviewers

\# of extra curricular activities per semester

\# of faculty teaching evaluations

\# of full-time equivalent students (FTES)

\# of full-time students admitted in the fall term semester

\# of graduate students with undergraduate degrees from us

9. Education

of graduating senior surveys

# of instructional faculty

# of integrated marketing communications plan

# of licensure exams (taken by all graduates of a program)

# of minorities student groups graduating

# of new graduate programs

# of new programs or other educational services developed in order to satisfy students/learners

# of persons served through continuing education

# of portfolio analysis

# of portfolio evaluation

# of programs for teaching improvement

# of registrations per year/# of degrees granted

# of special recognition/honors received by students

# of student internships

# of student surveying and exit interviews

# of students enrolled in upgrading courses

# of students participating in academic enhancement activities

# of students participating in academic enhancement/ enrichment activities

# of students participation in using learning portal

# of thesis evaluation

# of videotape evaluation of performance

% academic performance of targeted student groups

% drop-out rate

% ethnic minority students

% of absent students per class

% of academic success of transfer students

% of adjunct teaching

% of admitted students requiring developmental/remedial courses

% of campuses compliant with regulations

% of course or program completion

% of courses that are web-based or web enhanced

% of departments with learning outcome maps for curriculum

% of employers satisfied with quality of graduates

% of existing exams, assignments, or projects common to a group of students in the major

% of expelled students

% of general university support generated by contract and grant activity for instruction, public service, and scholarship

% of improvement in students learning rate

% of international student load

% of minorities student groups graduating

% of parents satisfied with education programs and services

% of programs with assessment plans

9. Education

% of standardized tests

% of student evaluations of curriculum, instruction, and services

% of student learning outcomes for program in the university

% of student satisfaction with the student-centered support system

% of students engaged in internships

% of students engaged in research

% of students enrolled in upgrading courses

% of students entering post graduate programs who complete those programs in specified time

% of students entering programs who successfully complete first year

% of students entering undergraduate programs who complete those programs in minimum time

% of students master 90% of course competencies

% of students meeting full admission requirements and prerequisites

% of students who enroll in excursions

% of target teaching hours per annum

% of undergraduate classes with <20 students

% of undergraduate classes with >50 students

% of writing samples completed

% percentage attending per course

% questions measuring participation in research with faculty

Alumni ratings of the quality of instruction, counseling, and curriculum

Alumni ratings of the quantity and quality of preparation for career or other post-graduation activities

Alumni surveying

Attrition rate of online courses

Average # of students by course or tutored

Average class size

Average course experience

Average course grade of individual students

Average GPA

Average grades of students

Average of students overall rating on the quality of their courses

Average student load (full time)

Average student time to graduation

Average time to graduate

Capstone course evaluation

Capstone courses for graduating seniors

Certification and licensing pass rates

Class attendance %

Classroom climate satisfaction rate

Comprehensive strategic enrollment management plan

Course-embedded assessment

Dropout rate

9. Education

Dropout rate for a program / course

Early graduation rate

Failure rate for a program / course

FTE student / FTE Faculty ratio

Graduate school admission rate

Graduated student ratio/ divided by # of students accepted

Graduation rate

Late graduation rate

Median teacher experience

Post-graduate pass rate

Pre-test/Post-test evaluation rate

Professional to academic staff ratio

Program accreditation and re-accreditation review results

Rates/times of completion

Rating by students of pedagogy, counseling services, staff programs, courses

Ratio of students to places

Ratio of students to teaching staff

Student persistence rate

Student retention rate

Teaching skills satisfaction rate

Student Support

of prizes or other recognition given to service personnel

# of students receiving counseling services

% effectiveness in minimizing student anxiety and help students matriculate into college

% extracurricular activities

% of alumni rating of services and programs

% of creating campus climate that supports retention

% of student satisfaction with co-curriculum

% of student satisfaction with placement testing experience

% of students receiving counseling services

% of total operating funds allocated to provision of student services

% of web enhanced service delivery

% student connectedness to campus

% students per computer

% students supported by scholarship schemes

Average professional fee rate of staff

Average rating of student on the adequacy of academic counseling

Productivity rate of services

Rating by students of staff, procedures and administrative staff

Ratio of students to administrative staff

10. Energy Supply

Direct Energy

Gas production volumes

Total direct power generated

Total wind off take commitment

Distribution

Amount of supplied water

Commercial power sales as % of total sales

Connection density per km network

Connection density per service area

Industrial power sales as % of total sales

Network overhead %

Own power generation as % of total power

Residential power sales as % of total sales

Total amount of radioactive waste

Energy Generation

% of coal energy generated

% of natural gas energy generated

% of nuclear energy generated

Renewable power installed capacity

Renewable power purchased under long-term contracts

Total power generated

Total renewable power generated

Wind energy generation utility under construction / consented

Exploration & Production

Fuel consumption/ktoe produced

GHG emissions/ktoe produced

HSE expenditure/hydrocarbon production

HSE investments/capital expenditure

Oil concentration in water discharges

Re-injected water/production discharges

Gas & Power

CO_2 emissions/distributed gas

CO_2 emissions/toe consumed

CO_2 emissions/transported gas – transport activities

Energy consumption indicators

Energy consumption/(transported energy * average distance) – transport activities

Energy consumption/distributed energy – gas distribution

Energy consumption/transported energy – transport activities

Energy performance index

GHG emissions/transported gas – transport activities

Natural gas emissions/distributed gas

Natural gas emissions/transported gas - transport activities

Net specific consumption

10. Energy Supply

NOx emissions/distributed gas

NOx emissions/kWheq produced

NOx emissions/transported gas – transport activities

Oil reserves claimed to be recoverable under existing economic conditions

Re-gasification energy consumption/LNG fed into the network

SO2 emissions/kWheq produced

Social Programs

of advice packs distributed

# of customers on 'Essentials' social energy tariff

# of customers on 'Winter Warmer' initiative

# of grants awarded

# of thermometers distributed

Cumulative value of unclaimed benefits identified

Value of grants awarded

11. Engineering

Cost Reduction

of debtors

% deviation from budget

% of Inventory (Raw Material + Work-In-Progress)

% return on capital employed

% variation to cost estimates

Total amount of capital employed

Total cost reduction due to global sourcing

Total cost reduction due to value engineering projects

Total liability due to outstanding funds until previous year

Customer Satisfaction

of contact plan with customers

# of customer meets

# of new area offices

# of principals' feedback

% of defects during warranty period

% of fast moving parts availability

% of satisfactory business performance

Export distributor satisfaction index

Loyalty index

Mean time to recovery

Design Cost

of person-months per released print

% of bills of material that are released in error

% of errors in cost estimates

Average cost of input errors to the computer

Customer cost per life of output delivered

Total spare parts cost after warranty

11. Engineering

Design Quality

of days for the release cycle

# of days late to pre-analysis

# of errors in publications reported from the plan and field

# of meetings held per quarter over quality and defect prevention

# of misused shipments of prototypes

# of off-specifications accepted

# of off-specifications approved

# of problems that were also encountered in previous products

# of products that pass independent evaluation error-free

# of restarts of evaluations and tests

# of times a print is changed

# of unsuccessful pre-analyses

% accuracy of advance materials list

% effectiveness of regression tests

% of corrective action schedules missed

% of data recording errors per month

% of drafting errors per print

% of error-free designs

% of errors found during design review

% of evaluations that meet engineering objectives

% of field performance of product

% of prints released on schedule

% of repeat problems corrected

% of reports with errors in them

% of requests for engineering

% of requests for engineering action open for more than two weeks

% of special quotations that are successful

% of test plans that are changed(change/test plan)

% of total problems found by diagnostics as released

% product meets customer expectations

% simulation accuracy

Average cycle time to correct customer problem

Average time required to make an engineering change

Average time to correct a problem

Forklift Business

of crane needed

# of forklift population

# of forklift sales - exports

# of forklift sales - high end

# of forklift sales-domestic

Cost of cranes per year

11. Engineering

Maintenance

of hours lost due to equipment downtime

# of hours used on scheduled maintenance

# of repeat call hours for the same problem

# of unscheduled maintenance calls

% of equipment maintained on schedule

% of equipment overdue for calibration

% of warranty parts dispatch within 48 Hours

% rework due to calibration errors

% scrap due to calibration errors

Average maintenance cost/equipment cost

Average parts delivery period - current

Average parts delivery period - non-current

Materials Handling

% materials handling solution turnover

% materials handling solution turnover - parts

% materials handling solution turnover - service

Project Engineering

of changes to layout

# of errors found after construction had been accepted by the company

# of industrial design completions past due

# of mechanical/functional errors in industrial design artwork

% of accuracy of assets report

% of engineering action requests accepted

% of error in purchase requests

% of error in time estimates

% of manufacturing time lost due to bad layouts

% of on-time delivery of finished goods

% of production capacity

% of projects executed within approved budget

% of projects executed within scheduled time

% of total floor space devoted to storage

Suppliers Partnership

of SLAs met between the division and support functions

# of SLAs met between with suppliers

Annual service contracts

Parts business - actual versus potential

Waste Heat Engine

of manufactured engines

% gross margin of cranes

% gross margin of manufactured engines

% gross margin of own forklifts

% gross margin of traded engines

Equipment turnover

11. Engineering

Total gross margin

12. Financial

Accounting

acid test ratio
current ratio
of equipment sales miscoded
# of final accounting jobs rerun
# of hours per week correcting or changing documents
# of inventories
# of key performance indicators
# of open items
# of untimely supplier invoices processed
% of advances outstanding
% of deviations from cash plan
% of shipments requiring more than one attempt to invoice
Amount of intra-company accounting bill-back activity
Amount of time spent appraising/correcting input errors
Average # of days from receipt to processing
Average age of assets
Cash flow return on investments
Cash flow shares outstanding
Common stock equity
Cost of goods sold
Credit turnaround time
Cumulative annual growth rate
Direct costs
Earnings before interest, taxes, depreciation and amortization
Fixed costs
Gross profit
Gross profit margin
Income statement revenues & expenses goodwill
Income statement revenues & expenses retained earnings
Indirect costs
Interest cover
Marginal costs
Money owed to suppliers for goods or services purchased on credit
Net change in cash
Net fixed assets
Net profit margin
Net receivables
Operating income
Other current assets
Other current liabilities

12. Financial
Other non-current assets
Other non-current liabilities
Preferred stock equity
Short-term debt
Total accounting costs
Total assets
Total current assets
Total current liabilities
Total equity
Total expense accounts processed in three days
Total liabilities
Total of long-term debt
Total time spent correcting erroneous inputs
Total variable costs

Accounting Control

- # asset turnover
- # of complaints about inefficiencies or excessive paper
- # of complaints by users
- # of errors in input to information services
- # of errors reported by outside auditors
- % data entry errors in accounts payable and general ledger
- % discrepancy in line scrap reports
- % net interest margin (NIM)
- % of input errors detected
- % of late reports
- Free cash flow (FCF)
- Length of time billed and not received
- Length of time to prepare and send a bill
- Machine billing turnaround time
- Net cash flow
- Net debt
- Operating expenses
- Risk assessment value (RAV)
- Working capital

Accounts Payable

- # days of purchases in accounts payable
- # days of purchases paid
- # of days payable
- # of invoices disputed
- # of invoices outstanding
- # of overdue invoices
- # of unsettled (unpaid invoices)
- % of bad debts against invoiced revenue
- % of business partners performance satisfaction

12. Financial

% of electronic invoices

% of invoices disputed

% of invoices under query

% of low value invoices

% of overdue invoices

% of payable invoices without purchase order

% of payment made within time limit

% reduction of payroll errors

Accounts payable % effectiveness in payables management

Accounts payable turnover

Average monetary value of invoices outstanding

Average monetary value of overdue invoices

Average monetary value of unsettled (unpaid invoices)

Cost of passing up discount by paying invoice after discount period

Cycle time to resolve an invoice error

Debtor days

Entry errors per week

Expenses claims processed per staff

Invoicing processing costs

Monetary value of invoices outstanding

Sum of monetary value of unsettled (unpaid invoices)

Total monetary value of overdue invoices

Total non-current liabilities

Variable costs

Accounts Receivable

days in accounts receivable

of creditors

% of invoices requiring special payment

Accounts receivable collection period

Accounts receivable turnover

Average value of overdue invoices

Cash at hand

Creditor days

Receivables against product

Receivables against product, region, sales office

Total sum of monetary value of outstanding invoices

Total value of overdue invoices

Budgeting

of budget deviations

# of days taken to close the budget

# of years with a balanced budget

% accuracy of periodic financial reports

% of budget cuts achieved

% of budgeting deviation of planned budget

12. Financial
% of budgeting forecast accuracy of budget
Time by which budget closed before the year end
Total managed expenditure (TME)

Expense Reimbursement

% of expense report exception line items
% of expenses violating corporate policy
% of travel and entertainment expenses on expense claims
Average # of expense claims per employee or FTE
Average value of expense claims
Average value of travel and entertainment expenses per expense claim
Cycle time in days to approve and schedule reimbursement
Expenses claims processed per FTE

Financial Costs

of projects completed on time and on budget
% wages cost from total sales
Actual expenses
Average cost per store
Budget variance
Budgeted expenses
Computer program change cost
Cost of equity (COE)
Cost of goods sold
Cost of insurance
Cost of sales
Cost variance as per budget
Direct operating cost
Interest on overdraft
Inventory turnover
Inventory value
Material costs
Operating cost
Operations costs
Payables turnover ratio
Receivables turnover ratio
Total inventory
Total overtime hours
Total payables
Warrantee costs

Financial Management

Altman Z-Score (for manufacturing public companies)
Altman Z-Score (for privately held non-manufacturing companies)
Annual equivalent rate (AER) %
Annual surplus
Capex ratio (cash flow by capital expenditure)

12. Financial
Cash flow
Cost of finance %
Cost per FTE
Creditor length (days)
Current ratio
Debt gearing ratio
Debtor length (days)
Fixed asset turnover
Gross profit %
Investments evaluation
Profit per FTE
Return on capital employed %
Return to shareholders
Revenue per FTE
Stock turn/year
Tax charge %
Total profitability
Total taxation paid
Working capital requirement

Financial Performance

Benefits cost per employee
Equity ratio
Gross margin for each product line
Gross profit % by department / team
Revenue by major customer
Sales generated by department / team
Sales growth rate
Sales per customer
Sales per employee hour
Total gross profit margin
Total sales generated
Total shrink (loss due to theft and breakage)

Financial Ratios

% of organic revenue growth
Average equipment costs per employee
Average revenue per employee (or FTE)
Average telephone/communication costs per employee
Average travel costs per employee
Bonus payout as a % of the total possible within the measurement period
Book-to-bill
Cash conversion cycle
Contribution margin ratio
Corporate credit rating
Cost of office space per employee

12. Financial
Cost/income ratio
Days payable outstanding
Days sales of inventory
Days sales outstanding
Debt ratio
Debt-to-capital ratio
Dividend yield
Economic value added
Enterprise value / takeover value
Financial ratios equity ratio
Fixed asset utilization
Gross profit per share
Internal financing ratio
Non-organic revenue growth
P/E to growth ratio
Payroll to net sales
Price/sales ratio
Price-to-book ratio
Price-to-earnings ratio
Profit per admin. staff
Profit per customer
Profit per employee (FTE)
Profit per product
Profit per project
Purchase price variance
Ratio of net debt to equity
Return on capital employed
Return on equity
Revenue won lost due to currency exchange rates as a % of total revenue
Reward-to-variability ratio
Risk-adjusted return of an investment asset
Sacrifice Ratio
Sales and financial ratios Earnings per share
Share price
Subsidy dependence ratio
Value to volume ratio

Financial Reporting

% of errors in reports
% of financial reports issued on time
Average costs of rework of financial statements due to inaccuracy
Average costs to produce financial statements
Cycle time in days to perform monthly / quarterly / annual close (at site level).

12. Financial

Delay (in days) in production of financial reports, based on target for production/delivery

Governance & Compliance

of audit finding closing more than two weeks

# of certifications held by a proposed newcomer

# of errors found by outside auditors

# of errors in financial reports

# of manual payroll payments

# of minor finding on ISO 9001 Internal Audit

# of overdue invoices

# of payroll errors per month

# of postponed ISO 9001 internal audit caused by auditee

# of postponed ISO 9001 internal audit caused by auditor

# of record errors per employee

# of years of industry specific experience of a proposed newcomer

% error in budget predictions

% of bills paid so company gets price break

% of error-free vouchers

% of errors in checks

% of errors in expense accounts detected by auditors

% of errors in travel advance records

% of expense report exception line items

% of financial reports delivered on schedule

% of financial reports issued on time

% of payable invoices that have not been matched to a purchase order

% of strategic objectives achieved within a given period

% of un-assessed identified risks

Computer rerun time due to input errors

Cycle time for expense reimbursements

Cycle time to perform periodic close

Cycle time to process payroll

Cycle time to resolve payroll errors

Health & Safety Costs

of initiatives raised to optimize health & safety costs

% reduction in costs of safety management

Health & safety cost reports produced - weekly / monthly

HR Costs

% of labor cost competitiveness

HR controllable cost

HR controllable cost by headcount

HR controllable cost by labor cost

HR related operating cost

HR related total operating expenditure

HR total labor cost by total headcount

12. Financial
Overtime headcount factor (for total employees)
Overtime labor cost ratio
Share schemes cost
Social security paid
Total direct labor costs
Total eligible headcount
Total headcount
Total HR revenue
Total HR revenue by total headcount
Total indirect labor cost
Total overtime cost
Total pensions and retirement benefits
Total wages and salaries

Legal Cost

# of legal staff per billion of company's revenue
% of legal budget spent externally
Cost per hour per in-house lawyer
Legal cost per hour per lawyer
Legal staff per size of revenue
Total legal spending expressed as a % of the company's revenue

Payroll

# of instances where statutory returns filed with the authorities are accurate
% of errors in payroll
% of manual payroll payments
% of payroll disbursements that include retroactive pay adjustments
% of untimely payroll payments
Average overall cost of producing a payslip per pay run
Cost of payroll process as % of total payroll cost
Cost per payslip issued
Cycle time (in days) to process the payroll
Cycle time to resolve payroll errors
Payment errors as % of total payroll disbursement
# of payment errors
Payroll processing time
Systems cost of payroll process as a % of total payroll cost
Timeliness in submission of statutory returns

Procurement & Supplier

Accounts payable days
Bought in materials and services
Purchasing department's administration costs as % of sales
Total spend with suppliers
Value of materials consumed
Value of supplies consumed

12. Financial

Revenues & Profits

breakeven point (BEP)
of new product / services
# of opportunities initiated
working capital turnover
% dividend yield
% earnings yield
% gross profit margin
% net profit margin
% return on equity (ROE)
% return on net assets (RONA)
% return on security investment (ROSI)
% return on total assets (ROTA)
% revenue generated from new products
% sustainable growth rate (SGR)
Annual loss expectancy (ALE)
Assets per FTE (Full Time Equivalent)
Book value per share (BVPS)
Cash cycle (days)
Cost income ratio
Creditors (days)
Cumulative growth rate
Earning per stock
Earnings before interest, taxes, depreciation and amortization (EBITDA)
Earnings before interest, taxes, depreciation, amortization, and restructuring or rent costs (EBITDAR)
Earnings per share (EPS)
EBIT (Earnings Before Interest and Taxes)
Economic value added (EVA ™)
Export sales volumes
Gross profit from the key supplier
Inventory value in team's area
Market Share
Net income after taxes (NIAT)
Net profit by region / office
Net profits
Product profitability
Profit after tax
Profit from direct energy
Profit from energy
Profit in dollars
Return on assets or investment
Return on capital employed (ROCE)
Revenue from new products and services

12. Financial

Revenue generated by team

Revenue per FTE (Full Time Equivalent)

Sales per share

Shareholders' equity

Total direct profit

Total revenues before tax

Savings

Savings "in year" revenue

Savings capital "in year"

Savings endowments "in year"

Savings full year revenue recurring impact

Savings next year revenue

Savings total "in year"

Shareholders & Creditors

Net interest payable

Ordinary dividend per share

Total dividend paid to shareholders

Taxes

% of disputed tax statements

% of error in placing tax right parameters

% of overdue tax statements (either not filed in-time or not paid in-time)

% of tax statements filed in-time

% of taxes paid in-time

Cost of tax penalties

13. Health & Safety

Employee Safety

of auditor/thousands of employees

# of carbon monoxide incidents

# of cases of work hours violations

# of health care staff/thousands of employees

# of major injuries

# of major/ serious accidents

# of safety accidents per 100,000 hours worked

# of staff who got medical treatments

# of total fatalities

% of carbon monoxide incidents

% of effective safety culture

% of eligible employees who signed the ethics policy

% of employee involvement and satisfaction.

% of employee perception of management commitment

% of employees covered by collective bargaining agreements

% of employees receiving regular safety performance reviews

% of staff demonstrates high priority to safety

13. Health & Safety
Average overtime hours per person
Contractor injury frequency index
Contractor injury severity index
Employee injury frequency index
Employee injury severity index
Light injury frequency index
Light injury severity index
Serious injuries frequency rate
Total accidents/100,000 hours worked
Total carbon monoxide incidents with death
Total health expenditure/employee

Environment

of business units analyzed for risks related to environment

# of environment violations

# of initiatives undertaken by the business to promote greater environmental responsibility

# of spills of liquid and accidental releases of substances

# of substantiated complaints regarding breaches of regulations

% and total volume of water recycled and reused

% of actual versus licensed water abstraction

% of business units analyzed for risks related to environment

% of materials used that are recycled input materials

% of natural light within buildings

% of products and services categories subject to procedures in which health and safety impacts are assessed

% of significant suppliers and contractors that have undergone screening on environment breaches

% of spending on environment-friendly suppliers

% of suppliers that affirmed business code of conduct

% of usage of water from non-traditional sources such as desalination and recycled water

Amount of energy saved due to conservation and efficiency improvements.

Amount of petrol and diesel used by fleet

Average carbon dioxide emissions by type of vehicle

Average carbon dioxide emissions of vehicles

Average fuel economy by type of vehicle

NOx emissions/toe consumed

Size of identified contaminated land sites

SO2 emissions/toe consumed

Water treatment expenditure/total treated water

Ergonomics

% employee satisfaction with ergonomics

% of practical impact of design

Accessibility rating

13. Health & Safety

Adaptability rate

Ease of employment rate

Level of consistence rate

Position/Location and convenience rate

Product liability rate

Rating on cognitive elements

Rating on contrast principles

Rating on physical elements

HSE Costing

of lost days

# of lost time injury cases

# of medical injury cases

% of warranty work costs recovered through claims

% of warranty work with submitted claims

% reduce cost of safety management

% reductions in costs and safety improvement

Cost of office space per HSE employee within measurement period

Cost of solved safety non-conformance per year

Cost of solved safety non-conformances by location

Cost of solved safety non-conformances for the month

Cost per HSE employee

Cost savings

Health and safety prevention costs within the month

HSE current expenditure/operating costs

HSE expenditure*100/year-end order backlog

HSE expenditure/productions

HSE expenditure/revenues

HSE expenditure/sales of natural gas to third parties and own consumption

HSE expenditure/sales of oil products

HSE facilities services total warranty work costs

HSE facilities services total warranty work hours

HSE prevention costs within the month

HSE staff/thousands of employees

Lost time (in hours) due to accidents (including fatalities) per 100,000 hours worked

Lost time (in hours) due to accidents (including fatalities) per year

Lost time (in hours) due to accidents per 1,000 hours worked

Lost time (in hours) due to non-fatal accidents per 1,000 hours worked

Lost time (in hours) due to non-fatal accidents per 100,000 hours worked

Lost time (in hours) due to non-fatal accidents per year

Steps taken to eliminate expensive system elements and training limitations

Total costs for health and safety prevention within a period

Total man-hours worked

13. Health & Safety

HSE Representatives
% of attendance at occupational HSE committee meetings
% of health and safety representatives positions filled
% of HSE representatives positions filled
% of issues raised by reps acted
% of issues raised by reps actioned
% of occupational HSE committee recommendations implemented
Total of hours in safety and health training in the month
Total of man-hours in safety and health training

Policies & Compliance
of completed relevant policies & procedures
# of implemented safety and health programmers
# of non-conformance with legal or internal standards in safety inspections
# of safety inspections for month
# of safety violations by department
# of security violations per audit
# of solved safety non-conformances from previous audit
% of solved safety non-conformances from previous audit
# of tests passed audit
# of violations committed
% implemented quality management standards and systems
% implemented safety and environmental standards and systems
% of audits conducted on schedule
% of corrective actions closed out within specified time-frame
% of implemented health, safety and environment policies and procedures
% of managers trained in accident investigation
% of noise level control
% of safety adherence to compliance
Contamination rating
Energy intensity index
NOx emissions/processed crude oil
SO2 emissions/processed crude oil

Productivity & Performance
of accidents per year
# of health management programs
# of measures of safety performance
# of non-conformance per year / quarter
# of reportable accidents year
# of reportable non-fatal accidents per year
# of safety accidents due to non-conformance per month
# of times work was stopped due to unplanned unsafe condition
% of clearance errors
% of documents classified incorrectly
% of fatal accidents relative to all accidents per year

13. Health & Safety

% of operating times with free accidents

% of participation in safety teams

% of safety equipment checked per schedule

% of security violations

% of sensitive parts located

Lost time injuries

Lost-time injuries/1,000 hours worked

Lost-time injuries/100,000 employees

Safety Awareness

of attendance to HSE courses/employee

# of circulars & Reports Distributed

# of health and safety reports produced

# of issued HSE news letter

# of safety certifications given

% effectiveness of communication methods

% effectiveness of safety training plan

% of attendance at occupational health and safety committee meetings

% of instructions facilitated and presented to users in a manners that is easy to interpret

% of personnel trained in safety, security and facilities measures

% of staff with adequate occupational health and safety training

% of staff with adequate environmental safety training

HSE training hours/employee

Total HSE training offered

Safety Improvement

of accidents

# of civil defense inspections

# of corrective actions within work group

# of days since last incident

# of executed safety plans

# of fatalities per 100,000 hours worked

# of fatalities per location

# of fires

# of hazards identified

# of incidents with actions taken

# of indicator to judge safety program effectiveness

# of initiatives for safety projects generated

# of joint drills

# of measure of proper resource allocation to safety

# of near misses

# of new guidelines implemented

# of occupational accidents

# of occupational accidents per million working hours

# of occupational illnesses

13. Health & Safety

of preventative and corrective maintenance backlog

# of property damage more than $x

# of reportable accidents per 100,000 hours worked

# of reportable non-fatal accidents per 100,000 hours worked

# of risks mitigated

# of safety inspections

# of safety problems identified by management versus total safety problems identified

# of safety suggestions

# of spills

# of tasks assessment

# of vehicle accidents

# of vehicular accidents per 100,000 driver hours

% of assessment of health hazards

% of carbon monoxide incidents investigated

% of corrective actions closed out within specified timeframe

% of emergency response covered

% of employee injuries treated in-house

% of fatal accidents

% of fatal accidents relative to all accidents (non-fatal and fatal) per 100,000 hours worked

% of maintained equipments safety

% of occupational health and safety committee recommendations implemented

% of products/services assessed for health & safety impacts

% of significant products and services are assessed for safety improvement

Accident rate in non-core time

Average # of square feet cleaned by an FTE

Average long and short-term span to fix severe violations

Average time to get safety clearance

Design rating/success

HSE index

Maintenance-rating index

Total preventive occupational safety cost

Social Responsibility

of full-time employees dedicated to social investment projects

% of employees who consider that their business acts responsibly in the society

Funds raised per FTE for non-profit and humanitarian organizations

Social contributions spent per employee

Social responsibility % of operating income dedicated to social contribution

Total investment in the community (company cash donations and staff volunteering)

Total value of financial contributions to social institutions

14. Healthcare

Bed Utilization

of bed days lost NHS Responsibility
# of bed days lost, LA responsibility
# of hospital beds capacity
# of total bed days per private sector
% accuracy of discharge predictions
% alternate level of care days (ALC)
% bed occupancy rate
% cases classified as may not require hospitalization
% days over/under expected length of stay
% of available critical and telemetry hospital beds
% of available hospital beds
% of bed occupancy
% of day-case basket performance
% of delayed transfers of care
% of emergency patients (not) hospitalized
% of stand-alone hospital beds
% of time that hospital beds remains occupied
Average length of stay
Average length of stay (elective inpatient and day case)
Average length of stay (LOS) in ER
Average length of stay (non-elective)
Average length of stay per ward
Projected versus actual hospital bed occupancy
Throughput per bed

Clinic Appointment

of clinic visits
# of referrals
# of social service referrals -dental
# of social service referrals -medical
# of social service referrals -mental health
% medical clinics finishing on time
% medical clinics starting on time
% of appointment referrals in a month receiving a response
% of clinic access (within x weeks)
% of no-shows at appointments
% of no-shows at follow-up appointments
% of no-shows at intake appointments
% of overall clinic utilization
% of referrals from other hospitals
Average booking response time (within x days)
Average clinic visit duration
Average time taken to type and dispatch dictated medical correspondence
Dictation turnaround

14. Healthcare

Elective day cases (% variance to plan)

Elective inpatients (% variance to plan)

First outpatient appointments (% variance to plan)

Follow-up visits per FTE physician

Non-elective (% variance to plan)

Patient discharge rate

Rate of patient attendance

Clinical Trials

of clinical trial protocols published

# of clinical trials completed

# of clinical trials opened during the grant year

# of observation patients

# of patients actively participating in clinical trials

# of patients assisted with the costs associated with clinical trial participation

# of patients currently active in clinical trials

# of patients enrolled in clinical trials

# of patients who have completed their participation in clinical trials

# of registered nurses and navigators educated about clinical trials

# of registered nurses and navigators participating in the enrollment process

Community Health

congregational health programs

individuals receiving hearing referrals

of after-school program participants

# of clients served

# of drug misusers in treatment, year to date

# of early intervention in pychosis. services

# of immunizations given

# of individuals receiving food or referred to food bank

# of individuals receiving medical referrals

# of individuals receiving vision referrals

# of program participants

# of smoking quitters (proxy for smoking prevalence)

# of smoking quitters per 100,000 population aged 16 and over

receiving immunizations

% children with BMI recorded in reception

% children with BMI recorded in year 6

% increase in drug misusers sustained in treatment

% infants with breastfeeding

% integration of older people

% of children and young people who have learning disability

% of children who complete immunization by recommended ages

% of infants breastfed at 6-8 weeks

14. Healthcare

% of women who have seen a midwife or maternity healthcare professional by 12 completed weeks of pregnancy

% people where health affects the amount/type of work they can do

% prevalence of breastfeeding at 6-8 weeks from birth

% primary school age children in reception

% primary school age children in year 6

% reduction in cancer mortality rate in people age under 75

% reduction in CVD mortality rate in people age under 75

<75 yrs cancer mortality rate

<75 yrs CVD mortality rate

All-age all cause mortality rate per 100k population - Females

All-age all cause mortality rate per 100k population - Males

Annual under 18 conception rate per 1,000 females aged 15-17

Childhood obesity rate - reception year

Childhood obesity rate - year 6

Mortality rate per 100,000 from causes considered amenable to healthcare (< 75)

Teenage conception rates per 1,000 females aged 15-17

Dental Care

in need of dental service

of dental screenings

# of individuals in need of dental services

# of individuals receiving dental services

who received dental care

Facility Management

of implemented quality of service standards

# of public safety violations

# of service and repairs done / year

# of unplanned initiatives

% adherence to compliance

% efficiency of equipment in facilities

% of occupant concerns addressed

% of planned developments on schedule

Building occupancy requirements

Financial Management

% margin

% of plan achieved

% of revenue from charitable sources

Average age of discharged not final billed accounts

Cost per patient day

Financial benefit from operations (% variance to plan)

GP referrals (% growth vs. prior year)

Income performance (surplus)/deficit

Total support staff cost per physician

14. Healthcare

Health Awareness

of adolescents participating
# of adults participating
# of classes
# of clients in tutoring services
# of educational activities
# of group educational presentations
# of health fairs in which the organization participated
# of individual educational presentations
# of participants
# of patients educated about clinical trials
# of people educated on breast cancer and/or breast health
# of people to whom informational pieces were distributed
# of people with increased knowledge of a topic after the educational session
participating in health training classes
% of people educated on breast cancer and/or breast health who are medically uninsured or underinsured
% of people educated with increased knowledge of a topic after the session
Health training graduation rate

Health Insurance

% of children's health insurance plan
% of invalid patient demographic information
% of invalid patient insurance information
% of operating expenses paid from endowment proceeds
% of scheduled accounts with insurance verification completed on-time
% of scheduled patients with a self-pay liability

Healthcare Access

of maximum center's capacity level
# of patients benefiting from patient assistance programs
# of practices offering extended opening hours as per guidance
# of technology transfer initiative agreements with companies
% access to GUM clinics - offered
% access to primary care - GP
% access to primary care - patient survey
% access to primary care - PCP
% access to primary dental services
% breast symptom patients seen within two weeks of referral
% increase of extended opening hours of GP practices
% of all HIV/AIDS patients living in countries eligible for no-profit medicines
% of all HIV/AIDS patients living in countries eligible for reduced-price medicines
% of patient reported measure of primary care access
% of patients accessing primary dental services in 24 month period

14. Healthcare
% of people served within specified time after program completion
% patients seen within 18 weeks for direct access audiology treatment
% who have access to appropriate services
FTE registered nurses per physician
FTEs per occupied bed
New patients per full-time-equivalent (FTE) physician

Heart Attack

of- patients who spend at least 90% of their time on a stroke unit
% of higher risk TIA cases who are treated within 24 hours
% of patients "expired"
% of patients admitted with a heart attack who were prescribed a beta-blocker
% of patients admitted with a heart attack who were prescribed a stating
% of patients admitted with a heart attack who were prescribed an anti-platelet
% of heart attack patients given ACE inhibitor for left ventricular systolic dysfunction
% of heart attack patients given Aspirin at arrival
% of heart attack patients given Aspirin at discharge
% of heart attack patients given Beta Blocker at arrival
% of heart attack patients given Beta Blocker at discharge
% of heart attack patients given Fibrinolytic medication within 30 minutes of arrival
% of heart attack patients given PCI within 90 minutes of arrival
% of heart attack patients given smoking cessation advice/counseling
Heart attack mortality rate

Heart Failure

% of heart failure patients given ACE inhibitor for left ventricular systolic dysfunction
% of heart failure patients given an evaluation of left ventricular systolic function
% of heart failure patients given discharge instructions
% of heart failure patients given smoking cessation advice/counseling
Heart failure mortality rate

Hospital Management

# of all age all cause mortality - female
# of all age all cause mortality - male
# of commissioner national measures
# of crisis resolution/home treatment services
# of emergency bed days
# of hospital occupied bed days of patients aged under 18
# of hospital occupied bed days on adult psychiatric wards
# of hospital occupied bed days on adult psychiatric wards of patients under the care of a psychiatric specialist
# of hospital-acquired infections

14. Healthcare
# of incidence of clostridium difficile
# of national health indicators
% admitted pathway data completeness
% admitted pathway performance
% distance from target
% follow up DNAs adult
% follow up DNAs older people
% lst attendance DNAs adult
% lst attendance DNAs older people
% non admitted pathway data completeness
% non admitted pathway performance
% occupancy
% occupancy - by ward
% of data quality in database
% of good experience of patients
% of individuals who complete immunization by recommended ages (Children)
% of infection reduction in MRSA & other infections
% of patients spending more than 90% of hospital stay on stroke unit
% of staff satisfaction
% of TIA patients treated within 24 hours
% over achievement of activity when compared to capacity plan YTD figures
% readmissions <28 days
% variance demand vs. capacity
Average audiology waiting times
Average time to reperfusion for patients who have had a heart attack
Crisis resolution /HTT episodes

Maintenance Efficiency
# of trainings given to staff
% of maintenance issues resolved on time
Maintenance cost of statutory regulatory requirements for preventive maintenance
Maintenance costs of electro-mechanical systems
Maintenance costs of light service
Total annual maintenance resources required by the facility
Total cost of replacement and maintenance activities

Maternal/Child Health
# of immunizations up-to-date
# of fathers involved in parenting classes
# of mothers
# of normal birth weight
# of normal term pregnancy
# of normal weight gain
# of parenting class attendees

14. Healthcare

of parenting class graduates
# of pediatric well care up-to-date
# of prenatal patients
# of prenatal visits
# of social work referrals
# of social work visits
# of well woman well care up-to-date
# of women seen by M.D. during pregnancy

Mental Health

of children and adult getting mental health service
# of clients referred for mental health
# of individuals receiving mental health education and consultation
# of mental health screenings conducted
# of patients per month
# of patients reporting employment after receiving services
# of visits per month
Suicide rate among mental health patients

Nurse Performance

of C difficile cases in those aged over 65
# of cancelled operations on the day of or after admission due to staffing
% appointment centre calls answered within 5 minutes
% appropriate return to work dates
% attendance on time
% cancelled operations breaching the 28 day rule
% complaints responded to within 25 days
% discharge summaries sent within 48 hours
% nurse availability
% of allied health professional meeting occupational health standards
% of nurses fully compliant and assured against standards
% of ward audit cleanliness results
% punctuality and shift adherence
Average call handle time
Average work time
Hospital standardized mortality ratio (last 12 months)
Quality monitoring compliance
Readmission rate

Patient Services

of complete impact assessments
# of emergency admissions for ambulatory care sensitive conditions
# of emergency bed days
# of home visits
# of infections
# of infections clostridium difficile
# of issues received in question

14. Healthcare

of patient follow-ups

# of prescribing indicator

# of self reported bad experience of patients

# of staff survey measures of job satisfaction

% of acute readmissions

% of admissions screened for MRSA

% of patient-oriented time

% of patients leaving against medical advise

% of patients re-admitted after discharge

% of patients treated as day cases

% of patients without symptoms of cardiovascular disease but with an absolute risk of CVD

% of people with depression and/or anxiety disorders who are offered psychological therapies

% of public confidence

% of women who have seen a midwife or maternity healthcare professional for assessment of health and social care needs by 12 completed weeks of pregnancy

Average case load per physician FTE

Average cycle time of discharge of patients

Average cycle time of hospital beds

Average cycle time of medical assessment of patients

Average discharge time of patient

Average length of stay for patients

Average occupation time of hospital bed

Average time from discharge to final bill

Average time per patient

BME patients detained as a % of total detentions

Rate of hospital admissions per 100,000 for alcohol related harm

Ratio of full-time-equivalent (FTE) non-physician practitioners and physicians

Pneumonia

% of Pneumonia patients assessed and given influenza vaccination

% of Pneumonia patients assessed and given Pneumococcal vaccination

% of Pneumonia patients given initial Antibiotic(s) within 4 hours after arrival

% of Pneumonia patients given Oxygenation assessment

% of Pneumonia patients given smoking cessation advice/counseling

% of Pneumonia patients given the most appropriate initial Antibiotic

% of Pneumonia patients whose initial emergency room blood culture was performed Prior to the administration of the first hospital dose of Antibiotics

Pneumonia Mortality Rate

Preparedness & Response

of audit of suicide prevention

14. Healthcare
# of clinical evaluations
# of diabetic Retinopathy
# of environmental controls
# of equipments not meeting standards
# of evaluations done
# of hospital access controls
# of infection control and respiratory hygiene rules
# of major regulatory approvals received
# of major regulatory filings
# of patient isolation and cohering
# of patients waiting longer than 3 months for revascularization
% access to a GP within 2 working days
% access to a PCP within 1 working day
% access to abortion under 10 weeks
% access to crisis services (mental Health)
% ambulance category A calls meeting 19 minute standard
% ambulance category A calls meeting 8 minute standard
% ambulance category B calls meeting 19 minute standard
% ambulance distance from target
% cancer referral to treatment < 62 days (urgent refs)
% category A ambulance calls within 19 minutes
% category A ambulance calls within 8 minutes
% category B ambulance calls within 19 minutes
% increase in staffing needs to min standards
% of 24 hour cover is available to meet the urgent health needs
% of 48 hour access to clinic (appointments offered)
% of cancer 2 week wait (urgent refs seen in 2 wks)
% of cancer diagnosis to treatment < 31 days (urgent refs)
% of communication and reporting done on time
% of crisis resolution team implementation
% of delayed transfers of care at minimum level
% of early intervention for psychosis
% of first attendances in emergency room
% of follow-up attendances in emergency room
% of involuntary patient admissions
% of near misses during hospitalization
% of Thrombolysis 60 minute call to needle time
% of two week wait for rapid access chest pain clinics
% patients on the semi-urgent surgery list that waited longer than 90 days
% patients waiting over four hour maximum A&E
% reduction in 1st appointment at outpatients
% reduction in emergency admissions for long term conditions
% reduction in follow-up attendances
% unplanned readmission rate

14. Healthcare

Emergency triage rate

Rate of hospital admissions for ambulatory care sensitive conditions

Prescription Assistance

of clients receiving prescriptions

# of prescription received

# of prescriptions

# of prescriptions applied for

% of new prescriptions outside regular appointments

% of prescriptions not collected by patients

% of prescriptions that need unexpected repeat

% of repeat prescriptions outside regular appointments

Average # of prescriptions per patient

Total clients interviewed

Total prescription cost savings

Total prescription value applied for

Total prescription value reapplied

Total prescription value received

Total prescriptions reapplied

Regulations & Policies

of breaches

# of fines from regulatory bodies

# of non-conformities in the quality assurance system

requests for independent review

% Investigations completed <25 days

Hospitals national accreditation rate

Screening & Diagnosis

hearing screenings

of biopsies

# of biopsies provided

# of breast cancer screening for women aged 40-53

# of breast cancer screening for women aged 53-64

# of breast cancers detected

# of breast cancers detected by age: (Under 40, 40-49, 50-64, 65+)

# of breast cancers detected provided by Race

# of cases for Diabetes

# of cases for High Blood Pressure

# of cases for STDs

# of cases for Substance Abuse

# of cases for Wound Care

# of Chlamydia screening (as a proxy for Chlamydia prevalence)

# of clinical breast exams provided

# of clinical breast exams provided by age: (Under 40, 40-49, 50-64, 65+)

# of clinical breast exams provided by prior history: (first time, repeat)

# of clinical breast exams provided by Race

14. Healthcare

of diabetic retinopathy screening

# of diagnostic mammograms

# of diagnostic mammograms provided

# of excisional biopsies provided

# of health screenings

# of HIV screenings

# of individuals with early intervention in psychosis

# of individuals referred for HIV follow-up care/testing

# of individuals referred out for diagnostic follow-up

# of individuals referred out for diagnostic follow-up as a % of screenees

# of patients receiving biopsies as a % of screenees

# of patients receiving diagnostic mammograms as a % of screenees

# of patients receiving diagnostic services

# of patients receiving diagnostic services as a % of screenees.

# of patients receiving surgical consults as a % of screenees

# of patients receiving ultrasounds as a % of screenees

# of patients with diabetes

# of people receiving case coordination/management services through the screening and diagnostic process

# of people receiving case coordination/management services through the treatment process

# of people receiving navigation services through the screening and diagnostic process

# of people receiving navigation services through the treatment process

# of people to whom informational pieces were distributed in addition to providing screening services

# of screening mammograms provided

# of screening mammograms provided by age: (Under 40, 40-49, 50-64, 65+)

# of screening mammograms provided By prior history: (first time, repeat)

# of screening mammograms provided by Race

# of stereotactic vacuum assisted biopsies provided

# of surgical consults (including pre- and post-surgery care)

# of ultrasounds

# of ultrasounds provided

# of ultrasounds with core biopsy provided

# of ultrasounds with fine needle aspiration

# of vision screenings

% men and women aged 70-75 taking part in bowel screening program

% of follow up (by phone or face to face)

% of invalid diagnosis codes

% of nosocomial infection

% of the population aged 15-24 screened or tested for Chlamydia

% women aged 47-49 and 71-73 offered screening for breast cancer

% women receiving cervical cancer screening test results within two weeks

14. Healthcare

Surgical Care

% inpatient mortality

% medication error rate

% of surgery patients who received preventative Antibiotic one hour before incision

% of surgery patients who received the appropriate preventative antibiotic for their surgery

% of surgery patients who received treatment to prevent blood clots within 24 Hours before or after selected surgeries to prevent blood clots

% of surgery patients whose doctors ordered treatments to prevent blood clots (Venous Thromboembolism)

% of surgery patients whose preventative Antibiotic are stopped within 24 hours after surgery

% outpatient surgeries

% preoperative mortality

% surgical site infection rate

Surgical care mortality rate

Treatment Services

# of cancers one month diagnosis (decision to treat) to treatment (All Referrals)

# of cancers one month diagnosis (decision to treat) to treatment (GP Referrals)

# of cancers two month urgent GP referral to treatment (all referrals)

# of cancers two month urgent GP referral to treatment (GP referrals)

# of drug users recorded as being in effective treatment

# of patients receiving chemotherapy

# of patients receiving radiation therapy

# of patients undergoing a lumpectomy

# of patients undergoing a mastectomy

% of cancers two week wait

Average cost per patient for treatment services

Treatment Support

# of counseling sessions provided

# of days of hospice services provided

# of families receiving bereavement support

# of in-home health service visits provided

# of meals provided

# of navigation and care coordination/management services

# of one-time referrals for patients

# of patients actually receiving care coordination/care management services

# of patients actually receiving navigation services

# of patients assisted by a translator or bilingual breast health staff member

# of patients assisted with transportation needs

# of patients educated about a navigator program

# of patients educated about care coordination/care management services

14. Healthcare
# of patients for whom rides were provided for treatment-related services
# of patients participating in a navigation program with a high need (more than 10 hours of service)
# of patients participating in a navigation program with a low need (less than 3 hours of service)
# of patients participating in a navigation program with a moderate need (between 3 and 10 hours of service)
# of patients participating in a support group
# of patients participating in retreats during or immediately following treatment
# of patients receiving alternative and/or complementary therapies during treatment
# of patients receiving assistance in paying for medical insurance
# of patients receiving assistance in paying for medical services
# of patients receiving assistance with co-pays
# of patients receiving assistance with paying their medical bills
# of patients receiving childcare services during treatment
# of patients receiving counseling services
# of patients receiving financial assistance related to household expenses
# of patients receiving financial assistance related to housing costs
# of patients receiving financial assistance related to medical services
# of patients receiving financial assistance related to paying utility bills
# of patients receiving hospice services
# of patients receiving in-home health services
# of patients receiving meals during treatment
# of patients receiving non-medical financial assistance
# of patients receiving non-medical in-home services
# of patients receiving nutrition counseling
# of patients reporting an improved level of dignity from participating in funded project/program
# of patients reporting improved comfort from participating in funded project/program
# of patients reporting improved emotional well-being from participating in funded project/program
# of patients reporting improved physical well-being from participating in funded project/program
# of patients reporting improved quality of life from participating in a funded project/program
# of patients served by an exercise program
# of physicians actively participating in enrolling new patients in clinical trials
# of physicians educated about clinical trials
# of rides provided for treatment-related services
Average days per patient served
The average amount of financial assistance provided per patient

14. Healthcare

Waiting Time

# of inpatients waiting over 26 weeks
# of outpatients waiting over 13 weeks
# of patients waiting > 6 weeks for 15 key diagnostic tests
% of inpatients waiting longer than the 26 week standard
% of outpatients waiting longer than the 13 week standard
% of patients waiting longer than 3 months (13 weeks) for revascularization
% patients waiting no more than 31 days for second or subsequent cancer treatment (radiotherapy treatments)
% patients waiting no more than 31 days for second or subsequent cancer treatment (surgery and drug treatments)
% patients with suspected cancer detected through national screening programs who wait less than 62 days from referral to treatment
% patients with suspected cancer who wait less than 62 days from referral to treatment following a consultant decision to upgrade their status
Average waiting time for new patient to be admitted
Average waiting time for rapid access chest pain clinics
Average waiting time to follow up appointment
Average waiting time to new patient appointment
Average waiting time to treatment appointment
Cancer waits: 2 week wait from referral to first outpatient
Cancer waits: 31 day target diagnosis to treatment
Cancer waits: 62 day target referral to treatment
Delayed transfers of care - bed days as % of total
Delayed transfers of care bed days as % of acute (Adult & older) total
Thrombolysis- 30 minute door to needle
Thrombolysis- 60 minute call to needle time

15. Hospitality

Hotel

absent days per employee in high season (hotel)
average length of stay in hotel
complaints received (hotel)
guests per employee (hospitality)
of kilo-watt-hours (kwh) per room
technological competence of staff (hotel)
training sessions for hotel personnel
% decrease in cleaning cost per room
% hotel occupancy
% internet bookings
% of cancelled reservation requests
% of cancelled rooms occupied
% of guests who would rank stay as exceeding expectations
% of hotel beds occupied

15. Hospitality
% of non-room revenue
% of occupancy of rooms
% of reservation requests cancelled with penalty
% of reservation requests cancelled without penalty
% of rooms with maintenance issues
% room occupancy
% rooms booked through reservation channels
% rooms with maintenance problems
Annual operating profit per room
Average # of guests per room
Average cleaning costs per room
Average daily rate (hotel)
Average daily rate of rooms
Average length of stay of guests
Average revenue per available room
Gross operating profit per available room (GOPPAR)
Gross operating profits per available room
Revenue per available room (RevPAR)
Waste per night per occupied bed space

Restaurant

% canceled reservation
% frequent customers
% of pre-booked tables
% positive feedback from guests
% reservation channel revenue
Average # of guests per table
Average # of rotations per table
Average # of waiters per table
Food, dessert, and beverage sales per head
Kitchen labor %
Seating efficiency
Strike rate

16. Human Resources

Absenteeism

hours lost to absenteeism
of grievances per month
# of sick days (in hours) relative to # of work days (in hours)
time lost by starting work late
% of absenteeism
% of days that employees are absent from work
% of employees on long-term sickness leave (more than x working days)
% of employees that are too late at work
% of time cards that have errors on them signed by managers

16. Human Resources
% of time sheets in need of correction and/or validation by submitter
% of total hours lost to absenteeism
Absence cost per FTE
Absence Rate
Absenteeism rate due to health issues
Average # of sick days (in hours) per employee
Employee absence factor (days lost and absence rate)
Level of outstanding annual leave liability
Sickness absence rate
Total cost incurred

Compensation

# of employees on company secondment
# of manual payroll adjustments
# of share incentive plan
% compensation and benefits cost / sales turnover per year
% entry level wage to local minimum wage
% of complaints about salary
% of eligible employees purchased shares
% of employee share purchase plan
% of employee share scheme take-up rate
% of share bought by employees
% of total performance related pay
% total compensation revenue rate
% workforce on individual employment contracts
Average # of vacation days per employee
Average benefits
Average compensation
Average compensation per employee
Average employee salary
Average income per employee by hour
Average income per employee by month
Average income per employee by position
Average remuneration
Bonus payout
Compensation cost as % of revenue
Cost rate of benefits
Cost rate of medical insurance
Cost rate of social insurance
Cost rate of workers compensation
Pay for equity gaps
Pay for performance gaps
Range of ratios of standard entry level wage compared to local minimum wage
Ratio between standard level wage compared to local minimum wage

16. Human Resources

Ratio of female to male salaries including bonus

Salary rate / sales turnover

Total "frustration level" / # of employees

Total benefits/compensation

Variable compensation

Wage rate

Diversity & Inclusion

harassment and discrimination complaints received

of discrimination complaints received

# of female senior managers with more than 10 years in company

# of middle management

# of minority in senior management

# of physical harassment complaints received

# of sexual harassment complaints received

# of women in management positions

# of workforce who are persons with physical disabilities

# of workforce who are visible minorities

% gender ratio

% of female part-time

% of male part-time

% of staff who are disabled

% of staff from minority ethnic groups

% of women in management positions

% of women in total workforce

% of women returning to work after maternity leave

Average age range of employees

Average employee engagement score

Employee gender ratio (female/male)

Employees with a disability

Ethnic diversity ratio

Ratio of female appointments versus male

Employee Headcount

headcount

of employees (full-time equivalent - FTE)

# of employees aged 25–35

# of employees aged 35–45

# of employees aged 45–55

# of employees aged over 55

# of employees aged under 25

# of FTEs in HR

# of full time employees

# of part time employees

# of total staff by branch

# of total staff by Region

16. Human Resources

% HR outsource rate

% of affiliates with local general manager

% of senior employees

% of staff who are women

% of temporary contracted FTEs

% ratio of salaried staff to waged staff

% ratio of surplus

% ratio of surplus staff to required staff

Average length of service (current employees)

Average length of service (terminating employees)

Growth in full-time equivalent employees

HR FTEs as % of total workforce (FTEs)

Management-to-staff ratio

Ratio of direct to indirect employees

Total hours utilized

Employee Relations

hours volunteered by employees

intimidation, hazing, bullying or retaliation complaints received

of active flexible work agreements

# of active job sharing agreements

# of active teams

# of active working from home agreements

# of bulletins issued

# of company-wide meetings

# of emails issued

# of formal union grievances

# of formal grievances

# of internal communications campaigns

# of staff briefing sessions conducted

# of staff involved in company sponsored activities

# of team meetings

# of unfair dismissal claims

# of workforce on individual contracts

% of active flexible work agreements

% of employees participating in company-sponsored activities

% of error-free newsletters

% of executive interviews with employees

% of managers active in community activities

% of personnel problems handled by employees managers

% of retirees contacted yearly by phone

% of staff involved in company sponsored activities

% of unfair dismissal claims KPI

% of work/life balance

% operating income dedicated to social contribution

16. Human Resources
% workforce on individual contracts
Average time a visitor spends in lobby
Total workforce lost time (hours)

Employee Safety

accidents per 100,000 hours worked
lost time due to accidents per 100,000 hours worked
of accidents
# of health promotion
# of industrial accidents man days lost
# of initiatives for safety projects generated by site champions
% fatal accidents
% hospitalization leave factor
% of days with Zero doctors cases and lost time incidents
% of employees participating in voluntary health screening
% of employees trained in first aid

Employee Satisfaction

# of valuable feedback gained from Employee Satisfaction Surveys
% average satisfaction
% average satisfaction by each department
% average satisfaction by field
% average satisfaction by new employee
% employees to have a loyalty to company
% of day lighting in building
% of employees are in same job/function for 3+ years
% of employees who are willing to recommend the organization as an employer
% of employees who consider that their business acts responsibly
% of participation levels in improvement activities
% staff satisfaction in workplace facility
Average satisfaction % versus norm
Average satisfaction % versus previous survey
Average time employees are in same job/function
Job satisfaction score of employees measured by surveys
Opinion survey ratings

Employee Scheduling

Employee total scheduled time
Maximum overtime (OT) hours
Total of employee available time
Total overtime (OT) hours

Employee Turnover

employee tenure
of employee leaving with service time between 1 to 2 years
# of employee leaving with service time between 10 to 20 years
# of employee leaving with service time between 2 to 5 years

16. Human Resources

of employee leaving with service time between 5 to 10 years
% decrease in staff turn-over (dismissals, resignations)
% of early retirements
% of employee leaving less more than 10 years
% of employee leaving less than one year
% of employees that leave the organization in a given time period
% of employees who leave during the first year
% of staff turnover (fluctuation)
% of total workforce terminating
% personnel turnover
% reduction in turnover
% turnover in admin. Staff
% turnover in tech. Staff
Average age of employees that retire
Average tenure per employee
Employee attrition
Employee retention
Involuntary termination rate
Job leaving ratio per department
Job leaving ratio per year
Personnel turnover rate
Resignation rate by length of service
Resignation rate with 2 weeks notice
Turnover rate due to poor performance
Turnover rate for the year without notice
Voluntary turnover rate

Exit Interview

of employees who would recommend company
# of employees who would seek re-employment with company
% of employees who are willing to recommend company as employer
% satisfaction with conditions/physical work environment
% satisfaction with job
% satisfaction with opportunities for development
% satisfaction with participation and recognition
% satisfaction with personal relations
% satisfaction with wages/salary/benefits

HR Budget

% costs of FTE per division
% decrease in cost of training
% deviation to resource plan
% man hours available
% of salaries and wages
% training cost / sales turnover
Administration cost per employee

16. Human Resources

Average cost of recruitment per staff

Average cost of recruitment per year

Average cost of training per year

Average cost rate of social insurance

Average overtime cost per headcount

Average overtime hours per employee

Average paid time off

Average training cost per employee

Average training costs per employee

Compensation and benefit cost / sales turnover per year

Cost of office space per employee

Cost per FTE

Cost per hire

Cost per new employee

Error rates

FTEs per function FTEs

Function cost/total cost

Function costs per FTE

Health and safety prevention costs

Health safety cost per year

Hiring cost

HR cost as % of total workforce (FTEs)

HR department cost per FTE

HR department costs/total costs

HR labor cost as % of sales/revenue

Human capital return on investment

Human capital value added

Human resources (HR) department cost per FTE

Human resources budget spent on training

Human resources cost per sales turnover

Labor costs to sales

Overtime labor cost ratio

Personnel cost per employee

Prospect identification cost

Prospect to hire conversion rate

Salary budget ratio / sales turnover

Time spent on managing under-performing staff

Total cost of audio visual equipment rental

Total cost of training per year

Total employees' remuneration

Total employees' remuneration as % of sales

Total labor cost

Training cost headcount factor

Turnover cost

16. Human Resources

HR Department

FTEs per HR department FTE
% of HR staff with appropriate professional qualification
Average response time for routine HR inquiries
Average time to update employee records if changes in employee information occur
FTEs per HR department FTEs
HR department age of HR strategy
HR department EIS usefulness index
Human resources FTE to total FTE ratio

HR Process

Average tenure
FTEs per process FTE
Human capital ROI ratio
Recruitment headcount factor
Recruitment resignation factor
Share of employees below age X
Time to get security clearance
Time to process an applicant
Time to process insurance claims
Training hours ratio
Wait time in medical department

HR Ratio

% Managers
% of employees from minority groups managing x or more staff members
% of higher degree employees
% of management FTEs
% of or indexed to the salary range midpoint/market rate
% of part-time employees
% of part-time employees that are female
Average (annual) salary per employee
Average sickness days per FTE
Average span of control
Employer satisfaction (index)
Human capital ROI
Human capital value added
Independent contractors vs. employees ratio

Leadership Skills

# of best practice leadership programs and recommendation to CEO
# of business excellence champions/leaders
# of leadership development workshops conducted
# of management evaluation of management education courses
# of monthly once 1-on-1 coaching for GM / Director / Manager
% of knowledge shared between / within teams

16. Human Resources

Leadership effectiveness index

Medical Leave

of lost time days

# of lost time injuries

sickness absence days per FTE

% decrease in injury rates

% decrease in sick time used

% of employees on short-term sickness leave

% of lost time claims to total claims

% of MC issued by government hospitals and panel clinics

% of MC issued by non-government hospitals and non-panel clinics

% sickness

% staff in team with excess sick leave

Absence due to sick leave

Average cost per lost time claim

Average cost per medical only claim

Average cost per workers compensation claim

Average duration rate of lost time injuries

Average expense cost per lost time claim

Average indemnity cost per lost time claim

Average losses as a % of payroll

Average losses as a % of revenue

Average losses per full time equivalent employee (FTE)

Average medical cost per lost time claim

Average sick leave in working days per staff member

Average sickness period of employees

Cost of workers compensation

Frequency rate of LTI

Total lost time due to non-fatal accidents or accidents per year

Total time lost by work late

Performance Appraisals

of formal staff grievances raised

# of staff appraisals held

# of suggested improvements per employee

% high performing employees

% low performing employees

% monthly 1-on-1 program for all staff with performance rating

% of appraisals completed on time

% of appraisals done on schedule

% of appraisals with high quality

% of compliance survey for 1-on-1's completed with recommendations

% of employee output that is measured

% of employee time spent on first-time output

% of employee with their performance decreased compared to last year

16. Human Resources
% of employee with their performance increased compared to last year
% of employees above competence
% of employees below competence
% of employees receiving regular performance reviews
% of employees with their performance decreased compared to the previous evaluation report
% of employees with their performance increased compared to the previous evaluation
% of high performing employees
% of individual training plans completed
% of low performing employees
% of managers trained in key processes
% of peer reviews
% of personal goal achievement
% of staff given feedback on performance on time
% of staff having appraisal in last 12 months
% performance appraisals completed on time
% staff appraised by end of January
Employee satisfaction index
Employee's empowerment index
Normal appraisal distribution
Staff appraisals completion rate
Value added per employee

Productivity & Utilization
# of completed quarterly skills audits
# of credit returns (linked with employee error)
# of cross-functional assignments
# of customer complaints (employee related)
# of quality circles
% decrease in paper waste
% decrease in production time
% of complete training of skills through training programs
% of email newsletters received but not read
% of employee productivity
% of employees who can detect and repair their own errors
% of man days lost (in FTE) due stoppage of work
% of man days lost (in FTE) due to strike
% of meetings less than 30 minutes long
% of overdue work items
% of time spent on planned work items
% of time spent on priorities
Average age (in years) of workforce
Average overdue time of work items
Average planned workload per workforce member

16. Human Resources

Compensation/revenue

Compensation/total costs

Cycle time of regular tasks

Effective worktime index

HR ratios overtime rate

Human capital return on investment

Labor cost as % of sales

Labor cost as % of total revenue

Labor utilization rate

Level of training completed by all specialists

New staff versus experienced staff ratio

Profit per employee

Profits per employee

Quality reject rate (employee error)

Remuneration/revenue

Remuneration/total costs

Return on time invested

Revenue generated per FTE

Reward & recognition coverage

Sales per employee

Sales turnover per employee

Span of control

Suggestions implemented

Suggestions received

Task completion ratio

Unit production per FTEs

Recruiting

employment brand strength

of adjustments of manpower plan (MPP) per department

# of CVs / per channel

# of days recruitment activity required per employee

# of days to fill an employment request

# of days to respond to applicant

# of interviews from submitted applications/ CV's

# of job vacancies for (previously) filled positions

# of nationals recruited

# of open requisitions to current staff

# of qualified candidate compared to resumes

# of screened newly recruited employees

# of structure vacancies

open requisitions

responses (CVs received) per open position

time to recruit

% actual versus budgeted cost of hire

16. Human Resources
% applicants / appointees referred by current employees
% internally submitted CVs
% job offer acceptance rate
% new hire retention
% new hires achieving 12 months service
% new hires achieving 6 months service
% new hires achieving satisfactory appraisal at first assessment
% new staff with post-employment interview completed
% of 'wanted' new hire retention after certain period
% of converted submitted resumes to interviews
% of CVs that are worth screening compared to # received for an advertisement posting
% of employment requests filled on schedule
% of hires from "local" schools
% of hires from "top-10? targeted schools
% of hires that accepted an offer over offers from key talent competitors
% of job applicants that have received recommendations from current employees
% of job vacancies
% of job vacancies for (previously) filled positions
% of job vacancies for new open positions
% of job vacancies for new part-time positions
% of meet hiring plan
% of Nationalization achieved
% of new candidates for which a recruiting fee has been paid
% of new employee retention
% of new employee retention after x time
% of new employees with a recruiting fee paid
% of new hire retention
% of offers accepted
% of screened newly recruited employees
% of vacancies filled internally
% of vacancies filled within a period
% of vacancies filled within x days
% recruiter to open requisition ratio
% recruitment achievement meet hiring plan
% re-hired employees
% staffing rate
% vacancies
Acceptance Rate
Achievement %
Actual joinings vs. offers
Actual versus budgeted cost of hire
Average # of interviewees for open job positions

16. Human Resources

Average # of interviewees for open job positions within a given measurement period

Average # of interviews from submitted applications/ CVs

Average # of interviews from submitted resumes

Average # of responses for open job positions

Average cost of recruitment - management

Average cost of recruitment - staff

Average cost per vacancy filled

Average cost to recruit per job position

Average days of vacancy duration - management

Average days of vacancy duration - staff

Average feedback time on candidates

Average graduate compensation

Average interviewing costs

Average open time of job positions

Average sourcing cost per hire

Average time from job acceptance until job start

Average time from the moment a candidate submitted to hiring manager to receiving initial feedback from hiring manager

Average time to recruit manager

Average time to recruit per position

Average time to recruit staff

Average time to start

Cycle time from job acceptance until job start

Decrease open time in days per jobs

External addition rate

External recruitment rate

External replacement rate

Headhunter cost per hire

Internal promotion rate

Job offer acceptance rate

New employee satisfaction rate with recruiting quality

New hire satisfaction rate with recruiting process

New hire satisfaction rate with the recruiting speed

Performance evaluation average scores on hired candidates

Performance evaluation scores on hired candidates after 1 year

Ratio between internal versus external recruits

Ratio between local versus international recruits

Recruiting fee as % of annual budget

Recruiting fee as % of annual salary

Recruitment # of MPP adjustments

Recruitment costing per position

Recruitment costing per position per channel

Recruitment costs per year

16. Human Resources

Recruitment notice to sales budget delivery period

Recruitment source ratio - internal -v- external applicants

Time to acclimation for new employees

Total # of responses for open job positions per year

Total cost to recruit per year

Total costs for advertising

Total costs for agency

Total costs for referral

Total interviewing costs

Track # of converted submitted resumes to interviews

Turnover of new hire during 1 year

Turnover of new hire during 5 years

Redeployment & Retirement

% of employees taking ill health retirement

Average performance scores of departing employees

Average staff retirement cost

Cost of replacing a key worker vs. re-deploying

Cost of replacing a key worker vs. retaining

Cost of replacing a key worker vs. re-training

Performance scores of departing versus existing employees

Regulation Compliance

of big violations per year

# of HR policies and procedures

# of medium violations per year

# of small violations per year

# of violations by sector

Costing lost by violation

Time lost by violation

Violation rate by department

Rewards & Recognition

of days to answer suggestions

# of service stations recognized

# of suggestions resubmitted and approved

recognition events and awards to staff

% internal promotion rate

% of employees active in improvement teams

% of employees who have received recognition

% of professional employees active in professional societies

% of sales managers recognized

% of staff recognized

Succession Planning

% accession rate

% active job sharing agreements

% of employees cross-trained

16. Human Resources

% of employees nearing retirement age

% of employees of supervisory level who are not permanent in their role

% of employees promoted to better jobs

% of identified successor for various positions

% of identified successor with development plans in place on time

% of internal appointments above certain level

% of promotions and management changes publicized

% time (career) within company vs. time in other companies

Average lead time to promotion

Average length of service of staff appointed above level

Average time employees are in the same job or function

Average time to promotion

Average workforce age

Telecommuting

% active flexible work agreements

% active working from home agreements

% of employee satisfaction with teleworking/telecommuting

Average # of days of telecommuting per full-time equivalent (FTE)

Average estimated cost savings of employees that are teleworking/telecommuting

Satisfaction of managers of employees that are teleworking/telecommuting

Total cost savings of employer by having employees telework/telecommute

Training & Development

learning sessions held for top management

of conducted culture surveys for standards and recognition

# of courses implemented

# of courses offered

# of cross-training sessions

# of days training

# of employees completing sponsored MBA programs

# of employees completing sponsored tertiary studies

# of employees gone through training

# of hours of employee development

# of internet hours utilized

# of knowledge sharing sessions on brand identity

# of learning centers

# of managers with university degrees

# of new participants in training program

# of participants in development program

# of participants referred to the program by previous participants

# of participants that completed the program

# of participants that withdrew from the program

# of people already working at a company are considered for internal promotion

16. Human Resources
# of potential participants
# of sessions offered
# of skill matrices completed
# of training & development events per Head
# of training programs
# of training relevance
total hours employees spend in mentoring
training hours per employee
% decrease in customer service times
% decrease in error rates
% E-learning courses utilized
% employee attendance level in training sessions
% employee reach competence after training
% evaluating effectiveness of the training
% HR budget spent on training
% improvement in delivery culture
% improvement in staff health and safety at the workplace
% improvement in staff performance and morale
% improvement in team work
% improvement in the level of service
% improvement of staff competencies
% increase in accessibility of training by % of participation by branch office or region
% increase in product knowledge
% increase in productivity after the training
% increase in sales (after product knowledge training)
% increase in staff retention
% increase in team morale after the training
% increase of staff initiative, confidence and independent problem solving
% independent contractors
% of administrative and classified staff trained in process improvement
% of business continuity
% of conducive working environment
% of course participation
% of e-learning courses utilized
% of e-learning pass rate
% of employee probation reports completed x time before the due date.
% of employee satisfaction with training
% of employees assessed in an Assessment Center
% of employees certified for skilled job functions or positions
% of employees completing a course of training compared to # of employees employed
% of employees found their stress levels have decreased (feel more confident)

16. Human Resources
% of employees gone through training
% of employees gone through training in a given period
% of employees in self-managing teams
% of employees participating in career coaching
% of employees receiving regular performance and career development reviews
% of employees taking higher education
% of employees that are associated with a high performance band
% of employees that are associated with a low performance band
% of employees that have been assessed in assessment center
% of employees that participate in career coaching program.
% of employees with development plans
% of employees with higher education
% of enough time given to gain a comprehensive understanding of the subject
% of HR budget spent on training
% of human resources budget spent on training
% of new hire retention after a given period
% of outstanding employee probation reports
% of product knowledge
% of staff trained
% of staff who need to have qualifications that have appropriate qualifications
% of staff with management skills
% of technology skills of managers
% of training classes evaluated excellent
% of training course attendance
% of training course participant satisfaction
% of training courses requested, but not offered
% of training courses that match organizational requirements
% of women in training
% training certificates
% training for maintenance and support
% training goals met
% training hours imparted
% training on essential job skills
% training on knowledge improvement
% training penetration rate
% training return on investment
% training ROI of % training
% training scheduled to fit with operational constraints
% training to general staff
% training to management staff
Applied the learning on the job

16. Human Resources

Average # of training hours per employee
Average # of training hours per employee
Average # of training hours per employee
Average tenure per employee
Average test score %s
Average time it takes until expected competence level is reached
Average time to competence
Average time to planned competence
Average training cost per FTE
Average training hours per employee
Company training expenditure (% of salaries and wages)
Customer relations skills
Employee satisfaction with training
External cost per FTE
External hours per FTE hours
FTEs per L&D function FTEs
In-house training cost per FTE
In-house training hours per FTE hours
Learning rate of employees
Ratio of internal versus external training (cost)
Ratio of internal versus external training (hours)
ROI of training
Soft skills cost per FTE
Soft skills hours per FTE hours
Technical cost per FTE
Technical hours per FTE hours
Total human resources budget spent on training
Total training hours for all FTEs
Training cost
Training cost reduction
Training hours per FTE
Training investment / compensation
Training investment per FTE

Union Membership

formal union grievances
of employees in union
% lost time due to strike action
% of compliance against working time directive
% of employees in union
% of employees left union
% of man days lost due to strike

Vacation

% of employees that almost utilized their vacation balances
% of employees that are near or at max for their vacation balances

16. Human Resources

% of staff who have more than one year of annual leave owing

Average vacation hours utilized per employee by department

Department ratio of work days (or hours) to utilized vacation days (or hours)

Ratio of work days to utilized vacation days

17. Information Technology

Application Services

extra months spent for the implementation

fixed bugs

of alerts on exceeding system capacity thresholds

# of annual IT service continuity plan testing failures

# of business disruptions caused by (operational) problems

# of changes closed, relative to # of changes opened in a given time period

# of complaints received within the measurement period

# of failures of IT services during so-called critical times

# of incidents closed, relative to # of incidents opened in a given time period

# of incidents still opened

# of open incidents older than 15 days relative to all open incidents

# of open problems older than 28 days relative to all open problems

# of open service requests older than 28 days relative to all open service requests

# of overdue changes relative to # of open changes

# of overdue problems relative to # of open problems

# of requests closed, relative to # of requests opened in a given time period

# of Service Level Agreement (SLA) breaches due to poor performance

# of unmodified/neglected incidents

% accuracy of forecast against actuals of expenditure as defined in capacity plan

% accuracy of forecast against actuals of expenditure as defined in continuity plan

% applications with adequate user documentation and training

% bugs found in-house

% financial management processes supported electronically

% hosts missing high priority patches

% of (critical) infrastructure components with automated availability monitoring

% of actual uptime (in hours) of equipment relative to #s of planned uptime (in hours)

% of application / software development work outsourced

% of backlogged/neglected change requests

% of business process support of applications

% of closed service requests that have been escalated to management, relative to all closed service requests

17. Information Technology

% of Configuration Items (CIs) included in capacity reviews

% of Configuration Items (CIs) with under-capacity, relative to all CIs used to deliver services to end-customers

% of delivered changes implemented within budget/costs

% of efficient and effective technical business process adaptability of applications

% of incidents prior to the lifecycle

% of incidents solved within deadline

% of incidents that can be classified as a repeat incident, relative to all reported incidents

% of IT services that are not covered in the continuity plan

% of open service requests worked on

% of overdue incidents

% of overdue service requests

% of problems for which a root cause analysis was undertaken

% of problems resolved within the required time period

% of problems with a root cause identified for the failure

% of problems with available workaround

% of reopened incidents

% of reopened service requests

% of response-time SLAs

% of reviewed SLAs

% of service requests due to poor performance of services provided to end-customers

% of service requests posted via web (self-help)

% of service requests resolved within an agreed-upon/ acceptable period of time

% of SLAs with an assigned account manager

% of SLAs without service level breaches

% of time (in labor hours) used to coordinate changes relative to all time used to implement changes

% of unauthorized implemented changes

% of unplanned purchases due to poor performance

% of urgent changes

% of workarounds to service requests applied

ASL applications cycle management % of implemented changes without impact analysis

Average delay in SLAs review

Average problem closure duration

Average service request closure duration

Average spent duration of changes closed relative to the average allowed duration of those changes closed

Average time (hours) between the occurrence of an incident and its resolution

Average time (in days) between updates of Capacity Plan

17. Information Technology

Average time (in days) between updates of Continuity Plan

Average time spent (in FTE) on producing and keeping up-to-date of Capacity Plans

Average time spent (in FTE) on producing and keeping up-to-date of Continuity Plans

Business Value (BV) of application(s)

Change closure duration rate

Customer satisfaction (index)

First line service request closure rate

Gap between actual network usage and maximum capacity of the network

Problem queue rate

Ratio of # of incidents versus # of changes

Service request closure duration rate

Technical Value (TV) of application(s)

Time between reviews of IT continuity plan

Cobit Acquire & Implement

of application production problems (per application) causing visible downtime

# of bugs or software defects of applications (versions) that are in production

# of critical business processes supported by obsolete infrastructure

# of different technology platforms

# of infrastructure components that are no longer supportable

% of applications with adequate user and operational support training

% of business owners satisfied with application training and support materials

% of delivered projects where stated benefits were not achieved due to incorrect feasibility assumptions

% of development effort spent maintaining existing applications

% of feasibility studies signed off on by the business process owner

% of implemented changes not approved (by management / CAB)

% of infrastructure components acquired outside the acquisition process

% of key stakeholders satisfied with their suppliers

% of procurement requests satisfied by preferred suppliers

% of procurement requests satisfied by the preferred supplier list

% of procurements in compliance with standing procurement policies and procedures

% of projects on time and on budget

% of projects with a testing plan

% of Request for Proposals (RFP) that needed to be improved based on supplier responses

% of stakeholders satisfied with the accuracy of the feasibility study

% of systems that do not comply to the defined technology standards

% of users satisfied with the functionality delivered

Average # of responses received to Request for Proposals (RFP)

17. Information Technology

Average rework per change after implementation of changes

Average time to configure infrastructure components

Cost to produce/maintain user documentation, operational procedures and training materials

Satisfaction scores for training and documentation related to user and operational procedures

Software average time to procure

Time lag between changes and updates of training, procedures and documentation materials

Total rework (in FTE) after implementation of changes

Cobit Delivery & Support

of business compliance issues caused by improper configuration of assets

# of deviations identified between the configuration repository and actual asset configurations

# of formal disputes with suppliers

# of incidents due to physical security breaches or failures

# of incidents of non-compliance with laws due to storage management issues

# of incidents of unauthorized access to computer facilities

# of incidents outside hours where security staff are present

# of incidents where sensitive data were retrieved after media were disposed

# of SLAs without service level breaches relative to # of SLAs under management

# of training hours divided by # of employees (in FTE)

# of violations in segregation of duties

% of (major) suppliers subject to monitoring

% of applications that are not capable of meeting password policy

% of availability Service Level Agreements (SLAs) met

% of budget deviation relative to total budget

% of critical business processes not covered by a defined service availability plan

% of delivered services that are not included in the service catalogue

% of disputed IT costs by the business

% of IT service bills accepted/paid by business management

% of licenses purchased and not accounted for in the configuration repository

% of outage due to incidents (unplanned unavailability)

% of personnel trained in safety, security and facilities measures

% of scheduled work not completed on time

% of service levels (in Service Level Agreements) reported in an automated way

% of service levels (in Service Level Agreements) that are actually measured

% of successful data restorations

% of systems where security requirements are not met

17. Information Technology

% of telephone calls abandoned by the caller while waiting to be answered
% of transactions executed within response time threshold
% of user complaints on contracted services as a % of all user complaints
% of users who do not comply with password standards
Actual budget (costs) relative to the established budget
Amount of downtime arising from physical environment incidents
Average # of training days per operations personnel
Average time (in hours) for data restoration
Average time period (lag) between identifying a discrepancy and rectifying it
Downtime caused by deviating from operations procedures
Downtime caused by inadequate procedures
Frequency (in days) of physical risk assessment and reviews
Frequency (in days) of review of IT cost allocation model
Frequency (in days) of testing of backup media
Frequency (in days) of updates to operational procedures
Frequency of review of IT continuity plan
Unit costs of IT service(s) within measurement period
User satisfaction with availability of data

Cobit Monitor & Evaluate

of (critical) non-compliance issues identified
of (major) internal control breaches, within measurement period
of improvement actions driven by monitoring activities
# of IT policy violations
# of non-compliance issues reported to the board or causing public comment or embarrassment
# of recurrent IT issues on board agendas
# of weaknesses identified by external qualification and certification reports
% maturity of board reporting on IT to stakeholders
% maturity of reporting from IT to the board
% of critical processes monitored
% of metrics that can be benchmarked to (industry) standards and set targets
Age (days) of agreed-upon recommendations
Amount of delay to update measurements to reflect actual performance
Amount of effort required to gather measurement data
Average time lag between identification of external compliance issues and resolution
Average time lag between publication of a new law or regulation and initiation of compliance review
Cost of non-compliance, including settlements and fines
Frequency (in days) of board reporting on IT to stakeholders
Frequency (in days) of compliance reviews
Frequency (in days) of reporting from IT to the board
Frequency of independent reviews of IT compliance

17. Information Technology

Frequency of IT governance as an agenda item in the IT steering/strategy meetings

Stakeholder satisfaction with the measuring process

Time between internal control deficiency occurrence and reporting

Cobit Plan & Organize

# of conflicting responsibilities in the view of segregation of duties

% IT staff competent for their roles

% of budget deviation value compared to the total budget

% of IT budget spent on risk management (assessment and mitigation) activities

% of IT functions connected to the business

% of IT initiatives/projects championed by business owners

% of IT objectives that support business objectives

% of IT services whose costs are recorded

% of processes receiving Quality Assurance (QA) review

% of projects meeting stakeholder expectations

% of projects on budget

% of projects on time

% of projects receiving Quality Assurance (QA) review

% of projects with a post-project review

% of projects with the benefit (Return on Investment) defined up front

% of redundant and/or duplicate data elements as exist in the information architecture

% of repeat incidents

% of roles with documented position and authority descriptions

% of sick days (illness rate)

% of software applications that are not complying with the defined information architecture

% of software applications that do not comply to the defined technology standards

% of stakeholders satisfied with IT quality

% of stakeholders that understand IT policy

% of variation of the annual IT plan

Actual ratio vs. planned ratio of IT contractors to IT personnel

Average # of components under management per FTE

Delay in updates of IT plans after strategic updates

Frequency (in days) of enterprise IT control framework review/update

Frequency (in days) of review of the IT risk management process

Frequency (in days) of reviews of the existing infrastructure against the defined technology standards

Frequency (in days) of strategy and steering committee meetings

Frequency (in days) of updates to the information architecture

Frequency (in days) of updates to the technology standards

Overtime rate between employee overtime with the planned working times

Ratio of IT contractors to IT personnel

17. Information Technology
Direct IT Cost
# of maintenance contracts
% cost adherence
% hardware asset value to total IT value
Average age of hardware assets
Average cost to solve a problem
Average cost to solve an incident
Average costs of a release
Average costs of change implementation
Average costs of penalties paid on Service Level Agreements (SLAs)
Cost of CMDB reconciliation
Cost of consumable items such as ink, cartridges, cds etc
Cost of delivery
Cost of digital storage media
Cost of Infrastructure
Cost of leased equipment
Cost of maintenance per 1000 lines of code
Cost of producing and keeping up-to-date of Capacity Plans
Cost of producing and keeping up-to-date of Continuity Plans
Cost of purchase
Cost of security incidents
Cost of security incidents due to unauthorized access to systems
Cost of spares
Cost per device
Cost per PC
Cost per stored terabyte
Cost per terabyte transmitted
Costs associated to unplanned purchases to resolve poor performance
Costs of operating a call center / service desk, usually for a specific period such as month or quarter
Costs of operating call center / service desk
Costs savings from service reuse
Domain registrations costs
Facilities costs such as a dedicated server room with fire and air control systems
Financing costs
Hardware asset value
IT spending per employee
Labor cost for technical and user support
Net Present Value (NPV) of investment
Network costs determined by network demand and the bandwidth usage of the asset
Total cost of change implementation
Total cost of ownership

17. Information Technology

Total cost of release

Total cost to solve all incidents

Total cost to solve all problems

Unit cost of IT services

Unit costs of IT service(s)

Voice network - cost per minute

Green IT

% of energy used from renewable sources ("green energy")

% of recycled printer paper

% of servers located in data centers

Corporate average data efficiency (CADE) measures data center efficiency across the corporate footprint

Datacenter power usage effectiveness (PUE)

Help Desk

critical time outage

devices per FTE

incidents per PC

incidents processed per service desk workstation

IT service desk availability

mean time to repair (MTTR)

of complaints

# of training calls handled by the service desk

# of un-responded emails

% incidents resolved remotely, without the need of a visit

% incidents solved by first point of contact

% incidents solved within SLA time

% incidents which changed priority during the life-cycle

% IT incidents fixed before users notice

% IT incidents solved within agreed response time

% neglected incidents

% of (re)-assignments of service requests

% of calls transferred within measurement period

% of customer issues that were solved by the first phone call

% of first-line resolution of service requests

% of incorrectly assigned incidents

% of incorrectly assigned service requests

% of terminal response time

% service requests posted via web (self-help)

Average # of (re)-assignments of closed incidents within measurement period

Average # of calls / service request per handler

Average # of calls / service requests per employee of call center / service desk within measurement period

Average after call work time

17. Information Technology

Average after call work time (work done after call has been concluded)

Average amount of time (e.g. in days) between the registration of changes and their closure

Average amount of time between the registration of incidents and their closure

Average days for lease refresh/upgrade fulfillment

Average days for software request fulfillment

Average incident response time

Average overdue time of overdue service requests

Average problem closure duration

Average TCP round-trip time

Time before help calls are answered

Total service delivery penalties paid

Indirect IT Cost

% IT security budget

Average penalty costs per SLA

Cost of cleanup of virus/spyware incidents

Cost of CMDB reconciliation

Cost of finding and hiring one staff

Cost of managing processes

Cost of patches

Cost of producing capacity plans

Cost of producing continuity plans

Cost of professional certifications necessary

Cost of service delivery

Cost of skilled labor for support

Cost of support to the end users of IT assets

Cost per trouble report (man-hours)

Time for maintenance scheduled and unscheduled

Time of usage of assets for unrelated activities such a gaming, chatting

Training costs of both IT staff and end users

Use of assets for non-business purposes

IT Backup

applications data transfer time

data center infrastructure efficiency

deviations between configuration repository and actual configurations

time for configuration management database (CMDB) reconciliation

% backup operations that are successful

% corporate average data efficiency

% data redundancy

% of backup operations that are successful

% of changes that required restoration of backup

% of changes that required restoration of backup during the implementation

17. Information Technology
% of physical backup / archive media that are fully encrypted
% of test backup restores that are successful
Age of backup
Average time between tests of backup
Average time to restore backup
Average time to restore off-site backup

IT Business Performance

frequency of IT reporting to the board
of capabilities (services that can be rendered)
# of people working on a project versus the required #
# of services delivered on time
Service Level Agreements (SLA) breaches due to poor performance
terabyte managed by one Full Time Equivalent (FTE)
unique requirements
watts per active port
% facility efficiency (FE)
% growth in business profits
% growth in market share
% growth in sales
% improved SLA's
% IT projects with a testing plan
% Service Level Agreements (SLAs) reviewed
% SLAs without service level breaches
% stock price appreciation
% time coordinating changes
Actual capacity (# of people available & avoid new project traps)
Technology effectiveness index

IT Business Ratios

% IT budget of total revenues
% IT capital spending of total investment
% of current initiatives driven by IT
% of current initiatives driven by the business
% of growth of IT budget
% of IT contribution in ROTA
% of IT costs associated to IT investment
% of IT costs associated to IT maintenance
% of IT labor outsourced
% of IT time associated to IT investment
% of IT training on IT operational costs
% of spend on current IT capital projects that are considered driven by the business
Average IT-related costs per customer
IT to total employees ratio
Ratio of % growth of IT budget versus % growth of revenues

17. Information Technology

Ratio of fixed price projects cost versus T&M projects cost

IT Infrastructure

maximum memory usage
of compliments received
# of incidents caused by changes vs. total # of incidents
# of incidents caused by inadequate capacity
# of open IT Infrastructure incidents older than 28 days relative to all open incidents
# of open IT Infrastructure problems older than 28 days relative to all open problems
# of open service requests older than 28 days
# of outstanding actions against last SLA review
# of printers divided by # of staff
# of problems closed
# of repeated incidents
# of untested releases
# of urgent releases
power usage effectiveness
propagation delay
% availability (excluding planned downtime)
% data center infrastructure efficiency
% disk space quota used
% incidents solved within SLA time
% of audited Configuration Items (CI)
% of changes closed before deadline
% of closed service requests that were incorrectly assigned relative to all closed service requests
% of Configuration Items (CI) mapped onto IT services in the CMDB
% of Configuration Items (CI) monitored for performance
% of Configuration Items (CI) under maintenance contract
% of Configuration Items (CI) with under-capacity
% of customers given satisfaction surveys
% of delivered services not in the service catalogue
% of end user computers
% of end user printers
% of escalated service requests
% of fully documented SLAs
% of implemented changes without impact analysis
% of inaccurately registered Configuration Items (CI) in CMDB
% of incidents not solved in-time due to inaccurate configuration data
% of incidents which change classification during the lifecycle
% of incidents which change priority during the lifecycle
% of internal hosts which are centrally managed & protected
% of IT staff that is ITIL trained

17. Information Technology
% of IT staff with (advanced) ITIL certification
% of money spent on maintaining the IT infrastructure versus the total IT spent
% of money spent on new IT developments (investments) relative to the total IT spent
% of open service requests that are not owned by a person or group
% of open service requests unmodified/neglected
% of overdue changes
% of overdue problems
% of project files containing cost-/benefit estimates
% of refused changes
% of routine changes indicates the maturity level of the process
% of security-related service calls
% of Service Level Agreements (SLAs) in renegotiation relative to all SLAs that are in production
% of Service Level Agreements (SLAs) requiring changes
% of service requests closed before deadline
% of services covered by SLA
% of SLA breaches caused by underpinning contracts
% of SLA reviews conducted on-time
% of software licenses used
% of successful software installations
% of successful software upgrades
% of time coordinating changes
% of unmodified/neglected incidents
% of unmodified/neglected problems
% of unregistered changes
% of vendor services delivered without agreed service targets
% on-time service level changes
% reduction of IPCS's (Incident, Problem, Change, Service Request)
Average # of (re)-assignments of closed incidents
Average # of (re)-assignments of closed service requests within measurement period
Average change closure duration
Average rework (in FTE) per change after implementation of changes
Average size of discounts in procurement of items
Average time between audits of Configuration Items (CIs) as residing in the CMDB
Average time between CMDB reconciliation
Average time between urgent releases of software
Average time spent on CMDB reconciliation
Average time to procure an item
Balance of problems solved
Change queue rate
Delay in production of financial reports

17. Information Technology

First-call resolution rate

Forecast accuracy of budget

Growth of the CMDB

Incident impact rate incomplete CMDB

Mean Time To Detect (MTTD)

Overall cost of IT delivery per customer

Ratio of # of incidents versus # of problems

Service call abandoned rate

Service request backlog

Service request queue rate

Support costs of all software based on their support contracts

The actual costs relative to the budgeted costs of an activity

Time lag between request for procurement and signing of contract or purchase

Total critical-time outage

Total rework after implementation of changes

Total service delivery penalties paid within a period

IT Network

link transmission time

network latency

of bytes received since the system started

# of bytes sent out to connections

# of commands sent

# of connection attempts made since the system started

# of connections currently waiting in the queue to be processed

# of connections that have failed to complete successfully

# of connections that successfully completed their transfer and confirmation

# of messages received by the system

of the currently active connections that are open and sending information

retransmission delay

voice network minutes per FTE

% Internal servers centrally managed

% network bandwidth used

% network packet loss

% utilization of data network

Accuracy rate

Average connection time

Average network round trip latency

Average response speed

Connections per customer

Cost per byte

Total amount of time the system has been running in milliseconds

Total time the system started in UTC (days)

17. Information Technology

IT Operations

# of business disruptions caused by problems
# of compliments
# of deviations between configuration repository and actual configurations
# of incidents first month
# of outstanding actions of last SLA review
# of overdue changes
# of overdue incidents
# of overdue problems
# of overdue service requests
# of problems in queue
# of problems with available workaround
# of reopened incidents
# of reopened service requests
# of repeat incidents
# of reviewed SLAs
# of service requests posted via web (self-help)
# of SLA breaches due to poor performance
# of SLAs with an assigned account manager
# of SLAs without service level breaches
# of software licenses used
# of time coordinating changes
# of unauthorized implemented changes
# of unplanned purchases due to poor performance
# of unregistered changes
# of untested releases
# of urgent changes
% growth of the CMDB
% incidents assigned to a level of support
% incidents closed unsatisfactorily
% incidents resolved using a change
% incidents resolved with workaround
% of audited Configuration Items (CI)
% of availability SLAs met
% of backed-out changes
% of calls transferred
% of Configuration Items (CI) included in capacity reviews
% of escalated service requests
% of implemented changes not approved by management
% of incident classified as 'major'
% of incident impact rate incomplete
% of incidents bypassing the support desk
% of incidents caused by a workaround
% of incidents closed by service provider

17. Information Technology
% of incidents closed satisfactorily
% of incidents expected to close next period by scheduled workaround or change
% of incidents for which a first interview completed
% of incidents for which entitlement is unconfirmed
% of incidents inbound versus outbound
% of incidents incorrectly classified
% of incidents incorrectly prioritized
% of incidents involving third-party agreement
% of incidents recorded 'after the fact'
% of incidents rejected for reassignment
% of incidents resolved with non-approved workaround
% of incidents resulting from a service request
% of incidents resulting from previous incidents
% of incidents solved within deadline
% of incidents which change during the lifecycle
% of incidents with unmatched agreements
% of licenses purchased and not accounted for in configuration repository
% of obsolete user accounts
% of open service requests worked on
% of problems with a root cause analysis
% of problems with a root cause identified
% of response-time SLAs not met
% of service requests due to poor performance
% of service requests resolved within an agreed-upon period of time
% of services not covered in Continuity Plan
% of un-owned open service requests
% of unplanned outage/unavailability due to changes
% of workarounds to service requests applied
Accuracy of expenditure as defined in Capacity Plan
Accuracy of expenditure as defined in Continuity Plan
Availability
Availability (excluding planned downtime)
Average # of (re)-assignments of incidents
Average # of (re)-assignments of service requests
Average audit cycle of Configuration Items (CI)
Average change closure duration
Average cycle time between urgent releases
Average incident closure duration
Average service request closure duration
Average time between same reconciliations
Average time between updates of capacity plan
Average time between updates of continuity plan
Average time period between identifying and rectifying a discrepancy

17. Information Technology

Average time spent on continuity plans
Change closure duration rate
Change queue rate
Critical-time failures
Critical-time outage
Deviation of planned budget for SLA
Email backlog
First line service request closure rate
First-call resolution rate
Frequency of review of IT continuity plan
Incident backlog
Incident queue rate
IT service continuity plan testing failures
Mean time in postmortem
Mean time in queue
Mean Time to Action (MTTA)
Mean Time to Escalation (MTTE)
Mean time to repair
Mean Time to ticket (MTTT)
Total changes after implementation
Total rework after implementation of changes
Total time in postmortem
Total time in queue
Total time spent on CMDB reconciliation
Total time to action (TTTA)
Total time to escalation (TTTE)
Total time to ticket (TTTT)

IT Quality Assurance

incident efficiency
missing patches
of back up & testing of computer systems
# of changes after the program is coded
# of changes to customer requirements
# of coding errors found during formal testing
# of cost estimates revised
# of defects found over period of time
# of documentation errors
# of error-free programs delivered to customer
# of errors found after formal test
# of keypunch errors per day
# of process step errors before a correct package is ready
# of reruns caused by operator error
# of revisions to checkpoint plan
# of revisions to plan

17. Information Technology

of revisions to program objectives

# of test case errors

# of test case runs before success

untested releases

% assignment content adherence

% availability errors

% change in customer satisfaction survey

% compliance issues caused by improper configuration of assets

% critical processes monitored

% critical time failures

% error in forecast

% error in lines of code required

% failed system transactions

% false detection rate

% fault slip through

% hours used for fixing bugs

% incidents after patching

% incidents backlog

% incidents queue rate

% of changes caused by a workaround

% of changes classified as miscellaneous

% of changes incorrectly classified

% of changes initiated by customers

% of changes insufficiently resourced

% of changes internal versus external

% of changes matched to scheduled changes

% of changes recorded 'after the fact'

% of changes rejected for reassignment

% of changes scheduled outside maintenance window

% of changes subject to schedule adjustment

% of changes that cause incidents

% of changes that were insufficiently documented

% of changes with associated proposal statement

% of customer problems not corrected per schedule

% of defect-free artwork

% of input correction on data entry

% of problems uncovered before design release

% of programs not flow-diagrammed

% of reported bugs that have been fixed when going live

% of reports delivered on schedule

% of time required to debug programs

% of unit tests covering software code

Errors per thousand lines of code

Mean time between system IPL

17. Information Technology

Mean time between system repairs

QA personnel as % of # of application developers

QA personnel as a % of # of application developers

Time taken for completing a test of a software application

Total rework costs resulting from computer program

IT Security

detected network attacks

exceeding alerts capacity threshold

of detected network attacks

# of occurrences of loss of strategic data

# of outgoing viruses/spyware caught

password policy violations

security control

time to detect incident

unauthorized changes

viruses detected in user files

% compliance to password policy

% computer diffusion rate

% downtime due to security incidents

% e-mail spam messages stopped

% employees with own ID and password for internal systems

% host scan frequency

% intrusion success

% IT security policy compliance

% IT security staff

% IT systems monitored by anti-virus software

% licenses purchased and not accounted for in repository

% modules that contain vulnerabilities

% of downtime due to security incidents

% of email spam messages stopped/detected

% of email spam messages unstopped/undetected

% of incidents classified as security related

% of patches applied outside of maintenance window

% of spam false positives

% of systems covered by antivirus/antispyware software

% of systems not to policy patch level

% of systems with latest antivirus/antispyware signatures

% of virus incidents requiring manual cleanup

% of viruses & spyware detected in email

% overdue incidents

% repeated IT incidents

% security awareness

% security incidents

% security intrusions detection rate

17. Information Technology

% servers located in data centers

% spam not detected

% trouble report closure rate

% virus driven e-mail incidents

% viruses detected in e-mail messages

Distribution cycle of patches

Latency of unapplied patches

Spam detection failure %

Time lag between detection, reporting and acting upon security incidents

Weighted security vulnerability density per unit of code

IT Services

e-mail backlog

of alerts on exceeding system capacity thresholds

# of transactions executed within response time threshold

% delivered services not in the service catalogue

% fully patched hosts

% of "dead" servers

% of (assigned) disk space quota used

% of disk space used

% of dropped telephone calls

% of failed transactions

% of network bandwidth used

% of network packet loss

% of transactions executed within response time threshold during peak-time

Adoption Rate

Application performance index

Average # of virtual images per administrator

Average % of CPU utilization

Average % of memory utilization

Average network throughput

Average response time of transactions

Average retransmissions of network packets

Average size of email boxes/storage

Corporate average data efficiency (CADE)

Datacenter power usage effectiveness

Maximum CPU usage

Maximum memory usage

Maximum response time of transactions

Mean opinion score (MOS)

Mean time to provision

Mean-time between failure (MTBF)

IT Systems Availability

of developed new systems without downtime issues

17. Information Technology

of integrate IT systems
# of outage due to incidents (unplanned unavailability)
# of reviews of management information systems (MIS)
% downtime (hours)
% effective usage of IT systems
% improvement of capacity of current systems
% mainframe availability
% of outage (unavailability) due to implementation of planned changes, relative to the service hours
% of outage (unavailability) due to incidents in the IT environment, relative to the service hours
% of outage due to changes (planned unavailability)
% of system availability
% of unplanned outage/unavailability due to changes
% suitability of IT Systems
Customer database availability
Total outage from critical time failures in IT services

IT Training

of attendees at user training sessions
# of hours users have spent on training services
# of incidents caused by deficient user and operational documentation and training
# of incidents caused by deficient user training
# of users turned out successfully
Hours of user training
IT investment to IT staff training
Satisfaction scores for training and documentation
Time lag between changes and updates of documentation and training material

Programming - Class

of logical code lines (One logical line may be split on several physical lines by a line continuation character)
# of all statements
# of ancestor classes
# of classes to which a class is coupled coupling is defined as method call or variable access
# of comment lines
# of constructors defined by class
# of control statements
# of declarative statements (procedure headers, variable and constant declarations, all statements outside procedures)
# of events defined by class (This metric counts the event definitions)
# of executable statements
# of executable statements
# of immediate sub-classes that inherit from a class

17. Information Technology
# of interfaces implemented by class
# of logical lines of whitespace
# of methods that can potentially be executed in response to a message received a class counts only the first level of the call tree
# of methods that can potentially be executed in response to a message received a class counts the full call tree
# of non-control statements, which are executable statements that are neither control nor declarative statements
# of non-private variables defined by class VARS excluding private variables
# of physical source lines (including code, comments, empty comments and empty lines)
# of procedure calls going outside of a class (each call is counted once, whether it's early bound, late bound or polymorphic)
# of subs, functions and property procedures in class
# of variables defined and inherited by class
# of variables defined by class (does not include inherited variables)
Size of class (# of methods and variables)
Size of class interface (# of non-private methods and variables)

Programming - File

# of code lines count
# of constants (excluding enum constants)
# of control statements divided by # of all executable statements
# of files that a file uses
# of files that use a file
# of logical source lines
# of procedures (including subs, functions, property blocks, API declarations and events)
# of variables, including arrays, parameters and local variables
% of comment lines counted as full-line comments per logical lines
% of whitespace lines counted from logical lines
File size in kilobytes
Full-line and end-of-line comments that have meaningful content
Meaningful comments divided by # of logical lines of code

Programming - Procedure

# of distinct procedures in the call tree of a procedure
# of execution paths through a procedure (Cyclomatic complexity)
# of formal parameters defined in procedure header
# of global and module-level variables accessed by a procedure
# of input and output variables for a procedure (including parameters and function return value)
# of parameters used or returned by a procedure (output parameter)
# of procedure local variables and arrays (excluding parameters)
# of procedures that a procedure calls
# of procedures that call a procedure
% complexity inside procedures and between them

17. Information Technology

% external complexity of a procedure (# of other procedures called squared)

% internal complexity of a procedure (# of input/output variables)

% of Cyclomatic complexity without cases

Code lines count

Comment lines count

Fan-in multiplied by fan-out multiplied by procedure length (logical lines of code)

Length of procedure name in characters

Logical lines of code in call tree # of lines that may potentially execute in a call to this procedure

Logical lines of whitespace

Maximum # of nested conditional statements in a procedure

Maximum # of nested loop statements in a procedure

Maximum # of nested procedure calls from a procedure

Physical source lines (including code, comments, empty comments and empty lines)

Total amount of data read (procedures called + parameters read + global variables read)

Total amount of data written

Programming - Project

of abstract classes defined in project

# of actual couplings among classes in relation to the maximum # of possible couplings

# of class attributes (variables) hidden from other classes

# of class methods hidden from other classes

# of classes defined in project

# of concrete classes defined in project (a concrete class is one that is not abstract)

# of days passed between versions

# of enumeration constant names

# of enumeration names

# of files in project

# of global and module-level variables and arrays

# of interfaces defined in project

# of leaf classes defined in project (a leaf class has no descendants)

# of Physical lines in dead procedures

# of procedure call statements (including calls to subs, functions and declares, accesses to properties and the raising of events)

# of read instructions from global and module-level variables

# of reads from and writes to global and module-level variables

# of real forms excluding any User Controls

# of root classes defined in project

# of standard modules: bas files and Module blocks

# of unique names divided by # of names

# of unused constants

17. Information Technology

of unused procedures

# of unused variables

# of user-defined types (or structure statements)

# of write instructions to global and module-level variables

% comment density (meaningful comments divided by # of logical lines of code)

% of actual polymorphic definitions of all possible polymorphic definitions

% of code lines counted from logical lines

% of enum constants among all constants

% of parameterized classes (generic classes)

% of reuse benefit reuse of procedures)

Amount of data flow via global and module-level variables versus procedure parameters and function return values

Average # of calls on a code line (measures the modularity or structuredness)

Average # of constants in an Enum block

Average # of variable access instructions per logical line of code

Average file date

Average length of all constant names defined in VB files

Average length of names of variables (arrays and parameters defined in VB files, excluding parameters in event handlers and implementing procedures)

Average system complexity among procedures

Classes that do access attributes / Classes that can access attributes

Classes that do access operations / Classes that can access operations

Date of newest file in project

Deadness index

Density of decision statements in the code

Length of names

Length of procedure names

Maximum depth of call tree

Maximum depth of inheritance tree

Maximum size of call tree

Project size in kilobytes (includes all source files)

Reuse ratio for classes (a class is reused if it has descendants)

Specialization ratio for classes (a class is specialized if it inherits from a parent class)

Sum of SYSC over all procedures (measures the total complexity of a project)

The average # of times reused constants and enum constants

The relative amount of internal inheritance (internal inheritance happens when a class inherits another class in the same system)

The sum of inherited methods divided by # of methods in a project

The sum of inherited variables divided by # of variables in a project

Programming - Variable

of data flows into and out of a variable

17. Information Technology

of modules that use a variable
# of read instructions from variable
# of reads and writes A single instruction may count both as a read and as a write
# of write instructions to variable
Length of variable name in characters

Software Development

of bugs per release
# of critical bugs compared to # of bugs
# of defects detected in the software divided by # of function points (FP)
# of defects per function point
# of defects per line of code
# of defects per use case point
# of escaped defects
# of realized features compared to # of planned features
# of software defects in production
# of successful prototypes
software defects in production
unapplied patch latency
% critical patch coverage
% defects reopened
% of application development work outsourced
% of bugs found in-house
% of hours used for fixing bugs
% of overdue software requirements
% of software build failures
% of software code check-ins without comment
% of software code merge conflicts
% of time lost re-developing applications as a result of source code loss
% of user requested features
% on time completion (software applications)
% overdue changes
% patch success rate
% routine changes
% schedule adherence in software development
% software build failures
% software code check-ins without comment
% software licenses in use
% software upgrades completed successfully
% unauthorized software licenses used
% unique requirements to be reworked
% user requested features
Average # defects created per man month
Average number of software versions released

17. Information Technology

Average progress rates (time versus results obtained)

Cyclomatic software code complexity

Halstead complexity

Lines of code per day

Rate of knowledge acquisition (progress within the research)

Rate of successful knowledge representation

System usability scale

Time ratio design to development

Time-to-market of changes to existing products/services

Time-to-market of new products/services

Work plan variance

Web Client

of type of client (browser, robot, etc)

% of Java-enabled

% renderable mime-types

Click-generation functionality (address window, favorites list, history list)

Client-side filtering capability (Internet content ratings, certificates)

HTML fluency (the latest version of HTML recognized by the client)

Web Page

and type of embedded non-text objects (images, video, streaming data, applets)

of content access scheme (free, pay-per-view, subscription)

# of type of collection (online journal, photo gallery)

# of Web pages in collection

% breakdown of mime types in hyperlinks

% breakdown of protocols in hyperlinks

% of textual description of page's content

Aggregate size of constituent Web resources (in bytes)

Average # of hyperlinks per page

Birth and modification history (major revisions of content - from HTTP header)

Ratio of internal to external links on page

Web Server

buffer size of router

host latency

of domain name (and aliases)

# of files on server

# of geographical locations

# of internet nodes mapped to same domain name

# of sub-sites

# of Web pages on server

refused sessions by server

server connection time

server response time

17. Information Technology

Files by traffic % (e.g., % of files account for % of traffic)

HTTP node classification (inaccessible, redirection, accessible; these classifications will be time-sensitive; see volatility metric below)

Internet node identification (IP address and port)

Pages by traffic % (e.g., % of pages account for % of traffic)

Ratio of explicit clicks to implicit clicks for server

Server-side filtering (robotstxt, firewalls)

Top-level domain (com, edu)

Volatility level (summarizing the accessibility of the server during a given time period)

Web User

of files transferred per user

# of pages transferred per user

# of unique files transferred per user

# of unique pages transferred per user

# of unique Web sites visited per user

# of user access method (ISP, dial-up modem, wireless network, etc)

# of Web sites visited per user

Data filtering imposed by user (which client filters have been activated by the user)

Inter-request time per user (request to request time)

Inter-session time per user (session to session time)

Intra-request time per user (request to render time)

Path length of sessions per user

Path length of visit per site per user

Ratio of embedded clicks to user-supplied clicks, per user per session

Ratio of explicit clicks to implicit clicks, per user per session

Reoccurrence rates for files, pages, and sites

Sessions per user per time period

Stack distance per user

Temporal length of sessions per user

Temporal length of visit per site per user

User classification (adult, child, professional user, casual user, etc)

User response rate and attrition rate

Website

of bytes

# of cookie supplied

# of levels in site's internal link structure (depth)

# of pages served per time period

# of search engines indexing the site

# of type of Web collections

# of unique Web sites (filter out Web sites located at multiple IP addresses)

# of user Web page requests per time period

# of Web collections

17. Information Technology

of Web pages

# of Web servers

# of Web site publisher

# of Web sites

% breakdown of protocols across the periphery

% of site devoted to CGI/dynamic content

% of textual description of site's content

Byte latency

Bytes transferred per time period

Network traffic (bytes transferred, Web pages accessed)

Ratio of size of core to size of periphery

18. Insurance

Claims

insurance claims processed

of days open of insurance claims

% of claims where initial liability decision is not made within statutory time frame

% of fraudulent insurance claims

% of in-time medical expenses entitlement notices

% overdue claims

Average claim processing time

Claim reserves

Claims forecast versus actual

Claims solvency (%)

Combined cost and claims ratio

Clients

new insurance policies issued

% policy renewal rate

Average insurance policy size

Average speed of underwriting

Best insured / client GPI forecast vs. actual

Not taken up (NTU) ratio

Policy renewal rate

Underwriting speed of insurances

Worst insured / client GPI forecast vs. actual

Revenues & Costs

of new insurance policies

policy sales

% combined ratio

% loss ratio (insurance)

% missed payments or lapses

% not taken up (NTU) ratio

% of overdue premium

18. Insurance
Average policy size
Gross Premium Income (GPI) forecast vs. actual (%)
Loss ratio (%)
Net written premium

19. Internal Process

Increase Efficiency

# of audit requirements
# of days taken in finance for processing
# of new products introduced
# of on time delivery
# of waste reduction initiatives taken
% equipment utilization
% improve space utilization
% minimize downtime
% of pay runs in banks on time
% plant utilization
% reduction of payroll errors per month
Administrative expense per customer
Average lead time
Average time for decision-making
Hours spent on product re-work
Pay runs in banks on time (< x% error)
Productivity rate
Response time to customer

Process Improvement

# of contracts filed without error
# of ISO 9001 certifications
# of ISO auditors
# of new ideas to reduce processing time
# of new policies and procedures
# of new products/services developed
# of positions outsourced
# of process changes per operation due to error
# of processes improved
# of systems upgrades
# of users accessing system
% of inventory turnovers
% of manual pays
% of process operations where sigma limit is within engineering specification
% of targets met
% on-time delivery
% planning accuracy

19. Internal Process

% using electronic links for communication with carriers

% using electronic links for delivery advice information

Audit requirements (% rating)

Break-even time for new products

Cycle time improvement

Defect rates

Delivery vehicle routing and scheduling

Distribution resource planning

In-process yields

Lead time for product development

Lead time for suppliers

Lead time from order to delivery

Product return rate

Rework rate

Relationship Management

of hours spent with external parties

# of SLA's signed

% of complaints resolved within agreed time

Existence of Service Level Agreement (SLA) with 3rd party service provider

20. Leisure & Recreation

Museum

of attendances per 1,000 population

# of members as % of visitors

% of art objects deemed worthy of display

% of artworks on loan from other institutions

% of artworks on loan to other institutions

% of children in attendance

% of endowment restricted to art acquisitions

% of estimated art collection value covered by insurance

% of new artworks on display

% of non-members who visited the museum x or more times

% of total building size dedicated to permanent collection galleries

% of trustees who donated sum greater than x % of operating budget

% of visitors who would rank visit as exceeding expectations

% of works on display from the museum's most significant collection

Average length of time spent in a noteworthy gallery

Average length of time spent with significant works

Sports

of international appearances

# of replica shirt sales

% of attendees of non-match-day events

% of TV viewing figures

% utilization of corporate facilities on match-days

20. Leisure & Recreation
Batting average (BA)
Conversion rate to professional contract
Conversion rate to transfer fee
Earned run average (ERA)
Match-day spend per spectator
Merchandise spend per head
On base % (OBP) / On base average (OBA)
On-base plus slugging (OPS)
Program penetration rate
Walks plus hits per inning pitched

Travel agent

Cost per transaction / ticket
Productivity per travel consultant
# of travel agents

21. Livestock & Dairy

Animals

% animal born alive per female
% of livestock born alive per female farrowed
% of mated females
% of mummified livestock per female farrowed
% of stillborn livestocks per female farrowed
% of tonnage landed at ports checked against log sheet
Average parity of livestock
Feed cost/ 100 lb of milk
Livestock culling rate %
Livestock mortality %
Livestock per female farrowed
Livestock survival % after born
Mummified livestock per female farrowed
Total livestock born per female farrowed

Dairy Industry

% community response to promotional campaign
% growth in white and low fat milk sales
% of market occupied by imports
% of white and low fat milk market supplied by us
Average milk yield per cow
Cost of marketing campaign per liter of milk sold
Cost of promotion
Energy-to-milk ratio
Per capita consumption
Sales compared to national average
Water-to-milk ratio

22. Management

Administration

# of iterations of strategic plan
# of meetings starting on schedule
# of open doors per month
# of tasks for which actual time exceeded estimated time
% increase in output per employee
% of action plan schedules missed
% of delinquent suggestions
% of documents that require two management reviews
% of meetings that start on schedule
% of target dates missed
Average time required to solve a problem

Clerical

# of kg of paper waste
# of misfiles per week
# of period reports not completed on schedule
# of times messages are not delivered
% data integrity
% of action items not done on schedule
% of clerical personnel support
% of coding errors on time cards
% of impressions reprinted
% of inputs not received on schedule
% of pages retyped
% of phone calls answered within two rings
% of phone calls dialed correctly

Cost & Budget

# of variances in capital spending
% of output delivered on schedule
% projected cost reductions missed
% revenue/expense ratio below plan
% variation from budget
Return on investment
Revenue actual versus plan
Revenue generated over strategic period
Total amount saved per employee due to new ideas and/or methods
Total cost of poor quality
Warranty costs

Error & Deviation

# of administration errors due to not using the right procedures
# of delays because process instructions are wrong or not available
# of errors in operator training documentation
# of errors per type
# of pages processed error-free per hour

22. Management

of security violations per year

# of user complaints per month

% correlation between testers

% correlation between testers delivered on schedule

% error in manufacturing costs

% error in output product quality

% error in personnel records

% error in planning estimates

% error in test equipment and tooling budget

% error in yield projections

% of drafting errors found by checkers

% of errors that escape the operator detection

% of testers that fail certification

% of time program plans are met

% of tools that are networked due to design errors

% of tools that fail certification

Motivation & Innovation

of employees dropping out of classes

# of employees participating in cost effectiveness

# of formal reviews before plans are approved

# of hours per year of career and skill development training per employee

# of job improvement ideas per employee

% functional test coverage of products

% improvement in customer satisfaction survey

% improvement in opinion surveys

Department morale index

Labor utilization index

Procedures

of decisions made by higher-level management than required by procedures

# of procedures violations per month

# of procedures with fewer than three acronyms and abbreviations

# of waivers to manufacturing procedures

% of changes to process specifications during process design review

% of departments with disaster recovery plans

% of designed experiments that need to be revised

% of manufacturing used to screen products

% of procedures less than 10 pages

Direct/indirect ratio

Volume actual versus planned

23. Manufacturing

Assets & Equipment

of critical equipment availability

# of damaged equipment and property reports

# of problems that test equipment can't detect during manufacturing cycle

% asset utilization

% equipment utilization

% of changes to project equipment required

% of equipment ready for production on schedule

% of overall equipment effectiveness (OEE)

% of tools and test equipment on change level control

Average age of equipment

Average useful life of equipment

Equipment availability as % of overall operation time

Equipment performance %

Equipment quality %

Automation

of evaluations of software by performing usability testing

# of evaluations on alternative designs through the use of equipment mockups and software prototypes

# of improvement, enhancement or additions in the existing applications

# of software development requests completed on time

% deployment of storage area network

% deployment of supplier portal

Data application across multiple functions

Data integration across multiple functions

Evaluations on predecessor systems and operator tasks

Human Factors Engineering

of analysis of tasks and workload

# of design and testing and evaluation

# of hours provided training for systems

# of modeling tools to evaluate station design and operator procedures

# of requirements specification

# of tasks and associated workload analysis

# of training requirements

% for operations

% of functions allocation

% of system performance and reliability

% of undesirable design or procedural features identified

% operator stress

% reduction of operational errors

% training for sustaining manpower skills

Ease of use rate

User fatigue rate

User satisfaction rate

23. Manufacturing

Maintenance

facility age

maintenance efficiency indicator

of approved work orders over 3 months old

# of assets in the condition monitoring program

# of breakdowns

# of breakdowns per year or per department

# of candidate items for condition monitoring

# of defective steam traps found

# of devices surveyed

# of direct maintenance personnel on shift

# of emergency maintenance jobs

# of emergency priority service calls

# of failures

# of failures causing downtime

# of faults found

# of hours the equipment was available to run at capacity

# of immediate corrective maintenance man-hours

# of immediate corrective maintenance work-orders completed

# of incomplete work orders

# of internal direct maintenance people using software

# of internal direct maintenance personnel

# of internal maintenance personnel

# of internal multi-skilled maintenance personnel

# of jobs

# of maintenance internal personnel man-hours for training

# of maintenance work-orders causing downtime

# of major assets/systems

# of major assets/systems with preventive maintenance routines

# of man-hours for continuous improvement

# of man-hours used for planning in a systematic maintenance planning process

# of material requisitions

# of material requisitions met from stock

# of modification proposals registered

# of modifications completed

# of outstanding work orders

# of overdue preventive maintenance work orders at the end of the period

# of planned and scheduled maintenance man-hours

# of plant stoppages due to failure

# of PM/CM backlog items

# of preventive maintenance + emergency maintenance jobs

# of preventive maintenance jobs completed

# of preventive maintenance jobs scheduled

23. Manufacturing
# of preventive maintenance tasks completed
# of preventive maintenance tasks planned
# of priority 1 service calls
# of priority 2 service calls
# of production operator maintenance man-hours
# of repeated breakdowns
# of rework jobs
# of scheduled work orders
# of service calls
# of service calls within the target response time
# of steam traps surveyed
# of stoppages due to failure
# of systems
# of systems covered by a critical analysis
# of unexpected equipment failures resulting in downtime
# of urgent priority service calls
# of work orders closed during the period
# of work orders completed during the period
# of work orders performed as scheduled
# of work orders registered
or maintenance work-orders completed
time spent performing preventive maintenance (PM) work
% after action review usage
% critical equipment availability
% of adherence to preventive maintainers schedule
% of critical equipment availability
% of failed maintenance
% of maintenance hours of operating time
% of maintenance hours of operating time (maintenance efficiency)
% of maintenance rework
% of preventive maintenance cost
% of scheduled maintenance man hours planned
% repairs completed within time limit
% unplanned maintenance
% work orders closed within the specified time period (maintenance)
Achieved up time during required time
Actual available hours to schedule each week
Asset replacement value
Average cost to resolve a breakdown
Average inventory value of maintenance materials
Average loading time
Average preventive maintenance man-hours / day
Average required travel time
Backlog of maintenance work

23. Manufacturing

Cumulative response time of all customer calls

Cumulative response time of all emergency priority service calls

Cumulative response time to all service calls

Cumulative response time to all urgent service calls

Cumulative safe repair time of all emergency priority service calls

Cumulative safe repair time of all service calls

Maintenance cost per unit

Maintenance cost per unit

Maintenance shutdown cost

Mean time failure

Monthly depreciation of equipment

Net maintenance parts turnover

Preventive inspection effectiveness

Quantity of output

Ratio of value adding time to lead time

Schedule completion effectiveness (%)

Time taken to answer maintenance calls

Total actual man-hours for completed work orders

Total annual maintenance expenditure per square meter

Total assets value

Total budget implemented / budget planned

Total condition based maintenance man-hours

Total corrective maintenance man-hours

Total direct maintenance personnel man-hours

Total direct man-hours worked

Total emergency jobs worked

Total estimated cost of work

Total estimated man-hours for all outstanding work orders

Total estimated man-hours for completed work orders

Total hours in the reporting time period

Total internal direct man-hours available

Total internal direct man-hours worked

Total internal maintenance man-hours

Total internal maintenance personnel man-hours

Total jobs worked

Total maintenance cost / month

Total maintenance cost per equipment

Total maintenance cost per year

Total maintenance man-hours available

Total maintenance personnel man-hours

Total man-hours worked on shift

Total off-site maintenance man-hours

Total operating time

Total overtime maintenance man-hours

23. Manufacturing

Total overtime man-hours worked by indirect maintenance personnel during period

Total preventive maintenance hours

Total regular man-hours of indirect maintenance personnel during period

Total stoppage time due to failure

Total time of failures

Total time of failures costs

Total time to restoration

Total value of parts inventory

Total value of parts on sites

Minimize Cost

% cost of quality

% cost reduction

% increase in inventory turnover

% of corrective maintenance cost

% of statutory compliance

% reduction in variable cost

% residual (scrap) value

Average production costs of items

Cost of poor quality (COPQ)

Cost of replacing obsolete items

Cost reduction %

Engineering costs are not more than x$ per tone

Interest cost reduction

Labor costs per unit production

Power consumption per hour production

Price of non-conformance

Ratio of actual to projected unit production costs

Total actual cost of work

Total contractor cost

Total cost of all jobs

Total cost of contractors

Total cost of direct labor

Total cost of equipment parts

Total cost of maintenance

Total cost of maintenance materials

Total cost of planned and estimated jobs

Total cost of preventive maintenance

Total direct maintenance personnel cost

Unit cost

Water used per amount of product manufactured

Mining & Metals

Ratio of actual dilution of ore to dilution stated in the feasibility study

23. Manufacturing

Ratio of actual impurities content to impurities content stated in the feasibility study

Ratio of actual recovery to metallurgical recovery stated in the feasibility study

Trim optimization efficiency

Operational Excellence

of elements affecting other functions

# of elements related to other functions

% of improved uptime of machines

% of planned monthly shuts completed within planned time

% of rejects

% of respond to breakdowns in < 30 minutes

% of undamaged goods

Achieve uptime of x% by x date

Average # of quality checks vs. targeted #

Increase output to x tones per day

Less % waste

Manufacturing cycle time

Quality Assurance

Truck turnarounds reduced to x mins

Order Management

of issues inquired into arising out of the data applied or integrated

% maintained price with value to customer

% of efficiency of control structures

Average sales turnover / customer

Average time from dock to dock

Average time from order to cash in bank

Average time from raw material to dispatch

Average value of the order

Profit rate / each order

Rate of profit from each customer

Value of the minimum order

Process Improvement

of manufacturing steps

takt time

unit production time

units per man-hour

% adherence to processes

% downtime

% lost manufacturing capacity

% process validation

% production orders finished late

% total time yield

Manufacturing schedule adherence

23. Manufacturing

Ratio of actual to design input required to produce one unit of output

Production Control

failure rate

of items exceeding shelf life

# of new change orders

# of open change orders

production lead time

regression testing

% machine scheduled time

% of errors in work in process records versus audit data

% of manufacturing jobs completed on schedule

% of products that meet customer orders

% of stock errors

% work in progress

Average cycle time (ACT)

Cost of inventory spoilage

Employee work center loading

Production targets

Ratio of actual capacity to rated capacity

Ratio of downtime to projected operating time

Spare parts availability in crib

Time required to incorporate engineering changes

Time that line is down due to assembly shortage

Productivity

of deadlines/milestones met

# of metrics relating to specific team tasks

# of orders produced by individuals

# of orders produced by section

# of orders produced by week or day

# of staff off work

# of units produced

% changes to the weekly schedule

% uptime

Attendance rates

Average time to manufacturing

Length of time staff are off work

Output rates

Overall equipment effectiveness

Schedule compliance

Total machine available time

Total machine work center loading rate

Total sales turnover / total employee

Turnaround time for jobs

23. Manufacturing

Products Improvement

# of new products introduced per month
# of review of product design
% first time right
% standardization of products

Quality Assurance

areas of improvement
emissions from production
of customer feedback
# of internal customer complaints
# of kaizen applications
# of non conformances
# of product realization projects implementation
# of products defects at customer site
# of products warranty failure – OEM
production rejects
startup rejects
% defects per million opportunities
% final products which do not meet quality criteria
% first time yield (FTY)
% hazardous operational waste
% mean time between failures
% must do it again - rework
% of defect goods
% of defect goods of department
% of defect goods of individual
% of rejection in products due to packing & handling
% production losses
Amount of time lost due to rework
First time through quality yield
Internal customer satisfaction
Products having first tuning above 100,000 cycles in endurance test
Quality rates
Response time to customer queries
Rework rate of department
Rework rate of entire company
Rework rate of worker

System Safety

# of injurious accidents due to human or machine errors or failures
# of safety considerations applied in a system acquisition
% high quality for all customer point of interaction

24. Procurement

Business Control

# of documented issues
# of hubs (logistics network)
# of returns/ customer complaints
# of suggestions per employee
# of supply chain disruptions
% contracted staff
% correct forecasting
% lean logistics
% of employees trained to do the job they are working on
% of logistics outsourcing
% product return rate
% reduction of waste
% supply/demand imbalance
% use of technology
% warranty claims rate
Average project time frame
Gross margin
Lead time
Maintenance, repair and operating supplies (MRO)
Procurement employees as % of total employees
Procurement operating expense as % of sales
Procurement operating expense as % of total spend
Procurement operating expense per procurement employee
Procurement spend per procurement employee
Radio frequency identification (RFID)
Total operating revenue

Contracts

contract complaints
contract variations
identified contract breaches
% cancelled and suspended contracts
% contract compliance
% contracts delivered within original budget
% contracts reviewed
% retention rate of active contracts
Contract terminated billed value with contractors
Contract terminated remaining value
Total contract value
Value of activated contract renewals

Costs

warranty claims per item
% of internal logistics cost
% outsourced logistics costs

24. Procurement

% return rate (RR)

% total distribution cost of delivered sales value

% warranty expenses

Cost avoidance savings

Cost of purchasing units

Cost of rush implants

Cost of rush shipments

Cost per unit

Cost to schedule product deliveries

Direct labor cost

Direct material cost

Direct product cost

Distribution costs (warehousing)

Insurance and taxes cost

Internal logistics cost

Inventory carrying costs

Inventory holding costs (IHC) as % of gross sales

Inventory holding costs (IHC) as % of inventory value

Inventory management cost as % of gross sales

Opportunity costs

Outsourced logistics cost

Parts costs per total costs

Repair cost per return

Scrap and rework cost

Shrinkage cost

Stock costs

Stock value

Total backorder costs

Total costs

Total logistics wage

Total obsolescence

Total spend expenses

Total value of goods returned

Travel & entertainment costs as % of gross margin

Travel & entertainment costs as % of increased revenue

Unit cost per batch

Warranty cost per item sold

Cycle Time

Cash to cash cycle time

Customer order actual cycle time

Customer order cycle time

Customer order promised cycle time

Cycle Time of purchase order

Expected customer order cycle time

24. Procurement
Finished product cycle time
Internal cycle time receipt of material
Inventory replenishment cycle time
MRP exemptions cycle time
Order fulfillment cycle time
Production cycle time
Purchase order cycle time
Schedule product deliveries cycle time
Schedule production activities cycle time
Supply chain cycle time

Inventory

Altman Z-Score for privately held manufacturing companies
anticipation stock
consignment stock
days sales of inventory (DSI)
decoupling stock
inventory turnover
of finished goods in hand
# of inactive Stock
# of line items picked
# of obsolete stock
orders picked per hour
pick-to-ship cycle time for customer orders
piece variance
pipeline stock
reorder point (ROP)
safety stock
stock level
theoretical inventory
warehouse network surface
warehouses
working stock
% distressed stock
% inventory quality ratio (IQR)
% obsolete items in inventory
% of correctly picked line items
% of duplicate stock #s
% of Inventory items incorrectly located
% of inventory items with incorrect stock balances
% of safety stock used
% of safety stock used in measurement period
% of slow moving products
% of stock available at customers first request
% of stock controlled SKUs

24. Procurement
% of warehouse shrinkage
% out of stocks
% part of flow which is through stock
% sales order cancellation rate
% scrap rate
% slow moving stock
% spoilage rate
Actual inventory turnover for period
Average age of inventory
Average picks per order
Beginning inventory (BI)
Early PO Receipts to PO due date
Early receipts to MRP date (required date)
Ending inventory
Gross margin return on inventory
Independent demand ratio
Inventory carrying rate
Inventory lead time
Inventory months of supply
Inventory service level
Inventory turnover rate
Inventory turns ratio
Planned inventory turnover for period
Sell through %
Size of safety stock
Stock cover
Stockouts in period
Surplus inventory
Value of obsolete stock

Materials
# of material and other accessory
# of material defect
# of material spent in using ratio of material allowed
% of damage material by error of workers
% of material defect by causes
% of perfect order measure / fulfillment
% time spent picking back orders or stock-outs
Lost ratio of material per order
Material value add
Raw materials availability

Outsourcing
% actual vs. estimated savings
% of invoices disputed
% of key stakeholders satisfied with suppliers

24. Procurement
% of suppliers screened on human rights
% of user complaints due to contracted services
Outsourcing and off-shoring production
Vendor/client quality calibration variance

Purchasing

# of items billed but not received
# of items on the hot list
# of new suppliers per year
# of orders received with no purchase order
# of suppliers accounting for 80% of the value of goods
# of suppliers be removed per year
# of suppliers of goods per year
# of times per year line is stopped due to lack of supplier parts
requisition, purchase order, or invoice transaction volume
% decrease in parts cost
% key suppliers accounting for 80% of spending
% local suppliers
% of defect-free supplier model parts
% of discount orders by consolidating
% of errors in purchase requisitions
% of errors in stocking
% of late deliveries
% of lots received on line late
% of parts with two or more suppliers
% of purchase orders returned due to errors or incomplete description
% of suppliers with 100 % lot acceptance for one year
% of supplies delivered on schedule
% of time parts are not in stock when ordered from common parts crib
% quantity bought over required
Actual purchased materials cost per budgeted cost
Average time to fill emergency orders
Average time to replace rejected lots with good parts
Customer dissatisfaction index - replacement
Customer satisfaction index - OEM
Errors per purchase order
Expediters per direct employees
Labor hours per $10,000 purchases
Negotiated cost reduction savings
Purchase order cycle time
Purchase price variance
Purchasing cost
Ratio of material allowed
Routing and trace errors per shipment
Supplier parts scrapped due to engineering changes

24. Procurement

Suppliers rating

Time of product in shipment

Time required to process equipment purchase orders

Time to answer customer complaints

Total products blended for third parties

Total products manufactured for third parties

Transaction cost unit of purchasing

Shipping

of accidents per month

# of bill of lading errors not caught in shipping

# of complaints on shipping damage

# of operating forklifts

# of orders shipped

# of orders shipped inline with requested date

# of orders shipped on time

% delivered in-full, on-time

% deliveries on behalf of other branches

% delivery in full on time

% delivery on time

% delivery with not enough quantity

% driver utilization

% items delivered

% items tracked with radio frequency identification

% of control charts maintained correctly

% of daily reports in by 7 am

% of facilities on schedule

% of invalid test data

% of jobs that meet cost

% of jobs that meet schedule

% of late shipments

% of on time ship rate

% of on-time delivery

% of operators certified to do their job

% of orders shipped inline with requested date

% of output that meets customers orders and engineering specifications

% of parts not packed to required specifications

% of product defect-free at measurement operations

% of products defective at final test

% of products error-free at final test

% of shipments below plan

% of shipping errors

% of time log book filled out correctly

% of utilities left improperly running at end of shift

% of vehicle utilization

24. Procurement
% on time deliveries
% on time in full (OTIF)
% orders delivered with damaged products/items
% packaging to product ratio
% part of logistics flow which is cross-dock
% performance against standards
% pilferage rate
% reduced deviation to advance shipment notification
% reduced deviation to transport routing
% supplier on-time delivery
% unplanned overtime
Cases fill rate
Count of on-time stock keeping units
Delivery performance - OEM
Quantity per shipment
Replacement parts defect rates
Stock keeping units fill rate
Time and/or claiming errors per week
Time between errors at each operation
Value of fill rate
Value of orders shipped on time

Supply Chain

# of active suppliers per supply employee
# of missed deliveries per million
% of (preferred) suppliers not used in last 12 months
% of active suppliers that are e-procurement enabled
% of backorders
% of EDI transactions
% of emergency purchases
% of forecast Accuracy
% of in advance procured travel booking expenses
% of inventory accuracy
% of lowest air fare acceptance
% of orders based on framework/standard contract
% of orders delivered in full
% of orders delivered to customer in the committed date
% of orders that were captured with incorrect attributes
% of orders that were delivered with requested documentation
% of payable invoices without purchase order
% of preferred hotel usage
% of procurement requests satisfied by preferred suppliers
% of purchases made from contracts/frameworks
% of receipts of formal bids & proposals via the Internet
% of schedules changed within supplier's lead time

24. Procurement
% of standard tender/bid procedures
% of suppliers that are responsible for 80% of spend
% of time spent picking back orders
% of total procurement spend offshore
% of total procurement spend onshore
% of total spend managed/controlled by procurement
% of total spend via e-auctions
% of total spend via e-procurement
% of total spend with diversity suppliers
% of uninterrupted orders
% of value of orders based on standard/framework contract
% requested time in full (RTIF)
Average # of modifications to orders
Average # of requests for information to suppliers for orders
Average days per engineering change
Average days per schedule change
Average release cycle of engineering changes
Average size of discounts of items
Average time to procure
Average value of orders
Delivery schedule adherence (DSA)
Fill rate
Managed procurement spend outsourced as a % of total spend
Product lead time
Production equal to demand (supply vs. demand curve)
Scrap value %
Test cycle time
Time needed to obtain additional capital
Time needed to obtain additional equipment
Time needed to recruit/hire/train additional labor
Total negotiated cost reduction savings
Total procurement spend as % of sales
Total supply chain management cost
Total value of orders
Upside supply chain flexibility
Write-off %

Tendering

of quotations invited
# of single source tenders
# of suppliers accounting for % of spend
# of suppliers paid
# of tenders invited
% of RFPs that needed to be improved based on supplier responses
% value of orders covered by contracts

24. Procurement
Average # of responses received to RFPs
Average cost of a tender/bid procedure
Average time to complete tendering/bidding

25. Project Management

Project Administration

milestones per project plan
of milestones missed
# of new project/program issues
# of non conformities during vendor inspection
planned hours per task
% of "killed" projects
% of assigned FTE actually working on project
% of early no's on project proposals
% of FTE actually working on project that were not initially assigned
% of milestones missed
% of time coordinating project
% progress reports submitted as planned
% resource planning
Asset Yield
Average # of interdependencies between project tasks
Average # of projects managed by project managers
Average # of years working as project managers
Break-even time
Deviation of planned break-even time
Deviation of planned hours of work
Deviation of planned time schedule for project/program
Effective planning %
Estimate at completion (EAC)
Internal rate of return (IRR)
Modified internal rate of return (MIRR)
Net present value (NPV)
Project issue queue rate
Project issues addressed ratio
Ratio of project managers to total project staff
Requisition to item issuance time
Schedule variance (SV)
This can be applied to (IT) projects/programs Source

Project Control

conflicts arisen during the project
of un-staffed hours
% decrease in complaints after project execution
% of delivered projects with incorrect feasibility assumptions
% of overdue project status reports

25. Project Management

% of overdue project tasks

% of projects "in control"

% of projects following standards

% of projects on time

% of projects or resources allocated through business unit approval

% of projects receiving Quality Assurance review

% of projects that are prioritized according to business needs

% of projects with a testing plan

% of projects with high risk profile

% of projects with missed milestones

% of projects with non-ideal resource assignment

% of projects with post-project review

% of projects with scope changes

% of projects without deviation of planned hours of work

% of projects without deviation of planned time schedule

% of projects/programs with company sponsor

% of under-staffed projects

% overdue project tasks

% project schedule variance

% projects on time

% time spent as planned

Average # of alterations made to project definitions

Average # of interdependencies between projects

Average # of milestones per project plan

Average # of people assigned per project/program

Average age of project status reports

Average amount of overspending on project time

Average break-even time of projects

Average budget size of projects

Average delay in production of progress reports

Average deviation of planned budget of projects

Average deviation of planned duration of projects

Average deviation of planned net present value (NPV) of projects

Average overdue time of project status reports

Average project duration

Average risk profile for projects/programs

Average stakeholder satisfaction with outcome of projects

Average stakeholder satisfaction with project management

Estimate to complete

Project time predictability

Resource utilization (%)

Total deviation of time in projects

Total project/program delay

25. Project Management

Project Cost & Budget

project cost performance index
project cost schedule index
% budget allocated to budget spent ratio
% of projects on budget
% of projects on time and on budget
% of projects without deviation of planned break-even time
% of projects without deviation of planned budget
% of projects without deviation of planned ROI
% project budget variance
% projects on budget
Actual cost of work performed (ACWP)
Average amount of overspending on project budget
Average deviation of planned break-even time of projects
Average deviation of planned ROI of projects
Average project/program ROI
Budget at completion (BAC)
Budgeted cost of work performed (BCWP)
Budgeted cost of work scheduled (BCWS)
Cost performance index (CPI)
Cost schedule index (CSI)
Cost variance
Cost-/benefit estimation %
Deviation of planned budget
Deviation of planned ROI
Engineering costs as % of total installed costs (TIC)
Project cost predictability
Sum of costs of "killed" projects
Total deviation of planned budget of projects

Value Management

project schedule performance index
to complete schedule performance index (TSPI)
to-complete performance index (TCPI)
% of projects with non-positive ROI
% of projects with pre-defined ROI
% of projects without deviation of planned net present value (NPV)
% profitable projects
% successful projects
Average net present value (NPV) of projects
Deviation of net present value (NPV)
Earned revenue to total expenses
Return on investment (ROI)
Schedule performance index (SPI)

26. Quality Improvement

Benchmarking

of benchmark survey

% of benchmarking activities that result in implementation of enhancements

Average cost of benchmarking study

Average time to complete benchmarking study

Document Management

of documents that have not been removed after end-of-life

% of documents in non-enterprise repositories

% of documents not accessed regularly

% of documents not stored in document management system

% of duplications/document variations

% of enterprise documents accessible to search engine

% searches resulting in a document being opened

Average frequency of updates of documents

Document storage costs

Ratio of paper to electronic documents

Time to respond to legal discovery of records

Improvement

of (internal) control improvement initiatives

% of time of employees available for improvement activities

Average age of knowledge assets

Average lead time to respond to ideas / suggestions

Average value of ideas / suggestions implemented

Frequency of use of knowledge assets

Idea conversion rate

Total turnaround time (per business process)

Training penetration rate

Performance

% of goals accomplished from most recent strategic plan

% of KPIs outside set objectives

% of KPIs that are automatically measured

% of KPIs that are improved

% of KPIs that are worsened

% of KPIs that do not reflect business goals

% of KPIs within set objectives

% of measured KPIs

% of strategic budget cuts vs. % budget cuts through across-the-board cuts

Average data collection costs per KPI

Average KPI improvement

Cost of KPI measurement

Quality Assurance

of audit finding closing more than two weeks

# of audits performed on schedule

26. Quality Improvement
# of committed supplier plans in place
# of complaints from manufacturing management
# of customer calls to report errors
# of customer complaint due to quality of services
# of customer complaints
# of customer surveys
# of engineering changes after design review
# of errors detected during design and process reviews
# of errors in reports
# of manufacturing interruptions caused by supplier parts
# of minor finding on ISO 9001 Internal Audit
# of postponed ISO 9001 Internal Audit caused by Auditor
# of problems identified in-process
# of process changes after process qualification
# of reject orders not dispositioned in five days
# of requests for corrective action being processed
% error in predicting customer performance
% error in reliability projections
% of correlated test results with suppliers
% of customers given satisfaction surveys
% of employees active in professional societies
% of errors in defect records
% of field returns correctly analyzed
% of improvement in early detection of major design errors
% of lab services not completed on schedule
% of lots going directly to stock
% of part #s going directly to stock
% of problems identified in the field
% of product that meets customer expectations
% of QA personnel to total personnel
% of QE to product and manufacturing engineers
% of qualified suppliers
% of quality inspectors to manufacturing directs
% of reports published on schedule
% of responses to survey
% of suppliers at 100 % lot acceptance for one year
% product cost related to appraisal scrap and rework
% size of the sample group that is surveyed
% skip lot inspection
Cost of scrap and rework that was not created at the rejected operation
Receiving inspection cycle time
Time required to process a request for corrective action
Time to identify and solve problems
Variations between inspectors doing the same job

26. Quality Improvement

Six Sigma
of defects
# of opportunities for a defect
% of cost savings attributed to use of Six Sigma
% of internal Black belts
% of internal Greenbelts
% of profit increases attributed to use of Six Sigma
Average experience with Six Sigma
Defects %
Defects per million opportunities (DPMO)
Defects per unit (DPU)

27. Real Estate

Property Management
of crisis housing
# of long term housing
# of new properties
# of properties removed
# of tenants requesting maintenance
# of transitional housing
# of urgent repairs
space usage efficiency
% of homes which are non-decent
% of Repairs completed within timeframe
% office capacity ratio
% real estate capital ratio

Property Sales
% construction cost in use
% price-to-income ratio
Average fee per property sale
Average length of time property takes to sell
Average property management fee per property manager
Real estate cost per sales lead
Real estate sales leads generated per ad per day

Rental
of rental properties
# of tenancy units
# of tenants dissatisfied with maintenance
# of tenants providing feedback
price-to-rent ratio
% late rent payments
% of empty rental properties (vacancies)
% of revenue from booked flat to the total cost to be incurred
% of revenue from customer to % completion of project

27. Real Estate
% of tenants evicted as a result of rent arrears
% of tenants in arrears who have had notices of seeking possession served
% of tenants with more than x weeks of arrears
% vacancy ratio
Average # of tenancies managed per property manager
Average property management fees per tenancy
Average relet time
Average time taken to relet empty homes
Housing energy efficiency
Rent arrears as % of rent due
Rent collection as % of rent due

28. Research & Development

Cost & Budget

% change in administrative and operational cost
% expenditure by introducing innovations
% hours with innovations
% idea conversion rate
% license costs of total R&D cost
% license revenues to total R&D costs
% market share increase due to R&D
% product design cost accuracy
% products meeting cost target
% R&D budget allocated to new product development
% R&D budget allocated to product improvements and extensions
% R&D budget from total budget
% R&D budget spent on new innovations
% R&D projects involving customers
% R&D staff involved in customer contacts
Average development costs per new product

Enterprise

frequency of meetings per group
% of products capturing 50% or more of the market
% of R&D expense as a % of revenue
Average engineering change cycle time
Breakeven time or time-to-profitability
Current year % of revenue from products developed in the last "X" years
Development cycle time trend (normalized to program complexity)
Proposal win rate
R&D headcount and % increase/decrease in R&D headcount
Total patents filed/pending/awarded per year

Innovation

e-public sector as an active partner in the innovation system
new product/service ideas proposed

28. Research & Development
# of collected ideas that were developed further
# of collected ideas that were implemented
# of ideas developed
# of new products
# of new techniques identified
# of new technologies adopted
# of system improvements implemented
% dedicated resources for radical innovation
% of ideas from outside the organization
% of ideas that are funded for development
% of ideas that are killed
% of investment in non-core innovation projects
% of new customers from new products / services
% of sales due to launched product/services
% of senior management time invested in growth innovation
% retained or evaluated ideas
% training programs for newly introduced innovations
Average # of prototypes per new product
Average age of patents
Average number of patents per researcher
Average prototyping speed
Average time-to-profitability for changes to existing products/services
Average time-to-profitability for new product/service
Customer satisfaction with new products / services
New product sales cannibalization ratio
New product turn around time
Ratio of # of concepts to actual products
Research idea conversion rate
Total funds invested in non-core innovation projects

Knowledge Management

drop in time due to knowledge management
knowledge management briefings and communication sessions facilitated
% employees trained in Knowledge Management (KM) practices
% savings due to knowledge management initiatives

Monitor Competitors

# of new techniques/innovations patented
# of new techniques/innovations patents pending
Perceived advantage in the market against actual
Perceived degree of competition

Organization/Team

bulletins distributed to employees
divisions represented per group
employees in R&D
ideas put forward by individuals to team leaders

28. Research & Development

members per group

of program management

time to respond to ideas / suggestions

% academic scientific staff

% core team members physically collocated

% cost performance

% employees involved in the innovation process

% meetings involving external experts

% new academic research recruits in R&D

% of balanced team scorecard

% of milestone dates met

% of schedule performance

% project personnel receiving team building/team launch training/
facilitation

% staff involved in groups

% students participating in research activities

Actual staffing (hours or headcount) vs. plan

Average training hours per person per year or % of payroll cost for training
annually

IPT/PDT turnover rate or average IPT/PDT turnover rate

Milestone or task completion vs. plan

On-schedule task start rate

Personnel ratios

Phase cycle time vs. plan

Ratio of experts to practitioners to novices per group

Staffing ratios (ratio of each discipline's headcount on project to # of design
engineers)

Time-to-market or time-to-volume

Process Development

of services processes

% data loss cases that affected the operational effectiveness

% electronic files backup

% growth of input in knowledge base

% of proof of concept accepted/rejected

% paper to electronic document ratio

% R&D alliance to meet expected standards

% safety testing

% success in determining ideal levels

% success of performance delivery mechanisms

% time d for data gathering

% time for completing standard documents

% time to correct the loss due to mismanagement of data

Average time to break-even

Efficiency of product processes

28. Research & Development

Product Assurance

# of open action items
# of parts procurement
% of build-to-packages released without errors
% of parts with no engineering change orders
% of testable requirements
Actual MTBF / predicted MTBF
Cost of safety certifications
Design review cycle time
Field failure rate
Process capability
Product yield

Product Cycle

concept approval cycle time
of design/build/test iterations
# of parts / # of parts for last generation product
% of parts or part characteristics analyzed/simulated
% of parts that can be recycled
% of parts used in multiple products
Average # of components per product
Breakeven time
Defects per million opportunities or per unit
Engineering changes after release by time period
Expected commercial value
Failure rate per unit of hours of operation
Field failure rates per unit of time
Labor hours or labor hours / target labor hours
Material cost or material cost / target material cost
Mean time between failures (MTBF)
Mean time to repair (MTTR)
Net present value of cash outflows for development and commercialization and the inflows from sales
Product general availability (GA) date vs. announced GA date or planned GA date
Product performance or product performance / target product performance
Product ship date vs. announced ship date or planned ship date
Production ramp-up time
Production yield
Unit production cost / target cost

Product Design

# of approved projects ongoing
# of design review changes / total terminations or connections
# of design review deficiencies / # of parts
# of development work-in-progress

28. Research & Development
# of drafting errors / # of sheets
# of ideas/proposed products in the pipeline or the investigation stage (prior to formal approval)
# of post-design release changes / total terminations or connections
# of print changes / total print features
# of prototype designs developed
# of prototype iterations
# of prototypes designs abandoned
# of prototypes designs pending
# of R&D units active
# of R&D units inactive
% drawing growth (unplanned drawings / total planned drawings)
% fault coverage or # of faults detectable / # of possible faults
% fault isolation
% hand assembled parts
% innovations for customer use
% of parts modeled in solids
% of projects approved at each gate review
% of understanding the requirement through market research
% R&D resources/investment devoted to new products (versus total of new products plus sustaining and administrative)
Cancelled projects and/or wasted spending last 12 months
Cost of investment
Development turnover (annual sales divided by annual average development work-in-progress)
Expected cost of investment
Failure rates of prototypes
First silicon success rate
New applications devised
New products completed/released to production last 12 months
Pipeline throughput rate
Portfolio balance by project/development type
Producibility rating or assembly efficiency
Ratio of research and development
Transistors or gates designed per engineering man-month

Research

ideas submitted per researcher per year
of invitations to address and participate in conferences/year
# of patent applications per R&D spend per year
# of patents
# of patents/year
# of peer-reviewed articles published
# of publications/year
patents issued at national level

28. Research & Development

% increase in searches per repository

% influences of culture of society

% of higher degree employees

% of hours spent on R&D

% of license costs of total R&D cost

% of license income to total R&D cost

% of patents for sale

% of R&D cost related to new product development

% of R&D cost related to product improvements and extensions

% of R&D financing by third party

% of R&D projects involving customers

% of R&D projects involving pre-competitive research with competing companies

% of R&D projects involving universities / research institutes

% of R&D resources by total resources

% of rejected patents

% of researchers moving from R&D to start up own business

% of researchers supported with grants

Average application time for patents

Average time from idea to first patent filing

Design to cost accuracy

Patent applications as a % of invention disclosures

R&D costs as % of total costs

R&D expense

R&D expense by total expenses

R&D productivity based on gross margin

R&D resources by total resources

R&D spend as % of revenue

Total investment in research

Software Engineering

double customers in the master data

of software defects per week

Code review errors per KSLOC

Design review errors per KSLOC

Man-hours per 1,000 software lines of code

Man-hours per function point

Software problem reports (SPR's) before release per 1,000 software lines of code (KSLOC)

SPR fix response time

SPR's after release per KSLOC

Specifications

of customer needs identified

# of discrete requirements identified (overall system and by subsystem)

# of in-process design changes / # of parts

28. Research & Development

of requirements/specification changes (cumulative or per unit of time)

# of to-be-determined (TBD) requirements / total requirements

prototypes per new product

steps to modify a document

% of requirement deficiencies at qualification testing

Requirements change rate (requirements changes accepted / # of requirements)

Requirements creep (new requirements / # of requirements)

Verification % (# of requirements verified / # of requirements)

Suppliers Involvement

of parts per supplier

# of suppliers

% of certified suppliers

% of standard or preferred parts

% of suppliers engaged in collaborative design

Technology

of possibilities identified to make

# of possibilities identified to sell

# of repackaged technologies

% of documents accessible through search engine

% of documents digitally archived

% of team members with video-conferencing/desktop collaboration access/tools

% team members with full access to product data and product models

% unnecessary data duplicates

% use of groupware

% use of intranet

Analysis/simulation intensity (analysis/simulation runs per model)

CAD workstation ratio (CAD workstations / # of team members)

Technical rating of product

29. Sales & Marketing

Advertising

audience reach

of events participated

# of marketing communication tools

# of people asked after advertising program

# of people asked to buy products advertised after advertising program

# of people bought products

# of sales of products advertised before and after the advertising program

viewership of advertisements

% inquiries growth following campaign

% of advertising spend of total spend of main competitors

% of awareness of advertising messages

29. Sales & Marketing

% of awareness of the product

% of campaigns that fail to start in due time

% of effective reach

% of new revenue

% of people remembering message

% of people understanding message

% of preferred customers with messages and advertising program

% of sales after the promotion and sales turnover before the promotion

% of sales in promotion period and before the promotion

% of targeted-audience that is exposed to a particular ad

Average exposure to advertisement

Average response rates of campaigns

Awareness growth % following campaign

Contact rate

Gross rating point (GRP)

Inquiries growth % following campaign

Rating by customers of advertising messages

Sales lead value ratio

Target Rating Point

Turnover rate before and after the promotion

Brand Marketing

of brand strength level

# of negative media coverages

% audience share

% brand awareness

% brand knowledge

% consumer awareness

% of brand awareness

% of brand consideration

% of brand credibility

% of brand relevance

% of consumer retention of commercial messages

% response rate

Brand equity

Growth sustainability rate of brand

Q score to measure the familiarity and appeal of a brand

Return on investment (ROI) of brand

Revenue generation capabilities of brand

Transaction value of brand

Cost & Budget

of promotional costs

% coupon conversion

% product shelf-space profitability

Actual cost versus budget

29. Sales & Marketing

Average customer acquisitions costs

Average discount margin % of items sold

Average discount margin monetary value of items sold

Average new revenue per customer

Average pay per employee

Bad debts as a % of credit sales (ex VAT)

Bonus payout as a % of the total possible

Cash flows from operating activities

Core earnings per share (CHF)

Cost of advertising on the 1000 target audiences

Cost of all deliveries per month

Cost of lead - average

Cost of sales / customers

Cost of sales force

Cost of services per customer

Cost of wages

Cost per # of engaged prospects

Cost per broadcast hour

Cost per customer

Cost per delivery per customer

Cost per exposure

Cost per lead

Cost per mille (CPM)

Cost per sale - average

Cost premises / sales turnover

Customer acquisitions costs as % of sales value

Debtors outstanding (days)

Equity ratio

Income taxes

Income taxes as % of sales

Marketing expenses

Marketing cost as a % of sales

Net assets

Net cash

Net financial income

Notice to sales budget delivery period

Operating free cash flow

Operating free cash flow as % of sales

Operating profit before exceptional items

Operating profit margin

Profit from continuing business

Promotional sales premiums

Salaries & related costs as a % of gross margin

Salaries & related costs as a % of total sales

29. Sales & Marketing

Salaries and sales commissions

Salary costs / sales turnover

Sales compared to budget/target

Sales Costs

Selling hour value

Shortages/overages in cash registers

Support cost per customer in community

The cost of wages

Total cost of customer acquisition

Total sales revenues / year

Transport costs as a % of delivered sales

Customer Loyalty

of customers do not buy our goods again

% customer loyalty (>2 years)

% dormancy rate

% of customer loyalty loss

% of customer purchase up 2 / total customers

% of customers back

% of customers retained in a given time period

% of lost customers lost after purchasing first time

% of new customer

Average lag time between customer purchases

Life cycles of a customer

Sale increase % due to loyal customers

Total customer lost

Customer Satisfaction

of customer claims

# of customer satisfaction reports

# of dispute complaints

# of enquiries

# of individual customer service reports

# of initiated support tickets per customer per period

# of meetings

# of new customers

# of new service stations

# of purchase

# of recognition certificates

# of requirements identified through market study

# of visits to customers

% complaints are resolved in the first time

% complaints resolved within agreed time

% customer complaints due to quality of services

% customer satisfaction with new products and services

% documentation of customer feedback

29. Sales & Marketing

% good relationship with customers

% of applications approved

% of complaints by sector

% of customer claims

% of customer service requests answered in given time frame

% of market returns on total sales quantity

% of rapid response

% orders delivered in full

% orders delivered on time

% product damage

% product returns

% Sales turnover of new customers

% served market

% service performance against standard criterion

% users satisfied with service responsiveness

Alternative format bills sent

Average time from customer contact to sales response

Brand-image index

Customer satisfaction rate

Customer satisfaction rating

Delays in delivering to customers (customer goodwill)

First request versus agreements

First request versus negotiated

Mystery shopper index

Mystery Shopper rating

Order entry accuracy

Respond to customers in (< 30 minutes)

Retention rates

Successful visits

Time to turn round complaints

Travel time as a % of total planned time

Visits made - % to peers

E-Commerce

new customer on first visit ratio

of depts. using IT systems

# of depts. using websites

# of goods / order

# of invoices

# of orders

# of orders per customer per year

page per session

page redirect latency

session think time

unique authenticated visitors

29. Sales & Marketing

visitor regency
visits per visitor
visits to purchase
web traffic concentration
website success rate
% bounce rate
% conversion rate
% new visitors
% of canceled checkouts
% of low value invoices by #
% of low value invoices by value
% of low value orders by value
% of new customers
% of returning customers
% page exit rate
% revenue from new visitors
% visits under one minute
Average # of items per purchase
Average days to purchase
Average lifetime value of customers
Average order size
Average order value (AOV)
Average time on page
Average time on site
Average visits to purchase
Cart conversion rate
Checkouts per cart
Coupon conversion %
Frequency of sales transactions
Order session %
Shopping cart abandonment rate
Value of invoices
Value of orders

E-Marketing

of ads served
# of changes in product schedules
# of direct access increase
# of forecasting assumption errors
# of page views / visitor
# of project plans that meet schedule, price, and quality
# of reference site (from any site which links to our Website)
# of source access to our Website
# of upward pricing revisions per year
visitors of left page

29. Sales & Marketing
% left web just after visiting (Bounce Rate)
% of bounced emails
% of emails that are opened
% of out-of-office replies
% of responses to opened emails
% of responses to sent emails
% of return of the old visitors
Ad click-through ratio (CTR)
Advertising revenue
Average # of ad units served per visit
Average cost per click (CPC)
Average revenue per ad served
Cancellation rate of payment / cart
Conversion rate of marketing/sales campaigns
Cost per action (CPA)
Effective cost per mille (eCPM)
Forward Email to a Friend %
Opt-out %
Revenue from online ads
Spam report %
Success rate of campaign
Time to load web site
Value of the average order

Lead Generation
# of deals in the sales pipeline
# of junk leads
# of leads/period
# of new leads per week/month
# of pre-sales reference calls (to other customers)
# of qualified leads/period
# of sales leads to be generated to achieve revenue goal
selling opportunities
% of delayed opportunities
% of neglected opportunities
Average new appointments generated per sales rep
Average new-hire ramp-to-quota
Conversation-to-appointment ratio
Delays in addressing new leads
First appointment to sales proposal ratio
Ratio of qualified to non-qualified leads
Time to qualified lead - average

Market Share
market share rank
of geographical areas

29. Sales & Marketing

of research and development projects
relative market share
% market share
% of customer acquisition
% of customer attrition
% of sales turnover of the company compared with sales of the entire sector
% share of voice (SOV)
Compare market share to growth rate
Dealer sales in IG
Direct communications to customers per year
Exit # of unprofitable markets
Increased % of market
Introduce product to # of new market
Investment in development of new markets
Investment in new product support and training
Investment in training by # of customers
Launch of new products
Lost to competitors
Market share %
Market share against competitors
Market share gain comparison %
Market share of the company compared with the entire market
Research and development as % of sales
Sales per channel
Sales volume

Online Journal

of commentators
# of subscribers
% of new commentators
% of unique visitors / members commenting
Average # of new blog entries
Average # of trackbacks per blog post
Average comments per blog post
Average new visitors per blog post
Average returning visitors per blog post
Average thread length in comments
Average word count in blog post
Average word count of comments
Frequency of blog posts

Packaging

% corrective actions in production taken within 24 hours for each non-compliance
% quality of packaging (materials or other)

29. Sales & Marketing
% quality of presentation
% variation reports to production
Customer complaints packaging
Customer complaints undeliverables

Public Relations

of article placements in trade magazines
# of customer complained about the company
# of customer write about feelings sent to newspapers
# of customers who nominate recent media item as reason for their inquiry
# of media agencies has posted messages on business
# of phone calls to the company for more information
target rating points (TRPs)
% of awareness of customers and the public image of the product and business
% of awareness of the enterprise through the public relations
% of awareness of the product through the public relations
% of negative (bad) online buzz
% of positive (good) online buzz
% of press releases that are picked-up by media
Average # of media that pickup story per press release
Column-inches of articles appearing in publications
Minutes of airtime in TV/radio media
Ratio positive to negative editorial articles
Volume of online buzz

Retail

of contracts signed
# of sets of customer requirements identified
# of SLAs signed
stock rotation
% increase in volume of sales during promotion
% inventory turns
% invoice accuracy
% markdown goods
% of technology skills (e.g. POS Equipment)
% of perishable items with past due date
% of retail stores audited on hygiene and quality criteria
% of spaces occupied by tenants
% of spaces unoccupied
% of total stock that is not displayed to customers
% on time delivery to customer
% product share on shelf
% product visibility on shelf
% sales by department or product category
% same store sales growth

29. Sales & Marketing

% store conversion rate
Average lead time per order
Collected sales as a % of Ex stock sales
Conversion rate (customer into sale)
Delivered sales as a % of Ex stock sales
Direct sales as a % of total sales
Direct sales per employee
Ex stock sales as a % of total sales
Ex stock sales per employee
Markdown goods %
Price premium
Promotion share
Sales turnover / location
Scanning % in store
Total sales at stores open at least a year
Turnover of average stock
Units per customer/transaction

Sales

new customers
of customer deliveries
# of new product ideas
sales as a result of the average purchase
% converting enquiries into orders
% new products sales cannibalization ratio
% of ideas from customers/prospects/community
% of repeat business turnover
% of sales lost
% of sales revenue via partner channel
% of win backs
% sales quota attainment
% sell-through
Accuracy of the sales forecasting
Achieve x % price increase
Age of sales forecast
Average customer time spent before purchase
Average deal size in sales pipeline
Average sales per 100 customers
Closing ratio
Early sales growth %
Idea to development initiation cycle time
Involuntary customer churn
New account cycle time
New product / service analysis
New product / service launch adoption

29. Sales & Marketing
Numeric product distribution
Region
Sales by period
Sales by product line
Sales growth
Sales Increase / (Decrease) over pervious year
Sales of a product as % of total sales of the company
Sales order by FTE
Sales per hour
Sales per square foot
Sales per storefront
Sales productivity ratio
Sales to-date
Sell cycle
Sell-through %
Time taken to turn round
Total amount of deal size in sales pipeline
Total sales
Total sales per employee
Up sales/cross sales
Value of sales lost
Value of sales lost by reason
Value to volume ratio
Voluntary customer churn
Weighted sum of deal size in sales pipeline

Sales Representatives

hourly Sales
of average appointments per sale rep
# of clients on / sale staff #s
# of customers / employees
# of customers have received feedback
# of ideas generated
# of ideas implemented
% of customers gained / total client feedback
% of gaining customers
% of response / total sent
% of sale rep met sales targets
% of sales reps at or above sales quota
% sales team trained
Average response time to business partner request
Average sale turnover/ per sales staff
Average sales revenue per sales person
Average time for a coaching staff sale achieve the target sales of the company

29. Sales & Marketing

Average turnover / customer / sale staff

Cost to gain new customers

Members at team meetings

Opportunity success rate

Repeated lost sales by individual salesmen

Time to answer a request by customers

Total costs to gained a new customer

Total sales of sale staff / total customers of each sale staff

Total sales turnover of the entire staff / # of sale employees

Total savings generated

Total time to recruit and train sale rep to meet sale standards

Sales Revenue

gross rating points (GRPs)

% error in sales forecasts

% increase in re-purchases following the execution of the project

% of income from return customers

% of online sales revenue

% of profit / capital

% of profit / per shop

% of repeat business

Activated new business value

Annual sales per customer

Average customer size

Average product price (APP)

Average revenue per sale

Average sale per customer/transaction

Average sale per VIP customer

Average sales per customer per year

Average value of customer baskets

Average value of private-label

Average weekly sales per city

Average weekly sales per store

Customer profitability

Customer service expense per year

Customers per employee

Gross margin as a % of direct sales

Gross margin as a % of Ex stock sales

Gross margin as a % of selling price

Gross margin as a % of total sales

Gross margin return on inventory investment

Gross profit margin

Gross profit per Employee

Labor time as a % of total planned time

Lifetime value of a customer (LTV)

29. Sales & Marketing
Lifetime value of customers
Net profit after interest per employee
Profit per customer visit
Rate of profit of a customer
Rate of service charges / profits
Revenue per successful call
Revenue won/lost due to exchange rates as a % of total revenue
Revenue/adoption rate of new products from community vs. traditional sources
Sales forecasting accuracy
Sales turnover
Spend per customer
Total customer profitability

Shareholders & Investors

% issues raised by business partners that are satisfactorily resolved in 24 hours
% Reports submitted on-time
Dividend as % of sales
Dividend per share
Market capitalization
Payout ratio
Price of non-voting equity security
Total dividend
Total shareholder return

Telephone Sales

# of calls are not connected
# of calls canceled after the guests have to wait too long
# of guests answered out of 3 ring tone to your phone
# of incoming calls but can not connect because telephone is busy or tailoring
# of telephone sales made
# of time that customers must wait to resolve
% answer after time regulated (for example 5 seconds or 3 ring tone)
% of calls in the meantime
% of resolution in the first call
% unique received calls
Average time waited when transiting
The average cost per call / per transaction
Time to talk of an average phone calls

Website

# of active buyers
# of buyers
# of completed profiles
# of connections (between members)

29. Sales & Marketing

of friends met online that member has subsequently collaborated with

# of friends met online that users have met offline

# of groups (networks/forums)

# of ideas that the user has gotten and then used in their work

# of members

# of page views

# of unique visitors

% of visitors entering booking system

% unable to book (non-IE browser)

Average time spent on site

Booking income

Conversion rate

Cost per visit

Money lost from non-IE visitors entering booking system

New 'friends' after 30/60/90 days

Non buying visitors as % of total

Quality and speed of issue resolution

Quality of non-buying visitors (% entering booking system)

Quality of organic visitors (% entering booking system)

Ratio of member to buyer

Ratios of posts to comments to posts

Visitors as a % of total hits

Website word count

Website Access

of indexed pages

# of internet channel feedback

# of site access through search engines

# of times website shows a 404 page

# of unique visitors from all channels

# of visits from all channels

# of visits which access the site directly

% at which visitors initiate transactions but do not reach the 'submit' page

% of direct URL access

% of Google backlinks/deeplinks

% of new visitors

% of server availability

% of total visits arriving at the site from referral sites

% of visits from searches corresponding to brand name

% visitors initiate transactions at 'submit' page

Average time on web site

Average visit duration

Bounce rate

Heavy user share

Index-to-crawl ratios

29. Sales & Marketing

Keywords per page yield

Natural traffic per keyword

On-site search sessions %

Referral %

Revenue from organic search engine traffic

Revenue per Visit

Search engine keyword visibility ratio

Search engine optimization rate

Search engine ranking

Site error messages

Visitor per keyword yield

Website success rate

30. Telecommunication

Coverage

of new service connections

# of service connection

% of land covered with services

% of land covered with telecommunication services

% of population covered with services

% of population covered with telecommunication services

Access to customer service

Average land unavailable to services

Average population unavailable to services

Reliability rate

Customer Satisfaction

of responses generated

# of unresolved issues

% of orders provided on time

Average score from call monitoring

Average score from external surveys

Average score from internal surveys

Average time frame for repairs and installations

Average time to restore service

Mean opinion score

Mean time to detect problem

Revenue

% of non-voice revenue

Average revenue per employee

Average revenue per subscriber

Average revenue per user

Average revenue realization

Average revenue realization from each unit of usage

Minutes of usage (MoU) per subscriber

30. Telecommunication

Prepaid average revenue per user

Revenue per voice-minute

Systems & Network

Bit error ratio (data, bits and elements transfer)

Bit rate (data, bits and elements transfer)

Call completion ratio

Cost of operational systems

Cost of support systems

Grade of service

Service life of equipment

Utilities

of prepaid lines

Access lines per call centre employee

Access lines per employee

Average service life

Bit error ratio

Bit Rate

Broadband subscribers as % of fixed voice lines

Contract-based

Digital video subscribers as % of fixed voice lines

MoU per subscriber for voice usage

31. Textile Production

Dyeing

of fibers/yarn cross-section

Average % of fabric rejects

Color fastness

Energy consumption for drying and steaming

Levels of residues of heavy metal based dyeing salts

Pollution levels of chlorine-based dyeing agents

Pollution levels of Pesticide used in the garments

Uniformity in coloring

Water consumption for washing and dyeing

Processing

% of shrink resistance

Deviations in dimensions of the fabric

Variance in dye color

Variance in fabric specifications

Production Capacity

of new technologies introduced

% of current period / previous period

% supply / demand

Idle time

Technology rating compared to global standards

31. Textile Production

Time spent on repair and maintenance

Spinning

# of abnormalities

# of preventive measures taken

% density

% effectiveness of the measures

% non-recyclable solid waste

% process stoppage

Amount of air pollution

pH of sample

Textile Cost

Cost of maintenance

Cost of raw materials

Overheads

People costs

Weaving

% deviation in thread quality

% humidity of threads

% of harness of threads

% presence of carcinogens

% reduction of pollutants post treatment

32. Transportation

Airline Customer Satisfaction

baggage transfer time

of assistance to disabled passengers

# of bags handled per month

# of involuntary denied boarding per 10,000 passengers

# of lost and misplaced luggage

# of lost luggage reports per 1,000 passengers

# of passengers per employee

# of passengers per flight

# of security services and measures

% lost luggage

% maturity of workforce

% of e-tickets

% of lost bags/luggage

% of trained and qualified staff

% online booking adoption rate

% received with complete and accurate documentation

Lost and misplaced luggage rate

Work load units per employee

Airline Flight Cost

average fuel consumption

32. Transportation
revenue passenger-kilometer
% passenger seats sold
Actual passenger load factor
Average # of flight hours per crew member
Average aircraft landing fee
Average flight distance per crew member
Average ticket price
Breakeven passenger load factor
Cost per flight hour
Crew operating cost
Equity ratio
Fuel cost as % of total costs
Fuel costs as a % of operating costs
Fuel costs per gallon
Fuel per block hour
Liquidity Ratio
Lowest fare given
Staff costs as % of total operating costs
Staff costs as a % of turnover
Staff costs as per employee
Staff costs as per passenger
Total airplane maintenance cost
Total cost per available seat mile
Total cost per flight hour controlled
Total cost per Km controlled
Total fuel cost
Total operating cost
Total operating costs per hour flown
Total operating costs per passenger
Total operating costs per revenue flight
Total operating costs per work load units
Total revenue per available seat mile

Airline Flight Revenue

# of investment agreements
seat availability
% empty running
% fill rate
% of aircraft utilization
% of seats utilized (load factor)
% of total revenue from non-aviation activities
% of traffic revenue
% transport capacity utilization
Available seat per mile
Available seats per departure

32. Transportation
Average revenue per flight
Basic earnings per share
Freight or cargo revenue
Operating profit
Operating profit per passenger
Passenger volume
Revenue passenger per mile
Revenue per available seat
Revenue per available seat per mile
Revenue seat/passenger-kilometer
Revenue tonne/kilometre
Total assets per employee
Total cargo revenue
Total operating revenue per employee
Total operating revenue per passenger
Total operating revenue per revenue flight
Total operating revenue per work load units

Airline Ground Operation

# of improvements carried out
# of long-term relationships with suppliers
# of policies and procedures in place
# of service level agreements
# of spare parts on hand
# of staff in critical decision making position
# of workshop maintenance hours
% frequency of ground delays
% ground crew trained
% of staff motivated and satisfied
% on-time departure of transport vehicles
Air traffic control rate
Average turnaround time
Total incentives given to avoid delays
Vehicle time utilization

Airline Schedule

airplane block time
average minutes delayed per delayed flight
of aircraft fleet structure and reserve
# of unscheduled maintenance
% of air carrier delays
% of cancelled flights
% of flights diverted
% of national airspace system delays
% of on-time arrival of flights
% of on-time departure of flights

32. Transportation

Arrival defect rate

Average # of check-in counters per flight

Average # of weather delays

Average duration between off-block time and first-bag

Average duration between off-block time and last-bag

Average duration of total check-in

Average immigration time

Average stage length

Average stops per trip

Block hours

Cargo throughput

Departure defect rate

Direct delay cost

Indirect delay cost

Customers Partnerships

of successful partnerships acquired for maintenance contracts

% difference in pricing models

% improvement in customer retention

% partner collaborations

% preference of service by the customers - advantage over competitors

Service quality of partner

Land Fleet & Buses

of active vehicles in the fleet

# of miles per vehicle

# of passenger trips

# of public volunteer driver hours

# of public volunteer driver miles

# of public volunteer driver passenger trips

Average fuel economy of vehicles

Count of visits to service centres

Count of visits to service centres for repair

Farebox recovery %

Other operating revenues

Passengers per hour

Passengers per mile

Total revenue from fares

Total revenue from public volunteer driver program

Total revenue service hours

Total vehicle miles

Land Fleet Cost

% of accessorial cost of total freight cost

Average cost involved with import or export transaction

Claims as % of freight costs

Cost of freight per unit shipped

32. Transportation

Cost per passenger trip

Cost per service hours

Cost per vehicle mile

Freight cost per unit shipped

Maintenance cost per mile

Outbound freight costs as % of net sales

Total operating costs

Total public volunteer operating costs

Land Shipment

of carriers used per cargo transported

# of deliveries with past due goods issue date

# of empty miles

# of on-time pickups

% functioning rate of network structure

% implemented integrated planning

% of accuracy for freight bills

% of cargo accountable at any given time

% of deployment of block and slack time measures

% of orders delivered with damaged products/items

% of orders/items arrives at the right location

% of shipment visibility/traceability

% of truckload capacity utilized

% of undamaged goods after shipping/transportation

% optimized load fulfillment

Accessorials as % of total freight

Average age of fleet

Average time of import or export transaction

Average transit time

Damages as % of throughput

Freight bill accuracy

On time delivery and pickup [Load, stop and shipment]

On time line count

On time value %

On-time pickups

Total network recovery

Truck turnaround time

Turnaround time

Operational Excellence

of improve business processes

# of improve internal communication tools

# of improvement programs

# of inventory monitoring done per month

# of non-conformities (orders)

# of non-conformities QA-system

32. Transportation

- # of subjective assessment
- % improvement in operational efficiency
- % improvement in service delivery
- % improvement in staff performance and productivity
- % increase in freight traffic
- Total R&D expenses

Rail Business Expansion

- # of developed and introduced new business lines
- # of developed dry ports
- # of explored communications business
- # of hours of utilization per day
- # of introduction of total logistics and transport solutions
- # of new venture into property business
- % availability of appropriate rolling stock to meet customer needs
- % expanded current and export business
- % increase workshops capacity
- % reduction in frequency of outages of trains
- Maximize track availability
- Resource reliability - quality check %

Rail Costs & Expenditure

- % reduction in inventory costs
- Administrative overheads
- Human capital cost
- Infrastructure cost
- Maintenance cost of the rail system
- Marketing costs
- Platform annual maintenance
- Spares for infrastructure

Rail Quality Service

- # of certification for drivers
- # of quality checks conducted
- % improved quality and condition of rolling stock
- % replacement and renewal of signaling & telecommunication systems
- On-time reliability %
- On-time reliability % during peak times
- Seat availability %
- Seat availability % during peak times

Safe Services

- # of accidents with permanent disabilities
- # of death Accidents
- # of man hours due to lost time injuries
- # of meeting standards set for the safety
- # of safety measures taken
- # of safety standards

32. Transportation
# of sign-off injuries
% comfort to customers
% decreased work-related accidents
% improvement in reliability of services
% of injured passengers during passenger handling operations
% of injured passengers during sea voyage
Accidents per 100,000 flight hours
Accidents per 100,000 Miles

Ship Cost & Budget

# of hours downtime
% deviation from budget
% deviation from budget (cost control)
% deviation from budget (customer costs)
% net result
% of deviation from budget (docking)
% of profit margin crew agencies
% of total cost
% operating result
% profit margin
% reduction in unit prices
% return on revenue
Administrative cost
Computers cost
Cost of technical operation
Crewing cost
Daily running cost per ship
Fees paid for ship and crew management
Insurance cost
Off hire operations
Profit margin (vessel)
Quality cost
Revenue share from long-term contracts
Revenue share from spot contracts
Salaries cost
Service cost
Ship running costs
Software cost
Staff training cost
Total cost
Total quality cost index

Ship Customer Satisfaction

# of ad-hoc requests
# of cargo damage / loss
# of customer surveyed

32. Transportation
# of customized solutions
# of oil company vettings
# of port state inspection findings
% deviation from project plan
% of customer satisfaction
% of customized shipping solutions
% of lost or damaged cargo during sea voyage
% of pool utilization
% of ship availability
% of spot requests serviced
% of voyage deviation

Ship Market Share

# of ships
% increase in customer base
% increase in fleet size
% of shipments outsourced
% relative market share
% revenue share from new transport services
Growth through new customers
Growth through old customers
Trailer fill %

Ship Quality Standard

# of cargo claims reported
# of crew trained
# of detentions by port state control
# of experience report per event
# of improvement conferences
# of observations per audit
# of outstanding maintenance jobs
# of update web report
# of voyage deviation

Ship Regulations Compliance

# of navigational incidents
# of non-conformities
# of port state inspection
% of cargo damaged or lost during cargo operations
% of cargo incident rate
% of detention
Ballast water discharge violations
Deviation on discharge rate from Charter party
Deviation on speed/ consumption from Charter party
Pollution incident rate

Ship Sustainable Growth

# of applicants

32. Transportation

of contractual conflict

# of projects handled

# of undesired events

% growth from last period

% growth results vs. tonnage

% of key personnel turnover

% of new cadets assigned to vessels

% of profit growth

Demurrage and claims recovery rate

Ship Port Operation

of container dwell time (in days) in the port divided by total # of boxes

# of crane moves per working hour

# of TEUs stored per ha of storage area and year

# of TEUs handled per year and per crane

Average ship turn around time

Average waiting rate

Average yard utilization rate

Berth occupancy rate

Container dwell time

Total # of TEUs per year per linear meter of the quay

Total hours vehicles stay in terminal (terminal-in to terminal-out) divided by total # of vehicles

Total hours vessels stay in port divided by total # of vessels

Total hours vessels wait for a berth (anchorage-to-berth time) divided by total time at berth

Total time of vessels at berth divided by total berth hours available

Total time of vessels being serviced at berth divided by total time at berth

Social & Environmental

of pollution incident

% deployment of renewable energy resources

% of energy efficiency

% of environmental compatibility

% of total airline fleet that meets noise requirements

Aircraft emissions per payload capacity

CO_2 emissions of aircraft total

CO_2 emissions passenger per kilometer

CO_2 emissions per ton-kilometer

SECTION B

GOVERNMENT

8600 Key Performance Indicators

GOVERNMENT CHAPTERS
(33 to 65)

33. Agriculture & Food
Agricultural Land

# of agricultural holdings growing crops
# of agricultural holdings with agricultural area < 5 ha
# of agricultural holdings with agricultural area > = 50 ha
# of agricultural holdings with agricultural area 20-<50 ha
# of agricultural holdings with agricultural area 5-<20 ha
# of agricultural holdings with another gainful activity than agricultural production
# of agricultural holdings with broilers
# of agricultural holdings with laying hens
# of agricultural land types
# of cereals farms
# of common wheat farms
# of enterprises in the manufacturing of foodstuffs
# of enterprises turnover in the manufacturing of foodstuffs
# of farms and agricultural area
# of farms legal status
# of farms with arable crops
# of flowers and ornamental plants farms
# of fruit and berry plantations farms
# of grain maize farms
# of greenhouses farms
# of holding managers
# of industrial plants farms
# of irrigation equipments in farms
# of melons farms
# of olive plantations farms
# of persons at farm work by age of worker
# of potatoes farms
# of registered operators processing and importing products issued from organic farming
# of registered organic operators
# of strawberries farms
# of sugar beet farms
# of vegetables farms
total area of land cultivated
% land used
% legal status of holding
% of agricultural land (% of land area)
% of arable land
% of arable land (% of land area)
% of barley farms and area
% of fallow land

33. Agriculture & Food

% of land use
% of landscape preservation
% of mixed farming
% of specialized farming
Agricultural holders < 35 years old
Agricultural holders > = 65 years old
Average land prices per square meter
Average land rents per square meter
Average size of farm
Organic crop yields from fully converted areas
Selling prices of land
Total area of cereals
Total area under organic farming
Total crops products area
Total economic size of farm
Total grassland
Total organic crop area
Total organic crop area (fully converted area)
Total rape area
Total size of farms
Total sugar beet area
Total sunflower area
Total wheat area

Agricultural Products

of inputs to the food chain
# of miles area under glass
# of tones of apples production
# of tones of carrots production
# of tones of cereals production
# of tones of crop production
# of tones of fruits production
# of tones of onions production
# of tones of oranges production
# of tones of organic farming
# of tones of pears production
# of tones of potatoes production
# of tones of rape production
# of tones of sugar beet production
# of tones of sunflower production
# of tones of tomatoes production
# of tones of vegetables
# of tones of vegetables production
# of tones of wheat production
% degree of self sufficiency

33. Agriculture & Food

% of extra imports of all edible vegetables prepared and preserved

% of extra imports of all edible vegetables, fresh, chilled and frozen

% of extra imports of cereals and cereal products

% of extra imports of coffee, tea, cocoa

% of extra imports of dairy products and bird's eggs

% of extra imports of feeding stuffs

% of extra imports of fish, crustaceans and molluscs

% of extra Imports of food products

% of extra imports of fruit and nuts (not including oil nuts) fresh or dried

% of extra imports of fruit juices and vegetable juices

% of extra imports of fruit preserved and fruit preparations

% of extra imports of roots and tubers, fresh, chilled and frozen

% of extra imports of roots and tubers, prepared and preserved

% of extra imports of sugars, sugar preparations and honey

% share of sales of foodstuffs in supermarkets and other non-specialized stores

Average selling price of main crop potatoes

Average selling price of soft wheat

Average selling price of sugar beet (unit value)

Average time from production to distribution

Cereals balance sheet (crop year)

Cereals, yields

Crops products: supply balances sheets

Dried pulses balance sheet (crop year)

Fats and oils balance sheet (crop year/calendar year)

Fruit and vegetables balance sheet (crop year)

Gross human apparent consumption of main food items

Gross human apparent consumption of main food items per capita

Harmonized Indices of Consumer Prices

Index of producer prices of agricultural products

Index of purchase prices of the means of agricultural production

Organic livestock

Potatoes balance sheet (crop year)

Price index of agricultural products

Price index of the means of agricultural production

Products with distinctive marks (final consumer's perspective)

Purchase prices of the means of agricultural production

Relative price level indices of food products

Retail sales of foodstuffs

Rice balance sheet (crop year)

Selling prices of animal products

Selling prices of crop products

Sugar balance sheet (crop year)

Total crops products (excluding fruits and vegetables)

33. Agriculture & Food
Total food consumption
Total production and external trade of animal and vegetable fats and oils
Total production and external trade of baker's yeast and soups
Total production and external trade of cereal products
Total production and external trade of chocolate and confectionary
Total production and external trade of coffee, tea and cocoa
Total production and external trade of dessert preparations
Total production and external trade of fresh meat and meat products
Total production and external trade of fruit and vegetable juices
Total production and external trade of mineral waters and soft drinks
Total production and external trade of processed fruits
Total production and external trade of processed vegetables
Total production and external trade of sauces and condiments
Total production and external trade of sugar, jam, and honey
Total production of organic animal products
Total production of processed foodstuffs
Total sales of foodstuffs

Agricultural Sustainability

food production per capita
of high-value habitats conserved
% farmers using conservation farming methods
% of environmentally favorable extensification of farming
% of forest (% of land area)
% of GDP - agriculture value added
% of low-intensity pasture systems
Food production index
Government expenditure on R&D projects related to food safety
National road transport of foodstuffs, by distance
Total economically active population in agriculture (1000 inhab)
Total external trade of products used to package food and beverages
Total sold production of products used to package food and beverages
Value of agricultural output
Value of intermediate consumption in agriculture

Agriculture Sector

# of actors involved in the food chain
# of agricultural production of specified products
# of canteens enterprises
# of direct involvement from academia, private sector associations and consumer protection agencies
# of existing Quality Management System (QMS) in agriculture sector
# of family farm labor force
# of farm machinery
# of food retailers enterprises
# of food retailers enterprises total employment

33. Agriculture & Food

of full-time regular farm labor force

# of hotels and restaurants next to farm lands

# of international accreditation of services

# of part-time regular farm labor force

# of publishing through official website and Media

# of reduction in districts that are food insecure

# of regional distribution units producing foodstuffs

# of regular farm labor force

# of square meters of land cleared and restored to productive use in sponsored programs

# of storage facilities

# of total earnings

% automation of e-government

% farmers training level

% growth rate in the agriculture sector

% increase in farmer satisfaction levels with services

% increase in sharing information through website

% increase of IT software and hardware usage across the sector

% of farms joining Farmers' association

% of agricultural training of farm managers

% of completion of integrated plan for agriculture Sector

% of contribution of agriculture to foreign exchange

% of contribution of agriculture to GDP

% of data and statistics in centralized data repository

% of electronic data of food imports stored in Database

% of farmers satisfied

% of functioning strategic planning capability

% of identified farmers and livestock owners eligible for support payments

% of non-core operational activities transferred to the private sector

% of privatized non-core businesses of agriculture sector

% of services provided online

% of SMART performance measures for all strategies targets

% of the population assessed as food secure

% of vacant technical positions

% tailored automated applications for core businesses

% turnover of food retailers

Administrative cost as a % of total agency costs

Administrative positions as a % of total agency positions

Economic accounts for agriculture - agricultural income

Economic accounts for agriculture values at constant prices

Economic accounts for agriculture values at current prices

Gross value added of the agricultural industry

Standard gross margin coefficients used for typology

Standard output coefficients used for typology

33. Agriculture & Food
Total economic accounts for Agriculture
Total income from agricultural activity
Total labor force
Total output of the agricultural industry
Total value of agricultural exports

Animal Pest & Disease Control

- # of animal site inspections performed
- # of animals or samples submitted to the labs per year for surveillance/ healthcare
- # of avian influenza tests provided to poultry growers and hobbyists
- # of diseases, by agricultural area
- # of employee hours spent on animal and agricultural emergency activities
- # of notifiable animal diseases
- # of plant pests by agricultural area
- # of reports of suspected or positive dangerous, transmissible diseases received
- # of samples submitted to the poultry lab network yearly for diagnostic testing
- # of tests and/or vaccinations performed on animals
- # of violations detected per category
- % cow mortality
- % cow survival
- % farrowing rate
- % of animal production establishments are certified with evidence on good farming practices
- % of known pest introductions detected before they spread from the original area of colonization
- % of positive test results from livestock and poultry tested for specific diseases
- % stillborn cow

Aquaculture

- # of acres tested
- # of bushels of processed shell and live oysters deposited to restore habitat on public oyster reefs
- # of leases verified for compliance
- # of shellfish processing plant inspections
- # of shellfish processing plants inspected
- % of shellfish facilities in significant compliance with permit and food safety regulations
- Aquaculture production - Quantities (Tones live weight)
- Aquaculture production - Values ($)
- Total aquaculture production

Consumer Protection

- # of assists provided to consumers by the call center
- # of complaints investigated/processed

33. Agriculture & Food

of food borne disease reporting mechanism

# of identified risks for imported and domestic Food

# of Issued codes of practice for farms and abattoirs

# of law assists made to consumers

# of no sales solicitation calls processed

# of regulated entities licensed

# of risk based system implementation on borders of entry

# of successful programs / campaigns

% food and health certification for food Industry

% increase in food and health certification for 4 & 5 star hotels

% increase in involvement of various stakeholders

% increase in transparency through reports sharing and stakeholders satisfaction

% increase of qualified food inspectors with related degrees

% increase society awareness

% of all regulated entities where an investigation found a violation of consumer protection laws

% of fuel sold in meeting minimum quality standards

% of licensed food establishments maintaining compliance with regulations

% of risk management model fully deploy in local market

% of risk management model fully deploy on borders of entry

Dairy Facilities Compliance

average milk yield per cow

of analyses conducted on samples

# of dairy establishment inspections

% of dairy establishments meeting food safety and sanitation requirements

% of samples analyzed that meet standards

Environmental Services

of fertilizer sample determinations

# of official seed sample determinations performed

# of people served by mosquito control activities

# of pest control businesses and applicators licensed

# of pest control, feed, seed, fertilizer, and pesticide inspections conducted

# of pesticide products registered

# of pesticide sample determinations made in the pesticide laboratory

# of reported human/equine disease cases caused by mosquitoes

% of commercial pest control businesses and applicators inspected who are in compliance with regulations

% of feed, seed and fertilizer inspected products in compliance with performance/quality standards

% of licensed pesticide applicators inspected who are in compliance with regulations

% of pesticide ingredients evaluated and/or managed that are in compliance with regulations

33. Agriculture & Food

Fisheries

of catches in all fishing regions
# of fishing catches by fishing region
# of fishing vessels
# of vessels in fishing fleet
Average consumption of foodstuffs per inhabitant
Average time from farm to fork
Total engine power in fishing fleet
Total exports trade in fishery products
Total external trade of main fish products
Total fishery production - total all fishing areas
Total fishery production (catch + aquaculture)
Total imports trade in fishery products
Total landings of fishery products
Total production and external trade of fresh fish and fish products
Total tonnage of fishing fleet

Food & Health Risks

of animal diseases reported in a year
# of certified companies in a country
# of food safety alerts in a year
# of food safety incidents
# of violations
% of entry borders successfully implementing risk-based food inspection system
% of established food safety indicator
% of reduction in the violations during local market risk-based inspection
Establishment regulation compliance rate
Food products compliance rate

Food Safety Inspection

of chemical residue analyses conducted
# of food analyses conducted
# of implemented automated laboratory information management system
# of inspections of food establishments and water vending machines
# of tons of fruits and vegetables inspected
% accuracy in tests conducted in lab analysis timeframe
% completed in lab of received food samples
% of food establishment inspections conducted by inspectors
% of food establishments meeting food safety and sanitation requirements
% of food products analyzed that meet standards
% of food service establishments that have certified staff
% of individuals affected by a substantiated food borne illness per 100,000 population
% of produce or other food samples analyzed that meet pesticide residue standards

33. Agriculture & Food
% reduction in prevalence of food borne illness from meat, poultry, and egg products
Value of fruit and vegetables that are shipped to other countries that are subject to mandatory inspection

Forestry

of cooking apple trees
# of cooking pear trees
# of forest fires
# of forest increment and fellings
# of forest trees damaged by defoliation
# of lemon trees
# of orange trees
# of peach trees
# of removals
# of removals by ownership
# of removals by roundwood assortment
# of small-fruited citrus trees
# of trades for major forest industry products
% decrease in subdivision and development of wooded area
% increase in forest resources
% increase in roundwood production
% increase in sawnwood production
% increase in trade of roundwood
% of forest damage - defoliation
% of land used
% of secondary paper products
Gross value added of the forestry industry
Total apple trees area (in hectares)
Total area of apricot trees (area in hectares)
Total forestry values at constant prices
Total lemon trees area (in hectares)
Total orange trees area (in hectares)
Total paper and paperboard production
Total peach trees area (in hectares)
Total production of roundwood and fuelwood
Total production of sawnwood and wood based panels
Total production of wood pulp and paper and paperboard
Total secondary wood products / tones
Total small-fruited citrus area (in hectares)
Total subdivision and development of wooded area
Total trade value for roundwood and fuelwood
Total trade value for sawnwood and wood based panels
Total trade value for wood pulp and paper and paperboard
Total value of secondary processed wood and paper products

33. Agriculture & Food

Interdiction Stations

# of bills transmitted from agricultural interdiction stations

# of vehicles inspected at agricultural interdiction stations

# of vehicles inspected at agricultural interdiction stations transporting agricultural or regulated commodities

% of vehicles carrying agricultural related products that are inspected

Amount of revenue generated by agricultural interdiction stations

Legislations & Enforcement

# of borders using the system

# of completed risk analysis and benchmark studies

# of comprehensive training programs across the sector

# of developed and issued bylaws and regulations

# of law enforcement investigations initiated

# of monitored members of Farmers' Association

# of new food standards published

# of refrigerated food inspection centers

# of research and development to identify and implement the latest agriculture practices

# of research published

# of seizures of undeclared risk items at the border

# of studies / surveys conducted

# of surveys completed in food safety

% alignment of external processes with other entities

% alignment with other international entities

% imported foods for consumption that was rejected by source

% of awareness on basic food safety issues covering targeted audience groups

% of completion of policy document for the agricultural sector and food safety

% of criminal investigations closure

% of eligible farmers and animal owners receive the support payments

% of farms and abattoirs show evidence of compliance with health regulations

% of food establishment and hotels will utilize risk based system

% of food handlers certified on health practices

% of food handlers trained and certified

% of food premises complying with food safety regulations

% of food safety matters that is covered with regulations

% of fully consolidated regulations for all animal and plant care activities

% of plant and animal production facilities complying with agricultural regulations

% of policies and regulations are easily accessible to all stakeholders

% of products recalled in 3 days by crisis response team

% of staff meet or exceed the performance requirement criteria as defined by competency standard

33. Agriculture & Food

% of stakeholders engaged in dialogue on standards, regulations, and laws

% of the final legislations issued for the agricultural sector and food safety in the period of time

% staff and stakeholders receiving right communication

Livestock

# of agricultural holdings rearing animals

# of cattle

# of cattle farms

# of dairy cows

# of eggs production per year

# of fodder crops farms

# of goats farms

# of goats population

# of grazing livestock

# of hens

# of holdings with dairy cows

# of laying hens

# of laying hens population

# of livestock (heads)

# of livestock categories

# of livestock heads by of farm

# of poultry farming

# of poultry other than hens

# of sheep

# of sheep farms

# of slaugthered animals for meat production

# of total dairy cows

% increase in animal production

% increase in production of meat: cattle

% increase in production of meat: poultry

% increase in production of meat: sheep and goats

% of extra imports of live animals

% of extra imports of meat and meat products

Average selling price of barley

Average selling price of calves

Average selling price of chickens

Average selling price of fresh eggs

Average selling price of maize

Average selling price of oats

Average selling price of raw cow's milk

Average selling price of sheep

Landings of main species used for human consumption

Livestock density

Livestock density index

33. Agriculture & Food

Producer price index, animals and animal products

Purchase price indices, total means of agricultural production

Total cattle population

Total meat foreign trade

Total meat production

Total sheep population

Milk & Milk Products

\# of collection centers of milk collection

\# of dairies by size (volume of milk collected or treated)

\# of enterprises producing butter

\# of enterprises producing cheese

\# of enterprises producing drinking milk

\# of enterprises producing fresh products

\# of enterprises producing powdered dairy products

\# of milk products

% of fat contents and protein contents (cow's milk)

% utilization of milk on the farm

Average production of milk on the farm

Total collection of cows' milk

Total of enterprises volume milk collection

Total production and external trade of dairy products and eggs

Total production of butter

Total production of cheese

Total production of milk at farm

Total production of milk powder

Total quantity of milk collected by dairies

Total volume of milk treated

Plant Pest & Disease Control

\# of cartons of citrus certified as fly-free for export

\# of commercial citrus acres surveyed for citrus diseases

\# of enforcement actions taken per millions dollars of cost

\# of enterprises in the manufacturing of composite feedingstufs, fertilizers and pesticides

\# of enterprises turnover in the manufacturing of composite feedingstufs, fertilizers and pesticides

\# of food safety alerts

\# of grams of fertilizer consumption per hectare of arable land

\# of plant pests, diseases

\# of plant, fruit fly trap, and honeybee inspections performed

\# of plant, soil, insect, and other organism samples processed for identification or diagnosis

\# of seizures of undeclared risk items at the border and trends over time

\# of sterile med flies released

33. Agriculture & Food

of successful targeted consumers/ food handlers education campaigns/ programs

# of surveillance of food safety and animal and plant disease

# of total # of certified applicators

% chemical fertilizer reduction

% of animal and plant disease alerts that are effectively responded to

% of compliance actions taken as a result of inspection/enforcement

% of dealt with and solved alerts out of total # of food safety alerts

% of farm owners maintaining pest control on their farms to prevent the spread of harmful pests

% of farms implementing effective monitoring program

% of farms under pest control

% of newly introduced pests and diseases prevented from infesting plants

% of pesticide-sprayed samples within internationally accepted tolerance levels

% of samples sprayed with pesticides within internationally accepted tolerance levels

% of viable lead-based paint abatement certification applications that require less than established timeframes to process

% of violators committing subsequent violations

% reach of targeted groups by campaign

% reduction in chemical fertilizer from last year

% use of chemical fertilizers

% use of pesticides

% use of plant protection products in agriculture

Average consumption of fertilizers in agriculture farm

Nitrogen balances (in kg and kg/ha)

Sales of pesticides - Fungicides

Sales of pesticides - Herbicides

Sales of pesticides - Insecticides

Sales of pesticides - Other pesticides

Total consumption of fertilizers (tones of active ingredient)

Total consumption of pesticides (tones of active ingredient)

Total production of composite feeding stuffs (farm animals and pets)

Total quantity of commercial fertilizer consumed in agriculture: nitrogen

Total quantity of commercial fertilizer consumed in agriculture: phosphate

Total quantity of commercial fertilizer consumed in agriculture: potash

Total quantity of commercial fertilizer consumed in agriculture: Total of nitrogen, phosphate and potash

Total quantity of seeds used at the farm

Total quantity of seeds used at the farm from its own production

Total sales of pesticides

Total sales of plant protection products

Products Marketing

of buyers reached with agricultural promotion campaign messages

33. Agriculture & Food

of leased square feet at Farmers' Markets

# of marketing assists provided to producers and businesses

# of tons of federal commodities and recovered food distributed

% increase in total sales at the Farmers' Market

% increase in total users of the Farmers' Market

% of available square feet of Farmers' Markets leased

% of national transport of foodstuffs by air

% of national transport of foodstuffs by inland waterways

% of national transport of foodstuffs by rail

% of national transport of foodstuffs by road

Agricultural products as a % of the national market

Total sales of agricultural and seafood products generated by tenants of farmers markets

Water Policy

of acres enrolled annually in agricultural water programs

# of acres in priority basins or watersheds

# of gallons of water potentially conserved annually by agricultural operations pursuant to site-specific recommendations

# of irrigation methods

# of water policy assists provided to agricultural interests

% conversion of target fields into water efficient crops

% of agricultural water withdrawal as % of total water withdrawal

% of water reduction

% overall reduction in annual water use for agricultural purposes

% reduction of agriculture water consumption per hectare

Inland water(1000 ha)

Renewable internal freshwater resources per capita (cubic meters)

Total irrigable and irrigated areas

Total irrigable area

Yearly amount of water usage for agricultural purposes

Wildfire Prevention

of acres authorized to be burned through prescribed

# of acres of forest land protected from wildfires

# of person-hours spent responding to emergency incidents other than wildfires

# of wildfires caused by humans

# of wildfires suppressed

% of acres of protected forest and wild lands not burned by wildfires

% of threatened structures not burned by wildfires

% of wildfires caused by humans

34. Civil Rights

Advocacy

# of civil rights projects the civil rights commission participates/collaborates in

# of civil rights projects the civil rights participates/collaborates in

% survey responses from counsels to complaints

Average # of hours/month commissioners spend on civil rights related issues

Average # of hours/month commissioners spend on civil rights related projects

Total funds raised per FTE for non-profit and humanitarian organizations

Total investment in the community

Citizen Complaints

# of citizen complaints against police per 100,000 population

# of civil rights lawsuit filings per 100,000 population

# of civil rights violation lawsuit filings

Civil Rights Awareness

% of customers indicating they will use the educational information or materials they have received

% of customers rating materials satisfactory or better

% of customers rating presentations satisfactory or better

% of customers rating service satisfactory or better

Civil Rights Complaints

# of cases accepted for reimbursement by government agencies

# of cases investigated in less than 9 months from date of assignment

# of cases mediated in 90 or less days from date of assignment

# of cases screened in less than 120 days from date of filing

# of complaints regarding timeliness of response to requests for presentations/information

% of cases investigated in 9 months or less from date of assignment

% of cases mediated from date of assignment in 90 days or less

% of cases screened in less than 120 days from date of filing

Average # of days to complete cases processed

Electoral Commission

# of survey/observations

Election cost per elector

Informality rates

Referenda cost per elector

Rejection rate of declaration votes

Total cost per elector

Minorities Rights

# of participating communities

% of individuals attending training

% of individuals, organizations and agencies that are satisfied with products and services

34. Civil Rights

% of individuals, organizations and agencies that are satisfied with technical assistance and information provided

% of primary customers who report satisfaction with services

Average Income by racial and cultural background

Persons with Disabilities

disabled employees

% of client assistance program clients finding resolution to problems with rehabilitation agencies without legal action

% of complaints resolved

% of customers provided with services

% of customers resolving disputes through advocacy, mediation, and negotiation

% of recommended changes in policy that are implemented

% of requests from government agencies reviewed to determine physical and program access

% of youth and college leadership forum graduates with disabilities that are employed

Ranking of among top # counties in employment of persons with disabilities

Technical Training

% of individuals attending training that indicate training goals were met

% of media and public information inquiries responded to within prescribed timeframes

% of organizations and agencies that are satisfied with technical assistance and information provided

Women Rights

new data briefs per year on topics related to women and girls

of businesses that take the labor wage equity self audit

# of persons reached with wage equity information annually

% of agencies served that rate women commission services as helpful or very helpful

% of agencies that say women commission services are likely or very likely to improve their services to women in the future

% of attendees satisfied with female juvenile justice conference(s)

% of partner organizations working with women commission to achieve its mission through legislative action, per year

% of policy women priorities that are drafted into legislation

% reduction in # of cases of gender violence

Abuse rate against women

Total # persons to whom briefs are distributed

Total # of website visitors who download data briefs

35. Culture & Heritage

Arts, Literature & Film

of annual attendance (seats)

# of films funded

35. Culture & Heritage

of films promoting culture and heritage

# of films screened at the Festival

# of local writers trained

# of national regional and international awards won by activity

# of produced films

# of programs and events

# of programs and initiatives aimed at encouraging creativity in the fields of arts, literature & film among citizens

# of radio receivers per 1000 inhabitants

# of registered citizen participants in programs and initiatives in the fields of arts, literature and film

# of strands set-up.

% increase in theatre productions

% of film commission established

% of participation rates

% of success in creating visual arts grant, performing arts grant and design grant

Total # of community radio stations in country

Total # of daily news papers in country

Total # of radio and television institution in country

Cultural Education

of art courses designed and launched

# of establishment of community arts centers

# of exposure over local press

# of exposure over national press

# of extension programs in culture and arts management designed

# of instructors and candidate participants for Certified Program selected

# of people benefiting from educational programs about history, culture, and arts

# of people impacted by arts projects funded by arts council

# of programs created for children

# of programs developed

# of students trained

# of students/ local artists trained per year in arts and culture through internship programs

# of visitors at historical museum, historical libraries, historic sites, and archives

% implementation of the master plan for the establishment of new national art libraries

% of academies structure and program completed

% of art curricula content and teaching materials developed

% of artists training forum concept and synergies completed

% of implementation of framework

Total amount of arts and heritage funds launched

35. Culture & Heritage

Culture & Heritage Events

of initiatives and projects with international impact
# of international fairs and exhibitions
# of local and international heritage and cultural programs conducted locally, regionally and internationally
# of programs/events with full participation rates
# of visitors to events and cultural sites
Country index (Culture and Heritage exposure)
Total household expenditure on recreation and culture

Culture Institutions

of agreements in place
# of attendance by international exhibitors
# of collections built
# of feasibility studies for distribution system completed
# of improvement measures and management plans implemented
# of members in publishers association
# of new business concepts set-up
# of people participating in reading promotion events
# of translated works annually
# of visits to museums or galleries
% museums operated or supported by government authorities
% of completion of art exhibition
% of completion of construction for branches
% of completion of exhibition project
% of completion of museum
% of completion of national memorial
% of completion of rehabilitation project
% of memorials conserved and exhibition fitted-in
% of return on investment from projects supported

Intangible Cultural Heritage

of celebrated and enhanced family culture and traditions
# of interpreted and streamlined local identity and traditions
# of inventory completed for the identified intangible resources
# of local trained artisans engaged by projects
# of major manifestations organized
# of oral history and traditions/ traditional practices inventoried and sustained
# of re-developed craft products
# of traditional craft products marketed at a national level
# of translated works per year
% of architectural study completed
% of citizen population poll involved in our sponsored activities
% of compliance with UNESCO-WHC standards for nomination on the world heritage list

35. Culture & Heritage
% of intangible resources inventoried

International Promotion

of cities which displayed our cultural heritage exhibition

# of cultural exchange programs signed and implemented

# of cultural exchange programs signed and implemented with major cultural international institutions

# of exhibitions developed and toured

# of exposure over International press

# of exposure over regional press

# of images exposure over internet

# of international level events developed and launched successfully

# of nomination file and all necessary accompanying documentation submitted to UNESCO

# of participation in all relevant international forums on intangible world heritage

# of pavilion inaugurated

% of communication strategy provisions/initiatives accomplished successfully

% of promotion in international art newspapers

Legislation

of antiquities law drafted and approved by higher authorities

# of days required to provide initial response to constituents applying for historic tax credit

# of dedicated judges trained in cultural heritage cases

# of laws approved by higher authorities

# of legal experts trained in cultural heritage cases

# of policies drafted

# of policy standards developed to improve quality of programming of cultural events

% of culture and heritage framework policy developed

% of implementation decrees approved

% of key stakeholders informed and trained about the provisions of the new law

% of key stakeholders trained on the extents and provisions of the law

% of laws approved by higher authorities

% of policy framework for regularizing the art market developed

% of policy framework for the development of museum institutions developed

% of return on the state's investment of dollars into grant programs

Local Traditions

of culture and heritage school and university education courses

# of historic buildings, archaeological sites and cultural landscapes and their condition

# of oral history and traditions inventoried and sustained

# of sites on the Tentative List of World Heritage

35. Culture & Heritage

of World Heritage natural sites

% of historic buildings, archaeological sites and cultural landscapes, protected, and conserved

% of intangible cultural assets (oral history, traditions, traditional practices) recorded or maintained

% of people's increased awareness and involvement in the culture and heritage

% of tangible cultural assets (historic buildings, archaeological sites, cultural landscapes) conserved

Household expenditure on recreation and culture as % of GDP

Professional Capacities

of cultural workers receiving professional development

# of establishment of placement program for culture and heritage

# of people employed by arts, culture, and history projects

% of completion of certified courses in culture and heritage management

% of completion of institute for cultural projects

% of completion of short-term program in culture and heritage management

% of cultural sites manned with heritage interpreters

% of establishment of artists residency program

Amount of training fund for culture and heritage

Tangible Conservation

of cultural landscapes conserved and developed.

# of inventory completed for identified tangible cultural properties

# of inventory of historic buildings, archaeological sites and cultural landscapes

# of management plans drafted

# of properties listed in the National Historic Register that could qualify for tax benefits

% of completion of the central laboratory for the conservation of the tangible cultural heritage

% of completion of the inventory of tangible cultural properties

% of compliance with UNESCO standards

% of historic buildings and sites conserved

36. Customs

Clearance Time

Average time of arrival of goods at the border until their release to the importer

Average time taken from when goods arrive at the port of entry until the time they are claimed from customs

Average waiting time at borders

Maximum waiting time at borders

Weighted average customs clearance time

36. Customs

Confiscations

of confiscations of all dangerous, prohibited, and restricted goods

% increase in the weights of seized drugs in grams in all custom houses compared to last year

% increase of confiscations of all dangerous, prohibited, and restricted goods from last year

Total weights of seized drugs in grams in all customhouses compared

Customs Efficiency

of hidden import barriers other than published tariffs and quotas

% of customs authorities facilitation of the efficient transit of goods

% of trader base trained on the licensed customs brokers training program

% quality of facilities

Total # of declarations / # of customs employees

Total cost of transporting goods

Trade Volume /# of Customs Employees

Worse/best time to clear border crossing

Revenues Collection

% of duty payments made via e-payment system

Average of irregular known extra payment or bribes connected with export and import payments

Discrepancies as % of total # of declarations (Import, Export, Transit)

Revenue collected/import declaration

Revenue collected/value of imports

Total revenue collected/ Total # of customs employees

37. Economic Development

Balance of Payments

Balance of payments

Balance of payments by country

Balance of payments of institutions

Balance of payments, capital account

Balance of payments, current account

Balance of payments, financial account

Balance of payments, international investment positions

Balance of payments, international transactions

Current and capital account

External balance of goods and services

International investment position

International investment position of institutions

International trade in services, geographical breakdown

Total capital account

Total current account

Total direct investment flows, breakdown by economic activity

Total direct investment flows, breakdown by partner country

37. Economic Development

Total direct investment income, breakdown by economic activity

Total direct investment income, breakdown by partner country

Total direct investment positions, breakdown by country

Total direct investment positions, breakdown by economic activity

Total international trade in services

Total services, detailed geographical

Business Competitiveness

of license applications processed

% of agent applications processed within 7 days

% of chartered banks examined

% of completed paper renewals processed within five working days of receipt

% of qualified candidates examined

Competitiveness Index of economy (score)

Cost of Starting a business in % of income per capita

Creation of firms is supported by legislations (scale from 1 to 10)

Ease of doing business is supported by regulations (scale from 1 -10)

Global ranking in international investment

Global ranking of country in international investment (On a 0 - 3 Scale)

Gross return on capital employed, before taxes, of non-financial corporations

Growth rate of private sector contribution to GDP

Increase in productivity and competitiveness index

Investment rate of non-financial corporations

Net debt-to-income ratio, after taxes, of non-financial corporations

Net return on equity, after taxes, of non-financial corporations

Private sector as % of GDP

Profit share of non-financial corporations

Real private consumption

WB doing business country ranking

Businesses & Jobs

of active projects and leads for possible business projects

# of bushels of corn and soybean to be processed per year by companies

# of businesses attracted per year, per region

# of businesses served per year per business accelerator

# of continuous training and educational programs

# of downtown jobs

# of employed by age

# of employed by occupation

# of employed by sector of economic activity

# of employees with tertiary education, by field of education

# of employees with tertiary education, employed, by field of education and occupation

37. Economic Development

of employment in technology and knowledge-intensive sectors at the national level

# of enterprise deaths presented by legal form

# of enterprise deaths presented by size class

# of external service provider broken down by activity

# of feature films produced

# of graduation from tertiary education

# of high-paying jobs created/retained through Business Development programs

# of hours supplied by labor recruitment services

# of jobs created

# of jobs created or retained

# of jobs created with employer sponsored health care

# of jobs per year retained through the efforts of regional economic development organizations

# of jobs retained with employer sponsored health care

# of jobs sustained by tourism activities

# of jobs to be created (break out full-time and part-time)

# of jobs to be created for low and moderate income persons

# of jobs to be retained (break out full-time and part-time)

# of jobs to be retained for low and moderate income persons

# of job-to-job mobility of highly qualified personnel (aged 25-64)

# of leads developed to create business opportunities for companies

# of main economic variables

# of new bioscience companies created over 5 years

# of new businesses in cities

# of new businesses in downtown client communities

# of new community-based seed funds

# of new investment per year through the efforts of regional economic development organizations

# of new location announcements

# of persons employed by enterprises

# of purchases of advertising space or time for resale

# of purchases of services belonging to enterprises

# of service providers broken down by activity

# of service providers broken down by sector

# of service related investments broken down by product

# of service related investments broken down by sectors

# of types of purchase made from external service providers

# of unemployed by gender

# of unemployed, by age

% annual job growth

% growth in assets of permanent endowment funds at accredited community foundations and their affiliates

% increase in # of new workers completing post-secondary training

37. Economic Development

% increase in # of persons recruited to fill skilled positions

% increase in export sales per year by all firms

% increase in jobs in industries in biosciences, advanced manufacturing, and information solutions

% increase per year in # of bioscience start-up companies that obtain investment funding

% increase per year in firms' participation in foreign trade shows and trade missions

% increase per year in tourism generated sales tax

% internal and external customer satisfaction

% of applications processed within 21 days of receipt of all required documentation.

% of businesses still operational after 12 months in operation

% of loans that receive initial disbursements within 5 days of loan closing

% turnover by client specialization

% turnover by employment size class

% turnover by nationality of client

% turnover by product and economic activity

% turnover by product and employment size class

% turnover by product specialization

% turnover by residence of client

% turnover by type of client

% turnover by type of media for advertising services

% young worker population growth

Amount of investment from new small business announcements

Amount of private investment leveraged for regional economic development projects

Barriers for purchasing services outside the country broken down by sector

Business demography indicators presented by legal form

Business demography indicators presented by size class

Business demography statistics - all activities

Data on barriers for purchasing services outside the country broken down by activity

Demand for services - all activities

Employer business demography presented by legal form

Employer business demography presented by size class

Employment by Sector

Ratio of # of small businesses initial certifications compared to the previous year

Ratio of % increase/year in gross product to world rate

Ratio of % increase/year in per capita income (PCI) to world rate

Ratio of downtown housing units to jobs

Total estimated # of jobs created or retained

Total value added by enterprise size

Unemployment rate

37. Economic Development

Commerce & Trade

of current account transactions, exports

# of current account transactions, goods

# of current account transactions, imports

# of current account transactions, services

# of customer's trade license

# of enterprises by importance of barriers met in cross border trade

# of enterprises carrying out cross border trade by economic activity

# of enterprises carrying out cross border trade by employment size class

# of enterprises carrying out cross border trade by reasons

# of enterprises carrying out cross border trade by type

# of international transactions in air transport services

# of international transactions in communications services

# of international transactions in computer and information services

# of international transactions in construction services

# of international transactions in financial services

# of international transactions in government services

# of international transactions in insurance services

# of international transactions in other business services

# of international transactions in other transport services

# of international transactions in personal, cultural recreation services

# of international transactions in royalties and license fees

# of international transactions in sea transport services

# of international transactions in transportation

# of international transactions in travel

# of market integration by type of trade activities

# of new car registrations

# of partner countries and regions of OECD merchandise exports

# of partner countries and regions of OECD merchandise imports

# of partner countries and regions of OECD merchandise trade

# of SME enterprise statistics broken down by size of trade

# of tons of alternative energy source consumption

# of trade in goods and services

% analysis of data made available by surveys

% increase in exports (%)

% increase in gross fixed capital formation (%)

% knowledge by local firms in the supporting services provided to local firms

% of electronic renewal of trade licenses.

% share in the world trade

% share of motor, wholesale and retail trades in total distributive trades

% turnover by product - total trade

% turnover by product in motor trade

% turnover by product in retail trade

% turnover by product in wholesale trade

37. Economic Development

% turnover in retail sale of food by specialized and non-specialized stores

Balance of international trade in goods

Balance of international trade in services

Balance of the current account

Balance of trade

Current account balance (% of GDP)

Current account balance (US millions)

Current account balance of payments

Exchange rate

Exchange rates versus national currency

External trade of chemicals and related products

External trade of food, drinks and tobacco

External trade of machinery and transport equipment

External trade of mineral fuels, lubricants and related materials

External trade of other manufactured goods

External trade of raw materials

External trade, by declaring country, total product

Increased # of hits on the website

Increased # of special events

Increased satisfaction % of users

Industrial labor input - total industry

International trade of candidate countries

International trade values by main third countries

National currency exchange rate

Other multi-yearly statistics - trade

Other services - turnover

Real effective exchange rate

Retail trade - operating costs

Retail trade deflated turnover - automotive fuel

Retail trade deflated turnover - food, beverages and tobacco

Retail trade deflated turnover - non food

Retail trade deflated turnover - total

Retail trade turnover - automotive fuel

Retail trade turnover - food, beverages and tobacco

Retail trade turnover - non food

Retail trade turnover - total

Services trade balance (exports of services minus imports of services)

Total # of exports of goods

Total # of exports of services

Total # of imports of goods

Total # of imports of services

Total amount # of imports

Total distributive trades broken down by employment size classes

Total distributive trades broken down by turnover size classes

37. Economic Development

Total goods export value of chemicals and related products

Total goods export value of food, drinks and tobacco

Total goods export value of machinery and transport equipment

Total goods export value of mineral fuels, lubricants and related materials

Total goods export value of other manufactured products

Total goods export value of raw materials

Total goods export value of total

Total goods import value of chemicals and related products

Total goods import value of food, drinks and tobacco

Total goods import value of machinery and transport equipment

Total goods import value of mineral fuels, lubricants and related materials

Total goods import value of other manufactured products

Total goods import value of raw materials

Total goods import value of total

Total sales space for retail stores

Total wholesale trade

Trade balance (exports of goods minus imports of goods)

Trade to GDP ratio

Trade unit value, by declaring country

Trade volume, by declaring country

Unit value of exports

Unit value of imports

Value of export earnings coming from non traditional exports

Volume of trade - merchandise exports

Volume of trade - merchandise imports

Consumer Protection

of the customers requesting direct support

% customer's satisfaction on the consumer's protection services

% of claims settled within 30 working days

% of claims that received a response within 2 working days

% of consumers informed about consumer protection services

% of consumers informed about protection services

% of customers satisfied with consumer protection services

% of response to claims received within two working days at least

% of settlement of the issues within 30 working days

% response to the claims received within two working days

% satisfaction of committees requirements and standards

% settlement of the issues within 30 working days

Cost of Living Index

Exchange rates

Indices of price levels

Nominal effective exchange rates

Overlapping property tax bill

Purchasing power parities

37. Economic Development

Relative consumer price indices

Development Loans

of accounts linked to CPA categories

# of branches in other countries

# of enterprises and balance sheet total broken down by legal status

# of enterprises and balance sheet total broken down by residence of the parent enterprise

# of enterprises and persons employed broken down by category of credit institutions

# of enterprises broken down by size classes of balance sheet total

# of financial subsidiaries in other countries

# of loans and advances to customers

# of million per year

% clear formulas of lending policy

% of compliance to international best-practice

% of factors achieved (factors are determined at project appraisal stage)

Credit institutions: # of enterprises

Credit institutions: # of persons employed

Credit institutions: balance sheet total

Credit institutions: interest payable and similar charges

Credit institutions: interest receivable and similar income

Interests payable and similar charges by product

Interests receivable and similar income by product

Total commissions payable by product

Total commissions receivable by product

Total of local wages and salaries by region

Direct Investment

of classification of the targeted foreign investor

# of global ranking of nation in international investment

# of investment risks

# of jobs created or retained in distressed communities as a result of investments

# of press campaign, regional international media, TV interviews, and newspaper articles

# of review of proposals related to the free trade agreements

% completion of planned promotional campaigns

% increase in Foreign Direct Investment (%)

% of foreign investors that view us as a favorable investment destination

% of free trade agreement proposals reviewed

% of international customers (e.g., investors) satisfied with the level of services provided

% of international customer's satisfaction as to investment information to the desired subject

% of international customer's satisfaction as to the level of the provided services

37. Economic Development

% of international customers satisfied with the pertinence of the investment information

% of new foreign investors informed about promotional campaigns

Direct investment flows abroad (% OF GDP)

Direct investment flows abroad (USD Bn)

Direct investment flows inward (% OF GDP)

Direct investment flows inward (USD Bn)

Direct investment stocks inward - Growth (%)

Direct investment stocks inward (USD Bn)

Foreign control of enterprises - breakdown by controlling countries

Foreign control of enterprises - breakdown by economic activity

Foreign-exchange reserves

Moody's investors service bond rating

Total direct investment flows as % of GDP

Total direct investment inward flows by main investing country

Total direct investment inward stocks by main origin of investment

Total direct investment outward flows by main country of destination

Total direct investment outward stocks by main destination

Total direct investment stocks as % of GDP

Diversified Economy

of sectors included in economic plan

# of SMEs (enterprises with <50 employees) in manufacturing as % of total enterprises in manufacturing

% growth in non-oil sector contribution to GDP

% growth in non-oil sector value added

% increase in contribution of non-oil sectors to GDP

% increase in value added of non-oil sectors (nominal) to GDP

% increase in value added of non-oil sectors (real) to GDP

Diversification of the economy (on a scale from 0 - 10)

Employed population in agriculture sector as % of total employed population

Employed population in construction & utilities sectors as % of total employed population

Employed population in financial services sector as % of total employed population

Employed population in government & other services sectors as % of total employed population

Employed population in manufacturing sector as % of total employed population

Employed population in mining, quarrying & energy sector as % of total employed population

Employed population in trade, restaurants, & hotel as % of total employed population

Employed population in transport & communication sector as % of total employed population

37. Economic Development

Government Consumption Expenditure (% of GDP)

Population Growth

Real government consumption

Real value added in agriculture, forestry and fishing

Real value added in industry

Real value added in services

Small and Medium Enterprises (SMEs) efficiency by international standards

Small and Medium Enterprises Output or Export value per worker

SME Efficiency (on a scale of 0 - 10)

Unemployment rate by nationality (%)

Value added in agriculture, hunting, forestry and fishing

Value added in banks, insurance, real estate and other business services

Value added in construction

Value added in government, health, education and other personal services

Value added in in transport, trade, hotels and restaurants

Value added in industry, including energy

Economic Policy

of advanced analytical tool to support policy development

# of consultation with private sector representatives for economic policy development

# of implemented new policy in the private sector

# of initiatives recommended that have been identified through public-private communication forums

# of internal staff with capabilities to develop policy recommendations

# of partners external experts/consultants in recommending policies

# of policy issues raised/identified economic committee

# of policy recommendations issued

# of reviews conducted by private sector board members

% data accuracy in key national accounts

% of local comprehensive plans and similar reviews completed within designated 30-day timeframe

% total national public spending expenditure on services

Private sector representatives policy recommendation participation satisfaction ratio

Economic Prosperity

of areas in which economic data has been acquired & compiled out

# of businesses assisted that provide goods/services to meet service area/local need

# of businesses assisted with commercial façade treatment/building rehab

# of department with attestation by ISO

# of enquiries received from prospective investors showing interest

# of first mortgage loans purchased

% completion of data acquisition & compilation process

% completion of development & launch of investment promotion campaign

% completion of implementation of the land use plan

37. Economic Development
% completion of Industrial zone creation plan by deadline
% completion of socio-economic database
% decrease rate of staff
% growth in active enterprises
% Increase in # of priority projects implemented over the previous years
% increase in contribution to federal budget
% increase in employment in the private sector
% increase in exports
% increase in foreign direct Investment (FDI)
% increase in future purchases of services broken down by activity
% increase in future purchases of services broken down by sector and size class
% increase in future purchases of services of enterprises
% increase in gross fixed capital formation (GFCF)
% increase in non oil and gas sector
% increase in population in targeted cities
% increase in volume of land under private & government ownership
% labor productivity by sector
% land used that fit the needs of communities
% of 25-34 year-olds in the total population
% of 5-year sector strategies implemented within timeframe/budget limits
% of automation of manual procedures
% of business in major centers
% of capacity utilization in manufacturing industry
% of more people shopping downtown
% of stakeholders' satisfaction
% of strategies in practice satisfy its contemplated goals within the preplanned time frame and budget limits
% progress of developing ready-to-go investment packages
% satisfaction of citizens on the economy and commercial environment
Average turnaround time since filing of application till getting approval for establishing new businesses
Competitiveness index of country economy
Competitiveness index of nation economy
GDP deflator
GDP growth (nominal, real)
GDP per capita (nominal, real, PPP)
Gross debt-to-income ratio of households
Gross fixed capital formation
Gross fixed capital formation: housing
Gross fixed capital formation: machinery and equipment
Household investment rate
Household net saving rate
Household saving rate

37. Economic Development

Increase in # of SMEs

Inflation rate

Per capita income

WB doing business ranking

Energy Sector

of new industries in the energy sector

% increase in contribution of downstream production industries to oil GDP

% increase in gas production per day

% increase in oil production per day

% increase in value added exports

% increase in value added of downstream production industries

% increase in value added of downstream production industries (real)

Oil production per day

Total gas production per day

Total purchases of energy products

Total purchases of energy products by industry and construction

Foreign Relations

of barriers met for engaging in international sourcing

# of foreign investors who's initial point of contact was a foreign mission

# of general agreements of cooperation signed and implemented

# of implanted projects /year in other countries

# of missions in strategic regions

# of motivation factors for international sourcing by enterprises currently planning to go outside

# of plans for international sourcing

# of visas issued by foreign missions

% increase in exports

% of customers (local businesses) receiving supporting services in a suitable time

% of customers (local businesses) satisfied with the access to export and regional data

% of customers satisfied with the supporting services

% of events and promotional campaigns carried out

% of increase exports value per year

% of local businesses aware of supporting services

Level of technical assistance accrued as a direct initiative of missions

Total international sourcing by enterprises currently planning to go outside

GDP Growth

% of labor productivity

Average compensation of employees

Average monthly national household income

City Competitiveness Index

Contribution of labor productivity and labor utilization to GDP per capita - GDP per capita

37. Economic Development
Contribution of labor productivity and labor utilization to GDP per capita - GDP per hour worked
Contribution of labor productivity and labor utilization to GDP per capita - labor utilization
Contributions to GDP growth: GDP growth
Contributions to GDP growth: ICT capital
Contributions to GDP growth: labor input
Contributions to GDP growth: multi-factor productivity
Contributions to GDP growth: non-ICT capital
Effective interest rate (%)
Final consumption aggregates - current price
Final consumption aggregates - volumes
Final consumption expenditure of general government
Final consumption expenditure of households and non-profit institutions serving households
GDP Growth - real (%)
GDP nominal growth
GDP per capita (nominal)
GDP per capita (PPP)
GDP per capita (real)
GDP per hour worked
GDP real growth
Government final consumption expenditure, current prices
Government final consumption expenditure, volumes
Gross domestic product
Gross domestic product at market prices
Gross domestic product, current prices
Gross domestic product, volumes
Gross domestic savings (% of GDP)
Gross fixed capital formation (investments)
Gross fixed capital formation, current prices
Gross fixed capital formation, volumes
Gross national income per capita
Gross national savings rate (%)
Growth rate of real GDP per capita
Inflation rate (%)
Inflation rate: GDP deflator/ CPI
Labor productivity per hour worked
Labor productivity per person employed
Nominal GDP (US$ at PPP)
Private final consumption expenditure, current prices
Private final consumption expenditure, volumes
Real GDP growth rate
Real unit labor cost growth

37. Economic Development
Total investment
Total taxes on production and imports less subsidies
Unit labor cost
Volume index of GDP per capita

Insurance

# of insurance companies broken down by gross premium written size class
# of insurance companies broken down by legal status
# of insurance companies broken down by products
# of insurance companies broken down by technical provisions size class
# of insurance companies by geographical breakdown
# of insurance companies by type of enterprise
% of consumer and industry stakeholders satisfied services through postcard follow up
% of customer responses indicating satisfaction with the service provided during the handling of their complaint
% of modernization initiatives implemented
% of regulatory investigations with full cross-sectional database searches
Average # of examiners compared to total supervised assets (in millions)
Insurance, # of persons employed by type of enterprises
Insurance, gross claims payments by type of enterprise
Insurance, gross premiums written by type of enterprise

Legislation & Regulations

# of audit comments
# of educational press releases issues
# of legislation and regulation reviewed
# of papers prepared & submitted with comments on legislation & regulations
# of private-public workshops & meetings organized
# of regulations and economic laws that protect local institutions and business corporations
# of studies completed and recommendation proposed
% accuracy of projections related to key national accounts
% completion of 5-year economic plan
% examine of companies and industries as required by law
% licenses issued according to the laws and regulations
% of complaints resolved in 80 days
% of effectively applied federal regulations locally
% of execution of internal policies and legal requirements
% of legislations that requires amendments that have been addressed with amendment proposals
% of local businesses satisfied with the application of laws and regulations
% of products acted upon within 30 days of a completed applications
% of requirements fulfilled under policy

Licensing Process

# of new licenses within 1 working day

37. Economic Development
# of transactions of license renewal within 1 working day
% of customers satisfied with trade license services
% of electronic renewal of licenses
% of issued trade licenses conforming to laws and regulations
% of new trade licenses processed within 5 working days
% of trade license renewals processed electronically
% of trade license renewals processed within 2 working days

Local Economy

of carried out promotional campaigns
# of changes of circumstances which affect customers' entitlements within the year
# of enterprises by sector
# of entry level qualifications in numeracy achieved
# of level 1 qualifications in literacy (including ESOL) achieved
# of local bus and light rail passenger journeys originating in the authority area
# of non-principal classified roads where maintenance should be considered
# of persons employed by sector
# of persons employed in services
# of previously developed land that has been vacant or derelict for more than 5 years
# of principal roads where maintenance should be considered
% access to services and facilities by public transport, walking and cycling
% entered employment rate (following preparation program)
% flows on to incapacity benefits from employment
% impact of local authority regulatory services on the fair trading environment
% local suppliers that affirmed the business code of conduct
% of bus services running on time
% of enterprises with 20 persons employed and more
% of food establishments in the area which are broadly compliant with food hygiene law
% of population aged 19-64 for males and 19-59 for females qualified
% of skills gaps in the current workforce reported by employers
% of small businesses in an area showing employment growth
% overall employment rate
% processing of planning applications
% satisfaction of businesses with local authority regulatory services
% share of gross operating surplus
% spending on local suppliers
% youth unemployment rate
Average journey time (congestion) per mile during the morning peak
Average personnel costs by sector
Intangible investment and subcontracting
Median earnings of employees in the area

37. Economic Development
New business registration rate
Overall employment rate (working-age)
Total net value of on-going cash-releasing value for money gains
Working age people claiming out of work benefits in the worst performing neighborhoods
Working age people on out of work benefits
Working age people with access to employment by public transport

Macroeconomics

of time environment was an important point of discussion
% of departments whose total actual expenditures is within +/-5 of the total funding
% of variance between original budget and primary budgeted expenditure
Debt service to export ratio
Domestic borrowing as % of GDP
Domestic tax revenue as a % of GDP
General government deficit (-) and surplus (+)
General government fixed investment
General government gross debt
General government primary balance
Government final consumption expenditure
Population density by regions
Stock of domestic suppliers debt as % of GDP
Total area and land area
Total tax revenue
VAT reimbursements taking less than 30 days

Manufacturing

employment in manufacturing in enterprises with 10-19 employees
employment in manufacturing in enterprises with 20 or more employees
employment in manufacturing in enterprises with less than 10 employees
employment in manufacturing in enterprises with less than 20 employees
of enterprises in manufacturing with 10-19 employees
# of enterprises in manufacturing with 20 or more employees
# of enterprises in manufacturing with less than 10 employees
# of enterprises in manufacturing with less than 20 employees
# of industrial new orders for capital goods
# of industrial new orders for durable consumer goods
# of industrial new orders for heavy transport equipment
# of industrial new orders for intermediate goods
# of industrial new orders for non-durable consumer goods
# of new products entering the market that are certified
# of persons employed in manufacturing
volume of steel production
% employment increase in manufacturing sector
% growth in manufacturing activities contribution to GDP

37. Economic Development

% growth in manufacturing activities value added

% increase in contribution of manufacturing activities to GDP

% increase in value added of manufacturing activities (nominal)

% increase in value added of manufacturing activities (real)

% of industrial turnover of capital goods

% of industrial turnover of consumer durables

% of industrial turnover of consumer non-durables

% of industrial turnover of intermediate goods

% of industrial turnover of manufacturing

% of industrial turnover of mining, quarrying and manufacturing

% share of gross operating surplus in turnover

% share of value added in production

Annual capacity (in 1000 Tones per year)

Balance sheet for electrical energy in the steel industry (in MWh)

Direct foreign investment in manufacturing in $ million

Employment in affiliates under foreign control, share of employment in manufacturing

Fuel and energy consumption (gas products in GJ, other: metric tones)

Growth rate of manufacturing GDP

Industry labor input index

Industry new orders index

Industry production index

Industry turnover index

PPI: manufacturing

Relative unit labor costs in manufacturing

Steel and cast iron scrap balance sheet (in metric tones)

Total industrial labor input in capital goods

Total industrial labor input in consumer durables

Total industrial labor input in consumer non-durables

Total industrial labor input in energy

Total industrial labor input in intermediate goods

Total industrial labor input in manufacturing

Total industrial new orders

Total industrial production of capital goods

Total industrial production of consumer durables

Total industrial production of consumer non-durables

Total industrial production of energy

Total industrial production of intermediate goods

Total industrial production of manufacturing

Total industrial production of total industry (excluding construction)

Total investments in the iron and steel industry

Value added in manufacturing

37. Economic Development

Mining

of large scale mining companies contributing to the improvement of social welfare of the communities

# of local manufacturing companies processing minerals into finished products

# of small scale mines in production

% of mining companies complying with environmental regulations

Annual growth rate of the mining sector

Value of receipts generated by small-scale mining in dollar equivalent

Patent & Trademark

of # of patent applications by institutional sector

# of biotechnology patent applications at the national level

# of co-patenting according to applicants' country of residence

# of co-patenting according to inventors' country of residence

# of co-patenting: crossing inventors and applicants according to applicants' country of residence

# of co-patenting: crossing inventors and applicants according to inventors' country of residence

# of domestic ownership of foreign inventions in patent applications

# of high-tech patent applications

# of high-tech patents granted

# of high-technology patents

# of ICT patent applications

# of ICT patents granted

# of innovating enterprises having applied for a patent

# of innovating enterprises supported by government

# of international co-patenting

# of Nanotechnology patent applications

# of ownership of inventions

# of patent applications

# of patent applications by IPC sections and classes

# of patent applications by sector of economic activity

# of patent applications with foreign co-inventors

# of patent citations

# of patent citations according to applicants' country of residence

# of patent citations according to inventors' country of residence

# of patents granted by the United States patent and Trademark Office (USPTO)

# of triadic patent families

% foreign ownership of domestic inventions in patent applications

% foreign ownership of domestic inventions in patents granted

% of biotechnology patents granted at the national level

% of domestic ownership of foreign inventions in patents granted

Average patent pendency

Average trademark pendency

37. Economic Development

Cost per patent disposed

Cost per trademark registered

Total income from intellectual property rights for computer services

Prices & Interest Rates

3-month-interest rate

Bilateral exchange rates

Central bank interest rates

Central bank lending rates

Central bank refinancing operation rates

Central government bond yields

Consumer price index - alcohol and tobacco

Consumer price index - all items

Consumer price index - all items excluding energy

Consumer price index - all items excluding tobacco

Consumer price index - clothing

Consumer price index - communications

Consumer price index - country weights

Consumer price index - education

Consumer price index - energy

Consumer price index - food

Consumer price index - hotels and restaurants

Consumer price index - household equipment

Consumer price index - housing

Consumer price index - Item weights

Consumer price index - transport

Consumer price index at constant tax rates

Contribution (in % points) to GDP change

Convergence of interests rates by type of loan

Day-to-day money market interest rates

Final consumption expenditure of households by consumption purpose

Food supply chain - annual rates of price change

Food supply chain - Price indices

Government bond yields - 10 years' maturity

Gross disposable income

Gross national income

Gross value added - total, current prices

Harmonized index of consumer prices

Harmonized MFI interest rates

Industrial domestic output prices - capital goods

Industrial domestic output prices - consumer durables

Industrial domestic output prices - consumer non-durables

Industrial domestic output prices - energy

Industrial domestic output prices - intermediate goods

Industrial domestic output prices - manufacturing

37. Economic Development
Industrial domestic output prices - Mining, quarrying and manufacturing (except MIG energy)
Industrial domestic output prices - total industry (excluding construction)
Industrial import prices - capital goods
Industrial import prices - consumer durables
Industrial import prices - consumer non-durables
Industrial import prices - intermediate goods
Industrial import prices - manufacturing
Industrial import prices - total industry
Industry - domestic output prices
Industry import prices index
Industry producer prices index (PPI)
Long term government bond yield
Long-term interest rate
Long-term interest rates
Median household / Family Incomes
MFI interest rates - deposits
MFI interest rates - loans to households
MFI interest rates - loans to non-financial corporations
Money market interest rates
National currency exchange rates
Official deposit rate
Official lending rate
Official refinancing operation rate
Producer prices index (PPI)
Retail bank interest rate
Share price index
Short-term interest rate
Stock market capitalization
Treasury bill rates
Yield curve
Yield curve by maturity (1, 5 and 10 years)

Public Facility & Service
# of acres of brownfields remediated
# of independent subsidiary to handle, implement and operate projects
# of persons assisted with improved access to a facility or infrastructure
# of persons assisted with new access to a facility or infrastructure
# of persons served by a public facility or infrastructure that is no longer substandard
# of persons with improved access to service
# of persons with new access to service
# of persons with service that is no longer substandard
Increase # of citizens using facilities

37. Economic Development

Real Estate

net additional homes provided

of affordable homes delivered (gross)

# of affordable units

# of building permits

# of building permits in centers and corridors

# of downtown housing units

# of downtown properties maintained and developed

# of establishment types in major activity centers

# of first-time home buyers receiving housing counseling

# of households living in temporary accommodation

# of owner occupied units created

# of owner occupied units rehabilitated

# of qualified Energy Star units

# of rental units created

# of rental units rehabilitated

# of tax benefit new claims

# of total building permits issued

# of units brought from substandard to standard condition

# of units brought into compliance with the lead safe housing rule

# of units created through conversion of nonresidential building to residential

# of units occupied by elderly (62 years of age or above)

# of units occupied by first-time homebuyers

# of units subsidized with project-based rental assistance

# of units with appropriate wiring for broadband access

# of years affordability guaranteed

served receiving down-payment assistance and/or assistance with closing costs

% non-decent council homes

% of building permits issued in centers and corridor

% of downtown homes sold compared per year

% of leases executed at or below prevailing market rate

% of local authority tenants' satisfaction with landlord services

% of market rate units

% of supply of ready to develop housing sites

% of surplus property disposed at or above market rate

Average # of mortgage licensees and registrants

Average time taken to process housing benefit

Construction cost of new residential buildings

Construction labor input

Construction new orders index

Construction production

Cost per household

37. Economic Development

Increased # of feet of streets repaired

Median price per square foot

Median sales price of downtown homes

Median single family home prices

New residential buildings - prices index

Value of new commercial building permits

Research & Surveys

of buyouts

# of cooperation in innovation activity

# of educational attainment of 25-64 years old by country of citizenship

# of educational attainment of internationally mobile 25-64 years old

# of educational attainment, by gender and age group

# of enterprises in manufacturing technology sector

# of enterprises with innovation activity

# of enterprises with innovation activity in manufacturing sector, by sector of technology

# of entrepreneurs using developed technologies

# of factors hampering innovation

# of innovating enterprises with abolished projects

# of innovating enterprises with innovation cooperation

# of innovating enterprises with not even started projects

# of innovating enterprises with progress problems

# of innovating enterprises with seriously delayed projects

# of innovating firms' engagement in R&D

# of innovation survey done

# of knowledge intensive services at the national level

# of participation in tertiary education

# of participation of foreign students in tertiary education

# of partners, by size class

# of R&D professionals Receiving further training

# of R&D units developed

# of R&D units rehabilitated

# of real and potential inflows of employees

# of researchers in government and higher education sector

# of study dealing with the economy as a whole

# of technologies developed by R&D institutions for commercialization

% compatibility with international statistics standards

% completion comprehensive and sector-specific research studies

% employment in high- and medium-high-technology manufacturing sectors

% employment in knowledge-intensive service sectors

% of customers (stakeholders) satisfied about the accessibility of studies

% of customers (stakeholders) satisfied about the pertinence of studies

% of deviation of main statistics with those from other sources

% of enterprises with innovation activity

37. Economic Development

% of registered local government authorities completing the annual report of registered authority finances

% of release of all social and economic statistics in accordance with the approved timetable.

% of release of all studies and surveys in accordance with the fixed timetable

% of released social and economic statistics in accordance with the approved timetable

% of socio-economic studies released according to fixed timetable

% share of female researchers by sector

% share of government budget appropriations or outlays for research and development

% share of total government budget appropriations or outlays for defense and for civil research and development

% share of women researchers (FTE): all sectors

% turnover due to innovative products

% world market share of high-tech trade by high-tech group of products

Business enterprise R&D expenditure by high-tech groups

Business enterprise R&D personnels

Government budget appropriations on R&D

Gross domestic expenditure on R&D

High-tech trade by high-tech group of products

Innovating firms' level of export intensity

Innovating firms' level of R&D intensity

Innovation expenditures

Innovation intensity in manufacturing sector

R&D expenditure at national and regional level

R&D personnel at national and regional level

Research and development expenditure

Research and development personnel by sectors

Total business enterprise R&D expenditure by economic activity

Total business enterprise R&D expenditure by size class

Total business enterprise R&D expenditure by source of funds

Total business enterprise R&D expenditure by type of costs

Total earnings in high-tech industries

Total exports of high technology products as a share of total exports

Total high-tech trade as a % of total

Total human resources in science and technology as a share of labor force

Total innovation co-operation in absolute value

Total innovation expenditures

Total innovation in high-tech sectors and SMEs

Total intramural R&D expenditure by sector

Total intramural R&D expenditure by source of funds

Total of doctorate students in science and technology

Total public funding of innovation

37. Economic Development

Total R&D personnel and researchers (FTE), in business enterprise sector

Total R&D personnel and researchers as % of total labor force and total employment

Total R&D personnel and researchers by economic activity

Total R&D personnel and researchers by fields of science

Total R&D personnel and researchers by qualifications

Total R&D personnel and researchers by region

Total R&D personnel by occupation

Total researchers (FTE) by sector

Total venture capital investments

Total venture capital investments - early stage

Total venture capital investments - expansion and replacement

Total venture capital investments by type of investment stage

Turnover due to innovating products in manufacturing sector, by sector of technology

SMEs Development

citizen entrepreneurs trained

increase in new start up enterprise

investment capital amount

of building code clarifications/technical assistance provided to public and private sector customers

# of business partners engaged in international sourcing

# of enterprises by economic activity

# of existing businesses assisted

# of existing businesses assisted - expanding

# of existing businesses assisted - relocating

# of found barriers preventing or obstructing inter-enterprise relations

# of job creation as a result of international sourcing activity

# of job loss as a result of international sourcing activity

# of link with more organizations

# of members awarded contracts Internationally

# of members awarded contracts locally

# of mining and quarrying broken down by employment size

# of new businesses assisted

# of services broken down by employment size

# of SMEs - electricity, gas and water

# of SMEs - industry and construction

# of SMEs - services

# of zoning for "family business"

% brand awareness (yearly)

% of construction broken down by employment size

% of customers' satisfaction about the accessibility to statistics

% of customers' satisfaction about the accessibility to studies

% of customers Satisfaction about the pertinence of available data

37. Economic Development

% of customers' satisfaction about the pertinence of studies

% of customer's satisfaction of the supporting services

% of customer's satisfaction on the simplicity of obtaining information related to export and regional data

% of enterprises having received orders on-line

% of enterprises managed by the founder - broken down by birth size class (number of employees)

% of enterprises managed by the founder - broken down by branch experience

% of enterprises managed by the founder - broken down by education of the entrepreneur

% of enterprises managed by the founder - broken down by entrepreneur age class

% of enterprises managed by the founder - broken down by experience managing an enterprise

% of enterprises managed by the founder - broken down by gender of the entrepreneur

% of enterprises managed by the founder - broken down by survival size class (number of employees)

% of enterprises using the Internet for interacting with public authorities

% portfolio profitability of funded companies over 3 years

Cumulative capital intensive industrial fund portfolio

Cumulative SME loan fund portfolio

Growth rate of private sector contribution to GDP

Increased # of council men having meetings outside of city hall

Total manufacturing broken down by employment size

38. Education

Administration

of assets inventoried and tagged

# of audit exceptions

# of lunches served through the summer food service program

# of plans presented annually

# of policies and procedures developed

# of quality manuals developed

# of survey of the parents of students regarding the quality of the services and care provided

% of accountability reports completed

% of community colleges participating in the management information system

% of districts participating in a student record system

% of districts reporting all data required under the education data exchange network

% of federal programs approved for funding

% of jobs with job descriptions and grading structure

38. Education

% of local and federal reporting requirements met by the Department for accountability

% of local districts receiving desk audits annually

% of organizational structure developed and in place

Adult Education

% of relevant age group receiving full-time education

Adult educational achievement rate

Enrollment rates - secondary school

Net enrolment ratio in primary education

Early Learning

of awards given

# of centers attaining center of distinction or recognition

# of early school leavers by gender

# of events and programs

# of license to child care learning centers and group day care homes each fiscal year

# of meals served per year by providers in the Child Care Food Program

# of pre-K program enrollment

# of providers participating in the homes program

# of standards of care program training attendees

# of technical assistance to child care learning centers and group day care homes each fiscal year

# of visits to child care learning centers and group day care homes each fiscal year

% increase child care teachers tracking their training and professional development online system

% of children entering kindergarten with basic early literacy skills

% of eligible providers reviewed with no missing meal components in the Child Care Food Program

% of four-year-olds in education

% of programs meeting or exceeding pre-K quality assessment standards

% of student survey completed results

Educated Population

of awards given in recognition of national identity to both teachers and students

# of educational attainment by sex

# of foreign languages taught

# of mathematics, science and technology enrolments

# of mathematics, science and technology graduates

# of persons with low educational attainment

# of qualified engineers

# of students at each institution in comparison to the demographics of the country

# of tertiary education graduates

# of tertiary education participation

38. Education
% educational attainment of the population (25-64 year olds) by highest level of education
% enrolment of 15-19 years olds
% enrolment of 20-29 years olds
% enrolment of 3-4 year olds
% enrolment of 5-14 years olds
% of citizens with second language
% of enrolment in education as a % of the age group (from 4– 40+)
% of labor market alignment
% of population that has attained at least tertiary education for persons 25-34
% of population that has attained higher education achievements
% of population with illiteracy
% of qualified engineers available in the labor market
% of recent vocational college and university graduates in employment
% of students accepted in schools
% projected increases in student population by region
% spread of educational facilities across the country
% unemployment by educational attainment
Distribution of pupils/ students by level
Educational attainment of the population - % by age group
Graduates in agriculture (% of total graduates, tertiary)
Graduates in agriculture, female (% of total female graduates, tertiary)
Graduates in education (% of total graduates, tertiary)
Graduates in engineering, manufacturing and construction (% of total graduates, tertiary)
Graduates in engineering, manufacturing and construction, female (% of total female graduates, tertiary)
Graduates in health (% of total graduates, tertiary)
Graduates in health, female (% of total female graduates, tertiary)
Graduates in humanities and arts (% of total graduates, tertiary)
Graduates in humanities and arts, female (% of total female graduates, tertiary)
Graduates in science (% of total graduates, tertiary)
Graduates in science, female (% of total female graduates, tertiary)
Graduates in services (% of total graduates, tertiary)
Graduates in services, female (% of total female graduates, tertiary)
Graduates in social science, business, law (% of total graduates, tertiary)
Graduates in social science, business, law, female (% of total female graduates, tertiary)
Graduates in unknown or unspecified fields (% of total graduates, tertiary)
Graduates in unknown or unspecified fields, female (% of total female graduates, tertiary)
Illiteracy - Adult (over 15 years) - illiteracy rate as a % of population
Literacy rate of 15–24 year-olds

38. Education
Participation rates in education by age
Participation/ enrolment in education by sex
Total # of enrolment - secondary school
Total participation/ enrolment in education
Total population having completed at least upper secondary education
Total workforce by educational level attainment in % of total workforce
Total workforce by educational level attainment in % of total workforce (primary education)
Total workforce by educational level attainment in % of total workforce (secondary education)
Total workforce by educational level attainment in % of total workforce (tertiary education)

Educational Institutions
# of advanced placement courses offered
# of awards per annum
# of based educational institution with environmental partnerships
# of charter schools
# of comparative spend
# of educational institutions
# of international research projects undertaken per year
# of learning resources for curriculum is available in schools
# of new higher education institutions that conform to higher education standards
# of new schools in all districts
# of publications in quality peer reviewed journals per annum
# of publications made in quality journals per annum by educational institution
# of schools on the needs improvement list
# of schools removed from the needs improvement list
# of students enrolled at academy for the blind
# of students enrolled at school for the deaf
# of teachers
# of teaching hours per school year
# of total educational institutions enrolment
# of universities
% accredited educational institutions
% of charter schools making adequate yearly progress
% of community college student who complete an award within three years
% of community college student who transfer to a four-year institution
% of community colleges meeting accreditation standards
% of free healthy meals
% of free stationary
% of free transportation
% of graduates from vocational colleges and university in employment
% of knowledge transfer developed between companies and universities

38. Education

% of new centers are licensed according to standards

% of new universities providing profiles and required data

% of private schools in relation to % public schools

% of professional development being undertaken by teachers

% of recent school leavers (not in further education) in employment

% of students completing courses

% of students passing the appropriate end of course test

% of university education meets the needs of a competitive economy

% pass rate overall by institution

% spread across the country

% utilization rate of educational institutions (seats)

Average annual boarding fee

Average capital costs per student by college

Average class size

Distribution of recent higher education graduates (by qualification major)

Educational spend in real terms as a % of GDP

Occupancy rates for different colleges

Operating costs per student by college

Staffing costs per student by college

Total college graduation Rate

Total educational spend in real terms

Expenditure

education fund spend in total (% of GDP)

education fund spend in total and trends over time

of schools (per million people)

# of students in primary, secondary and post-secondary non-tertiary education

# of students in tertiary education

% of government funds distributed according to formula prescribed by the funding source

% of government funds distributed using the correct data to determine distribution

% of internal operations in accordance with generally accepted accounting principles

% of school districts participating in individual student record system

Amount spend per student overall, by level (primary, secondary and university) and by institution

Annual expenditure on public and private educational institutions compared to GDP per capita

Annual expenditure on public and private educational institutions per pupil/student

Expenditure in institutions per student

Expenditure in primary, secondary and post-secondary non-tertiary education

Expenditure in tertiary education

38. Education

Expenditure on education as % of GDP or public expenditure

Expenditure on education in constant prices

Expenditure on education in current prices

Expenditure on public and private educational institutions

Expenditure on public educational institutions

Expenditure per student in primary, secondary and post-secondary non-tertiary education

Expenditure per student in tertiary education

Index of change in public expenditure on educational institutions

Private expenditure in institutions as % of public and private funding

Private expenditure on education as % of GDP

Private expenditure on educational institutions for all levels of education

Private expenditure on educational institutions in primary, secondary and post-secondary non-tertiary education

Private expenditure on educational institutions in tertiary education

Public education expenditure as % of public expenditure and GDP

Public education expenditure spent as students aid, by type of aid - %

Public expenditure on educational institutions for all levels of education

Public expenditure on educational institutions in primary, secondary and post-secondary non-tertiary education

Share of public expenditure on educational institutions

Total expenditure on educational institutions for all levels of education

Total expenditure on educational institutions in primary, secondary and post-secondary non-tertiary education

Total expenditure on educational institutions in tertiary education

Total financial aid to students

Total funding of education

Total investments in education and training

Total public expenditure on education

Total public expenditure on education (% of GDP)

Total public expenditure on education (per capita)

Total public expenditure on education per capita - US$ per capita

Total spending on national human resources

Trends in relative earnings for age group 25-64 with tertiary education: females

Trends in relative earnings for age group 25-64 with tertiary education: males

Formal Education

of participations in formal education by age

# of participations in formal education by degree

# of participations in formal education by educational attainment

# of participations in formal education by sex

Fields of study in formal education by working status

Informal Learning

of participations in informal learning by age

38. Education
# of participations in informal learning by degree
# of participations in informal learning by working status
Computer based learning participants by age
Computer based learning participants by educational attainment
Participants studying by making use of educational broadcasting
Participants studying in libraries or learning centers
Self studying (with printed materials) participants by age
Self studying (with printed materials) participants by working status

Life Long Learning

# of participations in any learning activities by age
# of participations in any learning activities by degree
# of participations in any learning activities by economic activity
# of participations in any learning activities by educational attainment
# of participations in any learning activities by occupation
# of participations in any learning activities by size of the local unit

Non Formal Education

# of participation in job-related non formal education/training by size of the local unit
# of participation in non formal education/training by # of activities
# of participation in non formal education/training by # of taught activities
# of participation in non formal education/training by age
# of participation in non formal education/training by degree
# of participation in non formal education/training by educational attainment
# of participation in non formal education/training by main reason for participating in the taught activity
# of participation in non formal education/training by sex
# of participation in non formal taught activities within paid hours
# of participation in non formal taught activity within paid working hours
# of participation of employed persons in non formal education/training activities on computers
# of participation of employed persons in non formal education/training activities on foreign languages
# of participation of employed persons in non formal education/training by field of study
# of participation of employed persons in non formal education/training by occupation
# of participation of employed persons in non formal education/training by sex
Mean volume of hours per employed participant in non formal education
Mean volume of hours per employed participant in non formal training
Mean volume of hours per participant in non formal education/training by field of learning
Mean volume of hours per participant in non formal education/training by sex

38. Education

Public Libraries

maturity of online public service delivery
of annual visits per 1,000 Population
# of average daily visits
# of circulations in public libraries
# of print materials available
# of public searches of electronic databases
% of accredited public libraries
% of certified public library directors
% of customers who get the information they need
% of libraries submitting annual survey data
% of overall satisfaction with library services
% of people with access through their public library to electronic informational databases
% of public and academic libraries participating in resource sharing programs
% of public libraries meeting key standards
% of public libraries open 45 hours or more per week
% of public libraries participating in direct aid program
% rate of library circulation
% use of public libraries

Research & Innovation

# of companies served
# of curriculum ready with internship component
# of established student exchange programs
# of grants and contracts received
# of industry investments in direct strategic research
# of interface between educational institutions and industries
# of internationally significant research contributing to industry social and the strategic economic needs
# of journal articles published to support economic development
# of major research projects undertaken and progress made versus investments applied
# of recommendations issued
# of researches developed in schools
# of start up research initiatives
# of survey that address national identity
# of technology jobs provided by companies (members and graduate)
% increase in income through the application of new technology
% of districts with approved career development plans
% of labor market needs by specialization in comparison with students undertaking required courses
% of local school districts visited annually by school improvement team
% of persons surveyed who attended education workshops who reported that the programs were beneficial

38. Education

% participation rate in service area

# of classroom cards distributed

# of graduates by age

# of graduates by age and field of education

# of graduates by sex

# of migrant education students

# of new entrants by sex

# of pupils in upper secondary education enrolled in vocational stream

# of pupils learning Arabic

# of pupils learning English

# of pupils learning French

# of pupils learning German

# of science and technology graduates by gender

# of students by age

# of students by level of education

# of students by modern foreign language studied

# of students by study intensity (full-time, part-time)

# of students by type of institutions (private or public)

# of teens not attending school and not working

# of tertiary students by field of education

# of youth in after-school educational programs

% female entrants by field of education

% graduates from abroad (foreigners/mobile students)

% net entry rate by age

% of 18-year-olds in education

% of education attainment of persons aged 25-39

% of education attainment, by age

% of education attainment, by sex

% of students in tertiary education who are non-citizens

% of students in tertiary education who are non-residents

% of students in tertiary education with prior education from another country

% of teens not attending school and not working

% share of women among tertiary students

% students studying part-time by age

Average attendance rates in x grade

Completion rate

Entrants in % of secondary school graduates

Foreign languages learnt per pupil

Foreign students as % of total students by origin

Foreign students in tertiary education by country of citizenship

Gross graduation rate

High school dropout rate

38. Education

High school graduation rate

High school graduation rate for African-American students

High school graduation rate for Hispanic students

High school graduation rate for White students

Median age

Net entry rate

Pupil/teacher ratio in primary education

Student - teacher ratio

Students abroad as % of students in country of origin

Student Assessment

of educational assessment / Mathematics (survey of 15-year olds)

# of educational assessment / Sciences (survey of 15-year olds)

# of educational assessment completed

% of produced standardized test for student performance

% tertiary attainment for age group 25-34

% tertiary attainment for age group 25-64

% tertiary attainment for age group 55-64

% tertiary entry rates

% tertiary graduation rates

Mean scores on the mathematics scale in PISA

Mean scores on the mathematics scale in PISA: females

Mean scores on the mathematics scale in PISA: males

Mean scores on the science scale in PISA

Mean scores on the science scale in PISA: females

Mean scores on the science scale in PISA: males

Score difference on the mathematics scale in PISA: difference (males - females)

Score difference on the science scale in PISA: difference (males - females)

Standard error on the mathematics scale in PISA

Standard error on the mathematics scale in PISA: difference (males - females)

Standard error on the mathematics scale in PISA: females

Standard error on the mathematics scale in PISA: males

Standard error on the science scale in PISA

Standard error on the science scale in PISA: difference (males - females)

Standard error on the science scale in PISA: females

Standard error on the science scale in PISA: males

Student Outcomes

of advisory body established for industries

# of industry linked programs with student destinations following graduation

# of school graduates that are recruited by local industry

# of school leavers that are recruited by local industry

# of schools making adequate yearly progress

38. Education

of students

% distribution of graduates by qualification major

% of children out of school, primary

% of children out of school, primary, female

% of children out of school, primary, male

% of International curricula developed and implemented

% of recent school graduates in further education

% of school graduates in further education (by type of education)

% of school leavers not in education (by employment status)

Annual dropout rate

Educational attainment of the population

Literacy rate, adult, 15 years and above, female (in %)

Literacy rate, adult, 15 years and above, male (in %)

Literacy rate, youth, 15 - 24 Years, female (in %)

Literacy rate, youth, 15 - 24 years, male (in %)

School completion rate as scheduled (time)

Teaching Quality

of approve surveys for all students

# of customer satisfaction surveys established

# of demographic report for existing teaching workforce

# of establishments with employment manual

# of full time professional advisers and trainers

# of high school with on-time graduation

# of marketing plan to promote education and success

# of national, regional and international awards received

# of new curriculum standards established in schools

# of newly certified teachers in meeting the highly qualified criteria

# of performance appraisal and reward system in place

# of policies and procedures for the implementation of the research accountability mechanism

# of school net hours by level of education (primary, secondary)

# of survey measured

% completion rate at grade 12

% completion rate at grade 7

% completion rate at grade 9

% curricula redesigned to meet international standards

% of 11th graders proficient or higher in mathematics

% of 11th graders proficient or higher in reading comprehension

% of 11th graders proficient or higher in science

% of 4th graders proficient or higher in mathematics

% of 4th graders proficient or higher in reading comprehension

% of 8th graders proficient or higher in mathematics

% of 8th graders proficient or higher in reading comprehension

% of 8th graders proficient or higher in science

38. Education
% of practitioner preparation programs meeting requirements
% of practitioners who are appropriately licensed
% of school districts meeting accreditation standards
% of schools inspected per year
% of schools meeting accreditation standards
% of students completing school (by primary, secondary and higher education)
% students achieving reading and numeracy by x grade
Average # of hours applied in renewing teacher knowledge per annum
Education district performance index
Net Enrolment ratio - from grade x - to grade x
Retention rate
Student teacher ratio from grade x - to grade x
Total loss of funds due to noncompliance with program requirements
Total pass rates

Teaching Staff
# of teachers and academic staff by age
# of teachers and academic staff by employment status (full-time, part-time)
# of teachers and academic staff by sex
# of teachers and trainers by age distributions
# of teachers recruiting events held annually
# of teaching certificate transactions annually
% of new teachers certified
% of teacher qualification and certification
% of teachers in core academic areas appropriately licensed and assigned
% of teachers meeting the definition of highly qualified teachers
% of teachers stays abroad as % of academic staff
% of teachers who have completed training
% of teachers with technology certification
% overall teacher qualification level
% teachers who have passed their ICT test
Pupil-teacher ratio (primary education)
Pupil-teacher ratio (secondary education)
Ratio of students to teaching staff

Transportation
# of buses operating daily
# of students transported

Youth Educational Services
# of performance learning centers
% mentored youth who establish themselves in employment
% mentored youth who improved their academic results
% of at-risk youth that graduate from the youth challenge academy

38. Education

% of graduates that meet standard for success 6 months after graduation from the youth challenge academy

Graduation rate for students

Youth education attainment level by gender

39. Energy

Alternative Fuels

of initiated community biodiesel fueling station

% of construct electric vehicle recharging facilities in new large parking facilities

% of conversion to biodiesel (B20)

% of conversion to compressed natural gas (CNG)

% of conversion to electric vehicles

% of conversion to ethanol

% of utilize hydrogen or fuel cell vehicles

Carbon Credits

% of carbon tax

% of purchase carbon credits

Energy Consumption

energy used per unit of production

total energy consumption

% energy dependency

% share of biofuels in fuel consumption of transport

Amount of energy saved due to conservation and efficiency improvements

Average electrical consumption per employee or product sold

CO_2 produced from gas consumed

CO_2 tones per employee per month

Energy costs per unit of production

Fuel gas consumption

Gross inland consumption of primary energy

Gross inland energy consumption by fuel

Total diesel used

Total electricity consumption

Total energy consumption (TJ/year per mCHF sales)

Total energy consumption (TJ/year)

Total energy used per unit of production

Total gas consumption

Total of final energy consumption

Total of final energy consumption by households

Total of final energy consumption by industry

Total of final energy consumption by sector

Total of final energy consumption by services

Total of final energy consumption by transport mode

Total of final energy consumption of electricity

39. Energy

Total of final energy consumption of natural gas
Total of final energy consumption of petroleum products
Total office energy consumption
Total on-site created energy
Total organic carbon (TOC) (t/year)
Total purchased energy per month
Total supply of transformation and consumption of heat

Energy Infrastructure

% improvement on infrastructure - electricity
% improvement on infrastructure - gas
% improvement on infrastructure - oil
% improvement on infrastructure - renewables
% of implement district heating and cooling
% of install energy-efficient cogeneration power production facilities

Energy Prices

Crude oil import price
Electricity price
Energy price
Gas - domestic consumers - half-yearly prices
Gas - industrial consumers - half-yearly prices
Gas price
Gas prices by type of user
Implicit tax rate on energy
Natural gas prices for large industrial standard consumers
Petroleum products - half-yearly prices
Prices of diesel oil
Prices of premium unleaded gasoline

Energy Saving-Equipment

% of certified wood stove
% of Energy Star clothes washers
% of Energy Star computers
% of Energy Star copiers
% of Energy Star dishwashers
% of Energy Star monitors
% of Energy Star printers
% of Energy Star refrigerators
% of Energy Star vending machines
% of Energy Star water coolers
% of Energy Star window air conditioners
% of energy-efficient boilers
% of energy-efficient chillers
% of geothermal heat pump
% of high efficiency water heaters
% of HVAC fan upgrades

39. Energy

% of HVAC maintenance tune-ups

% of switch electric heat to natural Gas

Energy Saving-Facility

% of adopt a high performance local energy code for new construction of community facilities

% of adopt strict commercial energy code requirements

% of adopt strict residential energy code requirements

% of distribute loans to citizens to make energy efficiency improvements

% of implement energy efficient new public/affordable housing projects

% of implement energy efficient weatherization of low-income housing

% of perform energy efficiency retrofits of existing facilities

% of require energy upgrades of facilities at time of sale

Energy Saving-Lighting

% of decrease average daily time street lights are on

% of distribute free CFL bulbs and/or fixtures to community members

% of install LED exit signs

% of install LED street lights

% of install LED traffic signals

% of install occupancy sensors

% of institute a lights-out-at-night policy

% of LED holiday lights

% of offer a halogen torchiere lamp exchange to community members

% of retrofit T-12 lamps to T-8 lamps

Energy Saving-Promotion

% of energy conservation through campaigns targeted at businesses

% of energy conservation through campaigns targeted at residents

% of green building practices through a local green building assistance program or incentives

% of participation in a local green business program

Energy Saving-Roofing

% of install green roofing

% of install reflective roofing

Energy Saving-Transportation

% of limit idling of government operations vehicles

% of limit idling of heavy equipment vehicles

% of limit idling of local transit buses and school buses

Energy Saving-Trip Reduction

# of car sharing program

# of Initiated car sharing program

% of allow bikes on trains/buses

% of bicycles for daily trips

% of create high-occupancy vehicle (HOV) lanes

% of educate citizens on options for utilizing local low-carbon transportation

% of expand bicycling infrastructure (lanes, storage facilities)

39. Energy

% of expand local or regional bus service in range and / or frequency

% of high school students with free bus passes

% of implement a police on bicycles program

% of implement bus rapid transit or shuttle programs

% of implement parking cash-out program

% of improve / expand pedestrian infrastructure

% of increase bus ridership

% of increase mass-transit ridership

% of increase ride-sharing (carpools)

% of increase telecommuting

% of install new light rail systems

% of institute a "safe routes to school" program

% of reduce fleet size

% of transit-oriented development

Energy Saving-Vehicle

% of hybrid vehicles

% of parking or lane incentives for hybrid vehicles

% of procurement of hybrid vehicles

% of procurement of smaller fleet vehicles

% of retire old and under-used vehicles

% of retrofit school buses with oxidation catalysts

% of retrofit school buses with particulate traps

% of utilize fuel-efficient vehicles (scooters) for parking enforcement

Energy Supply

of alternative fueling stations

# of consumption of petroleum products (tones)

# of wind energy kWh consumed

% energy intensity of the economy

% of contribution of renewables to energy supply

% of electricity generation

% of purchase green electricity via the grid from solar, geothermal, wind or hydroelectric sources

% of purchase green tags / renewable energy certificates

Energy savings per household

Gas production volumes

Nuclear electricity generation, % of total production

Nuclear electricity generation, terawatts

Nuclear power plants connected to the grid

Nuclear power plants under construction

Primary production of coal and lignite

Primary production of crude oil

Primary production of natural gas

Primary production of nuclear energy

Primary production of renewable energy

39. Energy
Production of crude oil
Total combined heat and power generation
Total primary energy supply
Total primary energy supply per capita
Total primary energy supply per unit of GDP
Total production of energy
Total production of primary energy
Total supply all products
Total supply and transformation of all products
Total supply and transformation of electricity
Total supply and transformation of gas
Total supply and transformation of oil
Total supply and transformation of solid fuels
Total supply of natural gas
Total supply of petroleum products
Total transformation - solid fuels

Energy Trade

Net imports of crude oil and petroleum products
Net imports of natural gas
Net imports of primary energy
Total exports (by country of destination) of all products
Total exports (by country of destination) of electricity
Total exports (by country of destination) of gas
Total exports (by country of destination) of oil
Total exports (by country of destination) of solid fuels
Total imports (by country of origin) of all products
Total imports (by country of origin) of gas
Total imports (by country of origin) of oil
Total imports (by country of origin) of solid fuels

Fuel Quality Inspection

# of amusement ride safety inspections conducted
# of LP gas facility inspections and re-inspections conducted
# of petroleum field inspections conducted
# of petroleum tests performed
# of pipeline safety inspections
% of amusement attractions found in full compliance with safety requirements on first inspections
% of LP gas facilities found in compliance with safety requirements on first inspection
% of petroleum products meeting quality standards
% of regulated weighing and measuring devices, packages, and businesses with scanners

Innovation

# of technologies developed with a % increase in energy efficiency

39. Energy

of technologies with NOx emissions less than .15 lbs per MWh

Energy density of hydrogen storage system using solid state storage
technologies, in weight %

Oil Pipelines

of employment in oil pipeline enterprises

Total carrying capacity of pipelines operated

Total investment in oil pipeline infrastructure

Total length of pipelines operated

Total oil pipeline transport within the national territory

Renewable Energy

% energy produced from renewable sources

% energy used from renewable sources

% of energy generation from landfill methane

% of install solar photovoltaic (PV) panels

% of install solar water heaters

% of install solar water heating at swimming pool

% of install solar water heating panels (inc. via incentives)

% of install wind turbines

% of install wind turbines (inc. via incentives)

% share of renewable energy

% share of renewables in gross inland energy consumption

Cost of "binary power" from geothermal resources (cents per kWh)

Cost of "flash power" from geothermal resources (cents per kWh)

Cost of drilling geothermal wells based on program estimates ($/ft)

Program benefit-cost ratio excluding non-energy benefits

Ratio of value of energy saved to program cost

Total consumption of renewables

Total consumption of renewables (biofuels)

Total consumption of renewables (biomass)

Total consumption of renewables (geothermal)

Total consumption of renewables (hydro)

Total consumption of renewables (photovoltaic)

Total consumption of renewables (solar heat)

Total consumption of renewables (wind)

Total renewable energy primary production through biomass

Total renewable energy primary production through geothermal

Total renewable energy primary production through hydro

Total renewable energy primary production through solar energy

Total renewable energy primary production through wind

Total supply of renewables

Total supply of renewables (biofuels)

Total supply of renewables (biomass)

Total supply of renewables (geothermal)

Total supply of renewables (hydro)

39. Energy
Total supply of renewables (photovoltaic)
Total supply of renewables (solar heat)
Total supply of renewables (wind)

40. Environment

Air Quality

# of cars transferring to CNG
# of days during the ozone season that the ozone NAAQS is exceeded
# of days exceeded ozone Standards
% change in emissions per GDP and per capita (over time)
% consumption of CFCs and halons over time
% frequency of Sox, Nox, PM10, ground level ozone and CO concentrations not exceeding limits
% improvement in the population-weighted ambient concentrations of ozone
% improvement in the population-weighted ambient concentrations of PM2.5
% increase of cars transferred to CNG
% increase usage of cleaner diesel
% main road links with acceptable air quality levels
% of air quality levels – SO2, NO2, O3 and CO
% of cars transferring to CNG over time
% of citizen satisfaction with efforts to improve air quality
% of CO2 emissions from fuel combustion
% of consumption of HCFCs and methyl bromide
% of establishments complying with noise emission limits from stationary/ point source.
% of existing industrial facilities that is environmentally compliant
% of Lead level in Perth's air
% of new development and industrial complying projects that are environmentally compliant.
% of noise baseline established
% of submit NAAQS pollutant data and QA data to the air quality system
% reduction in NOx and primary PM10 emissions for better air quality
% reduction in NOx and primary PM10 emissions through local authority's estate and operations
% usage of diesel containing 50 ppm sulphur
Air quality levels – PM^{10}
Average ozone levels
Carbon monoxide levels in air
Cumulative % reduction in # of days with Air Quality Index (AQI) values over 100
Emissions per capita (based on CO2 tones-equivalent/capita)
Emissions per unit of GDP (based on CO2 tones-equivalent/1000US)

40. Environment

Environmental Performance Index

Greenhouse emissions per Capita

Greenhouse emissions per unit of GDP

Index of CO2, CH4, N2O emissions as well as PFC, HFC, SF6 emissions (measured in tones)

Index of greenhouse emissions

Noise levels at selected locations on main roads

Ozone level in air

SOx and Nox per unit of GDP

SOx and Nox per unit of GDP and % change over time of total emissions

Awareness

increase in awareness programs conducted

increase of people informed through outreach

of initiatives to promote greater environmental responsibility

# of people informed through outreach

# of press releases - media monitors

# of private and public sector environmental initiatives including corporate environmental responsibilities

# of programs developed for different target groups

# of respondents to the awareness campaign

sponsored organizations dedicated to CSR

% improvement in the level of awareness

% of society's environmental awareness

% of society's level of positive environmental behavior

Beaches Protection

decrease of marine violations

of tones of litter

# of total catch by species and gear

# of total catch fishing seasons

% increase of compliance of marine regulations

% increase of fisheries resource key species

% increase of key marine ecosystems and habitats

% increase of protected areas as % of total areas

% of all public beaches that are monitored and managed

% of days of the beach season that beaches are open and safe for swimming

% of state-owned coastal boat ramps in safe operational condition

Increase media monitors by 10%

Biological Diversity

of acres certified for public shellfish harvest

# of catch by species

# of fish catches from stocks outside of 'safe biological limits'

# of fisheries resources

# of key marine ecosystems and habitats

# of key marine endangered species

40. Environment
# of species assessed (status of species)
# of species in ex-situ programs
# of tones of fisheries production by capture & aquaculture
# of total catch per species
% decrease in fish stock biomass and potential yields
% loss of coastal and marine habitats
% of area under forest plantation
% of compliance: marine
% of compliance: terrestrial
% of fish catches taken from stocks outside'safe biological limits'
% of fishing species distribution
% of protected areas as % of total area
% of total threatened species
% sufficiency of sites designated under habitats directive
Common bird index
Farmland bird index
Length of fishing seasons (# of days)
Marine protected area (% of surface area)
Total protected areas for biodiversity: habitats directive

Clean Community

increase of private and public sectors environmental initiatives
of acres of real property successfully negotiated and acquired for conservation
# of brownfields properties assessed
# of improved street and environmental cleanliness – fly tipping
# of mode of transport usually used by children traveling to school
# of properties cleaned up using brownfields funding
# of residual household waste per household
% achievement in meeting standards for the control system for animal health
% adaptation to climate change
% CO2 reduction from local authority operations
% improvement in street and environmental cleanliness (levels of litter, detritus, graffiti and fly posting)
% of community satisfaction with the availability of public access to the swan-canning river system
% of household waste sent for reuse and recycling
% of households living in proclaimed townships/areas
% of improved street and environmental cleanliness (levels of litter, detritus, graffiti and fly posting)
% of local sites where positive conservation management has been implemented
% of municipal waste land filled
% of people receiving income based benefits living in homes with a low energy efficiency rating

40. Environment

% reduction in NOx and primary PM10 emissions through local authority's operations

Per capita reduction in CO2 emissions

Quality of life index

Climate Change

of household energy efficiency products provided

# of national communication campaign

# of policy endorsements

% eco-balance

% environment impact of product use

% of build capability to greenhouse gas emission inventory

Carbon intensity of power generation

Eco-efficiency rate

Green workplace/ Carbon footprint

Greenhouse gas (GHG) emissions per employee per month

Greenhouse gas emissions (tones CO2 equivalents per mCHF sales)

Greenhouse gas emissions (tones CO2 equivalents)

Heavy metals (kg/year)

Lifetime carbon savings for household energy efficiency products provided

Particulate matter (t/year)

Total emissions from production into the environment

Total energy saved due to conservation & efficiency improvements

Volatile organic compounds (VOCs) (t/year)

Compliance

of complaints (including noise)

# of environmental laws

# of environmental laws that do not hinder the competitiveness of businesses

# of fines

# of incidents

# of non-compliances

# of regulation fault findings

# of total ratified environmental treaties

# of violations (marine, terrestrial)

% of companies complying with radiation right practices

% overall regulatory compliance performance

Penalties resulting from environmental non-compliance

Emissions

carbon dioxide emissions per capita

of HAP inventories submitted

% emissions through local authority's estate and operations

% increase of establishments complying with noise emission limits from stationary/ point source

40. Environment

% increase of new development and industrial projects that are environmentally compliant

% increase of usage of Diesel containing 50 ppm sulphur

% of emissions through local authority's estate and operations

% of environmental emissions

% of Euro 4 vehicles

% of Methane flaring at local landfills

% of vehicles in line with target emission standards

% reduction of cancer causing toxic pollutant emissions

% reduction of non-cancer causing toxic pollutant emissions

Average carbon dioxide emissions of vehicles

Carbon dioxide emissions per capita (ODP tons)

Greenhouse gas emissions

Greenhouse gas emissions by sector

Greenhouse gas emissions from transport

HFCs emissions (1000 Tones CO2 Equivalent)

NOx emissions (tones per year)

SOx emissions (tones per year)

Total air emissions

Total air emissions accounts by activity (industries and households)

Total air emissions accounts totals bridging to emission inventory totals

Total CO2 emissions

Total gas from power generation

Total gas from production

Total Methane (CH4)

Total Nitrous Oxide

Total NOx emissions

Forest Protection

of acres burned by wildfires

# of acres covered by a forest management plan

# of acres of state forests managed by the department

# of environmentally important acres of forest protected

# of forest visitors served

# of hours spent providing forest-related technical assists to non-industrial private landowners

# of hours spent providing forest-related technical assists to public land management agencies

# of online and automated burn permits issued

# of water quality exams conducted on logging and forestry operations

% achieved thinning versus prescribed

% area of forest cut

% authorized removal of firewood from total firewood removals

% change in forest area

40. Environment

% increase in volume of timber per acre of land due to selection, testing, and breeding of genetically improved seedlings

% land use by main category

% of area of forest plantations

% of forest areas under protected status

% of forest timber producing acres adequately stocked and growing

% of land area covered by forest

% of maintained area of forest plantation

% of protected area under forest plantation

% of total removals of firewood compared to the authorized removal

% of tree planting for carbon storage & heat island

% of tree planting to shade buildings

% of water bodies with significant variance of biodiversity

Amount of revenue generated through seedling sales

Average fire response time in minutes

Cost per acre of environmentally important forest protected

Deforestation rate

Forecast strategic timber yield versus actual timber yield

Level of soil damage resulting from timber harvesting

Per capita public green space

Time to regenerate harvested areas

Total built-up areas

Hazardous Waste

of acres of property to be remediated under approvals

# of facilities with final remedies constructed

# of facilities with human exposures under control

# of facilities with updated controls for preventing releases

# of hazardous waste cleanup projects completed during fiscal year

# of hazardous waste facilities assessed

# of hazardous waste facilities with final remedies selected

# of hazardous waste facilities with migration of contaminated groundwater under control

# of hazardous waste facilities with new or updated controls

# of hazardous waste facilities with remedy construction completed

# of hazardous waste management facilities with permits or approved controls in place

# of high priority facilities with human exposures to toxins controlled

# of individuals in the regulated community reached

# of partnerships established with hospitals and other health facilities to reduce Mercury in waste streams

# of risk management plan audits completed

# of sites receiving approvals for remediation during the year

% completion and implementation of emergency management system

% gap in processing of industrial hazardous waste from the non–oil sector

40. Environment
% gap in processing of medical hazardous waste
% increase of facilities that are in significant operational compliance with release detection and prevention
% of hazardous operational waste
% of recycled hazardous operational waste
% of reduced gap in processing of industrial hazardous waste from the non–oil sector
% of reduced gap in processing of medical hazardous waste
% recycled hazardous operational waste
% reduction of releases of industrial hazardous chemicals to the environment
Total chemical waste (t/year)

Health & Safety

- # of calls within time limits stipulated in operating procedures
- # of economic sectors with EHSMS approved against system requirements
- # of implementation of EHSMS
- # of incidents: Fatal
- # of incidents: Ill-health
- # of incidents: Major Injury
- # of major injury
- # of occupational health incidents
- # of organizations with ISO 14001 certifications
- # of responding to external emergency notification
- # of total reportable case frequency (calculated per 1,000,000 hrs worked)
- # of total time injuries
- # of work place fatalities
- % completion of a implementation framework
- % completion of EHSMS regulatory framework
- % of soil salinity mapping
- % of soil surveying (classification, mapping, evaluation, degradation, assessment)
- % of targeted entities complying with EHSMS requirements
- % of targeted entities with EHSMS approved against system requirements
- Lost time injuries frequency rate
- Lost time Injury frequency rate (calculated per 1,000,000 hrs worked)
- Lost time injury over time
- Lost time injury severity rate (calculated per 1,000,000 hrs worked)
- OH&S system development

Indoor Air & Radon

- # of additional homes built with radon-resistant new construction
- # of additional homes with operating mitigation systems
- # of additional schools mitigated and/or built with radon-resistant new construction
- # of homes built with radon-resistant new construction
- # of homes mitigated

40. Environment

of schools mitigated or built with radon-resistant new construction

% of reports with performance measures that have clear linkages to those of EPA

Local Assistance

of agencies collecting data for the HAP emissions inventory

# of components of domestic material consumption

# of cumulative reduction in tons of toxicity-weighted (for cancer risk) emissions of air toxics

# of cumulative reduction in tons of toxicity-weighted (for non-cancer risk) emissions of air toxics

# of eco-label awards

% of affected entities who operate NATTS in accordance with national guidance

% of affected entities who submit data in accordance with law

% of cumulative reduction in # of days with Air Quality Index (AQI)

% of cumulative reduction in the average # of days during the ozone season that the ozone standard is exceeded

% of major permits issued within one year of receiving a completed permit application

% reduction in population-weighted ambient concentration of fine particulate matter

% reduction in population-weighted ambient concentration of ozone

Current environmental expenditure by industry

Current environmental expenditure by the public sector

Distribution of environmental investment by industry

Distribution of environmental protection expenditure by domain

Distribution of environmental protection expenditure by the public sector

Domestic material consumption by material

Total area under agri-environmental commitment

Total environmental expenditure by the public sector

Total environmental investment by industry

Total environmental investment by the public sector

Total environmental protection expenditure

Total environmental protection expenditure by industry

Total environmental protection expenditure by size classes

Total environmental protection expenditure by total environmental domains

Total environmental protection expenditure in industry

Total environmental protection expenditure: % of GDP

Total environmental protection expenditure: % of gross fixed capital formation

Total environmental protection expenditure: % of output

Total environmental protection expenditure: % pollution prevention

Total environmental protection expenditure: distribution by industries

40. Environment

Total environmental protection expenditure: distribution by total environmental domains

Total environmental protection expenditure: per capita

Total environmental protection expenditures by institutions

Natural Resources

of total annual green houses emissions in Co2 equivalent

# of total species population

% encroachment in wildlife protection area

% extent of protected forest areas (ha) million

% increase of amount of domestic waste ending up in dumps

% of deforestations (# of HAs per annum cut down)

% of domestic waste generation per capita (in tons per annum)

% reduction in the rate of infestation of invasive alien species

Organizational Efficiency

of environmental performance Indicators

# of governance indicators (sustainability management)

% completion of corporate performance management reporting

% completion of environmental data sets

% completion of guidelines

% completion of noise baseline data project

% completion of recruitment of required manpower

% completion of soil classification

% completion of the database system

% implementation of the system at Federal level

% installation of radiation detection gates

% response to external emergency notification & calls within limits

Excellence model score

Parks & Recreation

of open space trails

# of park attendance

# of park, recreation and historic site visitation

% average annual occupancy at park cottages

% of customer comments indicating their overall park experience was good, very good, or excellent

% of hunters who rate their hunting experience as satisfactory or better

Pollution Control

of combined sewer overflow (CSO) permits

# of enforcement of environmental regulation

# of environmental laws

# of facilities covered by an overlay permit that incorporates trading provisions with an enforceable cap

# of facilities covered under either an individual or general construction storm water site permit

# of facilities covered under either an individual or general permit

40. Environment

of facilities that have traded at least once

# of incoming chemical, and hazardous material (including radioactive) shipments complying with requirements

# of organizations with a registered environmental management system

# of pollution problems that affect the economy

# of pollution serious problems

# of pounds of pollutants reduced

# of significant industrial users with pretreatment programs that have control mechanisms in place

# of territories that are on schedule with a mutually agreed-upon plan to adopt nutrient criteria into their water quality standards

# of territories that have adopted and are implementing their monitoring strategies in keeping with established schedules

# of territories that have adopted approved nutrient criteria into their water quality standards

# of territories that submitted new or revised acceptable water quality criteria

# of water bodies identified as being primarily nonpoint source impaired that are partially or fully restored

# of water bodies identified as not attaining water quality standards where standards are now fully attained

% concentration of Sox, Nox, PM10, ground level ozone and CO not exceeding limits.

% improvement of permitted companies complying with radiation practices conducted

% improvement of re-exported radioactive material shipments through point of exit, complying with requirements

% improvement of storages facilities of permitted companies dealing with chemicals and radioactive materials

% of environmental health of waterways

% of established and approved entities on a schedule consistent with national policy

% of existing industrial facilities that are environmentally compliant

% of facilities covered by permits that are considered current

% of facilities covered under either an individual or general industrial storm water permit

% of gasoline lawnmower replacement

% of implementation of a long term control plan which will result in compliance with water quality law

% of major dischargers in significant noncompliance (SNC) at any time during the fiscal year

% of portable gas can replacement

% of significant industrial users with pretreatment programs that have control mechanisms in place

40. Environment
% of territories that submitted new or revised acceptable water quality criteria
% of use low-VOC cleaning products
% of use low-VOC paints
% of use non-asphalt pavements
Carbon monoxide level
Ecological footprints
Environmental tax revenue
Environmental taxes by industry
Total environmental tax revenues as a share of GDP
Total environmental tax revenues as a share of total revenues from taxes and social contributions
Urban population exposure to air pollution by ozone
Urban population exposure to air pollution by particulate matter
Weighted emissions of greenhouse gases

Recycling

bottles recycled
effective residual ink concentration
paper pages used per employee
recycled paper
% biodegradable carrier bags
% completion of an implementation plan
% consumption of recycled paper
% landfill volume in use
% of establish / expand business recycling programs
% of establish / expand curbside recycling programs
% of establish / expand recycling programs
% of reuse or recycling of construction and demolition materials
% overall paper reduction
% reduced paper consumption due to duplexing
Tons of recyclable material collected as a % of all refuse & recyclable material collected
Total volume of recycled wastewater
Volume of recycled waste

Sewer Maintenance

of cities that adopted the voluntary management guidelines for on site sewage management
# of feet of sewer pipe jet cleaned
# of public system backups per 1,000 service connections
Average cost per foot of sewer pipe jet cleaned
Customer satisfaction rating

Solid Waste

of residential waste disposed per household
# of residential waste tons collected

40. Environment

of vehicles and mechanical equipment in service

% of capacity of the landfill consumed per year

% of citizen satisfaction % with residential garbage collection services

% of citizen satisfaction with recycling collection services

% of organics composting

% of regulated solid waste facilities operating in compliance with environmental standards

% of residential waste stream diverted

% of yard waste collection and composting

Average % of vehicles and equipment in service

Average Kg of garbage collected per household per Week

Average tons of recycling collected per account

Multi-family recycling rate

Recycling diversion rate

Residual household waste per household

Single-family residential recycling rate (% of tons of waste recycled)

Storm Drainage

of cited violations under the clean water act

# of facilities covered under either an individual or general industrial storm water permit

Average cost per foot of drainage pipe cleaned

Flood insurance ratings

Sustainable Environment

of groundwater reserves

# of industries who have signed MOUs with government

# of innovative private sector partnerships

# of private & public sector sustainability reports

% completion of implementation of the plan to protect ecologically sensitive areas

% completion of water management plan

% cumulative reduction of chronic human health risk from releases of industrial chemicals

% decrease in water and energy consumption

% of customers seeking stream bank variances who rate the service they receive as good

% of data sets available

% of enforcement of environmental regulation

% of new development and industrial projects that are environmentally compliant

% of quality of natural environment (ranked on a scale of 1 to 10)

% of renewable energies used

% of reported radioactive material shipments through point of exit, complying with requirements

% of storages facilities dealing with chemicals and radioactive materials complying with requirements

40. Environment
% of surface area protected for biodiversity
% of sustainability plan implementation
% of total primary energy supply of cleaner energy source (Hydro, solar, wind and geothermal power)
% of water quality
% passes unit/activity environmental compliance inspections
% reduction in chronically acidic water bodies in acid-sensitive regions
% reduction in review time for registration of conventional pesticides
% release of incoming chemical and hazardous material shipments complying with requirements
% share of renewable and wastes in total energy requirements
% usage of diesel containing 500 ppm sulphur
Annual reduction in daily municipal and industrial water use (measured in gallons per capita per day)
Average # per year of waterborne disease outbreaks attributable to oceans, rivers, lakes or streams
Average % of green sourcing per money spent
Carbon dioxide consumption of ozone-depleting chlorofluorocarbons (ODP tons)
Environmental performance index (EPI)
Environmental sustainability index
Forest area as % of total land
Index of greenhouse emissions (total emissions- 1000 tones CO2 equivalent)
Level of compliance to sustainability plan guidelines involving energy/ water consumption targets
PM10 level (micrograms per cubic meter)
Quality of life index (Based on an index from 0 to 10)
Ratio of # of ecologically sensitive areas protected to the total # of ecologically sensitive areas identified
Reduce water consumption per capita per day
Reduced # of violations of environmental regulations
Time to establish acute exposure chemical guidelines value per chemical
Water consumption per day per capita (lit/day/person)
Water consumption per hector in agricultural zones
Water consumption per hector in the forestry sector
Water quality (salinity (ppm))
Wealth accounts (net present value)

Toxic Substances

# of asbestos inspections conducted under government authority
# of asbestos inspections conducted with EPA credentials
# of asbestos inspections conducted with EPA credentials that resulted in enforcement action
# of enforcement actions taken
# of inspections by region

40. Environment

of inspections conducted with EPA credentials that resulted in enforcement action

# of total inspections conducted

% increase in hazardous waste sites where human health risks and disease have been mitigated

Index of production of toxic chemicals

Underground Injection

% increase rate of significant operational compliance over the previous year's target

% of deep injection wells that are used for salt solution mining

% of deep injection wells that are used to enhance oil recovery

% of deep injection wells that are used to inject industrial, municipal, or hazardous waste

% of identified motor vehicle waste disposal wells that are closed or permitted

Waste Management

of approved laws

# of collections missed per 100,000 collections of household waste

# of household collections missed, per 100,000 refuse collections

# of Kg of household waste collected per head

# of laws concerning establishment of waste management policy

# of paper pages used per employee per month

# of waste treatment facilities

# of waste water treatments plants

% approval for waste management initiatives

% completion of waste management initiatives

% completion of waste management policy

% completion of waste management strategy (master plan)

% gap in processing/treatment of sewerage/waste water from households and industrial sites

% improvement in street and environmental cleanliness (levels of litter, detritus, graffiti and fly posting)

% increase of residual household waste per household

% of applications for authorization of industrial processes dealt with within statutory deadlines

% of authorizations of industrial processes reviewed within statutory deadlines

% of materials used that are recycled input materials

% of non-hazardous operational waste

% of on-site assessment clients that implement at least one waste reduction recommendation

% of people expressing satisfaction with household waste collection

% of people expressing satisfaction with waste disposal

% of people expressing satisfaction with waste recycling

% of people satisfied with the cleanliness standard in their area

40. Environment
% of population resident in the authority's area served by a kerbside collection of recyclables
% of recycled non-hazardous operational waste
% of re-use facilities/programs to foster solid waste reduction
% of the total tonnage of household waste arising used to recover heat, power and other energy sources
% of the total tonnage of household waste arising which have been landfillled
% of the total tonnage of household waste arising which have been recycled
% of the total tonnage of household waste arising which have been sent for composting
% reduction of residual household waste per household
% treatment of waste
Average water use per employee per month
Average water used per amount of product manufactured
Gross cost of refuse collection per premise
Gross cost of refuse disposal per premise
Municipal waste by type of treatment
Municipal waste generated
Per capita daily domestic waste generation
Total domestic and process water
Total general waste (t/year)
Total generation of hazardous waste by economic activity
Total generation of non-hazardous waste by economic activity
Total generation of waste
Total generation of waste by economic activity
Total generation of waste by waste category
Total hazardous waste generated by households
Total non-hazardous waste generated by households
Total of office and operational waste
Total packaging waste
Total recycle target
Total waste
Total waste recycled
Total waste sent to landfill & incineration
Total water consumption (cubic meters per year)
Total water used as cooling water
Waste disposed of per amount of product manufactured

Wastewater

# of landfill of sewage sludge from urban waste water
# of methods of disposal of sewage sludge from urban waste water
# of wastewater overflows per 100 miles of wastewater main
% agricultural use of sewage sludge from urban waste water
% capacity of urban waste water treatment plants

40. Environment
% capacity of urban waste water treatment plants with advanced treatment
% composting of sewage sludge from urban waste water
% gap in processing municipal waste (household waste)
% incineration of sewage sludge from urban waste water
% of Ammonia in treated wastewater effluent
% of Biochemical Oxygen Demand (BOD) in treated wastewater effluent
% of citizen satisfaction with the wastewater treatment system
% of generation intensities of municipal waste
% of implement methane flaring at wastewater treatment facility
% of install anaerobic digester at wastewater treatment facility
% of population connected to independent waste water collecting systems: total
% of population connected to independent waste water collecting systems: with treatment
% of population connected to urban waste water collection systems: without treatment
% of population connected to urban waste water treatment: primary treatment
% of population connected to urban waste water treatment: secondary treatment
% of population connected to urban waste water treatment: tertiary treatment
% of population connected to urban waste water treatment: total
% of population connected to urban wastewater collecting systems: total
% of population connected to urban wastewater treatment with at least secondary treatment
% of urban waste water treatment with at least secondary treatment
% resident population connected to wastewater collection and treatment systems
% treatment capacity of waste water treatment plants
Sewage sludge production and disposal per capita
Sewer overflows per 100 miles of collection system piping
Total amount generated of municipal waste
Total generation and discharge of waste water
Total sewage sludge production and disposal
Total sewage sludge production from urban waste water
Wastewater treatment effectiveness rate

Water Sanitation
# of new appropriate sanitary facilities provided
# of new appropriate sanitary facilities provided in rural areas
# of new appropriate sanitary facilities provided in urban areas
# of wastewater management categorization
# of wastewater quality monitoring systems
# of wells identified in significant violation of regulations
% of identified waste disposal wells that are closed or permitted

40. Environment

% of population with access to improved sanitation, urban and rural

% of sewerage service availability (% pumping station running)

% population with sustainable access to improved sanitation

% providing the community with sewerage services

% recycling (TSE and sludge)

% regulatory compliance

Average distribution per area per user

Population with adequate sanitary facilities (as % of total population)

Population with adequate sanitary facilities (as % of total population) in rural areas

Population with adequate sanitary facilities (as % of total population) in urban areas

Total cost of sanitation

Volume of treated water produced (m3) by commercial utilities

Waste projection (ton/day)

Waste water treatments plants network coverage in % of population served

41. Governance

Central Administration

of citizen contact center calls

# of emergency calls

# of government departments with a service delivery charter

# of public disclosure requests processed

# of records retrieval requests

# of total telephone calls placed to the "1-800-" call center requesting assistance

% of benefit payments processed in accordance with the relevant legislation compared with # of applications received

% of customers' perception of service quality

% of government departments where payroll management and establishment control is operational

% of government departments with staffing complements appropriate to their agreed mandates

% of government employees whose salaries is described as being "Performance Based"

% of letter mail processed at discounted postage rates as measured by the mail management system

% of major permits issued within one year of receiving a complete permit application

% of non-tax fiscal notes completed during the legislative session in comparison to # requested

% of performance related pay in use by all gov. entities

% of retirement certifications issued within five working days of initial request

41. Governance
% of savings generated by the competitive bidding process measured by comparing the bid selected to highest bid
% of state garage vehicle repairs completed correctly
% of time application development project work is delivered within documented time
% of time finance data warehouse services are available for customer usage
% of time finance services are available for customer usage
Cost per member to administer
Cost per mile of motor pool as a % of private vehicle cost benchmark
Total amount of restitution, savings and other financial benefits to consumers

Citizen Services

of days to start a business (days)
# of firms supported by new legislations
# of Km of backlog of roads eradicated
# of trips per capita on public busses
% of all requests for assets and mutual aid assistance handled successfully
% of citizen satisfaction with services provided
% of households with access to basic or higher levels of electricity
% satisfaction score from all customers and stakeholders for the provision of customer service
Gross cost of street lighting per lamp
Gross national happiness (GNH)
Rating of doing business is supported by regulations (on a scale of 0 -10)
Rating of government decisions are effectively implemented (on a scale of 0 - 10)
Rating of legal and regulatory framework that encourages competitiveness of enterprises (on a scale from 0 - 10)

City Council

of applicants for board/commission positions
# of board/commission positions filled
# of legislative issues tracked
# of regional committees or organizations on which council members participate
% of citizens rating city as "good" or "excellent" place to live
% of citizens saying city is heading in the right direction
% of items approved by council on consent calendar
% of registered voters compared to eligible voters
% turnout for local elections
Average voting age participation
Average voting age participation in election

Community Council

of council agenda items analyzed and scheduled on calendar
# of council for the arts grant awards
# of courtesy hearings held

41. Governance

of issues advocated before city council

# of public hearings held

# of referrals receives annually concerning the well-being of children

# of regular meetings held

% of cases that are closed within six months of opening

% of counties served by the council

% of resolutions adopted approving city Council land use decisions

% of schools that made adequate yearly progress

Average attendance record

Council Support

of contracts and documents processed

# of council agenda items analyzed and scheduled in packet

% of citizen issues/complaints resolved within 10 days

% of customers rating service at the satisfied to very satisfied level

% of targeted records available on reference server

Equal Opportunity Commission

of coverage of the fair employment practices

# of education, training, and outreach activities performed

% between human rights cases reported and investigated

% of employment discrimination complaints investigated within 90 days

% of key decision making positions in the civil service that are occupied by women

% of successful performance evaluations done

Government Decentralization

of devolved functions undertaken by the local authority

# of housing units constructed by local authorities

# of surveys of local councils to ascertain local governments views on the departments services

# of valuation roles updated on an annual basis

% annual increase in direct transfers to local authorities

Average cost per council of providing the different types of service

Value of revenues accruing to local authorities from collection

Government Efficiency

% of correspondence replied to on time

Bureaucracy rating

Employment-housing equilibrium index

Government effectiveness rate

Hindrance to business activity from bureaucracy (scale of 0 -10)

Independence of public service from political interference (scale of 0 -10)

Raring of ease of doing business with government agencies

Rating of bureaucracy (hinder business activity)

Satisfaction level with services provided

Hearing Office

of administrative appeals of civil violations appealed to Superior Court

41. Governance

- # of land use matters heard
- # of other civil violations processed
- # of sign code violations processed
- % of hearing examiner decisions delivered within 10 days
- Average # of matters assigned per Hearing Examiner

Insurance Commissioner

- # of cases against insurance companies, agents, and other licensees
- # of licensed insurance companies
- # of suspected criminal fire investigations
- % of penalties collected from violators
- Funds recovered on behalf of consumers and health care practitioners

Internal Control

- # of internal control improvement initiatives, within measurement period
- # of major internal control breaches
- Average time between internal control deficiency occurrence and reporting

Openness & Transparency

- # of agencies that produce audited accounts and performance reports which are accessible to the public
- # of entities whose accounts are audited and reported publicly
- # of verifiable interactions between top government officials and their constituencies/citizens
- # of website page views by citizens
- % of entities with risk management framework implemented
- % of government entities audited / year
- Rating of transparency level (citizen survey)
- Rating of transparency of government policymaking

Planning & Accountability

- # of improvement projects successfully launched and achieving results
- # of performance audits completed
- % of agencies that meet established requirements (strategic plans, performance plans, link to enterprise plan and performance measures)
- % of employees covered by and assessed against individual performance contracts
- % of government entities that have adopted a full scale individual performance management system
- % of recommendations from the Public accounts committee that have adequate action taken by responsible government institution

Regulation & Compliance

- # of audit reports issued
- # of controls to avoid corruption
- # of regulatory or legal noncompliance events
- # of subprograms that completed mandated or requested projects by specified guidelines
- % completion of new laws identified for drafting

41. Governance
% of actuarial investigations issued on or before the statutorily mandated deadline
% of appeal board claims process accurately
% of appeal board claims processed within 3 weeks
% of cases resolved within 6 months of filing
% of county government rates certified
% of external peer reviews that determines the department performs its engagements accurately and in compliance with standards
% of inspector general recommendations implemented by agencies
% of internal quality assurance reviews that determines the department performs its engagements accurately and in compliance with standards
% of investigations and preliminary inquiries completed within a six-month period
% of legal and regulatory framework implementation
% of major non-compliance issues unclosed / year
% of recommendations from performance audits that were implemented as determined by follow-up reviews
% of requests for Appeal Board information delivered accurately
% of requests for Appeal Board information delivered within 7 days
% of school aid payments that are accurate
% of school aid payments that are timely
% of school district rates certified
% of tax levies certified
% of unauthorized disclosures
Average time lag between new regulation and initiation of review
Average time taken to dispose of cases (criminal and civil) at each stage of the administration of justice process
Bribe payers Index
Corruption Perception Index
Rating of adaptability of government policy
Rating on bribing and corruption
Rating on government decisions are effectively implemented
Rating on policy direction of the government

Resource Management
# of audit exceptions contained in annual audit
# of citizens employed in the civil service
# of Km of backlog of storm water drainage systems eradicated
# of new creation of firms
# of non-core services privatized
# of reportable and non-reportable audit comments on the most recent report
# of time the city maintains the AA+ credit rating
% of citizens employed in the civil service
% of customers surveyed that rate us as meeting or exceeding expectations in billing experience

41. Governance

% of customers surveyed that rate us as meeting or exceeding expectations in notification/update experience

% of customers surveyed that rate us as meeting or exceeding expectations in quality assurance experience

% of customers surveyed that rate us as meeting or exceeding expectations in service installation experience

% of customers surveyed that rate us as meeting or exceeding expectations in service order experience

% of government spend on outside advice services

% of government tax collected

% of performance related pay for government employees

% of reports required submitted timely

% of results website measures trending in the desired direction

% of statutorily mandated sales ratio studies and reports available

Gross National Income (GNI)

Gross National Product (GNP)

Net National Income (NNI)

Net National Product (NNP)

Sovereign credit rating

Trade surplus (deficit)

42. Government Workforce

Appraisal & Performance

of electronic and hard copy publications accessed

# of employees receiving employee of the quarter awards

# of individual performance plans completed

# of national annual survey for government entity to evaluate the performance of the government workforce

# of occupational injury and illness rates

# of performance management integrated framework developed

# of performance meetings

# of services provided

% of completed appraisals out of the total # of the staff

% of completion of assessments of all existing staff members

% of design completion and implementation of the Performance Management System

% of individual assessments done

% of job competencies evaluated

% of performance management system completed

% of tasks completed successfully and on time

% satisfaction of employee with the performance appraisal

% workforce perceptions of government as equal opportunity employer

Average % of individual performance assessment results

Lost time accidents per 1000 employees

42. Government Workforce

Compensation & Rewards

# of time & attendance system is implemented in all government entities
% benefit checks written without error
% of participants who rate Benefits Plan as good or better
% of satisfied employees with Compensation & Rewards

Organization Excellence

# of annually reviews of the HR manual
# of communications plan for change
# of conducted HRM review by end of year
# of government entities that make use of core HR and HRMS modules
# of implemented ICT infrastructure & systems to support new HR initiatives tracking
# of implemented stakeholder communications plans
# of internal performance management systems
# of organizational improvement survey
# of proper HR performance management process documented
# of re-engineered HR Processes
# of resignation with reasons
# of revisions on structure approved
# of significant safety incidents (SSI)
% completion of authority matrix implementation
% completion of job descriptions and functional statements
% completion of new organizational structure
% development of new organizational processes
% employees satisfied with job
% employees satisfied with their developmental goals as per their performance appraisal
% employees which have received a performance assessment
% of completion of job descriptions
% of completion of the HR Strategy
% of employee satisfaction
% of internal structure and governance implemented
% of job descriptions include competency profiles
% of perceived attractiveness of employees amongst target groups
% of physical security at work location is satisfactory
% of roles/jobs have been given a performance appraisal annually
% of satisfied staff
% of the employees having a suitable working places and facilities
% response rate to employee survey
% staff turn-over
Average excellence award assessment score
Average score on employee job satisfaction surveys
Change readiness index
Employee satisfaction index

42. Government Workforce

Employee satisfaction rate

Employees overall satisfaction score

Lost time injury frequency rate

Retention rates

Policies & Standards

of bi-annual review of HR policy & procedures against HRM best practice

# of cases pending in appeal

# of external quality assurance audits of specific HRM elements each year

# of HR governance units & committees exist in all departments

# of implement organizational design manual to all departments

# of internal audit risk management assessment done

# of labor market policy changes suggested

# of new HR standards/policy proposals submitted for approval

% of complaints investigated

% of employed in the private sector

% of known complainants responded to

% unemployment among citizens

% unemployment among women

Time elapsed from hearing to decision

Time elapsed from petition to decision

Skills & Qualifications

of staff members professionally satisfied at work

# of work place accidents

% employee approved suggestions are implemented

% increase of local employees with technical skills

% of citizens in technical staff

% of competent senior managers

% of employees certified

% of practitioners hold a HRM certification

% of senior managers with computers

% of staff with professional qualification recognized globally

Average staff length of service

Rate of employee promotions

Staffing & Recruiting

of agencies and entities using websites for job vacancy posting and applicant tracking

# of applicants reviewed/processed

# of candidate assessments done through the assessment centre each year

# of career fairs attended and other outreach activities conducted

# of direct hire employees

# of job applicant in pool

# of job seekers provided with employment

# of labor contracts successfully negotiated and implemented

# of recruitment for new organization structure completed

42. Government Workforce
# of recruitments coordinated
# of re-registration of all existing job seekers completed
# of vacancies filled
% 'Data cleansing' of job seeker data base completed
% assessment of all existing job seekers completed
% change in # of jobs applied for on website
% composition of non white job applicants in the applicant pool who are interviewed
% employees relocated to permanent built office building
% employees relocated to temporary office building
% execution of recruitment plan within timeframe
% external counseling capacity in-sourced to achieve required operational capacity
% implementation of process 'Job seeker assessment'
% implementation of process 'Job seeker classification'
% implementation of process 'Job seeker counseling'
% implementation of process 'Job seeker matching'
% implementation of process 'Job seeker registration'
% increase of job applicants per annum
% of reduction of time to fill
% of achieved targets within yellow and green range
% of citizens among total # of employees direct hire
% of company data captured from all employer interfaces
% of core team positions vacant
% of detailed job seeker placement process documented
% of employees that voluntarily leave employment per year
% of high-level job seeker placement process documented
% of hiring authority survey ratings that indicate satisfied with the hiring process
% of implemented manpower reporting system
% of job seeker placed in private sector jobs
% of job vacancies captured and confirmed from all employer interfaces
% of management & technical positions filled
% of manpower plan completed
% of minorities promoted from total # of employees
% of minority candidates hired
% of new employee satisfaction ratio
% of positions are filled with internal postings
% of positions in new organizational structure that are filled
% of projected positions fulfilled
% of recruitment requirements fulfilled
% of reducing staff
% of required positions vacant
% of set-up of assessment facilities

42. Government Workforce
% of special needs employees
% of staff successfully redeployed internally and/or externally
% of staff turnover
% suitable organization structure developed
Attrition rate
Average # of applicants per recruitment
Average # of applicants per recruitment - internal recruitments
Average % of minority applicants per recruitment
Average employment period / per staff
Average weeks to fill a position
Employees retention rate 2 years and above
New employee turnover/attrition ratio
Retention rate of the skilled employees
Staff turnover %
Vacancy rate
Voluntary staff turnover

Training & Development

in-house training conducted by those attended external training
of conducted stakeholder / partner forums per year
# of employees receiving leadership development training
# of employees with 10 days training per year
# of graduates per year from training program
# of hits on HRM Knowledge Management Portal
# of hours training
# of HRM professional development training provided
# of increase scholarship candidates
# of knowledge sharing ideas generated per annum
# of knowledge sharing initiatives implemented
# of knowledge sharing programs developed and implemented
# of leaders performance plans completed
# of placement of existing staff members into other positions as per approved organization chart
# of professionals with access to HR knowledge management information
# of staff trained
# of trained citizen / per year
# of training classes facilitated or coordinated
# of training days implemented /# of training days planned
# of training days per employee per year
# of training days per staff member
# of training hours per employee
# of training opportunities provided
# of training programs aimed at developing staff implemented
# of trainings courses to # of staff
% achievement of training plan

42. Government Workforce

% career development plans developed for employees

% completion of training center plan

% employee satisfaction with training provided and able to implement the skills and knowledge learned

% employee training implemented per employee

% employees who have completed 10 days of appropriate specialized training

% employees who have received and completed their required and planned training

% employees with defined and approved career paths

% implementation of training records system

% increase in training offered per year

% individual performance assessment results

% management satisfaction with employee training levels

% of approved manager and above positions that have a succession plan

% of career development plans developed for leadership

% of competency based training completed

% of completion of training needs for each employees

% of employee satisfaction with training offered

% of employees in top management who have successfully completed leadership program

% of employees that attend 10 training days or more per calendar year

% of employees that attend role-relevant trainings and workshops

% of employees that underwent a training needs assessment

% of employees trained

% of employees who responded that their leadership skills improved due to development training

% of employees with complete development plans

% of employees' participations

% of evaluations that are current

% of execution of the proposed plan for training center

% of existing staff members for whom personal development plans have been created

% of health and safety procedures completed

% of implement a learning & development framework

% of implemented training programs in relation to the planned programs

% of knowledge management IT system implemented

% of learning & development programs are offered online

% of management personnel with career development plans

% of manpower plan completion

% of office employees are ICDL certified

% of participant evaluations of courses as helpful in performing the job

% of planned training programs designed and implemented

% of senior leadership undergoing training

% of staff satisfied with the quality of training

42. Government Workforce

% of staff satisfied with training mix

% of staff trained as per individual requirements

% of staff undergoing training

% of study leave participants have an career development plan

% of survey items rated as satisfactory by employees

% of survey items rated as satisfactory by HR managers

% of the employee training needs identified through the performance appraisals are met

% of training effectiveness

% of training plans established

% of training programs conducted vis a vis the individual personal development Plans

%of employees who have successfully completed at least 2 weeks training per year

Average # of training days / employee / year

Average hours of development training for staff per year

Average training spend per junior employee as identified in the staff development program

Average training spend per technical employee as identified in the staff development program

Competency investment ratio

Net increase in # of citizen women employed

Workforce Distribution

increase of special needs in management positions

increase of women in management positions

of 50+ of age as a % of total employees

# of citizen placed in public sector jobs

# of employees with special needs

# of handicapped working in the health system

# of people employed with special needs

# of public workforce by age bracket

# of public workforce by department/ entity

# of public workforce by gender

# of public workforce by level

# of public workforce by people with special needs

# of public workforce, by department/ entity - Total

# of total workforce

% increase of staff across various industries in private and public sectors

% national employees

% of classification and position reviews delivered within established timeframes

% of disabled people employed in public services

% of employees who are white

% of professional positions filled by citizens

% of public workforce by age bracket

42. Government Workforce

% of public workforce by department/ entity
% of public workforce by gender
% of public workforce by level
% of public workforce by nationality
% of public workforce by special needs
% of public workforce by specialty
% of special needs employments
% of staff that are minorities
% of stations in which resource allocation model has been implemented
% of technical staff who are female
% of total force deployed as front line, service delivery members
% of unemployment
% of women in senior positions
% special needs employees to total employees
% women employees to total employees
Ratio of employees to supervisor
Ratio of non-HR employees divided by HR employees
Span of control supervisor-employees
Workforce distribution index

43. Healthcare

Addiction

% of adults who are current smokers
% of high school youth who are current smokers
% of middle school youth who are current smokers
% of patients/clients substance free six- months following discharge from treatment
% of successfully discharged clients reporting no wagering in last 30 days (gambling treatment)

Causes of Death

of deaths
# of deaths - standardized death rate (per 100,000 inhabitants)
# of deaths by region - crude death rate (per 100,000 inhabitants)
# of deaths by region - crude death rate (per 100,000 inhabitants) - females
# of deaths by region - crude death rate (per 100,000 inhabitants) - males
# of deaths by region - crude death rate (per 100,000 inhabitants) - total
# of deaths by region - standardized death rate (per 100,000 inhabitants)
# of deaths by region- absolute # (3 years average) - females
# of deaths by region- absolute # (3 years average) - males
# of deaths by region- absolute # (3 years average) - total
# of teen deaths due to suicide
% of deaths due to accidents
% of deaths due to AIDS (HIV-disease)
% of deaths due to alcoholic abuse

43. Healthcare

% of deaths due to cancer

% of deaths due to chronic liver disease

% of deaths due to diabetes mellitus

% of deaths due to diseases of the nervous system

% of deaths due to drugs dependence

% of deaths due to homicide, assault

% of deaths due to ischaemic heart diseases

% of deaths due to pneumonia

% of deaths due to suicide

% of deaths due to transport accidents

% of deaths rate due to chronic diseases

Suicide death rate - females

Suicide death rate - males

Suicide death rate - total

Suicide rates and per capita GDP: GDP per capita

Suicide rates and per capita GDP: suicide rate

Suicide rates by gender: both men and women

Suicide rates by gender: men

Suicide rates by gender: women

Suicides rates and subjective life-evaluations: suicide rates

Child & Adult Protection

of deaths due to unintentional injuries

# of students & professionals participating in sexual & domestic violence prevention programs

# of substantiated maltreatment incidents

with brain injury that get information about living with it & preventing secondary disabilities

% distribution of deaths among children under 5

% of autopsy reports completed within 90 days from date of death

% of children receiving immunization/vaccination

% of fully immunized children under one year of age in 20 worst performing districts

% of initial assessments for children's social care carried out within 7 working days of referral

% of maltreatment incidents that were victims of a separate maltreatment incident within the past 6 months

% reduction rate of infant deaths

% using child safety seats

% with disabilities satisfied or very satisfied with life

Emergency Management

% implementation of multi-stakeholder action-plan to implement integrated command centre

% of all ambulance calls responded to in less than 16 minutes

% of all paramedics fully licensed to practice according to international standards

43. Healthcare

% of ambulance calls that submit a patient care report

% of categories of emergencies in the health system that have been reviewed by international accreditation institutions

% of emergency categories that have been drilled in each region

% of local public health agencies that participate in an annual test of emergency response plans

% of patients meeting the criteria of trauma protocol transported to a trauma care facility in 30 minutes or less

Ambulance response time in minutes

Average # of deficiencies per EMS site.

Environmental Hazards

of direct consultations provided to local boards of health or environmental health practitioners annually

% of children under the age of 6 years that receive a blood lead test

% of lead-tested children who are lead poisoned (^{3}10 micrograms/decilite)

Food & Nutrition

% of prevalence iron deficiency (6– 59 months)

% of prevalence Vitamin A deficiency (6– 59 months)

% of women attending ante-natal classes who are malnourished

Health Awareness

of authorized and promoted medical-scientific research projects

# of incidence of tuberculosis (per 100 000 population per year)

# of incident of communicable and non communicable diseases

# of preventative programs

# of public health priority areas where measurable improvement in mortality, morbidity, or behavior has been achieved and documented

% of births, death, and notifiable diseases accessible through secure 24/7 IT system within 12 hours of event/diagnosis

% of national population screened for cardiovascular risk factors

% of vaccination program that is fully accredited by the WHO

Pregnancy rate (per 1,000) among females ages 15-17

Health Expenditure

Average health expenditure per capita

Expenditure of health care functions by financing agents in health care, in %

Expenditure of health care functions by financing agents in health care, in millions

Expenditure of health care functions by financing agents in health care, per inhabitant

Expenditure of health care functions by providers of health care, in %

Expenditure of health care functions by providers of health care, in millions

Expenditure of health care functions by providers of health care, per inhabitant

Expenditure of providers of health care by financing agents in health care, in %

43. Healthcare

Expenditure of providers of health care by financing agents in health care, in millions

Expenditure of providers of health care by financing agents in health care, per inhabitant

Health care expenditure by financing agent

Health care expenditure by function

Health care expenditure by provider

Health care expenditure on long term care

Health care expenditure, in %

Health care expenditure, in millions

Health care expenditure, per inhabitant

Per capita total expenditure on health

Total cost of citizens going overseas for treatment by type of treatment over time

Total health expenditure on public hospitals

Health Professionals

of assistance to medical students

# of inhabitants per physician

# of licensed physicians

# of medical graduates, Per 1 000 practicing physicians

# of medical physicians across the country

# of medical professionals applying to join the health system (public and private)

# of medical school graduates enrolling in US or European board certified residency programs

# of medical students studying health topic

# of nationals training and working in allied health professions

# of nursing graduates per 1000 practicing nurses

# of physicians by age

# of physicians by medical specialty - # per 100,000 inhabitants

# of post graduate residency places in hospitals

# of practicing dentists

# of practicing physicians

# of professional accepted

# of professional applying to join the health system (public and private)

# of public health programs planned and conducted

% increase in # of citizens training and working in allied health professions

% increase in # of customer facing administrative staff working in hospitals and primary healthcare facilities

% increase in # of medical school graduates enrolling in US or European board certified residency programs

% increase in # of medical students studying abroad

% increase in # of post graduate residency places in hospitals

% of all employees participate in at least 3 days professional training per year

43. Healthcare

% of credentialed and privileged physicians and healthcare professionals

% of physicians who have met minimum ongoing training requirements

% of standards pertaining to the licensing of health professionals and providers are defined and published

Attrition rate (the turnover rate of medical staff in both public and private institutions)

Health personnel (excluding nursing and caring professionals) - # per 100,000 inhabitants

Health personnel (excluding nursing and caring professionals) - % per 100,000 inhabitants

Health personnel by region - # per 100,000 inhabitants

Health personnel by region - % per 100,000 inhabitants

Nursing and caring professionals - # per 100,000 inhabitants

Nursing and caring professionals - % per 100,000 inhabitants

Physicians by medical specialty - % per 100,000 inhabitants

Turnover rate of medical staff in private institutions

Turnover rate of medical staff in public institutions

Health Research

of conferences hosted and attended

# of licensed healthcare providers submit mandated raw data to allows tracking of system performance indicators

# of publication made

# of research projects being undertaken

# of research projects funded and undertaken

% mortality data consistently collected

% of date set for mobilization of new integrated command centre prepared and endorsed by hospitals and other relevant healthcare facilities

% of hospital acquired infection rates data consistently collected

% readmission data consistently collected

Total expenditure on health R&D (%of GDP)

Total expenditure on health R&D (US$)

Health Services

of health insurance providers introduce bonuses to providers with above average customer satisfaction ratings

# of hospitals integrated with electronic appointment system

# of magnetic resonance imaging units, per million population

# of medical facilities across the country

# of overseas treatment of citizens

# of patients on waiting lists

# of services for disabled children

% cost of overseas treatment quality

% hospital acquired infection rates data consistently collected by major diagnostic categories

% of accredited private facilities

43. Healthcare

% of all hospital beds managed by internationally experienced hospital groups

% of all staffing decisions based on market availability of qualified employees

% of deliveries assisted by midwives, nurses, doctors or clinical officers

% of health infrastructure that meets the needs of society

% of long term care complaints resolved

% of new healthcare related infrastructure financed and developed by the private sector

% of population very confident of getting high-quality care

% reduction of paper consumption

Average waiting times for key services

Breast cancer screening - mammography - by age (%)

Breast cancer screening - mammography - by educational level (%)

Cervical cancer screening by age (%)

Cervical cancer screening by educational level (%)

Consultation of a dentist during the past 12 months, by age (%)

Consultation of a dentist during the past 12 months, by sex (%)

Consultation of a medical doctor during the past 12 months, by age (%)

Consultation of a medical doctor during the past 12 months, by sex (%)

Day-patient hospitalization during the past 12 months, by age (%)

Day-patient hospitalization during the past 12 months, by sex (%)

In-patient hospitalization during the past 12 months, by age (%)

In-patient hospitalization during the past 12 months, by sex (%)

Process times for key services

Total cost of medical assistance

Total external dollars leveraged by Distinguished Cancer Clinicians and Scientists (in millions)

Total health expenditure by private sector

Health Services Access

of agencies that have received technical assistance, resources, or training that report progress towards increasing cultural competency

# of agreements between hospitals and other health facilities

# of beds per 1000 population and by category (primary, maternity, intensive, mental)

# of involved private investors in hospital construction projects

# of licensed hospital beds per 1'000 population versus G-7 Country average

# of medical facilities across the country

# of medical services across the country

# of patients accessing primary care centers

# of patients awaiting treatment (both elective and acute) by facility

# of patients awaiting treatment (both elective and acute) by specialty

# of people with unmet needs for dental examination

# of people with unmet needs for medical examination

# of physicians across the country

43. Healthcare

of practicing physicians density per 1000 population (head counts)

of the people living further than 25 minutes by car from nearest primary care facility

% of all infrastructure decisions based on financial feasibility assessment

% of core assessments for children's social care that were carried out within 35 working days of their commencement

% of eligible low income and uninsured provided access to cancer treatment services through the cancer aid program

% of families of adult consumers with developmental disabilities whose lives have improved as a result of supported community services

% of GP offer at least two alternative providers

% of initial assessments for children's social care carried out within 7 working days of referral

% of medical insurance coverage

% of patients on waiting lists for top-10 elective procedures

% of underserved & vulnerable citizens with access to health care services through community health centers

% reduction of citizens traveling abroad for treatment not available in country

% reduction of citizens traveling abroad or diagnostics not available in country

% reduction of hospital stays by type of treatment

% reduction of the population living further than 25 minutes by car from nearest primary care facility

% reduction of waiting times for top ten elective in- and out-patient specialist consultations

% reduction waiting times of top ten elective in and out patient consultations

% specialty service lines with average 12-months occupancy of specialty hospital beds in excess of 95%

Total # of beds

Utilization rate of medical facilities

Healthcare Providers

of care beds in hospitals

# of hospital beds

# of psychiatric care beds in hospitals

% mortality data consistently collected by major diagnostic categories

% of facilities achieving internationally recognized accreditation

% of total # of pay-rolled working days lost through sick-leave or disability reason

% readmission data consistently collected by major diagnostic categories

Hospital beds - # per 100,000 inhabitants

Hospital beds - % per 100,000 inhabitants

Medical technology - # per 100,000 inhabitants

Medical technology - % per 100,000 inhabitants

43. Healthcare

Healthy Population

of activity status by severity of disability

# of assistance needed for those with disability

# of assistance provided among those with disability (and employed)

# of causes of disability by economic activity

# of child deaths per 100,000 children age 1-14 years (child death rate)

# of estimated TB deaths (all forms)

# of infant deaths per 1000 live births (infant mortality rate)

# of salmonella infections

# of severities of disability

# of types of assistance needed

# of types of assistance provided

# of types of disability

% of adults eating five fruits & vegetables a day

% of adults participating in moderate physical activities for 30 minutes or more five or more times a week

% of adults rating their own health at good to excellent

% of adults with a BMI

% of children born with very low birth weight

% of children served by Title V who report a medical home, excluding children with special health care needs

% of disability by activity status

% of disability by economic activity

% of disability by education level

% of disability by marital status

% of disability by occupation

% of disability by region

% of medical aid-enrolled children, ages 1-5 years that receive any dental service

% of neighborhood residents often walk for exercise

% of people having a long-standing illness or health problem

% of people having a short-standing illness or health problem

% of people who drunk any alcohol the past 12 months by age

% of people who drunk any alcohol the past 12 months by sex

% of public health nursing & home health aide clients with congestive heart failure (CHF) who were not hospitalized due to an acute episode of CHF

% of total death caused by cancer

% of total death caused by cardiovascular disease

% of total death caused by communicable disease

% of total death caused by injury

% of total death caused by other chronic disease

% of workforce walking to work

% smokers by age

% with activity restriction for at least the past 6 months

43. Healthcare
Activity restriction for at least the last 6 months by sex (%)
Activity restriction for at least the last 6 months, by age (%)
Body mass index (BMI) by age (%)
Body mass index (BMI) by sex (%)
Cutdown in activities over the past two weeks because of health problems (%)
Distribution of deaths among children under 5 (by %) (for Diarrhoeal diseases, Pneumonia and Injuries)
Duration (in years) since onset of disability by cause of disability
Exercise rates
Government expenditure on health as % of total expenditure on health
Healthy life expectancy
Human development index
Infant mortality rate (per 1 000 live births) both sexes
Maternal mortality rate (per 100,000 live births)
Mortality rate by cause (per 100,000 population) (non- communicable diseases, cardio vascular, cancer, injuries)
Registration coverage of birth (%)
Self-perceived health by sex, age and income quintile (%)
Under-5 mortality rate (probability of dying by age 5 per 1000 live births) both sexes

HIV & AIDS

# of HIV+ pregnant women receiving a complete course of ARV prophylaxis
# of persons with advanced HIV infection on ART
# of workplaces with developed workplace policies and programs for HIV and AIDS
tested for HIV at VCT and receiving the test results
Amount of funds spent on HIV and AIDS in the past 12 months
Reduce rate of deaths due to HIV infection
Reduction in # of new HIV infections

Immunization

# of cases of vaccine-preventable diseases
% of children receiving immunization/ vaccination
% of members in families receiving annual health check screens and immunizations
% of two-year old children adequately immunized
% one-year-olds immunized with MCV
% one-year-olds immunized with three doses of diphtheria tetanus toxoid and pertussis (DTP3) (%)
% one-year-olds immunized with three doses of Hepatitis B (HepB3) (%)
% one-year-olds immunized with three doses of Hib (Hib3) vaccine (%), 2006

Leisure & Recreation

# of arrivals of non-resident tourists in hotels and similar establishments and at borders
Average leisure time across activities: other average leisure activities

43. Healthcare

Average leisure time across activities: participating and attending events
Average leisure time across activities: sports
Average leisure time across activities: TV or radio at home
Average leisure time across activities: visiting or entertaining friends
Average leisure time across demographic groups: ages 15-24
Average leisure time across demographic groups: ages 25-44
Average leisure time across demographic groups: ages 45-64
Average leisure time across demographic groups: ages 65 and over
Average leisure time across demographic groups: men
Average leisure time across demographic groups: total
Average leisure time across demographic groups: women
Government expenditure on recreation and culture
Household and government expenditure on recreation and culture

Life Expectancy

Infant mortality
Life expectancy at birth: men
Life expectancy at birth: total
Life expectancy at birth: women

Medical Insurance

of additional non-medical aid eligible family members with health insurance
# of children who are enrolled in medical aid expansion
# of medical aid-eligible individuals who use employer provided insurance
% decrease in ER visits for members receiving disease management and administrative services
% decrease in hospital days for members receiving disease management and administrative services
% decrease in hospital stays for members receiving disease management and administrative services
% health insurers offering products with bonuses to providers with above average customer satisfaction ratings and performance
% increase in collections of medical aid overpayments
% increase in member satisfaction with administration of medical aid program over prior year
% increase in provider satisfaction with medical aid provider services over prior year, based on survey results
% increase over the prior year in medical aid revenue collections from third parties
% of 15 month old children on medical aid with six well-child visits
% of all expats enrolled in health insurance plan with licensed health insurer
% of care enrollees who smoke
% of care members who access preventive health services
% of children on medical aid with a dental visit
% of children under 18 with health insurance coverage
% of citizens enrolled in comprehensive health insurance plan

43. Healthcare

% of claims paid within 30 days of initial receipt

% of clean medical aid claims accurately paid or denied on time

% of core business processes online

% of cost for insured patients recovered from health insurances

% of counties covered under at least one of the health plans

% of enrollees in consumer directed plan options

% of medical aid members with asthma where appropriate medications are used

% of members aware of medical aid Member Services

% of members receiving medical aid program services whose income is validated during the eligibility process

% of members who pay premiums or declare a hardship exemption

% of population covered by the medical insurance scheme and commentary on major gaps

% of women on medical aid receiving prenatal care from the first trimester

Reduced cost for medical aid resulting for Medicare and medical aid eligible's

Savings from medical aid surveillance and utilization review compared to contract cost

Savings from medical aid utilization and care management strategies

Mental Health

of hours per 1,000 patient hours spent in restraint or seclusion

% of all patients admitted that show an improvement in their ability to function

% of consumers who are not readmitted within 180 days following moving from the facility

% of consumers with a severe and persistent mental health condition receiving psychiatric inpatient services

% of MHI clients (or their guardians) who self-report they are satisfied with the treatment and services received during their stay

% of MHI clients who are not readmitted within 30 days of discharge

% of the children served that live in the family home

Mental health agency per capita spending

Obesity

of overweight population aged 15 or more

# of overweight population aged 15 or more: females

# of overweight population aged 15 or more: males

% obese population aged 15 or more

% obese population aged 15 or more: females

% obese population aged 15 or more: males

% of overweight population aged 15 or more

% of overweight population aged 15 or more: females

% of overweight population aged 15 or more: males

Decrease obesity rates for children

Total obesity Rate

43. Healthcare

Patient Choice

of GP elective referral situations in which GP offers at least two alternatives and describes trade-offs to patient
% of health professionals in licensed facilities for whom/which licensing status is published on public website
% of health system users surveyed
% of top ten specialties for which standardized/adjusted mortality, readmission, and infection rates are published

Public Health Risks

of incident of certain diseases in the country
# of Malaria case fatality rate among children below five years
# of Plague, West Nile Virus, and Hantavirus Outbreaks
# of Syphilis cases per 100,000 Population
% of infants vaccinated
% of seniors (65+) lacking flu vaccination
Cardiac arrest survival rate
Diabetes rates
Mortality rate by cause
Mortality rate by cause (per 100,000 population)
Mortality rates
Sexually transmitted disease rates
Smokers between 15 and 24
Smokers by # of cigarettes (%)
Smokers by gender

Regulation & Compliance

of healthcare inspection team members
# of neutral assessment by independent third party
# of shortcomings identified by inspection services followed up with appropriate enforcement measures
% of cases resolved within one year of receiving a complaint
% of health care provider inspections in which serious shortcomings are identified
% of licenses & certificates mailed to applicants within three working days after eligibility requirements are met
% of private sector healthcare providers inspected at least twice yearly
% of public sector healthcare providers inspected at least twice yearly
Average # of hours spent onsite auditing per facility
Average # of months between audits for care facilities
Rate of collection for moneys owed to care facility residents

Resource Management

% of contracts requiring a corrective amendment
% of facilities passing regular inspections and failure reasons
% of health statistics data requests delivered on or before target date
% of information management projects completed on or before target date
% of organizational operations issues rated positively by employee

43. Healthcare

Health expenditure as % of GDP

Spread of Disease

of infectious disease consultations provided to clinicians, local public health officials, hospital infection-control staff, & the public.

% of all children aged 19-35 months fully immunized

% of cases with an early diagnosis (HIV cases that did not convert to AIDS within 12 months)

% of children served in public sector clinics that are fully immunized by 24 months of age.

% of disease reports that are sent out to local public health for follow-up within 48 hours of receiving them

% of TB patients who complete treatment in 12 months.

Total cost of each program over time

Steering of Patients

of discharges from hospitals

# of hospital days of in-patients

# of hospital days of in-patients - females

# of hospital days of in-patients - males

# of main surgical operations and procedures performed in hospitals

% of non-emergency in-patients admitted via ER

% reduction of patients triaged CTAS levels 4 & 5 using ERs

% reduction of unnecessary bed days

% reduction of unnecessary procedures

Average length of stay

Hospital discharges by diagnosis, day cases, total #

Hospital discharges by diagnosis, day cases, total # females

Hospital discharges by diagnosis, day cases, total # males

Hospital discharges by diagnosis, in-patients, # Total

Hospital discharges by diagnosis, in-patients, per 100,000 inhabitants

Hospital discharges by diagnosis, in-patients, per 100,000 inhabitants - females

Hospital discharges by diagnosis, in-patients, per 100,000 inhabitants - males

Hospital discharges by diagnosis, in-patients, per 100,000 inhabitants - Total

Hospital discharges by diagnosis, in-patients, total #

Hospital discharges by diagnosis, in-patients, total # females

Hospital discharges by diagnosis, in-patients, total # males

In-patient average length of stay (in days)

In-patient average length of stay (in days) - females

In-patient average length of stay (in days) - males

Veterans Homes

increase in veterans receiving healthcare benefits

increase of filled beds in the domiciliary

increase of nursing care beds filled

increase of volunteer hours worked

43. Healthcare

of residents who successfully participate in the community program

% increase of resident satisfaction with housekeeping services

% increase of routine work orders that are completed within 3 days

% increase resident satisfaction with preparation, variety and taste of food

% of residents indicating an overall satisfaction with Veterans services

% reduction of medication dispensing errors

% reduction of residents receiving 9 or more medications

% reduction of residents who are affected by the behaviors of other residents

% reduction of residents who are obese

% reduction of residents who have moderate or severe pain

% reduction of residents with little or no activity

% reduction of the medication administration error rate per every 10,000 doses.

Reduce resident fall rate

Vocational Rehabilitation

of persons able to continue to live independently in their homes

# of persons with disabilities that achieve startup or expansion of a business

% of claims accurately determined per standards

% of persons meeting their goals

Access to services ratio of minority to non-minority clients

Youth Inactivity

of youths aged between 15 and 19 who are not in education nor in employment: females

# of youths aged between 15 and 19 who are not in education nor in employment: males

44. Human Services

Child & Family Protection

of children served by children-at-home program

# of children who do not experience re-abuse for at least 6-months from a previous occurrence.

# of community-level leadership programs held

# of finalized adoptions from foster care

# of kids served in aftercare program

# of people receiving personal assistance support

# of youth leaving paid foster care at 18 receiving medical aid

# of youth participating in post-secondary education/training or employed

% of adoptions finalized within 24 months of removal from home (timely adoption)

% of adults served in the community vs. congregate settings

% of all active child support cases that have a court order establishing the legal obligation of both parents to provide for the financial support of the child(ren)

44. Human Services

% of all child support owed in the current fiscal year which is collected in the current fiscal year

% of care facilities in compliance

% of cases with monthly face-to-face visit with child

% of cases with paternity established so that children have two parents legally responsible for their care

% of child support payments processed within 2 business days of receipt

% of children adopted timely

% of children exiting foster care who are re-unified with their families within 12 months from last removal from home (re-unification).

% of children re-unified timely

% of children safe from re-abuse

% of children served who remain at home

% of children who do not experience re-abuse for at least 6-months from a previous occurrence

% of children who do not re-enter foster care within 12 months of last foster care episode (re-entry)

% of community teen pregnancy and parenting grantees that do not have an increase in live births to mothers under age 18

% of complaint investigations initiated within required timeframes of 20 working days of receipt

% of founded cases of dependent adult abuse in long-term care facilities

% of maltreatment assessments that are initiated in a timely fashion

% of parents having monthly face-to-face visits with their caseworker

% of parents who maintain and improve the level of financial support to their children

% of parents who maintain or improve the frequency of visits with their children

% of reports submitted to the court within specified timeframes

% of resettled refugees placed in a job with health benefits available within 6 months of placement

% of surveys successfully completed within timeframe

Annual # of adults served through county funded programs

Annual # of children served in family support programs

Average monthly # youth with a self sufficiency plan

Average rating of the nursing home satisfaction questionnaire regarding the skill and professionalism of staff

Average score of teen pregnancy prevention participant responses to survey questions relating to abstinence and likelihood of postponing sex

Average wage for refugees placed in full time employment

Rate of confirmed child abuse (per thousand)

Rate of maltreatment for families referred to community care

Ratio of the average # of months between nursing facility surveys in comparison with timeframe guidelines.

Total child support collections

44. Human Services

Deaf Services

% of community services that become accessible after receiving assistance

% of primary customers (deaf, hard of hearing, deaf blind and late deafened people) have access to government services

% of primary customers who are deaf

% of primary customers who are deaf blind

% of primary customers who are late deafened people

% of primary customers who are satisfied with information and assistance provided

% of primary customers who gain access after receiving assistance

% of primary customers who report being prepared to self advocate

% of primary customers who report having independent living skills

% of primary customers with hard of hearing

Elder Affairs

of clients being discharged due to institutionalization or death

# of elders assisted though the senior living trust to continue living in their own homes

# of facilities which resolve 60% or more of identified resident issues

# of registered clients receiving assistance

% increase in savings from medical aid pharmacy cost saving strategies

% increase in the complaint resolution rate

% increase revenues available through the department for aging programs and services to elderly

% of dollars transferred through reconciliation or passthrough

% of elder per 1000 who access one or more services

% of high nutrition risk congregate meals and nutrition counseling clients who maintained or improved risk scores

% of high nutrition risk home delivered meals clients who maintained or improved risk scores.

% of long-term care resources devoted to home and community based care

% of medical aid members who are aware of available preventive health care resources

% of participants who receive employment in private business that lasts at least six months

% per 1000 of 60+ benefiting from one or more home and community bases service compared to previous years

Compare the ratio of confirmed abuse cases in initiative counties compared to non-initiative counties

Grant writing efforts represent as % of the annual fiscal year revenue

Increase % the ratio of expenditures for medical aid compared to those for medical aid Institutional for persons 65+

Maintain or improve the ratio of 65+ on medical aid

Maintain the rate of elder per 1000 reported to have received service through assistance and outreach

44. Human Services

Rate of 60+ persons per 1000 receiving congregate meals, home delivered meals or nutrition counseling

Rate of growth in pharmacy costs per member per month

Rate/1000 of 60+ persons receiving preventative health services

Family Assistance

of child care slots available

# of community action agencies participating

# of families receiving food assistance

# of households receiving food assistance

# of households served

# of providers at level 2 or higher in quality rating system

# of registered child development homes

% births to unmarried women

% of children and adults with access to managed care

% of children who are in regulated settings

% of families who leave and remain off assistance program for at least 12-months (recidivism rate)

% of households increasing their resources

% of households staying current on utility bill

% of 's population served

% of vulnerable people who are supported to maintain independent living

Average household benefit

Average monthly # of children served in child care assistance

Average monthly # of enrollees in medical aid

Average monthly # of families receiving assistance

Average monthly # of people served through food banks and soup kitchens

Average monthly # of people served through supplemental commodities

Hourly rate of earned income for families exiting assistance program due to income reasons

Monthly average # of elderly receiving food assistance

The average monthly # of children served in child care assistance for the fiscal year

Foster Care

% of adoptions finalized within six months of placement

% of children exiting foster care for adoption within 24 months of their last removal from home

% of children with substantiated reports of maltreatment that have a repeated report within six months

% of foster care children who have 2 or fewer moves in the first year after removal (placement stability)

% of foster care population who were discharged from a previous foster care placement in the past 12 months

% of foster required reviews conducted within specified timeframes

% of youth that turn age 18 in foster care with medical insurance

Median # of placements for a foster child within a 12-month period

44. Human Services
Total dollars collected per $1 of expenditures

Homeless
# of all homeless
# of chronically homeless individuals declines in %
# of cities on track to meet the goal of reducing homelessness by %
# of homeless - chronic homeless
# of homeless - domestic violence victims
# of homeless - dually diagnosed
# of homeless - elderly
# of homeless - families with minor children
# of homeless - farm workers
# of homeless - HIV/AIDS
# of homeless - in emergency shelter
# of homeless - in permanent supportive housing for formally homeless persons
# of homeless - in transitional housing
# of homeless - living outside/in car
# of homeless - mentally disabled
# of homeless - persons with substance abuse problems
# of homeless - physically disabled
# of homeless - sex offenders
# of homeless - single persons
# of homeless - veterans
# of homeless - youth
# of households at immediate-risk of homelessness who maintain their housing
% of formerly homeless individuals who remain housed in permanent housing projects for at least 6 months
% of homeless persons exiting the service system in one year and back to it subsequent year
% of homeless persons identified in a calendar year placed in affordable permanent housing
% of homeless persons identified in a calendar year placed in transitional housing
% of homeless persons who have moved from transitional housing into permanent housing
% of need for affordable housing not met
% of the population living in counties on track to reduce homelessness by %
% of total need for permanent supportive housing met
% of total need for transitional housing beds met
% satisfaction of homeless persons receiving housing/services
Average days between identification of a homeless person and their placement in transitional or permanent housing
Employment rate of persons exiting homeless assistance projects
Satisfaction of local government/non-profits providing homeless services

44. Human Services

Special Needs

of blind persons employed
# of citizenship & cultural Programs yearly
# of new centers or units
# of people with disability
% of disability benefit determinations shown to be correct in federal quality reviews
% of employed citizens with special needs
% of empowered family
% of empowered minors
% of integrated special needs in society
% of labor performed by individuals who are legally blind
% of new blind vendors
% of orphans integrated
% of patients with a physical disability who demonstrate an increase in functional gain between admission and discharge
% of people with special need not integrated in society
% of people with special need who attained formal education
% of public facilities and major private organization that accommodate citizens with special needs
% of return on investment on minor funds
% of returns on the investment of minors' money
% of served family
% of special needs labor force
% of students enrolled in schools
% of students with special need who attained the mainstream schools.
% of working age people with disabilities from total economically active population
Average time in days for processing a federal disability claim
Special needs unemployment rate

45. Information Technology

Applications Services

of applications
# of IT design completion & construction commencement
% of customers rating level of consulting services for business analysis and system design as good to excellent
% of customers rating the maintenance and support provided for their application(s) as good to excellent

Desktop Support

of PCs supported / # of technicians
% of customers rating satisfaction with desktop support services as good to excellent
% of Help Desk repair calls resolved at the time of the call

45. Information Technology

% of Help Desk repair calls resolved the next business day

% of Help Desk repair calls resolved within 4 hours

Government e-Services

of awards granted

# of deployed automated processes

# of e-Literacy programs implemented

# of enterprises using the Internet for interacting with public authorities

# of gov. employees with ICT certifications

# of individuals using the Internet for interacting with public authorities

# of IT concept designs per year

# of legal proposals submitted

# of users of central government portal

% of e-government availability (supply side)

% of e-government on-line availability

% of e-government usage by enterprises

% of e-government usage by enterprises (demand side)

% of e-government usage by individuals (demand side) in the last 3 months

% of e-government usage by individuals by gender

% of e-Services

% of IT business centre project completed

% of people aware of government service improvement program

Information technology expenditure as % of GDP

Information technology expenditure in millions

Level of Internet access (%)

ICT Capability

of employees trained

# of entities following information security policies and guidelines

# of hard-to-fill vacancies for ICT specialist jobs

# of ICT/IT specialists employed by enterprises

# of layers of information available on geographical information system platform

# of publications related to IT policies, standards and guidelines

# of training course on computer use

# of transactional services available on the Gov't Portal platform

# of ways of obtaining e-skills

% completion of IT procedures documentation

% demand for ICT skills

% E-skills of individuals

% IT project completion & implementation

% of enterprises where external suppliers performed ICT functions

% of enterprises who employed ICT/IT specialists

% of enterprises who provided training to develop/upgrade ICT skills of their personnel

45. Information Technology

% of enterprises who recruited or tried to recruit personnel for jobs requiring ICT skills

% of ICT competence in enterprises

% of IT government e-Procurement statistics available

% of users satisfied with shared contact centre services

% online public procurement

% public authorities present online

% staff not taken a computer course

Individuals' level of computer skills

Individuals' level of internet skills

ICT Industry

of advanced services

# of developments of broadband

# of public services e-Government

% adoption of ICT by businesses

% change of value added at current prices

% impact of adoption of ICT by business

% impact of ICT sector

% of households with access to the internet

% of persons employed with ICT specialist skills

% of persons employed with ICT user skills

% of the ICT personnel on total employment

% of the ICT sector on GDP

% point change in the share of ICT manufacturing in total manufacturing value added

% point change in the share of ICT services in total business services value added

% share of ICT manufacturing in total manufacturing value added

% share of ICT-related occupations in the total economy, broad definition

% share of other ICT services in total business services value added

% share of telecommunication services in total business services value added

% shares of ICT investment in non-residential fixed capital formation

Information Security

of complaints regarding breaches of customer privacy

# of days exhausted as a % of total days entitled of leave taken per employee

# of individuals having taken ICT security precautions within the last three months

# of information security-related risks at each significance level

# of repeat audit findings

% of backup operations that are successful

% of disclosures unauthorized

% of enterprises having taken ICT precautions

% of enterprises that have installed security devices on their PCs

45. Information Technology

% of enterprises that have updated security devices within the last three months

% of enterprises with Internet access having encountered security problems

% of individuals with Internet access having encountered security problems

% of information security policy deployment and adoption

% of information security risks for which satisfactory controls have been fully implemented

% of key controls

% of obsolete user accounts

% of past due corrective actions

% of physical backup / archive media that are fully encrypted

% of policies reported with non-conformances

% of risks identified assessed as high, medium or low significance, plus un-assessed

% of systems (workstations, laptops, servers) covered by antivirus/antispyware software

% of test backup restores that are successful

% of third party connections that have been identified , risk-assessed and deemed secure

% progressive reduction in # of breaches

Age (in days or hours) of backup

Average antivirus & antispyware corrective action response time

Average information security maturity level score from executive branch agencies

Average of time to implement corrective action

Average time (in hours or minutes) to restore backup

Average time (in hours or minutes) to restore off-site backup

Average time between tests of backup

Average time lag between detection, reporting and acting upon security incidents

Information security costs as a % of total revenue or IT budget

Internet Usage

computers per 1000 people

of computers in country

# of computers in households and enterprises

# of enterprises using Internet for interaction with public authorities

# of enterprises with broadband access

# of enterprises with connection to the Internet

# of households types of connection to the Internet

# of households with broadband access

# of individuals frequency of computer use

# of individuals frequency of internet use

# of internet users

# of internet users (per 100 population)

# of internet users (per 1000 people)

45. Information Technology

of mobile phone subscribers (per 100 people)

# of personal computers in use per 100 population

% growth of technology adoption

% individuals´ level of computer skills

% of citizens access to and use of the Internet

% of download of music and/or films from the Internet

% of employees - remotely working

% of employees with connection to the Internet

% of enterprises allowing remote working

% of enterprises having remote employed persons who connect to the enterprise's IT systems from home

% of enterprises having website/homepage

% of enterprises purchases with the software used for any internal function

% of enterprises sending and/or receiving e-invoices

% of enterprises sharing electronically information on sales

% of enterprises' turnover from e-commerce

% of enterprises using applications for employees to access human resources services

% of enterprises using automated data exchange with customers or suppliers

% of enterprises using Extranet/Intranet

% of enterprises using software solutions, like CRM to analyze information about clients for marketing purposes

% of enterprises using the Internet for filling forms to public authorities

% of enterprises using the Internet for interaction with public authorities

% of enterprises using the Internet for submitting a proposal in a public electronic tender system to public authorities

% of enterprises which have broadband access

% of enterprises whose business processes are automatically linked to those of their customers

% of enterprises whose business processes are automatically linked to those of their suppliers

% of enterprises with computers systems

% of enterprises with devices and communication systems

% of enterprises with Internet access

% of enterprises with persons employed accessing enterprise's IT systems from outside

% of enterprises with persons employed working part of their time away from enterprise premises

% of households access the Internet

% of households having access to the Internet, by type of connection

% of households level of Internet access

% of households which have broadband access

% of households with access to Internet via digital TV

% of households with access to Internet via mobile device

45. Information Technology

% of households with computers devices and communication systems

% of individuals by place of computer use

% of individuals by place of internet use

% of individuals computer use

% of individuals doing specific online activities in the previous 3 months

% of individuals frequently using the Internet

% of individuals Internet use

% of individuals paying for online audiovisual content

% of individuals regularly using the Internet

% of individuals regularly using the Internet, by gender

% of individuals use advanced internet services

% of individuals use mobile Internet access

% of individuals using a laptop to access the Internet

% of individuals using a mobile phone to access the Internet

% of individuals using Internet for interaction with public authorities

% of individuals using the Internet by place of use

% of individuals using the Internet for doing an online course

% of individuals using the Internet for downloading computer or video games or their updates

% of individuals using the Internet for downloading/listening to/watching music and/or films

% of individuals using the Internet for finding information about goods and services

% of individuals using the Internet for internet banking

% of individuals using the Internet for listening to webradio/watching web television

% of individuals using the Internet for looking for a job or sending a job application

% of individuals using the Internet for ordering goods or services

% of individuals using the Internet for reading online newspapers/magazines

% of individuals using the Internet for returning filled in forms to public authorities

% of individuals using the Internet for seeking health-related information

% of individuals using the Internet for seeking information with the purpose of learning

% of individuals using the Internet for selling goods or services

% of individuals using the Internet for sending/receiving e-mails

% of individuals using the Internet for specific purposes in the previous three months

% of individuals using the Internet for uploading self-created content to any website to be shared

% of individuals who have never used a computer

% of individuals who have never used the Internet

45. Information Technology
% of individuals who ordered goods or services over the Internet for private use
% of individuals with access to the Internet broken down by place of access (home, workplace, place of education, Internet cafe)
% of individuals with internet competence in enterprises
% of integration of internal business processes
% of integration with suppliers and/or customers
% of internet calls replaced other means of communication
% of internet regular users (per 100 people)
% of Internet use replaced time spent with off-line activities
% of PC-skilled government users
% of people not having broadband access at home
% of people not having Internet access at home
% of persons employed using computers connected to the Internet
% of persons employed using computers connected to the Internet in their normal work routine
% pay for online audiovisual content
% share of enterprises' turnover on e-commerce
Annual e-Maturity assessment score
E-literacy - social & cultural environment index
E-literacy rate
Government expenditure on ICT as a % of GDP
Mobile phone subscribers % of population
Use of the Internet for leisure activities related to obtaining and sharing audiovisual content
Use of the Internet for private purposes for advanced communication activities (excluding e-mail)

IT Communication

# of processes automated vs. actual # of processes
# of residents who have accessed portal to get information
# of telephone access
% completion of planned activities
% completion of workflow implementation
Total exports value of ICT equipment

IT Processes

# of activities utilized through intranet
# of quality systems implemented
# of systems implemented
# of unique website visitors
score of government excellence award
% completion of IT strategy & governance framework
% completion of IT systems implementations
% completion of property management and database systems with spatial data
% completion of property management database process and procedures

45. Information Technology

% implementation of investment back office IT system

% IT asset efficiency

% IT budget variance

% of automated key processes

% of automated processes from the total # of processes

% of entities reporting on-line

% of execution of information security management system initiatives

% of execution of IT platform initiatives

% of execution of generating revenues initiative

% of information systems and help-line utilization by customers/stakeholders

% of IT infrastructure implementation across municipality locations

% of IT project completion within time and budget

% of key manual procedures automated

% of key processes supported by the ERP system

% of milestones achieved according to plan for strategic IT projects

% of operations per functional area completed online

% of processes converted to paper-less

% of sectors receiving IT ISO certification

% of systems automated that are capable of being automated

% of workflow automation

% satisfaction of IT architecture and standards requirements

IT operational readiness rate for network infrastructure and programs

IT readiness score

Modern IT Platform

of entities connected to the central portal

# of government entities on-boarded to the contact centre

% broadband coverage

% broadband coverage use

% broadband penetration

% of enterprises having a broadband connection

% of enterprises having access to the Internet, by size classes

% of households equipped with home networking connections

% of households having a broadband connection

% of IT architecture completed

% of IT strategy completion

% of required information provisioned to employees and external users through developed information systems

E-Government readiness index

Government IT customer satisfaction index

IT architecture & standards readiness assessment score

Network Support

of phone line / # of technicians

# of servers supported

45. Information Technology

% Applications provided to the requesting sector within the agreed requirements and timescales

% network services uptime (server, network components, office network structures, internet and WAN connectivity)

% of approved mainframe and network system access requests which require creation of a new user account are completed within three work days

% of printing work done internally that is completed and delivered by the date requested

% of time core server (web hosting) services are available for customer use

% of time phone system fully functional during business hours

% of time servers are fully functional during business hours

% of time the network is available

Cost of phone line vs. phone company business line

Online Services

of barriers to buying/ordering over the Internet

# of individuals having ordered/bought goods or services for private use over the Internet

# of individuals having used the Internet in relation to training and educational purposes

# of individuals using Internet to seek health information whether for themselves or others

# of portal site visits per internet user

# of problems encountered by individuals when buying/ordering over the Internet

# of users of e-Government portal, contact centre and telecentres

% government basic services available online

% of automated services

% of enterprises having purchased on-line (at least 1%)

% of enterprises having purchased on-line over the last calendar year

% of enterprises having received on-line payments for Internet sales over the last calendar year

% of enterprises having received orders on-line (at least 1%)

% of enterprises having received orders on-line over the last calendar year

% of enterprises purchasing via Internet and/or networks other than Internet

% of enterprises selling via Internet and/or networks other than Internet

% of enterprises' total turnover from e-commerce over the last calendar year

% of enterprises using e-learning applications for training and education of employees

% of online services

Contact centre customer satisfaction survey

Customer satisfaction rate for online services

E-participation Index

45. Information Technology

Internet purchases by individuals

Total value of purchases and sales by Internet

Research & Development

of IT researchers

Gross domestic expenditure on IT R&D

R&D expenditure of businesses in ICT sector as % of total R&D expenditure

R&D personnel in ICT sector as % of total R&D personnel

Total investment in ICT Research

Total investment in knowledge systems

Technology Systems

% of ERP system implemented

% of GIS system established and maintained

% of management information reports implemented

% of time customers are able to access enterprise IT resources during business hours

46. Internal Process

Develop Technology

of IT MoUs signed

# of working days to issue IT financial management information reports

% approval of policies and procedures by management committee

% approval of risk management framework by the management committee

% of HR services online using oracle workflow

% of procurement requests submitted on line using workflow

Actual spend of IT budget

Custodians IT satisfaction overall score

Revised delegation of IT authority matrix is approved by management committee

Enhance Efficiency

% completion of structure review

% integration of IT systems

% of existing facilities incorporated into new business model

% of existing standards and codes documented

% of implementation of designed processes

% of standards and codes updated

% processes documented

Average time of financial reporting

Average time of performance evaluations

Compliance rate with municipality's processes

Government Performance

of acceptance of submission papers

# of achieved ISO certifications in government

# of activities added to the monthly newsletter

# of automated key core processes

46. Internal Process
# of contracts signed
# of development application review process manual for government entities published
# of development of ERP solutions
# of formal communication channels with concerned governmental authorities and departments
# of initiatives implemented into public private partnership
# of issues monitored and resolved
# of modules implemented
# of new premises operational
# of processes re-engineered
# of public awareness and community involvement events hosted
# of recruited internal counselors fully trained and ready to take over job of external counselors
# of survey reports on success of publicity campaigns
# of website visitors to performance reports
% achievement of development plan goals
% completion and implementation of authority matrix
% completion of corporate performance management reporting including application roll out
% completion of internal audit enhancement project
% completion of master plan phases as per to the project road map
% completion of outsourcing manual and guidelines project
% completion of process implementation
% completion of processes design
% compliance of internal bylaws and operating procedures pertaining to stakeholder communication
% development of document archiving and management system
% improvement of customer/stakeholder satisfaction
% improvement of municipal score
% increase in publicity budget per year
% management satisfaction with document archiving and management
% of customer issues resolved within specified timeframe
% of delivered items through the central logistics system
% of development proposals commented on in the pre-application stage
% of documented processes
% of employees work improvements suggestions implemented through employees suggestion scheme
% of enterprise architecture model completion
% of excellence award program criteria implemented
% of financial audits passed
% of follow-up calls
% of implementing revised approach to asset management
% of internal activities that are tracked through internal governance system
% of internal policies and legal requirements executed

46. Internal Process

% of knowledge management components established

% of monthly and quarterly performance reports automated

% of monthly and quarterly performance reports submitted on time

% of municipal services offered through e-government portal

% of optimally equipped branches

% of organizational processes and controls implemented

% of precedence-setting regulatory decisions incorporated into relevant documents within three weeks

% of processes mastered

% of programs driven by adequate research

% of project development applications reviewed across government within one month

% of publications produced

% of quality standards developed and implemented

% of reduction of informal requests received by municipality

% of standards enforced from total standards related to municipal services

% of variation between year to day planned and actual operating budget

% of yearly results from last results

% outfitting of new premises completed

% reduction in # of customer/stakeholder complaints against government agencies

% reduction in operating costs resulted by outsourcing

Average government excellence award score

Average score on customer satisfaction surveys regarding logistics service provision

Award assessment point score out of 1000 possible points

Customer satisfaction rate

Employee satisfaction ratio with ERP solutions

Employee satisfaction score on teamwork %

Execution rate according to each contract's construction plan

Expansion of customer/stakeholder access times to 10 most sought-after services

Logistics operational readiness rate

Net reduction in contract management overhead

Net reduction in contract net expenditure

Projects/programs delivered by the private sector

Top management and stockholders satisfaction rate

Internal Administration

of external audit items open for longer than four months

# of internal audit items open for longer than four months

% of key external audit areas externally audited

% of key internal audit areas internally audited

% of key management reports provided on time

Private Sector Partnerships

of corporate social responsibility initiatives implemented

46. Internal Process

of outsourced municipal services

# of research studies performed by strategic partners

# of services reviewed for privatization

% of revenues to expenditures

% of savings from outsourced services

% of suppliers fulfilling their agreements

Cost reduction per year as a result of outsourcing

Procurement Processes

% external customers satisfied with procurement services

% internal customers satisfied with procurement services

% procurement processes that have been automated

Stakeholders Collaboration

collaborations with non-profit organizations and NGOs

% of implementation of external stakeholders management process

% of implementation of internal stakeholders management process

47. Justice

Adjudication & Dispute

of restitution ordered

# of sentencing per year

% of appeals heard within 45 days of receipt of request for hearing

% of appeals proposed decision issued within 65 days

% of contractor registration decisions issued within 14 days of hearing by board

% of decisions issued within 14 days of Board hearing

% of decisions issued within 14 days of Board review

% of decisions not appealed to district court

% of pretrial evaluations completed for adult consumers within 45 days of receipt of court order

% of proposed decisions issued that were affirmed

Average age of pending unemployment insurance appeal cases

Board of Paroles

of Board pre-conditions of parole imposed on inmates before release from prison

% of parolees successfully completing parole supervision as compared to the national average

% of visitors' day participants who rate their overall experience as good or excellent

Average monthly rate of parolees employed

Counsel Legal Services

of convictions

# of final rulings upholding challenged notices of action

# of training sessions conducted

% of claims acted upon within 35 days

47. Justice

% of closed economic fraud investigations resulting in civil action

% of customer satisfaction response of good or better

Average claim processing time

Cost per hour as a % of outside counsel cost per hour

Rate of completion of professional standards investigations

Criminal & Juvenile

agencies assisted

events provided addressing disproportionate minority contact

local agencies/planning groups/communities assisted

of bait cars

# of grantees fully reporting service counts

# of illegal alien smuggling

# of illegal alien suspects

# of milestones in the 5-year plan implemented

# of open vehicle theft cases

# of possession of drugs/drug paraphernalia

# of repeat auto theft offenders

# of repeat offenders - other felonies

# of transportation of drugs cases

# of vehicle theft cases charged

# of vehicle theft cases closed

# of vehicle theft cases declined

youth served

% data exchange completed within 1 year

% field audits without major findings

% grantees fully reporting results

% juvenile court districts reporting improvement in outcome measures for youth

% juvenile court districts with comprehensive strategic plans for youth development & juvenile justice

% of juvenile Math academic grade level achievement (gain in grade level per month in school)

% of violence or weapons involved

% of youth arrested for committing a delinquent act within 6 months of program discharge

% of youth discharged from commitment to department that are recommitted or resentenced within one year of release

% of youth discharged from commitment to department that are recommitted or resentenced within three years of release

% of youth served in the community

% of youth who remain in the community for a 6- month period after discharge

Average jail sentence (days)

Average length of probation (months)

Average prison sentence (months)

47. Justice

Average utilization rate of available bed space

Psychologist/counselor services (hours per week)

Ratio of minority to non-minority youth held in detention

Total dollars allocated

Legal Representation

% of caseload expectations achieved

% of caseload performance expectations achieved

% of challenged Notices of Action on indigent defense claims that are upheld upon final judicial review

% of indigent defense claims reviewed and acted upon within 35 days of receipt

% of public defender cases where there have been ineffective assistance of counsel

%s of cases with final findings of ineffective assistance on direct appeal of convictions and post conviction relief

Average processing time for an indigent defense claim within an established standard

Prosecution

of criminal cases filed

# of vertical prosecutor positions filled

# of vertical prosecutor positions funded

Average prosecution cost per criminal case

Average review time in days

Conviction rate (convictions divided by cases closed)

Regulation & Compliance

of food assistance electronic benefit transfer recipient cases referred by law enforcement

# of founded dependent adult abuse criminal investigations referred for criminal prosecution

# of license plate reader

% of actions for noncompliance upheld on informal dispute resolution

% of applications returned for additional information

% of economic fraud investigation cases closed within statutory timeframes

% of Medical aid fraud investigation cases will be reviewed and receive proper disposition within statutory timeframes

% of new business applications submitted meeting the eligibility requirements

% of occupational licensees receiving no serious violations after licensure

Amount of cost savings resulting from front-end investigations

Money value recovered from misspent public assistance, resulting from error and fraud per year

Ratio of professional licensing investigations completed to total cases

Risk Management

% of risk losses recovered

% of self-insurance claims adjusted within timeliness standard

47. Justice

Victim Services

of correspondence sent to victims

# of people registered in the victim information and notification system

# of pubic legal awareness events sponsored

% of visitor days per year

48. Labor

Employment

of citizens currently employed for ten years or more

# of citizens currently employed for three years or more and progressing as per planned career path

# of citizens placed in jobs

# of days lost through industrial disputes

# of employed persons aged 15 and over by age

# of employed persons aged 15 and over by citizenship

# of employed persons aged 15 and over by detailed industry

# of employed persons aged 15 and over by detailed occupation

# of employed persons aged 15 and over by industry

# of employed persons with a second job

# of employer events/campaigns conducted

# of hours worked per week of full-time employment

# of hours worked per week of part-time employment

# of incidence of part-time employment

# of individuals covered by social security schemes

# of job seeker campaigns/events conducted

# of persons by qualification mismatch, 5 years after graduation

# of persons employed part-time - Total

# of public sector employees in different industries

# of sector committees established and operational

# of self-employment by age groups

# of self-employment by occupation

# of self-employment by sex

% employed in service sector and occupational status of recent school-leavers

% employment by economic activity

% employment by full-time/part-time

% employment by highest level of education attained

% employment by nationality

% employment by occupation

% employment by professional status

% employment growth - Annual averages

% employment growth by gender

% employment in agriculture (% of total employment)

% employment in industry (% of total employment)

48. Labor

% employment in services (% of total employment)

% of adults employed 90 days following workforce allocation services

% of citizens across various industries in private and public sectors

% of education / occupation mismatch of persons aged 25-34 by study field

% of expatriates (foreign labor) employed in key strategic sectors as % of total work force

% of labor force with primary education (% of total)

% of labor force with secondary education (% of total)

% of labor force with tertiary education (% of total)

% of youth who obtain a job, earn a credential, or further their education

% response rate to the federal occupational employment statistics survey

Amount collected in total sales

Average exit age from the labor force

Average exit age from the labor market, by gender

Average hours actually worked

Distribution by occupation of persons aged 25-34 with higher education

Employment - annual averages

Employment rate by gender

Employment rate by highest level of education attained

Employment rate of older workers

Employment rates by nationality

Employment rates for age group 15-24

Employment rates for age group 25-54

Employment rates for age group 55-64

Employment rates: men

Employment rates: total

Employment rates: women

Formal sector employment rate

Labor input index

Retail trade employment - total

Self-employment rates: men

Self-employment rates: total

Self-employment rates: women

Total # of private sector employment

Total # of public sector employment

Turnover index

Unemployment rate by field of study

Unemployment rate of persons aged 20-34

Unemployment rate of persons aged 20-34, by years since graduation

Youth transitions from education to working life (in # of months)

Job Vacancy

of quarterly job vacancies

Annual job vacancy rate

Quarterly job vacancy rates

48. Labor

Labor Compensation

of employees by economic activity corresponding to earnings data

# of employees by occupation corresponding to earnings data

# of hours paid

Annual earnings by quantiles for enterprises with 10 employed persons or more

Annual earnings for enterprises with 10 employed persons or more

Annual net earnings

Average annual earnings / staff

Average annual gross earnings by economic activity

Average annual gross earnings by occupation

Average annual gross income of workers with higher education

Average annual gross income of workers, by education level

Average gross annual earnings in industry and services

Average monthly earning

Gender pay gap in unadjusted form

Gender pay gap in unadjusted form by age

Gender pay gap in unadjusted form by economic control

Hourly earnings by contractual working time for enterprises with 10 employed persons or more

Hourly labor costs

Labor compensation per hour, total economy

Labor compensation per unit labor input, total economy

Labor cost index

Mean annual earnings by age

Mean annual earnings by collective pay agreement

Mean annual earnings by educational attainment

Mean annual earnings by employment contract

Mean annual earnings by length of service with the enterprise

Mean annual earnings by occupation

Mean annual earnings by sex

Mean annual earnings by size classes of the enterprise

Mean annual earnings by size of the enterprise

Mean hourly earnings by age

Mean hourly earnings by collective pay agreement

Mean hourly earnings by educational attainment

Mean hourly earnings by employment contract

Mean hourly earnings by length of service with the enterprise

Mean hourly earnings by occupation

Mean hourly earnings by sex

Mean hourly earnings by size classes of the enterprise

Mean hourly earnings by size of the enterprise

Mean monthly earnings by age

Mean monthly earnings by collective pay agreement

48. Labor
Mean monthly earnings by educational attainment
Mean monthly earnings by employment contract
Mean monthly earnings by length of service with the enterprise
Mean monthly earnings by occupation
Mean monthly earnings by sex
Mean monthly earnings by size classes of the enterprise
Mean monthly earnings by size of the enterprise
Mean monthly hours paid by age
Mean monthly hours paid by collective pay agreement
Mean monthly hours paid by educational attainment
Mean monthly hours paid by employment contract
Mean monthly hours paid by length of service with the enterprise
Mean monthly hours paid by occupation
Mean monthly hours paid by size classes of the enterprise
Mean monthly hours paid by size of the enterprise
Minimum wage
Monthly earnings by economic control for enterprises with 10 employed persons or more
Monthly earnings by quantiles and contractual working time for enterprises with 10 employed persons or more
Monthly labor costs
Monthly minimum wage
Monthly minimum wage as a proportion of average monthly earnings in industry and services (%)
Net earnings
Social security paid by employer
Tax rate
Tax rate on low wage earners - low wage
Tax rate on low wage earners - tax wedge on labor costs
Tax rate on low wage earners - unemployment
Tax rate on low wage earners by marginal effective tax rates on employment incomes
Tax wedge on labor cost
Total compensation of employees
Total wages and salaries
Unit labor cost, business sector

Labor Cost
# of apprentices
# of employees
# of employees hours actually worked and paid
# of employees hours worked and paid
# of hours actually worked and paid per employee
# of hours worked and paid per employee
# of hours worked by year

48. Labor
Coefficient of variation of labor cost
Direct cost
Direct remuneration
Hourly labor cost for temporary staff
Hours actually worked compared to hours paid
Hours worked compared to hours paid
Labor cost
Labor cost surveys
Labor cost, wages and salaries
Monthly labor cost for apprentices
Monthly remuneration of apprentices
Structure of labor cost as % of total cost
Structure of labor costs (%)
Temporary staff labor cost, # of employees
Temporary staff labor cost, # of hours worked
Total # of hours worked by temporary staff

Labor Dispute

of workers involved
# of workers involved by economic activity
# of working days lost
# of working days lost by economic activity
Workers involved per 1000 workers
Workers involved per 1000 workers by economic activity
Working days lost per 1000 workers
Working days lost per 1000 workers by economic activity

Labor Force

of active population by highest level of education attained
# of active population by nationality
# of active population by sex
# of adults by age
# of adults by age groups
# of adults by household composition
# of adults by level of education attained
# of adults by sex
# of adults by working status
# of adults with # of children higher than 3
# of employees by age
# of employees by age groups
# of employees by collective pay agreement
# of employees by economic control
# of employees by educational attainment
# of employees by employment contract
# of employees by length of service with the enterprise
# of employees by level of educational attainment

48. Labor
# of employees by occupation
# of employees by sex
# of employees by size classes of the enterprise
# of employees by size of the enterprise
# of full-time employment
# of full-time employment by age groups
# of full-time employment by highest level of education attained
# of full-time employment by occupation
# of full-time employment by sex
# of part-time employment
# of part-time employment by age groups
# of part-time employment by highest level of education attained
# of part-time employment by occupation
# of part-time employment by sex
# of persons by age groups
# of persons by sex
# of persons by working status
# of private households
# of private households by household composition
# of temporary employees by age groups
# of temporary employees by duration of the work contract
# of temporary employees by economic activity
# of temporary employees by occupation
# of temporary employment
% of employed adults having a second job
% of employed adults working at home
% of employed people having a second job by sex
% of employed people working at home by sex
% of employees working on shift work as a % of the total of employees
% of inactive population by main reasons for not seeking employment
% of part-time employment by age
% of part-time employment of adults by sex
% of population by household composition
% of population by labor status
% of population by nationality
% of population in employment having a second job
% of population in employment having a second job by highest level of education attained
% of population in employment having a second job by occupation in first job
% of population in employment having a second job by professional status of both jobs
% of population in employment working at night as a % of the total employment

48. Labor

% of population in employment working during asocial hours

% of population in employment working from home as a % of the total employment

% of population in employment working in the evening as a % of the total employment

% of population in employment working on Saturday as a % of the total employment

% of population in employment working on Sunday work as a % of the total employment

% of population, aged 15 to 74 years by highest level of education attained

% of population, aged 15 to 74 years by participation in education

% of population, aged 15 to 74 years by sex

% of self-employed adults by sex

% of self-employed by age

% of temporary contracts by sex

% of temporary contracts for adults by age

Activity rates by sex, age groups and highest level of education attained (%)

Activity rates by sex, age groups and nationality (%)

Average # of children per household by working status

Average # of persons per household

Average # of persons per household by household composition

Average size of households

Economic activity rates by sex

Economically active population by age

Economically active population by highest level of education attained

Economically active population in # of persons

Employment by # age of youngest child

Employment by household composition

Employment rate by household composition (%)

Employment rate of adults by highest level of education attained

Involuntary part-time employment as % of the total part-time employment (%)

Main reasons for part-time employment (%)

Main reasons for the temporary employment (%)

Part-time employment as % of the total employment (%)

Part-time employment as a % of the total employment (%)

Temporary employees as % of the total # of employees (%)

Temporary employees as a % of the total # of employees (%)

Total population

Labor Policy

of persons registered with public employment services

Public expenditure on labor market policies by type of action

Public expenditure on labor market policy interventions

Public expenditure on labor market policy measures

Public expenditure on labor market policy supports

48. Labor

Physical Safety

# of accidental injuries at work by type of injury
# of accidental injuries at work by work status
# of accidental injuries at work by year
# of accidents at work by contact
# of accidents at work by deviation
# of accidents at work by employment status
# of accidents at work by material agent of deviation
# of accidents at work by mode of injury
# of accidents at work by part of body injured
# of accidents at work by physical activity
# of accidents at work by severity
# of accidents at work by sex
# of accidents at work by size of enterprise
# of accidents at work by specific physical activity
# of accidents at work by type of injury
# of accidents at work by type of workstation
# of accidents at work by working environment
# of causes and circumstances of accidents at work
# of factory inspections taken in a year
# of fatal accidents at work
# of fatal accidents at work excluding road traffic accidents
# of industrial accidents in a year
# of labor inspections taken in a year
# of serious accidents at work by gender
# of work-related health problems by # of complaints
# of work-related health problems by activity
# of work-related health problems by age
# of work-related health problems by diagnosis group
# of work-related health problems by employment status
# of work-related health problems by severity
% fatal incidence rate
% incidence rate
% injuries at work at night work
% injuries at work by economic activity
% injuries at work by length of service in the enterprise
% injuries at work by occupations
% injuries at work by permanency of the job
% injuries at work by profession
% injuries at work by shift work
% injuries at work by working hours
% of accidents at work by contact
% of accidents at work by deviation
% of accidents at work by material agent of contact

48. Labor
% of accidents at work by specific physical activity
% of accidents at work by type of workstation
% of accidents at work by working environment
% of accidents at work by working process
% of employers inspected who are under the workers' compensation and rehabilitation policy
% of persons who receive vocational rehabilitation services and successfully return to work
% of serious accidents at work by gender
Average cost per return to work
Frequency of lost time injuries for mining operations
Frequency of lost time injuries for petroleum operations
Relative prevalence rate of work-related health problems
Relative prevalence rate of work-related health problems by employer
Relative standardized incidence rate of accidental injuries
Standardized prevalence rate of work-related health problems by diagnosis group
Standardized prevalence rate of work-related health problems by severity

Productivity Improvement

Capital productivity index
Labor cost competitiveness index
Labor productivity index
Profitability index

Retirement Transition

# of employed persons by planned age for stopping work
# of employed persons who reduced their working hours in a move to full retirement
# of employed persons who would stay longer at work if more flexible working time arrangements were available
# of employed persons who would stay longer at work if their workplace was healthier and/or safer
# of employed persons who would stay longer at work if they could update their skills
# of main reasons for retirement or early retirement
% of not employed persons having reduced their working hours in a move to full retirement
Average # of years spent working
Average # of years spent working by employed persons
Average age at which employed persons started receiving a retirement pension
Average age at which not employed persons started receiving a retirement pension

Training Cost

% of direct cost of CVT courses, by type of direct cost
Cost of training courses as % of total labor cost (all enterprises)

48. Labor
Cost of training courses as % of total labor cost by enterprises type
Cost of training courses per employee
Cost of training courses per participant
Cost of training courses per training hour
Costs of participation in education and training
Costs of training courses and size class
Mean amount of money spent by participant on education and training by age groups
Mean amount of money spent by participant on education and training by highest level of education attained
Mean amount of money spent by participant on education and training by labor status
Mean amount of money spent by participant on education and training by occupation
Structure of costs of training courses per employee in enterprises with training courses
Structure of costs of training courses per participant

Training Hours

# of hours in training courses per 1000 # of hours worked (all enterprises)
# of hours in training courses per employee
# of hours in training courses per employee by sex
# of hours in training courses per employee in enterprises with a joint training agreement
# of hours in training courses per employee in enterprises with 'new technologies'
# of hours in training courses per participant
# of hours spent on training courses
% of the total hours in external training courses
% of the total hours in training courses
% of the total hours in training courses by field of training
Distribution of education and training activities by field
Distribution of job related education and training activities by field
Distribution of non-formal education and training activities by provider
Instruction hours spent by participant on education and training
Mean instruction hours spent by participant on education and training by age groups
Mean instruction hours spent by participant on education and training by highest level of education attained
Mean instruction hours spent by participant on education and training by labor status
Mean instruction hours spent by participant on education and training by occupation
Share of total instruction hours in education and training activities by field

Training Participation

# of participations in job related non-formal education and training

48. Labor
% of persons not participating in education and learning
% of persons not participating in education and learning by age group
% of persons not participating in education and learning by degree of urbanization
% of persons not participating in education and learning by highest level of education attained
% of persons not participating in education and learning by labor status
% of persons not participating in education and learning by occupation
% of persons not participating in education and learning by sex
Distribution of reasons of participation in non-formal education and training
Participation rate in education and training
Participation rate in education and training by age groups
Participation rate in education and training by debree of urbanization
Participation rate in education and training by highest level of education attained
Participation rate in education and training by labor status
Participation rate in education and training by occupation
Participation rate in education and training by sex
Participation rate in job related non-formal education and training
Participation rate in job related non-formal education and training by highest level of education attained
Participation rate in job related non-formal education and training by sex

Unemployment

of jobless households by gender
# of jobless households with children
# of people living in jobless households
% long-term unemployment (12 months or more) as a % of the total unemployment
% of inactive population as a % of the total population
% of inactive population by highest level of education attained
% of inactive population by nationality
% of inactive population by sex
% of long-term unemployment
% of population in jobless households
% of unemployment with primary education (% of total unemployment)
% of unemployment with secondary education (% of total unemployment)
% of unemployment with tertiary education (% of total unemployment)
% of unemployment, female (% of female labor force)
% of unemployment, male (% of male labor force)
Average duration of unemployment
Harmonized unemployment - age class 15-24
Harmonized unemployment - age class 25-74
Harmonized unemployment by gender - total
Long-term unemployment (% of total unemployment)
Long-term unemployment rate

48. Labor
Long-term unemployment, female (% of female unemployment)
Long-term unemployment, male (% of male unemployment)
National unemployment rate
Previous occupations of the unemployed, by sex
Range in regional unemployment rate, small regions: maximum
Range in regional unemployment rate, small regions: minimum
Regional unemployment rates
Unemployment rate by nationality (%)
Unemployment rate by race (%)
Unemployment rates: men
Unemployment rates: total
Unemployment rates: women

Unemployment Insurance

# of adults receiving cash assistance
% of clients who obtain and retain employment for at least 90 days during the year
% of families leaving temporary assistance for employment who remain employed for at least 12 months
% of unemployment insurance benefits recipients who are paid accurately
% of uninsured employers detected
Average duration of unemployment insurance benefits in weeks

Vocational Training

# of participants in CVT courses
% of all enterprises providing CVT courses
% of all non-training enterprises, by reason for not providing CVT
% of employees (all enterprises) participating in CVT courses
% of employees (all enterprises) participating in CVT courses, by sex
% of employees (only enterprises with CVT courses) participating in CVT courses
% of employees in all enterprises by type of training
% of employees in enterprises with and without a joint CVT agreement participating in CVT courses
% of employees in enterprises with and without 'new technologies' participating in CVT courses
% of enterprises assessing the skills and training needs of employees as % of all enterprises
% of enterprises assessing their future manpower and/or skill needs as % of all enterprises
% of enterprises evaluating the effect of CVT courses
% of enterprises not evaluating the effect of CVT courses
% of enterprises providing any other form of training
% of enterprises that needed to obtain or develop new skills
% of enterprises undergoing technological or structural changes
% of enterprises with a training plan including CVT
% of enterprises with the need to obtain or develop new skills

48. Labor

% of enterprises without a training plan including CVT

% of participants in other form of CVT as a % of employees in all enterprises

% of reasons having an influence on the scope of the enterprise's CVT activities

% of training enterprises having a specific person or unit responsible for training

% of training enterprises making use of an external advisory service

Enterprises evaluating the effect of VT courses as % of all enterprises providing VT courses

Enterprises evaluating the effect of VT courses as % of training enterprises

Enterprises providing any other form of training as % of all enterprises

Enterprises providing 'other forms' of training, by form of training (%)

Enterprises providing VT courses by % of occupational group

Enterprises providing VT courses by % of participation of employees

Enterprises providing VT courses, by particular population category (%)

Enterprises providing VT courses, by type of contribution to collective funding arrangements (%)

Enterprises providing VT courses, by type of receipt from collective funding arrangements (%)

Enterprises where there was an impact of public measures on their VT plans as a % for all training enterprises

Enterprises who assess the future skills needs of the enterprise as a % of training enterprises

Enterprises who establish the training needs of their personnel as % of training enterprises

Enterprises with a training budget including provision for VT as % of all enterprises

Enterprises with a training budget including provision for VT as % of training enterprises

Enterprises with a training centre used exclusively or partly for VT as % of all enterprises

Enterprises with a training centre used exclusively or partly for VT as % of training enterprises

Enterprises with a training plan including VT as % of all enterprises

Enterprises with a training plan including VT as % of training enterprises

Enterprises with an agreement on VT as % of all enterprises type of agreement

Enterprises with an agreement on VT as % of training enterprises

Participants in other forms of CVT as a % of employees in CVT other form enterprises

Training enterprises as % of all enterprises

Work & Family Life

of employed persons having to make working time arrangements over the last 12 months to care for children

48. Labor

of employed persons regularly taking care of other children or people in need of care

# of employed persons taking time off over the last 12 months for family sickness or emergencies

# of employed persons who can take whole days off for family reasons

# of employed persons who can vary start/end of working day for family reasons

# of employed persons wishing to change the organization of their working life and care responsibilities

# of main childcare-related reasons given by employed persons for not working

# of persons regularly taking care of other children up to 14 in need of care

Average usual working hours of employed persons

Working Time

of annual holidays

% of employees finding it convenient for personal life on-call work

% of employees finding it convenient for personal life to do shift work activity

% of employees finding it convenient for personal life to work at night

% of employees finding it convenient for personal life to work in the evening

% of employees with variable working hours

% of employees working on call

% of employees working overtime

% of employees working paid overtime

% of self-employed persons who can control their own schedule

% of self-employed persons who can control their own work methods

% of self-employed persons who work for one single client or customer

Average # of actual weekly hours of work in main job

Average # of actual weekly hours of work in the second job

Average # of overtime hours of employees

Average # of paid overtime hours of employees

Average # of usual weekly hours of work in main job

Average usual working hours of employees

Mean annual holidays

Mean annual holidays by size of the enterprise

49. Military & Defense

Emergency Management

of responders trained in emergency management

% of county emergency management coordinators trained to established standards

% of emergency management employees trained to established standards

% of five-year security strategy projects funded and initiated

% of funded public assistance projects are successfully complete

49. Military & Defense

% of identified mitigation unmet needs projects that were funded

% of jurisdictions that have mitigation plans that meet the standards of the federal disaster mitigation act

% of jurisdictions that have recovery plans that meet standards

% of jurisdictions that have response plans that meet standards

% of jurisdictions that have strategic plans that meet standards

% of local governments that are sustainable for its citizens

% of public safety answering points capable of receiving and providing wireless emergency calls

% of state government that is sustainable for its citizens

% of wireless service customers that have public safety answering points areas that are capable of receiving and are providing calls

Facility Security & Utilization

of man days of utilization of training facilities

# of reportable security intrusions and appropriate actions

% of routine orders

Amount of losses of physical security equipment and appropriate action

Average cost of facility heating and cooling

Force Deployment

% national guard member and dependent processing

% of armories and facilities stationed and assigned for best utilization to improve readiness, and support and best utilize resources

% of members successfully reintegrated into employment after release from active duty

% of members that receive mandatory pre-/post-mobilization briefings that facilitate entry onto active duty

% of members that reintegration back into the civilian environment after release from active duty

% of national guard members utilizing educational assistance program

Military Readiness

of aircraft and other pieces of equipment restored

# of defense force volunteers for community support

% fill of qualified and trained personnel with available senior grade leadership to form a "ready pool" available for mobilization

% of armories requiring major repairs and renovations (more than x$)

% of fill of qualified and trained air patrol personnel

% of fill of selected equipment compared to wartime/primary mission requirements

% of fill of selected equipment on-hand that is maintained and considered operationally ready and fully mission capable

% of first responder jurisdictions with interoperable communication capabilities

% of national guard unit participation

% of network services availability to users during fiscal year

% of political subdivisions participation

49. Military & Defense

% of requests where information was successfully and accurately provided in response to inquiries from the media and other interested parties

% of successful responses within 24 hours to an "Alert Notice" by the emergency management agency and command post

% of units available for or serving on federal active duty

% of units fully trained, equipped, and deployable

% of units returned from mobilization and resetting in the three-year force generation cycle

% of units that achieve deployment latest mobilization station arrival date criteria as established by higher federal mobilization headquarters

% readiness level of the forward command posts

% readiness level of the state emergency operations center

Procedures & Leadership

% of capitals/military construction funding

% of increased federal support of national guard operations

% of total funding

% of units that meet quarterly unit status report readiness standards for equipment readiness

% of units that meet quarterly unit status report readiness standards for personnel on hand

% of units that meet quarterly unit status report readiness standards for personnel qualification

% of units that meet quarterly unit status report readiness standards for personnel training

Amount of funding acquired for new/upgraded facilities

Amount of funding support to national guard counter drug programs for schools and law enforcement agencies

Training & Exercises

of participants reached through special community events

% of available training periods scheduled

% of available training periods utilized

% of compliance with army standardized training requirements

% of local government exercises completed as required by rule or agreement

% of physical exercises completed as required by rule, regulation or agreement

% of units conducting training year of three-year force generation cycle

Veterans Affairs

of counseling referral education completed with returning active duty veterans

# of counties participating in grant funds to increase veterans programs

# of educational assistance grants to war orphans

# of grants provided to severely injured veterans

# of home grants provided to veterans

# of museum visitors

49. Military & Defense
# of veterans, spouses and or dependents receiving assistance payments directly
% of nursing home facilities that have reported the names of the veterans, spouses and widows in their facilities
Total # of bonuses to eligible veterans

50. Municipalities

Accountability & Transparency

# of annual service reports published on time
# of customer satisfaction measurement mechanisms to monitor satisfaction rate
# of defined and agree with municipalities on KPIs to be benchmarked across municipalities
# of internal mechanisms of governance framework to promote accountability and transparency
% budget variance
% completion of governance committees implementation
% completion of municipal boundaries identified, agreed and approved
% documented existing standards and codes used
% enforced non smoking policy in public buildings
% enforcement of existing standards
% financial self sufficiency
% of developed and issued financial regulations for municipal governance including municipal fees setting and revenue distributions
% of issued municipal governance regulations
% of leadership participating in international meetings and forums
% of municipal entities developed activity-based budgets as per department of finance guidelines
% of municipality services aligned with formal channels of services requisition, closure and regulation
% of projects completed on-time
% of projects completed with less than 20% budget variation
% of required IT systems in place

Building Inspection

# of complaints received
# of final inspections on all construction requiring permits
% of cases closed with initial response within target timelines
Average # of days for processing building permits
Total # of construction inspections performed
Total construction permit applications completed per year

Cleanliness & Safety

# of charges laid
# of cleanups
# of complaints about unsafe activities

50. Municipalities

of employees and employer's are active participants in the development of strategy

# of graffiti calls

# of graffiti clean-ups

# of lights installed

# of members respond to cleaning initiative

# of pieces painted per time period per person

# of repeat calls

# of responses to district issues

# of safety and security related calls

# of safety and security related complaints

# of safety incidents in downtown

# of viable solutions/alternatives developed

# of warrants executed

reduction of unsafe products and merchandise affecting public health

% achieved tourist and public satisfaction rate with city image

% increase in enforcement visibility in the city centre

% of citizen confidence that the centre city is a safe place to work and live

% of citizens satisfied with cleanliness

% of citizens satisfied with cleanliness in the city centre

% of citizens satisfied with public toilets accessibility

% of citizens satisfied with safety in city centre

% of citizens satisfied with safety in the city centre

% of citizens satisfied with safety while in public spaces

% of increased education service request in regards to response and file closure time

% of poles repainted

% of positive feedback in customer satisfaction survey

% of sidewalks meeting aesthetic standards

% of substandard poles replaced

% of suitable working places and facilities to municipality manpower

% of worn signs replaced

% reduction / elimination of homeless sites

% reduction in calls complaints regarding pathway snow removal

% reduction in complaints regarding social disorder concerns

% strategic locations with installed ashtrays

Average response time

Average response time to calls

Average response time to remove tags

Average response time to remove tags from both public and private property

Crime rate

Graffiti index

Increase lifespan of the average tree by 1 to 2 years

50. Municipalities
Increased # of education, and referral contacts
Litter Index
Litter index for city centre
Quality of life monitor index
Rate per million rides of summons issued
Rate per million rides of summons issued for nuisance behaviors
Resident satisfaction rating for clean streets
Safety index
Total spending per head of population on street cleaning

Community Facilities

frequency of services
of building rehabilitations
# of citizens took Municipal Services Survey
# of coordinated meetings with external stakeholders to ensure coordination in detailed planning
# of projects implemented that contributes to the development of the urban plan
# of solid waste transfer stations, sorting station, and compost factories
% buildings implementing Non-smoking in public buildings
% completion in new waste handling facilities construction
% completion of detailed planning for projects as defined by master plan
% completion of spatial data components
% controlling gas emission within the limit
% gap of medical incinerator, engineered landfill, and hazardous cell to protect the environment
% increase in green area per capita
% increase in waste processing capacity
% increase the life of waste landfill
% leakage from waste landfill rivers
% of citizens waiting on lands allocation waiting list
% of green areas per capita
% of major maintenance project funds expended by design & construction within 3 years
% of nationals, residents, visitors and investors approving the perception of City brand
% of non smoking policy compliance
% of parks project completed
% of population covered by easily accessible service centers
% of projects completed on-time and as per planned scope
% of projects completed within SLA budgets
% of public areas per capita
% of public buildings enforcing non smoking policy
% of roads project completed
% of roads that meet international standards

50. Municipalities

% of survey respondents rating their satisfaction with the department's customer service as good or excellent

% of work completed in conformance with industry standards

% population coverage where centers are within 1 hour travel time

% products that have passed certification

% reduction in cost of solid waste transportation

% reduction in energy consumption

Community satisfaction rate on beaches

Recycling cost per ton

Community Involvement

of community forums/meetings per city per year

# of community members attending meetings and events by municipality

# of community participation rate in municipal events

# of corporate social responsibility partnership with private institutions

# of council member participation rates in municipality/council meetings

# of council members attending council meetings by municipality

# of effective community initiatives implemented per year

# of local institutions involved in community forums/meetings

# of major corporate social responsibility initiatives

# of outreach activities to increase community's awareness

# of participation programs involving the municipal councils per year

# of residents attending community forums/meetings in each city

% civic participation in the local area

% increase of forums and meetings to increase the community's participation

% of customer complains resolved in pre-determined time

% of population awareness of municipal councils' roles and responsibilities

Community Services

of conducted field visits by municipality management

# of conducted programs of outreach activities

# of conducted town hall meetings

# of conducted training programs based on training needs analysis of staff

# of corporate social responsibility initiatives

# of new municipal services

# of new services to meet customer and community needs

# of public awareness program implemented to reduce waste produced per capita

# of sewer main backups/Km

# of solid waste collection/Ton

# of solid waste disposal/Ton

# of storm and wastewater/Km

of the community services - entertainment parks

of the community services - libraries

of the community services - rest areas

50. Municipalities

of the community services - sport facilities

# of water tests done / year

# of water treatment & distribution locations

% active participation of all municipal entities in excellence program

% completion of the CRM system implementation

% completion of the needed IT infrastructure across all municipality locations

% coverage of municipality services to citizens

% increase in customer frequency to municipality centers

% increase of services provided in centers to accommodate residents needs

% of services provided by area

% of area services centers developed as per master plan

% of cities with municipality area services coverage

% of communities covered by municipality services

% of contact channels running

% of customer complains resolved within predetermined time

% of customer satisfaction on municipal community services

% of employees with necessary training

% of municipal services through e-government portal

% of municipality services offered online

% of products and merchandise complying with international standards

% of products having quality mark

% of residents having access to municipal services in each city

% of satisfaction in city services among residents, visitors and investors

% of services introduced online

% of the customers are satisfied with municipal services

% of the enterprise architecture model completed and implemented

% of the municipality's internal and external processes re-engineered to improve efficiency of service delivery

% of transaction services conducted within predetermined time

% of transaction services for customer services within predetermined time

% processes designed and implemented according to international best practices

% rehabilitation for all areas served by municipality

% solid waste management processing and recycling facilities utilization rate

% waste and solid waste treatment and disposal

Customer satisfaction rate for services offered

Customer satisfaction rate on external municipality centers' services

Water main breaks/Km

Knowledge Sharing

of conducted research and development studies

# of international municipal conferences held

# of knowledge sharing initiative

# of knowledge tours

50. Municipalities
# of measures to monitor community's awareness about municipal systems
# of memberships in international knowledge centers
% completion of knowledge sharing system
% increase employees' participation in work improvement through the suggestion scheme
% of knowledge sharing system to be in place in order to facilitate inter-municipal coordination
% of property management and database systems implemented
% of required components for knowledge management system completed

Land

# of crusher plant and fallen stock incinerator
# of land use billable hours
# of land use hours per total # of applications reviewed
% increase the life of landfill by divert the construction waste
% of cadastral diagrams produced within the agreed time frame
% of complete review of all land use projects within 120 days
% of eligible citizens with access to land
% of eligible people with titled land
% of land applications processed within the agreed time frame
% of land mass of country covered by updated administrative maps
% of title deeds processed within the agreed time
Government land action cost

Outsourcing

# of customer services delivered within agreed customer service charters/SLAs
% of guidelines and manuals of effective use of outsourcing published
% of municipal services outsourced
% of municipal services outsourced reduced operational cost
% of outsourced contracts covered by Service Level Agreements (SLAs)
% of satisfaction with quality of outsourced services
% outsourced services are provided by more than one supplier
% saving from outsourced services
Total reduction in operating costs through outsourcing

Policies & Regulations

% completion of financial regulations for municipal governance
% completion of municipal fees and revenue distribution regulations
% completion of municipal governance regulation
% completion of real estate regulation
% completion of the enforcement monitoring system
% completion of updating necessary standards, codes and regulations
% implementation of internal audit and performance management in accordance with government requirements
% implementation of the new organizational structure
% of coordination and feedback mechanisms from municipalities, municipal councils and other relevant stakeholders

50. Municipalities

% of enforcement monitoring system to be in place

% of existing standards and codes to be reviewed and documented with input from municipalities

% of existing standards, codes and regulations reviewed and documented

% of extra staff needed according to the new organizational structure

% of monitoring system defined including multiple contact channels

% of municipal compliance with existing policies, regulations and standards

% of necessary standards and codes updated and adopted

% of recruiting requirements are fulfilled

% of the IT strategy in accordance with e-government standards

Public Housing

of dwelling/houses

# of house as per # of bedrooms

# of new dwellings started

# of outstanding applications

# of permanent dwellings started in a year

# of update to regulations relating to real estate registration

on land and housing waiting lists

% completion of public houses demolished and rebuilt, as needed by the residents

% completion of public housing compensation, as needed by the residents

% completion of public housing maintenance projects, as per plan

% completion the short term detailed plans

% of completed demolition and rebuilding of the buildings that are subject to collapse

% of public housing units requiring immediate maintenance are maintained on time

% of the additional public houses required to reduce the average # of residents per housing unit

% support of the infrastructure for the housing facilities

% urbanization growth

Average # of residents per public house

Average length of time of applications have been pending

Urban population (% of total population)

Recreation Services

of acres of city property managed

% accessibility to existing local community facilities

% community satisfaction with municipal recreation services

% of citizens surveyed rating appearance of parks as good or excellent

% of maintenance of public parks

% of municipal facility clients rating facility cleanliness and safety as satisfactory or better

% of on-time construction of new parks projects

% of parks constructed in each city as per the urban master plan

% of residents with access to parks and open spaces as per standards

50. Municipalities

% of secure clean, beautiful beaches with comprehensive services

% of services by category delivered within customer service charters/SLAs

Road Service

of public convenience sites provided by the authority normally throughout the year

% creation of new internal road networks to increase accessibility to all local communities

% of areas with accessible road networks as per international standards

% of communities with direct access to local roads

% of missed collections put right by the end of the next working day

% of road networks achieving volume to capacity ratio standards

% of roads fully meet specifications

% pedestrian crossings with facilities for people living with disabilities

% street lighting columns inspected for structural condition per annum

Public satisfaction with the roads in the region

Urban Development

of allocated land plots inline with the master plan to provide access to residents to parks and open spaces

# of public awareness campaigns per annum

# of waiting list for land distribution

% alignment between the detailed plans and the urban master plan

% compatibility of detailed plans with the urban master plan

% completion of needed infrastructure projects offered in each city

% completion of solid waste management project phases

% completion of the design requirements and construction of short term projects

% completion of underground storm water & irrigation maps

% compliance of the detailed planning with the urban master plan

% definition and demarcation of geographic boundaries between municipalities

% increase per capita green area

% of completed detailed plans

% of development of accurate information and efficient systems to support urban planning and development

% of housing facilities achieving acceptable safety standards as specified through criteria

% of housing facilities having access to community services in each city

% of infrastructure developed as per the urban master plan to provide community services in each city

% of internal roads as per safety standards

% of master and urban plans completed

% of municipal entities integrated their master and urban plans development into county level plan

% of sea front areas developed as per the urban master plan

% of sea front areas in coastal cities

50. Municipalities

% of the infrastructure upgrade in city areas in line with urban plan

% projects aligned with the urban master plan

Diversion rate of recyclable material and compost to reject waste

Length of newly constructed roads in each city as per the urban master plan

Public satisfaction rate

Tourist satisfaction rate

51. Pension Management

Asset Management

of approval of asset allocation by the board each year

# of updated governance framework

# of updated policies and procedures approved

% approved performance and monitoring framework

% of actual investment return exceeds investment policy benchmark

% of approved compliance monitoring system

Asset Allocation - bills and bonds issued by public and private sector (in %)

Asset Allocation - cash and Deposits (in %)

Asset Allocation - land and Buildings (in %)

Asset Allocation - loans (in %)

Asset Allocation - mutual funds (CIS) (in %)

Asset Allocation - of which: bills and bonds issued by public administration (in %)

Asset Allocation - of which: bonds issued by the private sector (in %)

Asset Allocation - other investments (in %)

Asset Allocation - shares (in %)

Asset Allocation - unallocated insurance contracts (in %)

Benefit Payments

of millions of dollars of assets under management

# of participants

# of retirees and beneficiaries currently receiving benefits

% customers satisfied with payment service

% distribution of disposable income amongst the post retirement population

% of applications processed in 3 days

% of e-payment system completed

% of member info requests to actuary in 5 days of request

% of payments on time

% of pensions are increased each year to keep pace with price inflation

% of retirees and beneficiaries currently receiving benefits manually

Amount of adequate absolute income at retirement

Benefit increase rate per year

Gross replacement rates by average earnings level, mandatory pension programs, men (in %)

51. Pension Management

Gross replacement rates by average earnings level, mandatory pension programs, women (in %)

Ratio of income level post-retirement to pre-retirement

Replacement rate for the median pensioner

Customer Services

of partnering program developed and adopted

% calculations completed accurately the first time

% member records analyzed & updated

% of customer relationship management (CRM) developed and implemented

% of customer service delivery framework developed and implemented

% of employee compensation & benefits system implemented

% of general public understand pensions and related matters

% of knowledge management framework implemented

% of members ranked satisfied or better based on member feedback surveys conducted

% of payments within 10 days of notification date

% of payments within 30 days of trigger date

% of performance management system enhanced

% of process management model & initiatives implemented

% of special needs members ranked satisfied or better based on member feedback surveys conducted

% of termination events notified within 5 working day

% of web services enhancement completed

% quality management model implemented

Average speed to answer incoming calls will be 30 seconds or less

Fund Investment

of enterprises broken down by size classes of members

# of enterprises broken down by size of investments

# of enterprises in other countries

# of identified and implemented new investment opportunities

# of members in pension funds

% funding by government

% invested in superior long-term risk-adjusted returns

% of benefit administrative costs are less than peer median administrative costs per active member

% of compliance with standards on monetary resource management

% of fund's fiduciary role validation exercise conducted

% of investment return meets the assumed actuarial annual rate of interest

% of non-autonomous pension funds

% of risk management framework developed and implemented

% of total fund market value spent on investment administration

Actual investment return exceeds actuarial discount rate

Employees' contributions, in % of total contributions

Minimum actuarial rate of return

51. Pension Management

Pension contributions as a share of GDP

Pension funds: total expenditure on pensions

Pension funds: total investments

Pension funds: total pension contributions

Rate of return required from the assets to maintain pension fund at a fully funded basis

Total investments broken down by currencies

Total pension fund

Policy & Legislation

of funding options presented to government

# of recommendations presented to government

% of accepted recommendations implemented prior to follow-up audit

% of final court orders reviewed and responded to in 10 working days

52. Population

Demography

of births

# of live births

# of private households by size

% of female population aged 15 and over

% of married population

% of population aged 15 and over living in private households

% of population aged 15-74

% of population aged 65 and over

% of population change

% of unmarried population

% of widowed population

Annual average population by sex

Average # of resident children in the family

Average age of mother

Average population by five-year age group

Crude birth rate

Crude rate of net migration

Deaths by age

Divorced population by age

Dwellings by # of building

Dwellings by # of rooms

Dwellings by total occupants

Dwellings by type of ownership

Old-age-dependency ratio

Population aged 15-74 by sex

Population by age

Population by citizenship

Population by country of birth

52. Population

Population by current economical activity

Population by employment status

Population by highest level of educational attainment

Population by marital status

Population by sex

Projected old-age dependency ratio

Women per 100 men

Fertility

of declared legal abortions by age

# of live births by month

% of live births outside marriage

Average mother's age

Fertility rate by age

Mean age of women at childbearing

Total fertility rate

Marriage & Divorce

of divorces

# of divorces by duration of marriage

# of marriages

# of marriages by month

% of marriages by previous marital status

Divorce rate by duration of marriage

First marriage rate by age

Migration & Asylum

of acquisition of citizenship

# of active population by citizenship

# of asylum applicants considered to be unaccompanied minors by citizenship

# of asylum applications

# of asylum by citizenship

# of asylum decisions pending

# of decisions on asylum applications by citizenship

# of decisions withdrawing status granted as final decision

# of decisions withdrawing status granted at first instance decision

# of foreign workers by citizenship

# of foreign workers by economic activity

# of immigration by age

# of immigration by country of previous residence

# of immigration by sex

# of new # of asylum applicants

# of persons subject of asylum applications pending

# of resettled persons

# of total emigration

% of asylum rejections

52. Population

% of non-national workers by citizenship

Population by citizenship - % of foreigners

Mortality

dying between exact ages

left alive at given exact age

of deaths by age

# of deaths by month

# of deaths by sex

# of infant mortality

Average life expectancy at age 65

Infant mortality rate

Life expectancy at 60

Life expectancy at age 65, by gender

Life expectancy at birth, by gender

Probability of dying between exact ages

Probability of dying by sex and age

Total person-years lived above given exact age

53. Prison Management

Administration

% change in dollars spent due to waste reduction / transformation efforts

% change in resources allocated due to waste reduction / transformation efforts

% of annual food requirements produced through prison farms

Administrative support costs as a % of total agency costs

Administrative support positions as a % of total agency positions

Annual occupancy rate

Cost of inmate litigation by issue

Cost per meal per offender

Total cost of correctional facilities maintenance and repair

Community Corrections

of court-ordered collected from offenders on community supervision

# of monthly personal contacts with offenders supervised in the community

# of monthly personal contacts with offenders supervised in the community compared to the department standard: community Control

# of monthly personal contacts with offenders supervised in the community compared to the department standard: maximum

# of monthly personal contacts with offenders supervised in the community compared to the department standard: medium

# of monthly personal contacts with offenders supervised in the community compared to the department standard: minimum

# of monthly personal contacts with sex offenders supervised in the community compared to the department standard

# of offenders that successfully complete their sentence

53. Prison Management
# of successful rehabilitations and early releases
% of community control offenders are still under supervision at the end of a two year measurement period
% of community control offenders that successfully complete their sentence at the end of a two year measurement period
% of court-ordered amounts collected from offenders on community supervision
% of offenders who successfully complete supervision and are not subsequently recommitted a new crime within 2 years (to prison)
% of post-prison release offenders that successfully complete their sentence or are still under supervision
% of pre-trial intervention offenders that complete their sentence or are still under supervision
% of timely delivery to court
% of value of community service provided to local communities
Status of offenders 2 years after the period of supervision was imposed: # absconded
Status of offenders 2 years after the period of supervision was imposed: # revoked
Status of offenders 2 years after the period of supervision was imposed: % absconded
Status of offenders 2 years after the period of supervision was imposed: % revoked
Three-year felony reconviction rate
Total of court-ordered amounts collected from offenders on community supervision

Inmate Education Skills

# of inmates in mandatory literacy programs
% of inmates in literacy programs who score at or above 9th 6th grade level
% of inmates needing special education programs who participate in special education programs
% of inmates who successfully complete GED education programs
% of inmates who successfully complete mandatory literacy programs
% of inmates who successfully complete vocational education programs
Average increase in grade level achieved by inmates participating in educational programs

Inmate Health Services

# of health care grievances that are upheld
# of offender deaths and/ serious Injuries
# of sexual violence occurrences in institutions
# of staff serious injuries
# of suicides per 100000 inmates in correctional facilities/institutions
% of facilities passing clinical audits
% of health care grievances that are upheld
Health care costs per inmate

53. Prison Management

Mental health cost per day per inmate

Physical health cost per day per inmate

Offender Control

\# of court findings for constitutional rights violations

\# of deaths or serious injury whilst in police custody

\# of disturbances/ serious incidents

\# of escapes

\# of escapes from police custody

\# of escapes from the secure perimeter of major institutions

\# of offender deaths not from natural causes

\# of prison population

\# of release plans completed for inmates released from prison

\# of transition plans completed for inmates released from prison

% of inmate suicide

% of inmates placed in a facility that provides at least one of the inmate's primary program needs

% of inmates who did not escape when assigned outside a secure perimeter

% of medium to high risk offenders that are receiving evidence based interventions for top four criminogenic needs

% of offenders who were medium/ high risk at time of admission who are convicted for a new aggravated misdemeanor/ felony within 3 years after discharge from system

% of release plans completed for inmates released from prison

% of technical violations resulting in Jail / prison

% of victim notifications that meet the statutory time period requirements

% of workload calculated demand per FTE staff

% utilization of all available bed space (prisons and centers)

Average time payment of jail subsidy

Average time taken to clear offences reported

Prison population as % of capacity

Parole Deliberations

\# of individuals on paroles

\# of parole release deliberations

\# of parole revocation hearings conducted

\# of paroles granted

Parole Executive Clemency

\# of executive clemency applications recommended

\# of executive clemency applications reviewed

\# of pardons recommended

\# of pardons reviewed

% of executive clemency applications processed timely

Parole Revocation

\# of GED's received

\# of paroles revoked

53. Prison Management

% of parole revoked

Parole Work Release

of work releases granted

# of work releases revoked

% of victims notified as designated

% of work release requested granted

% of work releases revoked

Probation Supervision

of jail days served on electronic home detention

% of contract goals met by contracted agencies

% of drug offender probation offenders that successfully complete their sentence or are still under supervision at the end of a two year measurement period

% of probationers that successfully complete their sentence or are still under supervision at the end of a two year measurement period

Jail cost savings from electronic home detention program

Public Service Work

of available work assignments

# of inmates available for work or program assignments

% of available inmates who work

% of those available for work or program assignments who are not assigned

Rehabilitation

of inmates participating in faith-based dorm programs

# of releases provided faith-based housing assistance

% of community supervision offenders who successfully complete transition, rehabilitation, or support programs

% of community supervision offenders without subsequent recommitment to community supervision or prison for 24 months after release

% of inmates participating in religious programming

% of inmates who successfully complete transition, rehabilitation, or support programs without subsequent recommitment to prison for 24 months after release

% of inmates without subsequent recommitment to prison for 24 months after release

Release Assessment

of risk assessments conducted

% of offender risk assessments calculated within timeframes

% of parole deliberations resulting in parole

Risk Identification

of offenders assigned / supervised in accordance with risk assessment/ classification instrum

% of medium to high risk offenders who's risk score shows significant drop prior to discharge from the system

53. Prison Management

% of medium/ high risk offenders who successfully complete case plan programming for each of their top four criminogenic needs before final release from corrections system

% of offenders who were medium/ high risk at time of admission who's score shows significant reduction at final discharge from corrections system

% required custody classifications completed

% required validated risk assessment

% risk assessments completed

Security & Operations

of batteries committed by inmates on one or more persons per 1000 inmates

# of inmates receiving major disciplinary reports per 1000 inmates

# of near security breaches

# of security breaches

% of reported criminal incidents investigated by the inspector general's office

Substance Abuse

of inmates who are receiving substance abuse services

# of substance abuse tests administered to offenders being supervised in the community

% of community supervision offenders who have completed drug treatment without subsequent recommitment to community supervision or prison within 24 months after release

% of inmates needing programs who successfully complete drug abuse education/treatment programs

% of inmates who have completed drug treatment without subsequent recommitment to community supervision or prison within 24 months after release

% of random inmate drug tests that are negative

% of substance abuse tests administered to offenders being supervised in the community in which negative test results were obtained

54. Public Finance

Accounting

% of claims not requiring pre-audit processed within 3 working days of receipt

% of deductions processed by required due dates

% of non-general fund money paid for unemployment claims

% of offset matches that are either released or applied to the liability within 45 days

% of paychecks rewritten per pay period

% of required (annual and monthly) accounting reports completed timely

% of unemployment compensation claims reimbursed within 30 days

Budgeting

% governor's recommendations delivered to the legislature on time

54. Public Finance

% growth in dollar value of grant application

% of accurate property valuations on file

% of agencies that submit budget on time

% of bill summaries/legislative action completed by deadline

% of city government rates certified

% of city requests for budget materials that are accurate

% of city requests for budget materials that are timely

% of county budget annual report materials delivered accurately

% of county budget annual report materials delivered on time

% of time budget system operational and accessible to departments for budget submission

% of utility tax replacement tax data delivered to the counties accurately

Budget variance

Central Assessments

of protests from board of review

# of replacement tax assessments completed

# of utility and railroad assessments completed

% of timely responses

Processing time for appeal process

Deficit & Debt

Debt by currency of issue

Debt securities

Debt securities issues in all currencies

General government debt

Government deficit/surplus

International debt securities

International debt securities, breakdown by currency

International debt securities, breakdown by sector

Public balance

Quarterly government debt

Quarterly non-financial accounts for general government

Social security funds debt

Total central government debt

Total derivatives

Equalization

% of agricultural jurisdictions within statutory assessment level tolerance

% of appraisals completed in a timely manner

% of commercial jurisdictions within statutory assessment level tolerance

% of residential jurisdictions within statutory assessment level tolerance

Reduction in # of equalization orders issued

Financial Management

of bank branches per 100,000 people

% effectiveness of payroll controls

54. Public Finance

% of modified departments implementing and applying the new Chart of Accounts

% of aggregate and sub-aggregate component level expenditure out-turn compared to original budget

% of cash flow resources borrowed from internal funds

% of ease of access to loans

% of modified departments implementing and applying standardized budget circular

% of modified departments applying and implementing decentralized accounting and reporting model

% of modified departments covered for the purpose of consolidation and reporting of financial data

% of modified departments implementing and applying new strategic planning procedures

% of received federal funds obligated and expended

% of variance between planned original budget and actual spending / per year

% return on average short-term cash holdings

Aggregate revenue out-turn compared to original approved budget

Average commercial banks prime lending % rate

Average time of accounts reconciliation and annual financial statements

Bank capital to asset ratio %

Bank credit stock to residents

Bank non-performing loans to total gross loans %

Cash surplus/deficit (% of GDP)

Deposit insurance coverage % of GDP per capita

Domestic credit provided by banking sector % of GDP

Employees' social security contribution rate

Government budget surplus/deficit

Government budget surplus/deficit (% of GDP)

Marginal analysis of sector credit growth vs. sector current GDP

Net foreign assets (current LCU)

Recording and management of cash balances, debt and guarantees

Revenue, excluding grants (% of GDP)

Total assets and market capitalization of top local banks

Total general government debt

Total general government debt (% of GDP)

Financial Operations

of receive unqualified audit opinion

Average # of days from requisition submitted to purchase order printed

Average # of days to close quarter in financial system

City bond rating (Moody's)

Customer service ratings "very good" to "excellent"

Local tax revenues from delinquencies, audits, and detection work (millions)

Tax returns billed per FTE

54. Public Finance

Financial Performance

% accuracy of budget forecasts

% development and implementation of monitoring and reporting application

% development of budgeting process and reports

% development of external processes and reports – excluding budgeting process

% deviation of total budget against plan

% deviation of total HR budget against plan

% Internal financial procedures and reports developed by the finance section

% Internal financial reports submitted and published on time

% of budget variance

% of deviation from final approved budget to actual spending

% of deviation from planned budget to actual spending (budget of modified departments)

% of modified departments implementing and applying new performance monitoring system

% of the real spending rate from the approved budget

% reports submitted on-time to the external entities

% return on average short term cash holdings

% variance between actual and planned operating budget

Elapsed days between receipt of internal budget change request and submission of request

Fund annualized return

Interest earned in excess of fees for gov. fund bank accounts held by government agencies (in millions)

Financial Planning

# of capital projects and subprojects per project manager

# of major special projects

% Initiated major maintenance projects

% of projects completed within budget estimates

Major maintenance cost per square foot

Variance of budget monitoring report at projecting year-end general fund expenditures

Variance of budget monitoring report at projecting year-end general fund revenues

Fiscal policy

% dependency of GDP Deflator on CPI-based inflation, monetary inflation, and imported inflation

% of claims in substantial compliance with finance rules and regulations

% of deviation from budget deficit/surplus against planned

% of diversification of revenues

Average budget performance as % of GPD

Capital adequacy ratio

54. Public Finance

Consumer price indices

Consumer price inflation (%)

Employees' social security contribution rate (% of GDP per capita)

Employers' social security contribution rate (% of GDP per capita)

Fiscal balance in % of current GDP

General government gross financial liabilities

Government net borrowing/net lending

Government non-discretionary spending as % of total expenditures

Highest marginal tax rate, individual rate (%)

Interest rate spread (Lending rate minus deposit rate % points)

Lending interest rate (%)

Multi year perspective in fiscal planning, expenditure policy and budgeting

Net domestic credit

Oversight of aggregate fiscal risk from other public sector entities

Producer price indices

Real interest rate

Risk unadjusted capital adequacy ratio

Tax evasion rate

Total collected social security contribution

Total collected social security contribution (% of GDP)

Total consolidated commercial bank assets as % of GDP

Total tax revenues (% of GDP)

National Accounts

of banking transactions

# of financial transactions

% changes in volume

Banks' balance sheet assets and liabilities

Foreign official reserves

Gross value added by agriculture, hunting and fishing

Gross value added by communication services

Gross value added by construction

Gross value added by energy

Gross value added by financial services

Gross value added by total, volumes

Gross value added by trade and transport

Gross wages and salaries

Household expenditure per inhabitant

Monetary gold in fine troy ounces

National accounts detailed breakdowns by industry

Net saving

Nominal holding gains/losses

Total consumption expenditure of households

Public Expenditure

of hearing cases by the board

54. Public Finance

of suppliers contracts

% of annual approval rate of all submitted policy advice

% of budget of strategic initiatives cost analyzed in details

% of capital projects assessed for opportunities for public private partnership arrangements

Current taxes on income

General government expenditure

General government expenditure (% of GDP)

General government gross fixed capital formation

General government output

Social benefits paid by general government

Stock and monitoring of expenditure payment arrears as % of total expenditure

Total expenditure on health

Total law, order and defense expenditure

Total public expenditure on health

Total public social expenditure

Total spend on procurement transformation initiative

Revenue & Taxes

of audit hours of investigative audit

# of contingent & evaluation reports completed

# of homesteads qualifying for the grants under the tax relief grant (in millions)

% of assessors meeting continuing education requirements

% of billed accounts resolved within 180 days

% of dollars deposited on the same day of receipt

% of electronic filed individual income tax refunds issued within 14 days of receipt

% of environmental and labor taxes in total tax revenues

% of federal legislation analysis published timely

% of income tax returns requiring review completed timely

% of internal audit project hours spent on high risk work functions

% of local option sales tax and school local option sales tax timely distributed each year

% of net debt collected within 365 days

% of net debt collected within 90 days

% of online tax system work time availability

% of paper filed individual income tax refunds issued within 60 days of receipt

% of protests resolved within 12 months

% of refunds and receipts reports completed timely

% of state fiscal impact estimates completed timely

% of tax revenues received by electronic funds transfer

% of utilization of electronic filing Program

% of utilization of the e-file services system

54. Public Finance

% tax collected

Amount of economic impact generated ($ millions)

Collections on delinquent and deficient accounts within the compliance division

Coverage ratio (operating revenue/operating expense)

Current wealth

Gross operating surplus

Implicit tax rate on labor

Income, saving and net lending / net borrowing

Net cost of tax collection

Net national income

Ratio of costs to collections

Taxes on goods and services

Taxes on income and profits

Taxes on production and imports

Taxes on the average worker

Total amount collected per audit enforcement dollar expended

Total amount of debt collected within 90 days

Total amount recovered for clients

Total general government expenditure

Total general government revenue

Total social contributions

Risk Management

of auto liability claims

# of property claims

# of workers compensation claims

Incurred cost of auto liability claims

Incurred cost of property claims

Incurred cost of workers compensation claims

Risk premium on lending (Prime lending rate minus treasury bill rate % points)

Support & Aid

Net amount official development assistance

Total amount of government financial transfers to fishing

Total amount to producer support

55. Regional Development

Attract & Retain Talent

of career management offices set up across the region

# of international education curriculum in region

% completion of housing program design

% decrease in land allocation time

% of citizens with university degrees

55. Regional Development
% quality of schools infrastructure with respect to capital city schools infrastructure
% satisfaction of private investors on effectiveness of land allocation programs
% satisfaction of stakeholders with access to jobs
% student performance compared with performance of students in capital city
% trainees satisfaction with technology courses
Average # of residents per room
Literacy rate
Women IT skills literacy rate

Communication

of events & activities attendees
# of events participation per year
# of feedback from readers
# of magazine copies distributed among residents
# of out reach surveys done
% completion of the process of setting up regional portal
% completion of the process of setting up regional radio
% completion of content & design stage of regional magazine
% satisfaction of events & activities attendees
End users satisfaction rate

Community Development

annual population growth
of active population
# of private households by economic activity
# of private households with children
% households with broadband access
% of employed persons aged 15 and over
% of households with access to the Internet at home
% population growth
% satisfaction of resident on community enablers
Average income of households
Average primary income of households
Expatriate to citizen Ratio
Gross fixed capital
Gross value added at basic prices
Ratio of female to male
Total active population by international migration
Total employment (in hours worked)
Total employment (in persons)
Total population by age
Total population by country of citizenship
Total population by economical status

55. Regional Development

Total population by household status

Total population by sex

Total population by size of household

Education & Health

of available beds in hospitals

# of deaths due to accidents

# of deaths due to cancer

# of deaths due to ischaemic heart diseases

# of deaths due to transport accidents

# of dentists per 1000 citizens

# of doctors per 1000 citizens

Regional differences in # of physicians, large regions: maximum

Regional differences in # of physicians, large regions: minimum

Regional differences in age-adjusted mortality rates, large regions: maximum

Regional differences in age-adjusted mortality rates, large regions: minimum

Regional differences is basic educational attainment, large regions: country average

Regional differences is basic educational attainment, large regions: maximum

Regional differences is basic educational attainment, large regions: minimum

Regions with the highest tertiary education attainment compared to the national average: country average

Regions with the highest tertiary education attainment compared to the national average: regional value

Effective Infrastructure

of human resources in science and technology

# of patent applications by year

# of road related accidents

# of traffic safety campaign completed

% completion of bus franchise

% completion of highway revamp plan

% of transport needs covered in transport master plan

% satisfaction of residents with the progress on highway revamp

% satisfaction of residents/businesses on the network service

% stakeholder's satisfaction on the road's compliance to highway safety

Accessibility index

Road network connectivity index

Travel time to reach international transport centers

Regional GDP

of researchers

% employment in high-tech sectors (high-tech manufacturing and knowledge-intensive services)

55. Regional Development

Dispersion of regional GDP per inhabitant

Disposable income of private household

Gross domestic product (GDP) at current market prices

Index of regional GDP per capita, small regions

Index of the population in regions with low GDP per capita, small regions: as a % of population

Range in regional GDP per capita, small regions: average

Range in regional GDP per capita, small regions: maximum

Range in regional GDP per capita, small regions: minimum

Real growth rate of regional GDP at market prices

Regional gross domestic product (millions)

Regional gross domestic product (per inhabitant)

Share of GDP increase of each region due to the % of most dynamic regions, small regions

Total intramural R&D expenditure

Regional Labor Market

% of long-term unemployment (12 months and more)

Differences in annual employment growth across regions: country average

Differences in annual employment growth across regions: maximum

Differences in annual employment growth across regions: minimum

Employment rate of the age group 15-64

Employment rate of the group 55-64 years

Share of national employment growth due to the % of most dynamic regions, small regions

56. Safety & Security

Alcohol Control

% alcohol related road fatality rates

% of 11th grade youth who believe there is great risk of harming themselves if they take one or two drinks of alcohol nearly every day

% of 11th grade youth who report drinking alcohol in the past 30 days

% of 11th grade youth who report driving after drinking alcohol in the past 30 days

% of 11th grade youth who report having 5 or more drinks of alcohol within a couple hours during the past 30 days

% of 11th grade youth who report that it would be very easy to get beer, wine or hard liquor

% of 8th grade youth who believe there is great risk of harming themselves if they take one or two drinks of alcohol nearly every day

% of 8th grade youth who report drinking alcohol in the past 30 days

% of 8th grade youth who report having 5 or more drinks of alcohol within a couple hours during the past 30 days

% of 8th grade youth who report that it would be very easy to get beer, wine or hard liquor

% of students self reporting current alcohol use

56. Safety & Security

Ambulance Services

of EMS services requests/unit responses generated

% of citizen overall satisfaction with EMS

% of first responder agencies with access to the center information system

% of life threatening calls responded to in less than 10 Minutes

% of local jurisdictions with interoperable communication capabilities for first responders

% of patients delivered to a hospital with a pulse and discharged from the hospital alive

% of patients delivered to hospital with a pulse

Community Confidence

increase in personal security and private property security

of community police officers

# of consultation by police members with key community stakeholder groups

# of discussion forums held by police

# of joint initiatives and projects between police and stakeholders

# of key community stakeholder groups

# of negative media messages

# of positive media messages

# of promotion for the public

# of provision of reports on policing with the community

# of public awareness campaigns

# of reports on police performance issued

# of reports on public consultation

# of times the police and local council dealt with anti-social behavior

# of victims served by grant funded programs

% attendance of police members in community meetings

% community perception of safety

% compliance with statutory obligations

% feeling unsafe or very unsafe on the street after dark

% increase of personal security and private property protection

% increase protection against terrorist attack

% of citizens' concern for human caused disaster

% of citizens concerned about natural disaster

% of community perceptions of public order, safety and security

% of customer satisfaction levels with wider policing services

% of people who have confidence in police services

% of public satisfaction with community police members

% of residents reporting a feeling safe outside in their neighborhood day and night

% public satisfaction of police ability to resolve problems

Citizens rating quality of neighborhood life as excellent or good

Net value of media coverage

56. Safety & Security

Public attitude survey, satisfaction with community policing

Community Safety

of campaigns

# of dealing with local concerns about anti-social behavior and crime issues by the local council and police

# of dogs/cats euthanized per 1,000 population

# of high threat level alerts

# of officers trained in critical incident command

# of prepared MOUs and signed with key stakeholders

# of protection activities against terrorist attack

# of public attitude survey regarding "how safe do you feel ?"

# of quarterly meetings held with community

# of relevant partnership initiatives

# of response times for a crisis-related incident

# of specialist to support victims of a serious sexual offence

# of thefts reported

# of unplanned public safety and security incidents dealt with by police

# of which child abuse is prevented

% adult re-offending rates for those under probation supervision

% awareness of civil protection arrangements in the local area

% building resilience to violent extremism

% citizen satisfaction with 911 emergency services

% citizen satisfaction with the livability of their neighborhoods

% of animal owner compliance/enforcement

% of community protection

% of critical infrastructure sites that have completed vulnerability assessment

% of critical infrastructure sites that have protective action plans

% of critical infrastructure sites that have surveillance detection plans

% of ethnic composition of offenders on youth justice system disposals

% of how safe people feel after dark

% of privatization of medical services

% of privatization of prisons for minor crimes

% of repeat incidents of domestic violence

% of residents who feel safe while walking alone

% of student awareness

% of workplaces that comply with occupational health and safety policy

% of young offenders' access to suitable accommodation

% of young offenders' engagement in suitable education, training and employment

% of young people receiving a conviction in court who are sentenced to custody

% perceptions of anti-social behavior

% perceptions of drunk or rowdy behavior as a problem

56. Safety & Security

% perceptions of parents taking responsibility for the behavior of their children in the area

% perceptions that people in the area treat one another with respect and consideration

% satisfaction of different groups with the way the police and local council dealt with anti-social behavior

% understanding of local concerns about anti-social behavior issues by the local council and police

Crime rates per 1,000 population

Rate of hospital admissions per 100,000 for alcohol related harm

Rate of proven re-offending by young offenders

Re-offending rate of prolific and priority offenders

Controlling Crime

of arson incidents

# of assault with injury crime rate

# of assaults or threats

# of attempted burglary

# of bicycle theft

# of burglary with entry

# of consumer fraud or corruption

# of conventional victimization

# of crime network

# of crime reports taken by patrol

# of crimes committed per 1,000 population

# of crimes recorded by the police

# of deaths or serious injury whilst in police custody

# of developed staff in terms of combating organized crime

# of domestic violence - murder

# of downtown offenses

# of homicides in cities

# of motor vehicle theft

# of motor-cycle theft

# of non-conventional crimes, consumer fraud

# of police officers

# of preventive crime initiatives

# of property crimes

# of recorded criminal cases per 10000 population

# of recorded domestic burglaries per 1,000 households

# of recorded offences cleared

# of robbery

# of serious acquisitive crime

# of serious knife crime

# of sexual offences against women

# of theft by pick-pocketing

56. Safety & Security

of theft from or out of cars

# of theft of cars by youth

# of vehicle crimes per year /per 10000 population

# of violent and property crimes committed per 1,000 population

# of violent crimes

# of violent crimes reported per 100,000 population

% change in crime rates

% crime prevention hours spent

% crimes against visitors

% increase in detected criminal cases

% of crimes cleared

% of major criminal investigations resolved from all divisions

% of recorded offences cleared

% of regions with completed plans for terrorism and all hazards
preparedness

% of serious violent crime done by women

% overall reported crime rate per 1000 population

% reduction in crime rate

% reduction in serious crimes per 1000 population

% reported light crime rate per 1000 population

% results of apprehension

Business-private crime ratio

Clear up rate

Clearance rate for offences

Detection rate

Gun crime rate

Index crime rate per 1,000 population

Prison population per 100,000 people

Total business costs of crime and violence

Total prison population

Victimization rate per household

Victimization rate per person

Criminal Investigation

of arrests by the investigative division

# of criminal investigations worked by the investigative division

# of judges per 100,000 residents

% of all incidents of known major corruption, fraudulent practices and
organized criminal activity investigated

% of cases investigated resulting in conviction

% of cases involving fires of suspicious or unknown origin in which the cause
is identified

% of criminal cases involving fire, explosives and incendiary devices which
are resolved

% of major investigations resolved

56. Safety & Security

Resolution rate of criminal offenses

Value of contraband seized by the investigative division

Criminalistics Laboratory

of service requests older than 30 days in the regional lab locations

% accuracy rate for all criminal lab work

% for all criminal history information processed by the crime information center repository

% of medical examinations completed same day

% successful completion by analysts of proficiency testing

% successful completion of at least one discipline specific training event annually for each lab analysts

Average lab-wide turn-around time on cases closed (days)

Critical Assets Risks

of detail hours

% decrease of security incidents

% of assets that have been identified and categorized in order of criticality

% of assets that have been identified and categorized in terms of vulnerability

% of completion of project

% of risk management units with information fusion capability

% of security audits passed successfully

% of site security plans completed

% of staff with risk management duties who successfully pass risk management analysis training

Drought

of "water shortage criteria" in all community projects to mitigate drought-related slow-downs during drought years

of "water-moving" equipment (including pumps, pipeline, tanker trucks)

of back-flow preventers/valves on residential structures

# of conditions that can lead to wasted water include garden hoses left lying in pools of water and spray nozzles left open

# of contingency plans for firefighting

# of crop insurance to preserve economic stability for farmers during a drought

# of developed drought contingency plans in the event of water shortages or rationing

# of education programs on cross-contamination

# of identified major "water-dependent" entities in the community, including large water usage employers, hospitals, and food services

# of identified opportunities in future water conservancies

# of implement plans to identify when a drought begins and ends

# of in drought plans to minimize fish and wildlife impacts

# of modify water rate structure to influence consumer water use

# of organized drought information meetings for the public and the media

# of policy to increase and protect instream flows and wetlands

56. Safety & Security

of pre-identified "drought planning teams" comprised of stakeholders in the community (including members from public works and utility, agricultural and ranching)

# of public information program designed to communicate the potential severity of a drought and the appropriate responses of the local population

# of statues governing water rights for possible modification during water shortages

# of temporary water supplies from inactive or dead storage or from ground water sources

# of voluntary water conservation measures the public can take

# of warning plans based on drought conditions and moisture measurements to alert officials of increased risk of wildfire

# of water conservation policies for inverted block water rate structure

# of water conservation policies for low flow plumbing devices

# of water conservation policies for moisture sensors on sprinkler systems

# of water conservation policies for the use of non-potable water for purposes that do not require treated water (landscape watering)

# of water main leak detection followed by repair and replacement to reduce water system losses

% information developed on drought tolerant grass varieties and xeriscapes

% of effects of the trees on groundwater recharge and loss of water table resources

% of fire department decreased water pressure and supply

% of information with community on water-saving appliances, shower heads, and toilets

% of low pressure in community drinking water lines that can lead to back-flow from residential gray water into primary lines

% of replacement program for aging and defective water meters

% of tertiary developed or extended water supply system

% reduction of water system losses

% shifting to uniform block rates and shifting to increasing block rates increasing rates during summer months

% use of non-potable water sources to meet community requirements

Total amount from imposing excess-use charges during times of water shortage

Drug Control

of drug users recorded as being in effective treatment

# of functioning county education programs

# of identification, awareness and education programs delivered

# of interdiction investigations

# of major drug trafficking organizations disrupted

# of multi-disciplinary drug endangered children response teams operational

# of narcotics arrests

# of pharmaceutical diversion investigations

56. Safety & Security

of reported clandestine methamphetamine lab incidents

# of responses to clandestine methamphetamine laboratories

# of students trained annually at the counterdrug regional training facility

% of agencies addressing drug use and related crime

% of counties served by performance based grant funded programs

% of drug affected offenders successfully completing substance abuse treatment in grant funded programs

% of drug investigations resolved

% of funded projects monitored for project effectiveness and financial compliance

% of past month illegal drug use

% of resources from sources other than grants

% of served by grant funded multi-jurisdictional drug enforcement task forces

% of students self reporting current drug use

% of students self reporting current tobacco use

% of validated government agencies requests for assistance and training that are supported and completed

% perceptions of drug use or drug dealing as a problem

Drug-related offending rate

Earthquake

of adopted residential building codes that require earthquake-resistant construction, such as using foundation piers

# of building reinforcements against earthquakes

# of public with earthquake insurance

Expansive Soil

of administrative procedure to check for expansive soils

# of builders apply for permits to build on expansive soils

# of educated builders on appropriate foundation types for soils

# of implemented a public information strategy for informing citizens and the building industry of the dangers to buildings of expansive soils

# of investigations done on construction of new foundations to mitigate expansive soil damage

# of provided information on landscaping techniques that can mitigate foundation damage

# of repair on facilities that show evidence of soils-related damage

% of facilities that show evidence of or have expansive soils-related damage

Total cost damage of buildings on expansive soils

Extreme Heat

identify public events scheduled during the hotter times of the year

of assists in installing window air conditioners for vulnerable population

# of community education campaigns on signs and symptoms of heat-related illness and steps that are available to prevent or respond to such illnesses

56. Safety & Security

of community hotlines for residents to obtain extreme heat-related information

# of developed a heat emergency annex to the emergency operations plan

# of extra extended hours when appropriate at designated community facilities

# of funds given to individuals or families on limited income to help offset utility bills

# of outdoor workers and other at-risk populations

# of promotions of actions to reduce the effects of community "heat islands"

# of promotions of urban vegetation and increasing the reflectiveness of urban surfaces

# of protocols with local utility providers to suspend utility shutoffs during extreme heat conditions

# of public facilities that can function as cooling shelters during heat waves and inform the public when they are operable

# of standardize protocols for identifying and disseminating information about impending high-risk weather

% increase urban vegetation and landscaping that can reduce the effects of heat

% of residents who get relief during the hottest part of the day at malls, community centers, libraries, recreation centers, and other air-conditioned facilities

Fire & Rescue

national fire academy "direct" and "regional" deliveries

of a fire department smoke detector installation and battery replacement program

# of annual fire inspections

# of annual individual training hours

# of certified firefighters

# of community facilities with fire extinguishers strategically placed and properly maintained

# of community fire alarm systems in place

# of contingency plans for evacuating population endangered by a wildfire

# of controlled burns done per year

# of developed fire emergency plan that assures access by fire vehicles to all areas included in the rural/urban interface fire danger area

# of emergency preparedness audiences reached

# of emergency preparedness response hands-on-skilled training programs

# of fire & rescue services

# of fire community certification given

# of fire hydrant meter backflow preventers

# of fire services requests/unit responses generated

# of firefighters receiving "live fire training"

# of homes with fire extinguishers or home sprinkler systems

56. Safety & Security

of implemented plans to provide sufficient water and water pressure

# of installed fire suppression systems in city / county facilities

# of installed water booster near the water tower

# of insurance companies that offer discounts for home sprinkler systems

# of primary fires and related fatalities

# of primary fires and related non-fatal casualties

# of proper evacuation plans exercises done for town buildings, businesses, offices, and residences

# of protocols for support by non-profit agencies during wildfire situations

# of public education project addressing the advantages of individual fire suppression in residences

# of replaced inadequately sized water lines and/or installing a water booster near the water tower and by developing a secondary water supply system

# of residential fires per 100,000 persons

# of secondary water supply systems

# of structure fires with a probable code-related cause

# of students receiving national fire academy training

# of training done to coordinate community fire, police, and public works departments on how to respond to a wildfire emergency

# of workshops to prepare fire departments to apply for grants

vehicles issued

% of agencies audited as required

% of brigades in local authority areas where fire appliances and equipment do not meet minimum determined standards

% of career firefighters in violation of annual training and certification requirements placed in non-compliant status

% of citizen satisfaction with fire protection and emergency response services

% of created fire breaks along fence rows

% of emergency calls with a response time of 5 minutes or less from dispatch to arrival on scene

% of emergency incidents with a dispatch to arrival time of 15 minutes or less

% of fire departments in which x% of fire fighters are trained to the fire fighter 1 level

% of fire departments with a certified fire instructor

% of fire stations found to be operating in violation of state requirements and placed in non-compliant status

% of fires confined to room of origin

% of fires confined to room of origin for all structure fires

% of incidents where call processing time is 1 minute or less

% of incidents where total emergency response time is 15 minutes and more

% of incidents where travel time is 4 minutes or less

56. Safety & Security

% of incidents where turnout time is 1 minute or less

% of public town buildings, businesses, offices, and residences with proper evacuation plans

% of routine orders filled within 24 hrs

% of structure fires contained to room of origin

% replacement of inadequately sized water lines with lines of sufficient size to provide proper fire protection to annexed and existing areas

% spread of trees which providing an environment prone to wildfire spread

Average service length in years

Average time to respond to emergency

Carrying out a substitution and change rate of % per year

Fire certification test "pass" rate

Fire death rate in inspected facilities (per 100,000 occupants)

Fire death rate per 100,000 population

Fire total loss in inspected buildings

Total amount of funds for education program to inform the public on proper evacuation plans

Fire Safety Inspections

of boiler and pressure vessel inspections conducted by inspectors

# of elevator and escalator inspections conducted by inspectors

# of investigations of fire-resistant materials for buildings

% of electrical installations inspected within 3 working days of receipt of request for inspection

% of electrical licenses issued within 10 working days of receipt of completed application and fee

% of health care facility inspection reports returned to facilities within ten calendar days

% of plan reviews completed within 60 calendar days of complete submission

% of required school and college fire inspections completed biennially

Median turnaround time (expressed in calendar days) of plans after complete submission

Flood & Dam Failure

of acquire accurate flood plain maps

# of adopted fee-in-lieu of on-site detention ordinance

# of amended floodplain regulations

# of beneficial uses of dams for park, recreation, and wildlife management

# of campaigns of public information letting people know they are in the dam failure inundation area

# of compensation for the impacts of new bridges and channel improvements

# of comprehensive basin-wide master drainage plans for watersheds within the community

# of constructed bridges to pass 100-year regulatory flood without overtopping

56. Safety & Security

of contingency plans for terrorist attacks on local dams

# of critical facilities elevated or flood-proofed

# of developed and enforced dumping regulations that may fill in or reduce the capacity of ditches and steams

# of distributed flood and flash flood safety tips to inform citizens of the dangers of flood waters

# of evaluated appropriate mitigation measures for homes located in the floodplain

# of identified and elevated important equipment inside buildings located in a floodplain

# of identified flooding problems within the community

# of implemented structural and non-structural flood mitigation measures for flood-prone properties

# of inadequate bridges

# of maintained habitat for flora and fauna in flood control projects

# of maintained or developed wetlands to receive or reduce floodwaters

# of master drainage plans identified acquisition as the most cost-effective and desirable mitigation measure

# of obtained elevation certificates for homes located in the floodplain

# of performed preliminary reconnaissance surveys of all buildings located in the floodplain

# of prepared elevation certificates for floodplain candidate properties for acquisition with positive benefit/cost ratios

# of programs to clean local streams of debris and waste

# of proposed hazardous material sites be taken to the floodplain board

# of recommended cost-effective and politically acceptable solutions to the flooding

# of reconciled addresses in flood zones entered into a database

# of recreation opportunities, off-street hiking and biking trails, and other enhancements in floodwater control and retention projects

# of removed flood plain where repetitive loss of properties in the community

# of residents who refuse to vacate the floodplain of flood proofing

# of safety measures to promote effective use of regulated downstream areas from dams

% computerized GIS modeling program for mapping appropriate cubic feet per second (CFS) dam release rates

% eliminated storm-water infiltration and inflow into the sanitary sewer system

% of "retrofitting" the shoreline with willow cuttings, wetland plants, or rolls of landscape material until the bank can be stabilized by plant roots

% of controlled erosion during development with vegetation or sediment capture

% of incorporated warning and evacuation procedures in dam emergency plans

56. Safety & Security

% of informed floodplain residents of the availability of flood insurance to eligible communities

% of inspected identified dams (shape of spillway, proper opening and closing of gates)

% of inventory done of inadequate bridges

% of new appropriate native vegetation along stream and river banks that resist erosion

% of people who know they are in the dam failure inundation area

% of performed benefit/cost analysis of floodplain buildings for acquisition

% of performed benefit/cost analysis of floodplain buildings for clearance from the floodplain

% of performed benefit/cost analysis of floodplain buildings for demolition

% of profile completed of who lives or works in the floodway below a high hazard dam

% of reduction of sedimentation which may fill in channels and lakes, reducing their ability to carry or store floodwaters

% of residents who know about flood mitigation alternatives

% update municipal dams and keep emergency action plan up to date and on file

% updated hydrology and hydraulics for Dams

Amount from storm water utility fee to fund maintenance of creeks and streams

Construct regional detention ponds to compensate for future urban development

Maintain culverts to adequately allow storm water drainage

Fugitive Apprehension

of felony arrests

% of fugitives captured

% of high-crime cities nationwide with a reduction in violent firearms crime

% of individuals found through general searches

% of offender wellbeing

% of total fugitives apprehended or cleared

Hailstorm

of hail-resistant measures/materials to protect existing public infrastructure

# of provided covered shelter for local government vehicles

# of public information programs for residents informing them of the advantages and costs of impact-resistant roofing and glass

Hazardous Materials

of community hazardous materials illustrations in schools

# of community hazardous materials illustrations through media

# of community hazardous materials illustrations through police, and fire stations

# of community hazardous materials illustrations through public offices

56. Safety & Security

of community-wide public awareness and collection program for household pollutants

# of designated hazardous materials route through a community to avoid heavily populated areas

# of developed plans for police and fire department personnel to expand their knowledge and capabilities relative to hazardous materials hazards and events

# of distributed information identifying hazardous materials to at risk citizens, such as the elderly, infirm, poor, and outside workers

# of emergency response units with equipments that deal with potential biological and chemical threats

# of evacuation maps and chemical details provided for emergency responders

# of identified populations around potential fixed-site hazmat hazards

# of local businesses and industry that manufacture, store, or transport dangerous chemicals in the community

# of pipeline routes and materials transported in the pipelines

# of provided public awareness campaign about household pollutants

# of trained dispatchers in the use of response programs

% of hazardous materials emergency equipments

% of labeled sanitary sewer drains to warn citizens against dumping chemicals and automotive fluids into the sanitary sewer drain

Intelligence Information

of current studies/projects

# of customers/stakeholders/groups services

# of databases held/managed

# of fiscal, policy and correctional impact analyses provided

# of individuals enrolled in e-mail notification service

# of key interagency partners with which has established memorandums of agreement (MOAs)

# of media personnel receiving press releases electronically

# of officers completing training school

# of sex offender research council and criminal and juvenile justice research issued

# of studies and evaluation projects complete

# of studies and evaluation projects initiative

% completion of digital linkage between government's agencies

% customers satisfied with BI products

% e-authentication across population

% of accurate submission and identification of fingerprints

% of alert broadcasts completed within 60 minutes of receipt required information

% of counties where case and disposition records are audited annually

% of existing records re-validated with in 12 months of previous validation

56. Safety & Security

% of fingerprints entered within 2 working days of receipt in the identification section

% of first responder agencies with access to information system

% of information provided to requesting person/agency which are accurate

% of law enforcement agencies rating intelligence services provided as "useful"

% of law enforcement agencies with access to agency website

% of mandated agencies reporting data to the police department

% of population in jurisdictions reporting data

% of records validated with in three months of initial entry

% of request for assistance regarding missing persons acted upon within 24 hours

% of requests for public information that are processed within 1 working day

% products delivered on or before target date

% time radio network available for voice communication

Average participant rating on the effectiveness of executive development programs

Ratio of outside funds received to agency funds

Lightning

of burned overhead electric power lines

# of constructed lightning rods (strike termination devices) for protection of critical facilities

# of designated individuals at community recreation facilities and schools that are educated in storm spotting and safety

# of educated people in the community about proper lightning safety through public service announcements and other media outlets

# of insurance companies offer discounts for homes with lightning protection

# of lightning warning systems for athletic directors and managers of outdoor sports areas, pools, golf courses, ball fields, parks

# of needed surge protection in existing critical facilities

# of provided educational demonstrations and information in whole-house surge protection technology

# of provided lightning injury and damage prevention materials and programs to vulnerable publics

# of provided surge protection and backup power generators for computer-reliant critical facilities (911 center, police stations, fire stations).

# of utilities that provide lightning prevention information materials and programs to their customers

# of warning systems that monitor lightning strikes used by local emergency managers

Planning

% of counties participating in the mutual aid compact

56. Safety & Security

% of funded public assistance projects are successfully completed projects to applicants

% of jurisdictions that have mitigation plans that meet the standards of the disaster mitigation act

% of local government that is sustainable for its citizens

% of local jurisdictions compliant with the national incident management system

% of municipalities participating in the mutual aid compact.

% of security strategy projects funded and initiated

Police

of accidents investigated

# of cases with fingerprint evidence processed

# of citations issued

# of emergency plans in existence

# of felony arrests by patrol

# of gang family interventions

# of misdemeanor arrests by patrol

# of vehicle stops performed

# of warrant arrests by patrol

% calls taken

% of citizens satisfaction with neighborhood policing

% of citizens satisfaction with traffic control/enforcement

% of citizens who feel safe or moderately safe

% of conviction of matters listed for trial

% of guilty pleads before trial

% of HIV and AIDS amongst prison inmates

% of investigations finalized within x days

% of police personnel doing administrative duties

% of positive stop and searches

% of search warrants issued that resulted in arrest

% of staff in key positions who are women

% of total police personnel on active crime duties

% reliability of police services

% satisfaction with the way the police and local council dealt with anti-social behavior

Annual % increase in # of arrests made as a result of reported offences

Annual % increase in # of arrests that result in prosecution

Annual % increase in reported offences

Annual % increase of # of prosecuted cases resulting in a successful verdict

Average patrol response time to critical emergencies

Average response times

Calls answered by call receivers within 10 seconds

Civil servants ratio to national archives

Commission for refugees staff ratio to refugees

56. Safety & Security

Community satisfaction % with police services

Community satisfaction rating with police attitude

Customer satisfaction indicating good or excellent service

Homicide rate per 100,000 population

Immigration officers ratio to total population

Injury accidents as a % of total accidents

National registration staff ratio to total population

Patrol staff ratio to total population

Police staff ratio to total population

Prison staff ratio to prison in-mates

Registrar staff ratio to societies

Reliability of police services (on a scale of 0 - 7)

Total # of callouts for S.W.A.T. assistance

Total # of juvenile arrests per 1,000 juvenile population

Police Support

of developed patrol deployment system based on the requirements

# of implemented police security policy

# of issued coordination report each month to senior management team

# of issued strategic threats assessment report

# of memoranda of understanding (MOUs) signed with key stakeholders within crises management

# of partnerships arrangements with key stakeholders and criminal investigation departments

# of statements issued by forensic evidence department for use in court

# of trained officers to be crises negotiators

# of trained police officers

% attained level of classification regarding e-government systems

% completion of DNA database project

% compliance with police security policy

% implementation of a scientific process to deploy staff to police stations by 100%

% increase in effectiveness of system utilization

% increase staff availability to respond to incidents

% of accreditation in own function

% of active peace officers seeking specialty certifications

% of cases for which forensic evidence presented at court

% of cases which have material submitted to the forensic laboratory

% of granted authorization to directorates to use the system

% of officers receiving mandatory training each calendar year

% of operational capability to deal effectively & efficiently with any incident involving massive casualties

% of operational capability to find any terrorism or criminal incident

% of operational staff with radios

% of police exercises completed as required by rule, regulation or agreement

56. Safety & Security

% of police sites with appropriate access control

% of system availability (uptime)

% of user satisfaction

% police data warehouse completed (central database)

% preparedness of the communication network with the embassies

% reduction in breakdowns of police systems and major programs

% satisfaction rate of police support

Port & Vessel Operations

of maritime fatalities/ injuries/ incidents in coastal waters, ports and marine facilities

% reduction in # of maritime fatalities/ injuries/ incidents in coastal waters, ports and marine facilities

Preparedness & Readiness

of acquired GIS and GPS technologies to record and maintain information on public infrastructure, private safe rooms and private water wells

# of certified disaster training for government employees and local team members

# of community partnerships involving local government leaders, civic, business and volunteer groups to work together to mitigate natural and man-made hazards

# of conducted regular testing of emergency communications, warning and response systems

# of developed debris management plan

# of developed emergency response and operations procedures

# of developed public schools emergency operations plans

# of distribution centers in local libraries and other public buildings where safety guidance on natural and man made hazards can be provided to citizens

# of educated businesses on the availability of insurance, in the event their business is impacted for a period of time by an unforeseen event

# of education courses to public on the importance of a family disaster plan

# of educational programs for town staff to recognize and render assistance for symptoms of life-threatening emergencies

# of emergency equipments for emergency response teams

# of enhanced 911 centers

# of established mutual aid agreements with surrounding communities for prevention and response to hazards and emergency situations

# of established working partnerships involving local government, civic, business leaders, and volunteer groups to create a safer community

# of hazard public information and awareness programs

# of identified vulnerable populations within the community and the agencies that work with those population

# of installed emergency communications network for fire, police, 911, EMS and other emergency operations

56. Safety & Security

of installed Reverse 911 System for mass call-outs to targeted areas of the community for emergency notification and/or information

# of message boards for travelers

# of new facilities for the 911 center and the emergency operations center

# of operators as communications source during hazardous events

# of programs through the school system to encourage children to think of people who require special assistance (elders, infants, and persons with disabilities) during severe weather conditions

# of provided security and surveillance equipments for police and fire stations

# of provided survival equipments and supplies for emergency response team members

# of supplied hazard radios to all local government buildings, schools, hospitals, and critical facilities

# of supply kit given during severe weather season

# of trained community employees on how to administer CPR and first aid

# of trained community employees on symptoms of common, life-threatening emergencies

# of trained emergency management staff at national emergency management

# of weather-warning systems for highway travelers

% of at-risk and vulnerable populations

% of decentralized location of water towers, utility power sources, and water treatment plants to lessen the potential for complete public utility failure in an major disaster event

% of educational materials for all hazards readily available off the shelf, and economical

% of installed continuity of operations systems within town utilities departments, and social service agencies so that operations during and after an emergency incident are still accessible and operable

% of installed street addresses on all buildings and curbs

% of recorded GPS locations of private water wells and underground storm shelters to rescue potentially trapped storm victims

% of updated GIS to include public utility infrastructure

Amount of obtained funding for development and distribution of public information and education plans for responding to natural and man-made hazards

Consider more stringent building codes that require all steel construction for public buildings and critical facilities.

Emergency centre performance index

Emergency management preparedness index

Regulate Private Security

private security ID card applications denied

private security ID cards issued

private security ID cards revoked

56. Safety & Security

Average # of days required to notify licensee of enforcement ID revocation

Road Safety

of children killed or seriously injured in road traffic accidents

# of commercial vehicle inspections

# of enforcement contacts

# of fatal crashes per 100,000 registered motor vehicles

# of major factors contributing to fatal road crashes

# of motorists assisted

# of pedestrian fatalities per 100K population

# of people killed on the roads

# of people killed or seriously injured in road collisions a year per 100,000 population

# of people seriously injured on the roads

# of serious traffic offences

# of traffic accident investigations opened

# of traffic fatalities per 100 Million vehicle miles traveled

# of traffic safety contracts administered

# of traffic violations per capita

# of vehicles found to exceed the speed limit

# of vehicles monitored for drivers and passengers not wearing seat belts

# of vehicles monitored for speeding that have been found to exceed the speed limit

% decrease of people killed or seriously injured in road accidents (per 100,000 population)

% increase in population awareness about traffic and road safety

% increase of people killed or seriously injured in road traffic accidents

% of alcohol involved crashes with fatality

% of child safety seat usage

% of drivers and front seat passengers using seat belts

% of people who have not worn a seat belt in the past six months

% of school buses found to have serious defects as a result of inspections

% of vehicles monitored for drivers and passengers not wearing seat belts

% of vehicles monitored for speeding that have been found to exceed the speed limit

% of vehicles weighed found to be in compliance

Amount from road toll

Crash and injury crash rate per 1,000 population

Fatalities per 100 million miles driven

Fatality rate per 100 million miles driven

Rate of alcohol-related fatalities per 100 million vehicle miles traveled

Rate of traffic crashes resulting in serious injury per 100 million vehicle miles traveled

Road fatalities per million vehicles

Seat belt usage rate

Traffic fatalities per 100,000 population

56. Safety & Security

Tornado & High Wind

inspected community schools for tornado, high wind, and earthquake vulnerability

of adopted building codes / incentives leading to construction that is more resistant to tornadoes, high winds, and earthquakes

# of adopted ordinances requiring roof-wall connectors be installed on all new residential construction

# of building reinforcements against wind and tornado damage

# of community tornado shelter programs implemented

# of developed public information and education programs bout construction methods and mitigation measures that protect building's roof an outside openings

# of educated citizens on the storm shelter certification seal for storm shelters

# of educated local builders on the low cost of adding roof-wall connectors and other mitigation techniques

# of educated school boards on safe rooms and the new law and funding opportunities

# of grants for storm shelters/safe rooms in mobile home parks

# of installed break resistant glass in government offices, public schools and other critical facilities

# of installed safe-rooms in daycare centers

# of mobile homes with provided nearby storm shelter / safe-room

# of provided manufactured home parks with community shelters/safe rooms

# of public and builder awareness on construction techniques for mitigating tornado damage

# of public with tornado damage insurance

# of retrofitted or remodeled buildings to make them more disaster resistant

# of upgrades on community-wide outdoor warning siren systems

# of utility company tree trimming program to keep trees out of power lines during high wind and ice storms

% certified and registered buildings

% completion of studies

% of exposed fluorescent lighting tubes in city and school facilities with impact resistant plastic coverings

% of performed tornado and high wind evaluations of schools

% of safe-rooms in schools

% of standards that could be incorporated into zoning and regulatory measures adopted by the community

Training & Education

# of intoxilyzer devices serviced/maintained

# of public school classes receiving instruction

# of students attending CPR courses

56. Safety & Security

of training hours

% increase of staff satisfaction in training

% increase the average training days / per staff

% of agency heads who state that their employees' job performance improved as a result of training provided

% of all staff appraisals are completed within agreed timescales

% of cases sent to council probable cause committee in under four months

% of customers stating that customer service rates good to very good

% of departmental policies reviewed

% of employees assessed as fully qualified

% of employees assigned to crisis management duties who have successfully passed crisis management training

% of employees who have received full role-relevant operational training

% of identified training requirements that are fully developed as courses

% of student registrations fulfilled to provide timely training

% the rate of staff satisfaction with training

% the rate of staff with secondary school degrees and diplomas

Mean rating of courses by course participants

Total # of certifications issued

Weapon Permit

of compliance inspections performed

# of concealed weapon/firearm licenses issued within 90-day statutory timeframe without fingerprint results

# of days required to process government employee and professional weapon permits

# of days required to process nonresident weapon permits

# of default concealed weapon/firearm licensees with prior criminal histories

# of investigations performed (security, investigative, recovery complaint and agency-generated inspections)

# of responses to inquiries

% of concealed weapon/firearm licenses issued within 90-day statutory timeframe without fingerprint results

% of inquiries responded to within 2 business days

% of license revocations or suspensions initiated within 20 days after receipt of disqualifying information

% of security, investigative, and recovery inspections completed within 30 days

% of security, investigative, and recovery investigations completed within 60 days

% of security, investigative, and recovery licenses issued within 90 days after receipt of an application

Average cost of administrative actions (revocation, fine, probation, and compliance letters)

Average cost of concealed weapon/firearm applications processed

56. Safety & Security

Average cost of security, investigative, and recovery applications processed

Average cost of security, investigative, and recovery compliance inspections

Average cost of security, investigative, and recovery investigations

Winter Storm

of contingency plans for responding to massive power outage due to severe storms and overload demands

# of critical structural "snow load" thresholds on flat-roofed on community or critical facilities

# of provided public awareness campaigns on effective ways to monitor and avoid ice damage, frozen pipes, and snow loads on roof systems

# of provided trimming of trees to reduce power outages during storms

% of educated public on the dangers of carbon monoxide pollution and the use of appropriate heating systems during power outages

% of upgraded communities' equipment and vehicles for combating ice storm damage/adverse impact to public infrastructure

57. Social Development

Children & Youth

of birth certificates issued

# of calls and online requests fielded by qualified family specialists

# of child and youth development workers trained

# of child protection plans lasting 2 years or more

# of children and youth equipped with relevant skills

# of children and youth trained in leadership skills

# of children enrolled in child enrichment activities

# of children's centers

# of grandparents that participate in intergenerational activities

# of initiatives implemented to promote dialogue between genders

# of looked after children cases which were reviewed within required timescales

# of placements of looked after children

# of quality time (in hours/week) mothers and fathers spend with their children

# of reported child abuse cases / year

# of sports administrators, coaches and community facilitators trained

# of young inventors supported

# of youths receiving training in small scale business

% effectiveness of child and adolescent mental health services

% gap between the lowest achieving in the early years stage profile and the rest

% of breastfeeding at 6 – 8 weeks from birth

% of child protection cases which were reviewed within required timescales

% of children and young people's participation in high-quality PE and sport

% of children and young people's satisfaction with parks and play areas

57. Social Development

% of children becoming the subject of a child protection plan for a second or subsequent time

% of children cared only by their parents

% of children in poverty

% of children who have experienced bullying

% of children who have run away from home/care overnight

% of children with at least one hour of care

% of Chlamydia in under 25 year olds

% of emotional and behavioral health of looked after children

% of emotional health of children

% of looked after children reaching level 4 in English at key stage 2

% of looked after children reaching level 4 in Math at key stage 2

% of referrals to children's social care going on to initial assessment

% of schools providing access to extended services

% of those identified as needing training who receive the identified training

% of young people's participation in positive activities

% under 18 conception rate

% under-five mortality rate

Average # of children with care

Average # of weekly hours of formal care

Average length of placement of looked after children

Average time of placements of looked after children for adoption following an agency decision that the child should be placed for adoption

Enrollment rates (primary school)

Formal childcare by duration

Rate of permanent exclusions from school

Family Lifestyle

of crime, violence or vandalisms

# of divorced persons

# of family health personnel

# of family surveys done on yearly basis

# of female over the age of 25 who have conducted a medical check-up within the past 2 years

# of local interest sites cultural family heritage

# of mothers who are able to articulate basic family nutritional requirements

# of new approved policies

# of new senior citizen community centers

# of single parents

# of traditional habits events and activities

# of unique marital cases attracted and managed at family counseling

# of unique non-marital cases attracted and managed at family counseling

% financial burden of the total housing cost

% level of noise from neighbors or from the street

57. Social Development

% of adults with above average incomes

% of births attended by skilled health personnel

% of city citizens by gender and age group in % of total citizens

% of divorce cases

% of divorced persons

% of enforcement of family policies in social institutions

% of financial burden of the repayment of debts from hire purchases or loans

% of household lack of a color TV

% of household lack of a computer

% of household lack of a personal car

% of household lack of a telephone

% of household lack of a washing machine

% of household lack of bath or shower in dwelling

% of household lack of indoor flushing toilet for sole use of household

% of household window frames of floor

% of household with damp walls, floors or foundation

% of household with leaking roof

% of housing costs in disposable household income

% of parents with post-secondary education

% of population aged 18 and over by education level

% of population aged 18 and over by health status

% of population aged 18 and over by occupation

% of population aged 18 and over by part-time or full-time employment

% of population by degree of urbanization

% of population by gender

% of population by household type and income group

% of population by tenure status

% of population by work intensity of the household

% of population living in households considering that they suffer from noise

% of population over 18 years

% of rent related to occupied dwelling in disposable household income

% of single mothers

% of single parents

% of under 18 conception rate

% reduction in women diagnosed with BC

% unable to afford a meal with meat, chicken, fish every second day

% unable to afford a meal with vegetarian equivalent every second day

% unable to afford paying for one week annual holiday away from home

% unable to face unexpected financial expenses

% unable to keep home adequately warm

Adolescent fertility rate (births per 1,000 women ages 15-19)

Arrears on hire purchase installments

Arrears on loan payments

57. Social Development

Arrears on mortgage or rent payments

Arrears on utility bills

Average # of rooms per person

Average hours/day mother spends with her kids

Average household size

Distribution of households by household income level

Distribution of households by household size

Divorce rate

Quality of life (on a scale of 0 to 10)

Total workforce by gender

Households Expenditure

Average consumption expenditure of private households

Average housing cost

Mean consumption expenditure by age

Mean consumption expenditure by degree of urbanization

Mean consumption expenditure by employment status

Mean consumption expenditure by income quintile

Mean consumption expenditure by type of household

Mean consumption expenditure of private households

Housing

of assist low income home buyers

# of beds created for overnight shelter or other emergency housing

# of customer satisfaction survey

# of first home buyers

# of mortgages purchased

# of multifamily units developed or preserved

# of new low income housing units per year

# of new shelter beds funded

# of non-point source loans

# of transitional housing units

# of units designated for persons with HIV/AIDS

# of units specifically designated for homeless persons & families

% compliance with terms of grant

% of certificates issued by abstractors and attorneys

% of home owners paying more than 30% of income for housing costs

% of loan funds committed

% of multi-family loans closed

% of renters paying more than 30% of income for rental housing costs

% of satisfied customers served in contract administration

% of scheduled low-income housing tax credit compliance reviews completed

% of substandard housing

% of tax credits awarded

Amount of clean loans closed

57. Social Development

Amount of down payment assistance provided

Amount of loans closed

Amount of planning and design loans closed

Average # of tenants served by the home and community based services or rent subsidy program

Average apartment price (per square meter per year)

Average apartment rent (per square meter per year)

Average office price (per square meter per year)

Average office rent (per square meter per year)

Average time of mortgage release

Citizen satisfaction % with the availability of affordable housing for low/moderate income families

Median gross rent as a % of household income in the past 12 months

S&P issuer credit rating (ICR)

Total amount of housing trust fund

Total amount of infrastructure grants

Total amount of revenue generated

Total amount of revenue transferred

Total funding for construction of new single family homes with low interest loans

Total funding of the rehabilitation of single family homes with low interest loans

International Migration

% of foreign population

% of foreign-born nationals

% of foreign-born population

Net migration rate

Students performance by immigrants status: % first-generation students

Students performance by immigrants status: % native students

Students performance by immigrants status: % second-generation students

Migration & Employment

Employment rates of foreign-born population: high education

Employment rates of foreign-born population: intermediate education

Employment rates of foreign-born population: low education

Employment rates of native-born population: high education

Employment rates of native-born population: intermediate education

Employment rates of native-born population: low education

Unemployment rate of native-born men

Unemployment rate of the foreign-born men

Unemployment rate of the foreign-born women

Unemployment rate of the native-born women

Non-Profit Organizations

of nonprofit arts and cultural organizations

# of recognized neighborhood associations

57. Social Development

of registered non profit organizations

% attendance at community and sporting events

% citizen perception community ratings

% of community support for nonprofit arts and cultural organizations

Non-profit organizations revenues as a % of community total personal income

Resident volunteer rate

Total donations to community organizations

Population Growth

of home based medical services

% distribution of the national population into rural regions

% distribution of the national population into small regions

% distribution of the national population into urban regions

Index of geographic concentration of population, small regions

Population growth rates

Regions with the highest population density in the country

Share of national population in the 10% of regions with the largest population

Total fertility rates

Poverty & Inequality

of households

# of point difference of poverty rate

% difference of poverty rate

% employment of disabled persons

% of adults with below average incomes

% of effects of taxes and transfers in reducing poverty: ages 0-17

% of effects of taxes and transfers in reducing poverty: ages 18-65

% of effects of taxes and transfers in reducing poverty: ages 65 and over

% of enterprise services cost recovery

% of household disposable income

% of inequality reduction

% of pension fund asset allocation

% of public cash transfers

% of residents living in poverty

% of young people from low income backgrounds progressing to higher education

% people at persistent risk of poverty

% poor people from households with a head of working age

% poor people from households with a head of working age and no workers

% poor people from households with a head of working age and one worker

% poor people from households with a head of working age and two workers

% poor people from households with children and a head of working age and a single parent

57. Social Development

% poor people from households with children and a head of working age and a single parent not working

% poor people from households with children and a head of working age and a single parent working

% poor people from households with children and a head of working age and couple parents

% poor people from households with children and a head of working age and couple parents both working

% poor people from households with children and a head of working age and couple parents not working

% poor people from households with children and a head of working age and couple parents with one parent working

Aggregate replacement ratio

At risk of poverty rate after social transfers

At risk of poverty rate anchored at a point in time

At risk of poverty rate before social transfers (pensions excluded from social transfers)

At risk of poverty rate before social transfers (pensions included in social transfers)

At risk of poverty rate before social transfers by gender

At risk of poverty rate before social transfers except pensions

At risk of poverty rate by age

At risk of poverty rate by education level

At risk of poverty rate by highest level of education attained

At risk of poverty rate by household type

At risk of poverty rate by main source of income

At risk of poverty rate by tenure status

At risk of poverty rate by work intensity of the household

At risk of poverty rate of elderly people

Average household taxes, concentration coefficients

Average of household disposable income

Children in poverty where no parent is working

Distribution of income by different income groups

Distribution of income by quantiles

Distribution of population by household types

In work at-risk-of-poverty rate

In work at-risk-of-poverty rate after social transfers

Income distribution and monetary poverty

Income inequality: Gini coefficient

Income inequality: interdecile ratio

Income inequality: mean log deviation

Income inequality: squared coefficient of variation

Income levels for people at different points in the distribution: average income of the bottom decile

57. Social Development
Income levels for people at different points in the distribution: average income of the top decile
Income levels for people at different points in the distribution: median income
In-work at risk of poverty rate by age
In-work at risk of poverty rate by education level
In-work at risk of poverty rate by full-/part-time work
In-work at risk of poverty rate by household type
In-work at risk of poverty rate by months worked
In-work at risk of poverty rate by type of contract
In-work at risk of poverty rate by work intensity of the household
Median earnings for full-time employed individuals
Median income by accommodation tenure status
Median income by age
Median income by education level
Median income by household type
Median income by main source of income
Median income by work intensity of the household
Pension replacement rate
Persistent at-risk-of-poverty rate
Poverty rate of children
Poverty rate of working age people
Poverty rates: poverty gap
Relative at risk of poverty gap
Relative median at-risk-of-poverty gap
Relative median income ratio
Social Inclusion indicators
Total amount of public cash transfers for inequality reduction
Trends in poverty rates: changes over 10 years
Trends in poverty rates: changes over 20 years

Recreation Services

# of girls up to age 18 who participate in sports activity that meets at least once a week
# of visits to recreation services programs
# of women who enroll in fitness facilities and come at least 2 times a week
% of clients who actually went to sports community clinics/organizations
% of cost recovery for merit programs
% of households that have visited a park or park facility in the last year
% of special community services participants rating programs as good or above
% of wellness clients who report learning about organizations and clinics in the community that they can go to for help if they need it
% of youth and their parents rating programs as good or above
% of youth who actually went to one sports community clinics/organizations

57. Social Development

% of youth who report learning about organizations and clinics in the community that they can go to for help if they need it

Cost per youth service visit

Senior Citizens

of home-based medical sponsored services

% of 65+ year-olds in the total population

% of elderly population by country

% of residents caring for elderly relative

% of senior citizens below the poverty level

At-risk-of-poverty rate for pensioners

At-risk-of-poverty rate of older people

Gender differences in the aggregate replacement ratio

Gender differences in the at-risk-of-poverty rate

Gender differences in the relative median income ratio

Index of geographic concentration of elderly population, small regions

Index of geographic concentration population, small regions

Ratio of inactive population aged 65 and over to the total labor force

Ratio of population aged 65 and over to the total population

Relative median at-risk-of-poverty gap of elderly people

Relative median income ratio (65+)

Share of national elderly population in the 10% of small regions with the largest elderly population

Social exclusion rate

Social Protection

of citizens on cash transfer schemes

# of citizens receiving fertilizer and seed

# of informal sector workers on social security scheme

# of street children reintegrated with families and communities

% of cases of sexual and gender based violence

Total expenditure on administration costs

Total expenditure on care for elderly

Total expenditure on pensions

Total expenditure on social benefits

Total expenditure on social protection

Total expenditure on social protection as a % of the total budgetary allocations to sector in a one year

Total expenditure on social protection per head of population

Total pensions

Total social benefits by function

Total social benefits per head of population

Total social protection expenditure

Total social protection receipts

Total social protection receipts by type

57. Social Development

Strong Community

of participations in regular volunteering
# of refused license applications leading to immigration enforcement activity
# of sponsored social, humanitarian and community events on monthly basis
# of sponsored university students
# of use of public libraries
# of visits to museums and galleries
% citizens engagement in the arts
% of adult participation in sport and active recreation
% of civic participation in the local area
% of customer contact that is of low or no value to the customer
% of migrants with English language skills and knowledge
% of people who believe people from different backgrounds get on well together in their local area
% of people who feel that they belong to their neighborhood
% of people who feel they can influence decisions in their locality
% of volunteer retention
% overall/general satisfaction with local area
Gini index
Median family income / year

Women Capabilities

of female students in university as % of total students' #
# of female workforce
# of newly established SME projects run by women
# of sectors with gender disaggregated data bases
# of women has assisted in participating in relevant activities
# of women successfully completing continuing education courses
reached by awareness campaign
% declarations and conventions domesticated
% of women with titled land
% women in decision making positions
Female who hold top/high level positions in government as % of the whole # of positions
Female work force as % of total workforce

Youth & Substances Use

% of current tobacco use among adolescents (13-15 years)
% of current tobacco use among adolescents (13-15 years) (%) female
% of current tobacco use among adolescents (13-15 years) (%) male
% of drug use among youth
% of students who actually reduced their use
% of students who report learning new information about the effects of using tobacco, alcohol and other drugs
% of students who reported attempting to reduce their use

57. Social Development

% of students who reported learning ways to reduce their use of tobacco, alcohol and other drugs

% of youth outreach workers who report learning new information about the effects of using tobacco, alcohol or other drugs

% substance misuse by young people

Youth Awareness

of student contacts

# of student service hours

# of students accessing wellness services

% of school staff who report consulting with a wellness staff member about a student

% of school staff who report referring a student to wellness services

Average hours of service per student

Youth Correction

of crime victims returning the survey

# of crime victims satisfied with program

# of crime victims served by the program that were satisfied with program

# of families satisfied with program

# of mentors who stopped working with the program

# of months of service for all mentors

# of new parents served

# of new youth served

# of program youth exhibiting desired

# of program youth exhibiting desired change in targeted behavior (antisocial behavior)

# of program youth with formal psychological / psychiatric evaluations

# of programs youth exhibiting desired change in targeted behavior (substance abuse)

# of service hours completed

# of surveyed youth exhibiting desired change

# of volunteer advocates/mentors remaining active until case completion

# of volunteer advocates/mentors working with the program

# of youth complying with the aftercare plan

# of youth satisfied with program

# of youth who exited

# of youth who exited the program

# of youth who exited the program after completing the program requirements

# of youth who exited the program before completing the program requirements

# of youth who had first meeting

#of program youth exhibiting desired change in targeted behavior (family relationships)

% of crime victims served by the program that were satisfied with program

% of families satisfied with program

57. Social Development
% of program youth exhibiting desired
% of program youth exhibiting desired change in targeted behavior (antisocial behavior)
% of program youth exhibiting desired change in targeted behavior (family relationships)
% of program youth exhibiting desired change in targeted behavior (gang activity)
% of program youth exhibiting desired change in targeted behavior (pregnancy)
% of program youth with formal psychological / psychiatric evaluations
% of programs youth exhibiting desired change in targeted behavior (substance abuse)
% of youth complying with the aftercare plan
% of youth satisfied with program
Average tenure length of mentors
Average time from assignment of case to first meeting with program youth
First time entrants to the youth justice system aged 10–17
Total # of days from assignment to first meeting

Youth Education

# of 14-19 learning diplomas
# of culture and traditions survey
# of enrolled students in religious School
# of enrolled students in School
# of graduates of vocational training programs
# of infants dying before reaching the age of one year per 1,000 live births in a given year
% achievement at level 4 or above in both English and Math at key stage 2
% achievement at level 5 or above in both English and Math at key stage 3
% achievement at level 5 or above in Science at key stage 3
% achievement gap between pupils eligible for free school meals and their peers achieving the expected level at key stages 2 and 4
% achievement of 2 or more A-C grades in Science
% achievement of 5 or more A-C grades in English and Math
% achievement of a level 2 qualification by the age of 19
% achievement of a level 3 qualification by the age of 19
% achievement of at least 78 points across the early years with at least 6 in each of the scales in personal social and emotional development and communication, language and literacy
% inequality gap in the achievement of a level 2 qualification by the age of 19
% inequality gap in the achievement of a level 3 qualification by the age of 19
% Key Stage 2 attainment for Black and minority ethnic groups
% Key Stage 4 attainment for Black and minority ethnic groups

57. Social Development

% of looked after children achieving 5 A-C at key stage 4 (including English and Math)

% of secondary schools judged as having good or outstanding standards of behavior

% of special educational needs achieving 5 A-C

% of special educational needs achieving key stage 2

% of special educational needs statements issued within 6 days

% of wellness clients reporting that there is an adult in the wellness program that really cares about them

% of wellness clients scoring high in school connectedness assets

% of wellness clients who report coming to school more often

% of wellness clients who report doing better in school

% of youth outreach workers scoring high in school connectedness assets

% of youth who prefer to speak other than national language

% participation of 17 year-olds in education or training

% post-16 participation in physical sciences (A level Physics, Chemistry and Math)

% progression by 2 levels in English between Key Stage 1 and Key Stage 2

% progression by 2 levels in English between Key Stage 2 and Key Stage 3

% progression by 2 levels in English between Key Stage 3 and Key Stage 4

% progression by 2 levels in Math between Key Stage 1 and Key Stage 2

% progression by 2 levels in Math between Key Stage 2 and Key Stage 3

% progression by 2 levels in Math between Key Stage 3 and Key Stage 4

% reduction of children drop out of schools

Ratio of boys to girls at primary school

Ratio of boys to girls at secondary school

Ratio of boys to girls at tertiary school

Reduction in # of schools judged as requiring special measures and improvement

Reduction in # of schools where fewer than 30% of pupils achieve 5 or more A-C grades

Reduction in # of schools where fewer than 50% of pupils achieve level 5 or above in both English and Math at KS3

Reduction in # of schools where fewer than 65% of pupils achieve level 4 or above in both English and Math at KS2

Secondary school persistent absence rate

Youth Health

of hospital admissions caused by unintentional and deliberate injuries to children and young people

# of medals won in international competitions / year

% obesity in primary school age children in reception

% obesity in primary school age children in year 6

% of clients who report learning information about how to improve their own health and well-being

57. Social Development

% of facilities with one ongoing program each in the areas of arts, sports and intellectual activities

% of people who use tobacco

% of school healthy lunches

% of students who report being better able to cope when things go wrong

% of students who report being more satisfied with their lives

% of students who report feeling better about themselves

% of students who report learning ways to reduce stress in their life

% of youth outreach workers who report learning new information about how to improve their own health and well-being

% of youth who smoke

% who planned to take steps to improve their health

% who reported they had taken steps to improve their own health

Suicide rate among youth

Youth delinquency rate

Youth inactivity rate

58. Sports

Football Clubs

of privatized football clubs

# of professional players in the football clubs

# of sports covered by academy pathways

% reduction of government finance to football clubs

International Sports

of international medals or titles won by athletes or teams

# of international sporting events held

Parks & Recreation

% of citizen overall satisfaction with parks and recreation

Total # of estimated youth participant hours (in millions)

Total park acres

Total park acres per 1,000 population

Professional Athletes

individuals gaining sports related qualifications

of sports conferences per annum

# of sports organizations or individuals rewarded per annum

% new athletes

% of events that are compliant

% of professional clubs not achieving management performance targets

% of professional clubs reporting using the performance management

Sport Participation

increase of citizen population participating in sport on a weekly basis

volunteers supporting the sport

% increase of elderly adults (over 65) participating in sport on a weekly basis

% increase of family sport participation on a monthly basis

58. Sports

% increase of female population participating in sport on a weekly basis

% increase of male population participating in sport on a weekly basis

% increase of non-citizen population participating in sport on a weekly basis

% increase of population participating in sport on a weekly basis

% increase of the special needs group participating in sport on a weekly basis

% increase of younger adults (under14) participating in sport on a weekly basis

Sport Teams

of international sports events held

# of medals won in international competitions

# of professional sports clubs

% increase of international sports events

% of professional sports clubs

Sports Activities

of major sports events executed by registered sport clubs

# of sport types offered by registered sport clubs

% increase of sport types offered by registered sport clubs

Sports Clubs

gym capacity

of registered sports

# of registered sports clubs

# of sport types offered by registered sport clubs

# of sports facility and planning meetings with urban planning

# of sports represented annual school championships

# of sports stadium capacity per million population

qualified coaches actively providing coaching in the sport

% accredited clubs within the sport

% increase in sports volunteers from last year

% of citizens registered in sports clubs

Total investment in exercise equipment

Sports in Schools

of education partnerships

# of mandatory sport hours in schools/ per week

% of kids classified as obese

% of teachers that have participated in the online healthy living program

59. Stock Exchange

Domestic Debt Market

of listed benchmark government bond

# of listed debt instruments

Economy Growth

of listed domestic companies

% change on index in national currency

59. Stock Exchange

% of stock traded turnover

Average value traded on stock market / per day

Bond market size (in USD billions)

Bonds trading value as % of total cash equity market

Cash or near cash form as a % of total assets

Equity market turnover ratio

Government bond market as a % of GDP

Increased # of listed securities

Local equity market access (scale from 1 to 7)

Market capitalization (as % of GDP)

Market capitalization as % of non-oil GDP

Stock market capitalization (in USD billions)

Stock market index

Stock market liquidity (%)

Stock market price index

Stock traded as % of GDP

Stock traded turnover ratio

Total stocks value traded as % of GDP

Total value of shares traded in stock exchanges as a share of GDP

Traded shares as % of total free float market capitalization

Trading to volatility ratio

Value of traded shares as a % of total market capitalization

Value traded on stock market (USD, Bn)

Value-traded-ratio divided by stock price volatility

Equity Market

of companies listed on stock exchange with capital equal to or exceeding 1 billion US

% of execution of initiatives

Disclosure ratio

Market liquidity ratio

Institutional Participation

of attracted strategic partners

# of international members operating remotely in stock exchange

# of operated custodians in stock exchange

% of execution of the investment survey project

% of institutional trading value

% of the increase in brokers' #

Share of ownership of institutional investors in stock markets (%)

Internal Process

% of reduction of overall time of stock exchange services

Brokers satisfaction survey overall score

Investors satisfaction survey overall score

Investment Products

of listed (ETF)s on stock exchange

59. Stock Exchange

of listed future contracts within the derivatives market

# of listed warrants in stock exchange

% change of investment literacy index

Future contracts trading value as % of total cash equity market

Market Intermediation

of brokers operating as market makers

# of brokers providing the service of portfolio managements to their clients

# of institutions/brokers providing the service of researches to their clients

# of stock traded per year

% change in market index, trend over time

% of clearing segmentation project completion

Average # of stock traded per day

Regulations

of rules on Foreign Direct Investment FDI

# of valued economic and/or financial researches that participated in the award and published by stock exchange

% compliance with IOSCO principles (Rank)

% compliance with World Federation of exchanges (WFE)

% of Business impact of rules on Foreign Direct Investment (FDI)

% of execution of rules and regulations initiatives

% of execution of the regulatory framework initiatives

% of prevalence of foreign ownership

% of property rights including financial assets

Corporate governance compliance Index

ETFs trading value as % of total cash equity market

Trading value of institutional investors in stock exchange (%)

Social Responsibly

% of actual donation & financial support

% of special needs staff

60. Telecommunication

Information Services

of community media organizations in operation

# of district centers linked to the sector wide network

# of districts able to receive TV and radio signal

# of media friendly laws implemented

# of provincial centers able to publish newspapers locally

# of total newspaper clips per year

Network Management

of access to networks (1000)

# of access to networks (per 100 inhabitants)

# of districts connected to fiber optic cables

% block error rate (BLER)

% data network availability

60. Telecommunication

% data network growth rate

% of backbone network ring reliability

Internet network reliability rate

Voice reliability rate

Public Television

of cumulative kids ages 2 to 11 using public television's broadcast services each week

# of individuals and families who support public television service through their membership

# of K-12 and adult literacy hours broadcast in a given year

# of students and school staff who will be served by interactive learning sessions through K-12 connections this year

# of subscribers accessing daily, weekly and seasonal weather forecasts

# of total contacts with businesses

# of total local production hours

# of unique viewers that use broadcast services a week

# of viewer awareness and engagement initiatives conducted each year

% of teachers that report that the content of the K-12 connections interactive learning activity was appropriate

% of time transmitters are on-air

Cumulative # of teachers and students who use public television's educational services

Telecom Services

of employment

# of international calls

# of media firms per 100,000 people

# of mobile phone

# of mobile phone subscriptions (1000)

# of mobiles per 1,000 people

# of operators and service providers

# of radio stations per 100,000 people

# of SMS (Short message service)

# of telephone lines per 1,000 people

# of TV stations per 100,000 people

# of wireless PCs per 1,000 people

telephone connections per number of inhabitants

% e-Commerce via Internet

% increase access to ICT services

% invoices issued by the 15th of each month

% of errors resolved in 30 days after receipt of the dispute

% of invoices without errors

% of rural telecommunications subscribers receiving new or improved service

% of services delivered within the customer negotiated service install date delivery for data

60. Telecommunication

% of services delivered within the customer negotiated service install date delivery for voice

Average prices of telecommunication

Average revenue per user (ARPU)

Average usage per telecom user (AUPU)

Broadband penetration rate

Household share of main telephone lines

ICT expenditure by type of product

Level of Internet access - % households

Market share in telecommunication

Market share of the incumbent in fixed telecommunications

Market share of the leading operator in mobile telecommunication

Mobile phone subscriptions (per 100 inhabitants)

Price of telecommunications by type of call

Telecom subscriber acquisition cost

Telecom subscriber retention cost (SRC)

Total international receipts and payments

61. Tourism

Economic Benefits

of tourism receipts

% contribution to GDP

% increase contribution to Employment (%)

% increase contribution to GDP

% increase in demand (tourism)

% increase in investment by tourism industry

% increase in the contribution of tourism to GDP

% increase in tourism GDP (nominal)

% increase in tourism GDP (real)

% occupancy in collective accommodation establishments: domestic and inbound tourism

% of increased restaurant revenues

% tourists entered through airports

% visitors growth rate

City tourism competitiveness index

Direct tourism earnings (US $ millions)

Estimated capital investment (USD Bn)

Estimated government operating expenditure (USD Bn)

Leisure tourist # per year

Total contribution to GDP (US)

Total contribution to investment

Total expenditure on tourism trips

Total investment in the tourism sector / per year

61. Tourism

Total tourism demand: domestic and outbound tourism (excluding day-trips)

Total tourism receipts for hotel and hotel apartments

Tourism receipts (as a % of GDP)

Tourisms' contribution value to local and foreign investment

Tourist average total spending

Tourist expenditure - package travel

Tourist expenditure - package travel - geographical breakdown

Tourist expenditure - total

Tourist expenditure - total - geographical breakdown

Travel & tourism exports as a % of total exports

Industry Stakeholders

of bed places in hotels and similar establishments

# of bed places in other collective accommodation establishments

# of bed-places in collective tourist accommodation establishments

# of bed-places in hotels and similar establishments

# of bulletin and year book published

# of establishments, bedrooms and bed places - national

# of hotels and similar establishments

# of presentations delivered which explain principals of correct alignment with tourism positioning

# of research topics and viewpoints issued

% of citizens who agree that tourism positively impacts on local culture

% of issues resolved satisfactorily

Gross utilization of bed places

Increased occupancy % in hotels

Monthly use of bed places

Net utilization of bed places

Total capacity of collective tourist accommodation - establishments, bedrooms and bed places

Marketing & Promotions

of exhibitions attended

# of international attractions

# of international promotion offices

# of major international events sponsored by government

# of MICE bids won

# of MICE events

# of national promotion offices

# of new information booths

# of new information kiosks

# of new offices/representation opened

# of support to projects that promote and preserve culture and heritage

# of tourists coming from promotion office countries

# of visitors coming from promoted areas

61. Tourism

of websites including tourism knowledge sharing

% of destination awareness levels

% of destination consideration levels

Awareness Index

Government prioritization of the tourism industry: rating on 1 to 7 scale

Governments efforts on marketing and branding for tourism industry:
Rating on 1 to 7 scale

Total # of tourists who came back again

Total hotel room / hotel apartments rented per year (# of days)

Travel and tourism competitive index

UNWTO tourism confidence index

Regulations & Enforcement

classification regulations set for new activities/businesses

licensing regulations set for new activities/businesses

of guest complaints handled

# of renewal licensing activity available online

# of tourism activities that are classified out of total # of tourism activities

# of tourism activities that are regulated & licensed out of total # of tourism
activities

# of tourism statistical bulletin and yearly statistical yearbook issued

% compliance level with classification standards

% compliance level with licensing standards

% Compliance levels with all inspected licensing and classification activities

% compliance with agreed engagement plans

% improvement in time for issuance of visas in partnership with relevant
stakeholders

% increase in awareness of licensing and classification regulations of
available channels

% licensing activities regulated to be processed online

% of audit risk points reduced

% of businesses inspected 2-3 times a year

% of classified businesses inspected

% of guest complaints handled

% of industry sector who consider the licensing and regulations to be
effective

% of industry who agree that information on licensing law is accessible

% of licensed businesses inspected

% of target market issued visas in under 24 hrs

% reduction of prior year's audit risk points

Tourism Jobs

of direct employment resultant from tourism

# of employed persons by age groups

# of employed persons by full-time / part-time activity

# of employed persons by level of education attained

# of employment in the tourism sector

61. Tourism

of new enrollments in tourism related programs
# of new jobs created in the sector
# of total tourism sector workforce
% contribution to employment
% increase enrollment levels in tourism college programs
% increase in employment by tourism industry
% of total tourism sector workforce
% tourism employment
Average seniority of work with the same employer
Employment levels in tourism (# people)
Total employment in the tourism sector

Tourism Products

nights of hotel stays sold
of hotel rooms per 100 population
# of major attractions
# of monthly newsletter
# of new leisure attractions
# of new leisure attractions developed
# of new major events and world class events launched
# of new rooms supplied
# of presence of major car rental companies
# of tourism research and viewpoints including existing studies
% of concept studies implemented by private sector
% of ideas implemented by private sector
Average # of rooms utilization per year
Hotel price index
Total amount of taxes from airport charges

Tourist Visits

hotel room nights generated (thousands)
of arrivals in hotels and similar establishments
# of arrivals in other collective accommodation establishments
# of arrivals of non-residents - world geographical breakdown
# of arrivals of residents and non-residents
# of nights spent
# of nights spent - national
# of nights spent (x1000)
# of nights spent by non-residents - world geographical breakdown
# of nights spent by non-residents in collective tourist accommodation establishments
# of nights spent by non-residents in hotels and similar establishments
# of nights spent by residents and non-residents
# of nights spent by total (residents and non-residents) in collective tourist accommodation establishments

61. Tourism
# of nights spent by total (residents and non-residents) in hotels and similar establishments
# of nights spent in hotels and similar establishments
# of nights spent in other collective accommodation establishments
# of theater days booked
# of tourism nights
# of tourism nights broken by age
# of tourism nights broken by length of stay
# of tourism nights broken by main mode of accommodation used
# of tourism nights broken by main mode of transport used
# of tourism nights broken by month of departure
# of tourism nights broken by sex broken annual and quarterly data
# of tourism nights broken by type of organization of the trip
# of tourism nights broken geographical breakdown
# of tourism trips
# of tourist arrivals
# of tourists
# of tourists (persons participating in tourism) by age
# of tourists (persons participating in tourism) by sex
# of trips
# of trips broken by age
# of trips broken by length of stay
# of trips broken by main mode of accommodation used
# of trips broken by main mode of transport used
# of trips broken by month of departure
# of trips broken by sex
# of trips broken by type of organization of the trip
# of trips broken geographical breakdown
# of visitors in sector (hotel guests) per year
Average day stay
Bed-places (x1000)
Business tourist arrivals per year

Travel Destinations

# of airlines with scheduled flights originating in country
# of ATMs
# of attended major tourism fairs
# of attracted tourists from new markets
# of extension of business trips recommended
# of flights
# of flights from target markets
# of international MICE Events
% of destinations with at least 1 daily flight
% of target market with at least 1 daily flight
% of visitors not meeting visa requirement

61. Tourism

Average tourism receipts

Average tourism receipts for hotel and hotel apartments

Average tourist arrivals / day

MICE events # of meetings

Ranking of country as a niche tourist destination

Tourism confidence index

Tourist/ visitor arrivals (in thousands)

Travel and tourism government expenditure as a % of total budget

Visitor Experience

of annual visitor survey conducted

# of national feedback surveys

# of repeated visitors

# of visitor booths opened and operated

# of visitor information centers opened and operated

# of visitor kiosks operated

# of visitor survey

% completion of the central complaints database

% of increase trainings offered per year to tourism employees

% of tourist satisfaction

% of visitor satisfaction with airport services

% of visitor satisfaction with stakeholder provided services

% positive attitude of population toward foreign visitors

% tourist satisfaction levels with transportation in partnership with relevant stakeholders

% tourist satisfaction related to provided government services

Visitor satisfaction ratings

62. Transportation

Air Mail & Goods

Total air transport of freight at regional level

Total freight and mail air transport between main airports

Total freight and mail air transport by country

Total freight and mail air transport by main airports

Total freight and mail air transport by reporting country

Total international freight and mail air transport by country

Total international freight and mail air transport by main airports

Total international freight and mail air transport by world regions

Total national freight and mail air transport by country

Total national freight and mail air transport by main airports

Total national freight and mail air transport by reporting country

Air Passengers

of air passenger transport by main airports

# of air passenger transport by reporting country

# of airline fleet capacity (passenger #s)

62. Transportation

of business flights

# of non-transit passenger movements in thousands at airport per year

# of passengers moved on flights - domestic

# of passengers moved on flights - international

# of tourists and visitors in thousands of airport arrivals

# of visitors per annum

Total # of national air passenger transport by country

Total # of national air passenger transport by main airports

Total air transport of goods

Total air transport of passengers

Total international air passenger transport by country

Total international air passenger transport by main airports

Airport Equipment

of commercial aircraft fleet by age of aircraft

# of commercial aircraft fleet by type of aircraft

Airport Infrastructure

of airport connections to other modes of transport

# of airports (with more than 15,000 passenger movements per year)

% completion of airport systems master plan

Airport infrastructures by type

Airports

of airline cargo capacity (tones)

# of airports per million population (air capacity indicator)

# of aviation and airport enterprises

# of aviation cargo tons originated and arrived

# of bilateral agreements with international connecting hubs

# of employment in aviation and airport enterprises

# of employment in main airports

# of tickets issued

% airport service quality indicators reported on a quarterly basis

% annual increase in connections

% completion of aviation sector strategic framework

% completion of comprehensive performance report of aviation sector

% critical service providers with whom the airport operator developed SLA

% development of key components in utilization plan

% development of procedures and clear interaction mechanisms with key aviation stakeholders that would allow to monitor safety and security standards at the airport

% development of procedures and regulations to monitor and measure the quality of airport passenger services

% implemented critical processes aligned to the objectives

% of adequate procedures to develop service standards and monitor quality of airport airline and cargo services

% of aircraft running on time

62. Transportation

% of airline cancelled/late

% of airports that meet facility and service objectives for their functional roles

% of commercial/ industrial cargo

% of customer satisfaction

% of developed processes to improve internal communication and flow of information between terminals

% reports regarding aviation sector performance submitted on-time and according to requirements

% required stakeholders with which coordination mechanisms have been established

% runway capacity versus aircraft usage

% stakeholders with which coordination and guidance mechanisms have been developed and implemented by the aviation sector

Air safety indicator

Airline capacity indicator

Airline growth rates

Airline ranking

Airline reliability indicator

Airport capacity indicator

Airport capacity planning indicator

Airport service quality index

Cargo growth rates

Connectivity index

Total # of carriers at airport

Total # of routes served at airport

Total air travel

Total value of cargo shipped

Volume of cargo transported on flights

Marine

of bulk flows at sea port in millions of tons

# of cargo processed per hour

# of days for vessel turnaround

# of employment by enterprises

# of employment in inland waterways transport enterprises

# of incidents on the water

# of inland waterway transport enterprises

# of ridership transit passengers

# of tonnage/TEUs handled in port

# of tons of waterway freight originated and arrived

# of vessels in enterprises

% completion of maritime sector strategic plan

% completion of pre-engineering studies

% of interaction mechanism regarding port tariffs and definition

62. Transportation

% of provided comments on maritime related requests within 15 working days of initial request

Average vessel turn around times

Minimum vessel turnaround time

Total investment and maintenance expenditure in vessels and infrastructure

Total of sea transport of goods

Volume of cargo transported on inland waterways

Marine Equipment

of inland waterways transport equipment

# of pushed vessels

# of self-propelled dumb vessels

# of self-propelled vessels

% completion of ferry infrastructure construction projects

% completion of ferry system plan and pre-engineering studies

Ship turnaround time at berth and total time

Total carrying capacity of the inland waterways transport enterprises vessels

Total carrying capacity of vessels

Total load capacity of pushed vessels

Total load capacity of self-propelled dumb vessels

Total load capacity of self-propelled vessels

Total power of self-propelled vessels

Total power of tugs and pushers

Marine Goods

of break bulk cargo

# of bulk cargo

# of containers handled

# of containers packed/unpacked per employee

# of gross tonnage of vessels in the main ports

Gross tonnage of vessels

Gross weight of goods handled in all ports

Gross weight of goods handled in main ports

Gross weight of goods in containers transported to/from main ports

Gross weight of goods transported to/from main ports

Maritime transport - data aggregated at standard regional levels (NUTS)

Maritime transport of freight at regional level

Total # of container transported

Total # of goods containers

Total # of vessel traffic (trips)

Total goods gross weight

Total goods handled in main ports

Total goods in short sea shipping

Total goods transport by inland waterways

Total transport of dangerous goods

62. Transportation
Total volume (in TEUs) of containers handled in main ports
Transport by nationality of vessel
Transport by type of vessel
Vessel traffic
Volume (in TEU's) of containers transported to/from main ports

Marine Passengers

# of maritime transport of passengers at regional level
# of passengers (excluding cruise passengers) transported to/from main ports
# of passengers embarked and disembarked in all ports
# of passengers embarked and disembarked in ports
# of passengers transported waterways
Total # of maritime transport of passengers - All ports

Planning & Integration

# of enplanements
# of integrated transportation options
# of miles of trails for public use
# of network congestion points
# of projects for strengthening highway links with other cities & adjacent countries
# of projects to enhance highway connectivity to other regions
# of road, rail and navigable inland waterways networks
% accessibility between industrial zones and main cities and airports
% completion of city transportation mater plan
% completion of the update transportation mater plan
% development of a comprehensive environment/emergency management system for all transport sectors
% development of a planning approach that integrates all transport modes/sectors, as well as transport and land use and strengthens regional linkages
% implementation of the transport master plan's recommendations for reduction of the ratio of traffic speed to bus network speed
% mode split between bus and train
% mode split between taxi and bus
% of car share of inland passenger transport
% of distribution infrastructure of goods and services generally efficient
% of highway transport needs resulting from economic growth and planned development projects
% of network density
% of network density (Roads)
% of projects reviewed and commented on
% of projects that support jobs with wages that meet or exceed average wage rate
% of quality of air in peak transportation points
% of quality of railroad infrastructure (on 1 to 10 scale)

62. Transportation

% of road share of inland freight transport

% of the port master plans are submitted for approval and integration with transport planning efforts in other sectors

% reduction congestion delays for forecast traffic

% transport sector contribution to GDP

%of transport sector contribution to employment

Amount of revenue from motor vehicle registration (in millions)

Journey time reliability

Modal split of freight transport

Modal split of passenger transport

Network adequacy in # of vehicle-kms (AM, PM peaks)

Network adequacy in vehicle-hrs (AM, PM peaks)

Planned passenger capacity at City airport in millions of passengers

Port reliability indicator as quality of port infrastructure (1 to 10 scale)

Ratio of car parking supply / demand

Total # of commercial vehicles in country

Total # of passenger cars in country

Total congestion cost per year

Transport services % of commercial services export

Transport system accessibility index

Volume of freight transport

Volume of freight transport relative to GDP

Volume of passenger transport

Volume of passenger transport relative to GDP

Public Transport

bus seats km per day (Bus capacity)

of 2 wheel vehicles per 1000 population

# of car ownership per 1000 population

# of completion of projects for construction of new bus shelters, stations and depots

# of driver-error incidents per 100,000 kms

# of minor accidents/incidents per 100,000 vehicle km

# of public transport buses

# of public transport kms travelled per capita

# of public transport taxis

# of public transport vehicle travelled per capita

# of taxis in peak time

# of taxis vehicles per 1000 population

# of travelled km per sq km of area (Density of public transport)

% availability of taxi services

% completion of sector governance definition

% completion of strategy, policies and high-level regulations for public transport sector

% completion of the framework for monitoring activities

62. Transportation

% customer satisfaction with passenger information

% customer satisfaction within .5 km of public transport route

% high quality vehicles in fleet

% increase the capacity of the bus network (million seat-km per day)

% increase the level of customer satisfaction for bus and hired vehicle quality

% increase the modal share of the bus sector

% new vehicles in fleet

% of bus and hired vehicle fleets to be compliant with emissions standards

% of public transport cancelled/late compared to total service

% of public transport vehicles running on time

% of rides with more than 2 transfers

% of routes where single ticket transfer between modes of public transport is available

% of service operated on time

% of special needs populations are actually served

% of special needs populations are capable of being served

% of stations where integrated network information is available

% on-time performance for public transport services

% overall customer satisfaction level

% regulatory compliance by franchisees with regulations for bus and hired vehicle sectors

% scheduled bus service actually run

Average fare revenue per day

Average operating costs per day

Average passenger expenditure for public transport

Average passenger income for lowest income quartile

Average time for frequency of services

Average time spent commuting in peak time

Average transfer time between two nodes of the public transport network

Bus services running on time

Coverage index of the service

Public transport safety indicator

Safety incident rate per 100,000 vehicle-km (vehicles)

Share of public transport individual journeys in the total # of individual journeys

Railway Enterprises

of employment in principal railway enterprises

# of principal railway enterprises

Total expenditure in principal railway enterprises

Railway Equipment

of hauled vehicle movements

# of hauled vehicle-kilometers

# of locomotives by tractive power

62. Transportation

of passenger railway vehicles
# of railcars
# of vans in railway transport
Hauled vehicles movements - # of seat kilometers offered
Hauled vehicles movements - # of Tkm offered
Max # of traffic flow of trains on the rail network
Total capacity of passenger railway vehicles - # of seats
Total load capacity of wagons
Tractive vehicle movements - # of vehicle and source of power

Railway Goods

Annual # of empty and loaded intermodal transport units carried on railways
Annual national and international railway goods transport
Annual railway transit transport
Annual railway transport of dangerous goods
Annual railway transport of goods in intermodal transport units
Annual railway transport using container and road/rail
Total goods transported
Total international annual railway transport
Total national annual railway transport
Total volume of goods transport by rail

Railway Infrastructure

Total # of tracks
Total length of electrified lines
Total length of railway lines
Total Length of tracks

Railway Passengers

of international railway passenger transport
# of passengers transported on railways / per day
# of rail passengers
# of total passengers carried (million passenger-km)
Accompanied passenger car railway transport (passenger cars)
Annual national and international railway passenger transport
Cost of producing a passenger kilometer
Total rail transport of passengers

Railways

of rail journeys
# of rail journeys distance
# of serious accidents/incidents per million train kilometers
# of tons of rail freight originated and arrived
# of total trains (engine)
# of trains cancelled/late compared to total service
# of trains running on time as a % of total trains
% completion of rail transit infrastructure construction projects

62. Transportation
% completion of rail transit system plan
% increase in passenger fares over ten years
% of rail miles capable of carrying heavy axle unit trains
% of railroads density of the network
% of railroads km in cities
% on time running
Customer satisfaction index
Customer satisfaction rating
Length of network (in km)
Total passengers transported/total passenger kilometers
Volume of cargo transported on railways

Road Asphalt Repair

# of asphalt repairs
# of asphalt repairs completed
# of asphalt repairs per 100 lane miles of streets
# of equipment hours by type of equipment (total hours including use and stand-by hours)
# of square feet milled
# of square yards of repairs per 100 lane miles of streets
% asphalt repairs requiring further repairs within two years
% of hazardous pavement conditions responded to within 24 hours
Average cost per asphalt repair
Average cost per cubic yard of concrete used
Average cost per ton of asphalt used
Average cost per ton of rock used
Pavement condition index within base repair area
Square feet of repairs made
Square yards of repair/DLH
Total contract costs for asphalt repair
Total cost/ton of asphalt used
Total direct costs for asphalt crew (hours multiplied by hourly rate)
Total direct costs for asphalt repairs excluding total direct costs for asphalt crew
Total direct labor hours/ton of asphalt used

Road Development

# of employment in goods road transport enterprises
# of journeys made by vehicles
# of kilometers of roads maintained - paved
# of kilometers of roads maintained - unpaved
# of kilometers of roads rehabilitated - paved Roads
# of kilometers of roads rehabilitated - unpaved Roads
# of regulations and policy guideline documents developed
# of vehicles of goods road transport enterprises
# of vehicles on road at peak road traffic

62. Transportation
% completion of annual maintenance plan
% completion of capital and special projects
% main road centerline-km constructed
% main road lane-km constructed
% main road lane-km constructed
% main road network length with international roughness index < 4.0
% main road network plan completed
% network with improved pavement marking
% network with improved ride quality
% of oversize permit requests filed electronically
% of purchases deployed within 45 days of receipt
% pavement markings with acceptable reflectivity
% priority main road projects developed
% projects completed (construction contracts awarded)
% projects prepared (feasibility/planning studies completed)
% reduction in unit road transport costs for selected goods movements
% regional development plans reviewed and aligned with main road plans
% signs improved
% signs with acceptable reflectivity
Average network speed during peak periods
Average peak period speed in metropolitan network
Stock of vehicles
Total investment expenditure
Total length of e-roads
Total length of motorways
Total length of side-roads
Total maintenance expenditure
Volume / capacity Ratio during peak hours
Volume / capacity Ratio on selected links

Road Driver Services

# of background investigations completed
# of driver improvement interviews conducted
# of driver's license fraud, immigrant, and internal affairs cases investigated
# of drivers placed out-of-service
# of makeup alcohol drug awareness program courses
# of programs audited per year
% of customers initially served within 30 minutes
Average % of calls answered within three minutes at the contact center

Road Equipment

# of company cars
# of company cars distance
# of lorries and road tractors
# of motor coaches, buses and trolley buses
# of new registrations of lorries

62. Transportation

of new registrations of lorries, road tractors, semi-trailers and trailers
# of new registrations of motor coaches, buses and trolley buses
# of new registrations of motorcycles
# of new registrations of passenger cars
# of new registrations of road tractors
# of new registrations of semi-trailers
# of operational vehicles
# of operational vehicles distance
# of passenger cars
# of passenger cars per 1000 inhabitants
# of seats on motor coaches, buses and trolley buses
# of vehicles on the road at peak time
# of vehicles per thousand people
% increase in private vehicles ownership
Motorization rate
Road tractors by type of motor energy
Semi-trailers load capacity (1000t)
Total load capacity of lorries
Total load capacity of semi-trailers
Total load capacity of trailers
Total lorries load capacity (1000t)
Trailers load capacity (1000t)

Road Goods

Annual cross-trade road freight transport
Annual road freight transport
Annual road freight transport by type of cargo
Annual road freight transport by type of operation
Annual road freight transport of dangerous goods
International annual road freight transport of goods loaded
National annual road freight transport
National road freight transport
Quarterly cross-trade road freight transported
Road sabotage by hauliers
Total road freight transport

Road Investigation

of commercial vehicle safety inspections
# of commercial vehicles inspected transporting hazardous materials
# of fraud investigations conducted
# of fraudulent document detection training seminars provided
# of motor carrier safety and hazardous materials regulation training sessions provided
# of new entrant carrier reviews performed
% of highway infrastructure is designed and constructed in accordance with best-practice standards

62. Transportation

% of light fleet into service within time standard

% of protected highway infrastructure from unnecessary damage from overloaded trucks

Annual % of officers' crash reports submitted electronically

Annual average time to hold incapable suspension appeal hearings

Road Public Work

of curb ramps constructed

# of days of temporary traffic controls or road closure on traffic sensitive roads caused by road works per km of traffic sensitive roads

% of paved lane miles assessed as satisfactory

% of street with good condition (in km)

% of the existing roads maintained to meet current needs

Average pavement rating for residential streets

Citizen satisfaction % with pedestrian accessibility

Citizen satisfaction % with road conditions

Road Safety

of accident countermeasures at high-accident locations

# of accidents /incidents at black spots

# of crashes and/or incidents

# of deaths on the road per 100,000 population

# of fatalities per 100 million vehicle-miles of travel

# of initiatives for safety improvement program for buses

# of initiatives for safety improvement program for hired vehicles

# of road accidents per year

# of road fatalities per million inhabitants

# of security breaches or loss due to theft, vandalism, or other incidents

# of serious injury on the road per 100,000 population

# of serious road injury rates

# of victims in road accidents

% of qualified roads as per safety standards

% of the internal roads achieve acceptable road safety standards

% of the internal roads are compatible with international standards

% updated road safety transport regulations

Causality rate

Crash rate

Frequency of casualties (fatalities and injuries)

People killed in road accidents

Rate of adherence to road safety

Rate of adherence to road safety specifications

Ratio of indirect spending on safety activities

Road fatality rates

Road Sweeping

of cubic yards collected

# of cubic yards collected per 1000 km of streets

62. Transportation

of equipment hours by type of equipment

# of lane miles of streets swept per month - total streets

# of street sweeping complaints

% customer satisfaction rating for clean streets

% of customers who rate street sweeping as good to excellent

% of highways that are either of an acceptable or high standard of cleanliness

% of residential streets rated as clean

% of routes completed on schedule

% of street miles meeting cleaning schedule

Average # of miles of streets swept per DLH

Average cost per mile of street cleaned

Total direct costs for street sweeping crew (hours multiplied by hourly rate)

Total direct costs for street sweeping expenses

Roads

of car parking spaces per 1000 cars

# of customer surveys on the satisfaction with the quality

# of institutional and technical requirements to maintaining the highway network in good condition

# of jobs accessible within # mile radius of residential areas

# of large trucks (semi-truck) vehicle miles of travel / per year

# of markets accessible within # mile radius of business area

# of new transportation research dollars secured

# of passengers transported on inland

# of people moved

# of recreational areas accessible by # mile radius of residential areas

# of shoulder miles of new paved shoulders awarded for construction on the primary highway system

# of special needs people evacuated during or after a disaster

# of special needs people evacuated prior to a disaster

# of tons of freight moved

# of viable alternative to highway travel for goods

# of viable alternative to highway travel for passengers

% of all highway miles returned to a reasonable, near-normal surface condition within 24 hours from the end of a winter storm

% of all highway miles returned to a reasonable, near-normal surface condition within three work days from the end of a winter storm

% of cities over 5,000 population with at least weekly scheduled transit access to health facilities and groceries

% of goods are actually served to reach activity center

% of goods are capable of being served to reach activity center

% of highway network length with international roughness index (IRI) of 6 or lower

% of non-committed right of way parcels returned to private, commercial, or public uses

62. Transportation

% of originally programmed projects let for construction in the current fiscal year versus programmed projects

% of passengers are actually served to reach activity center

% of passengers are capable of being served to reach activity center

% of road roughness

% of roads exceeding roughness standards

% of structure inventory and appraisal values for our bridge system that meets last year's values

% of third party claims involving unregistered motor vehicles

% of total dollars paid to the total awarded amount for all contracts dollars

% of vehicle kilometers travelled on roads that exceed roughness standards

% reduction in transfer time

Average # and length of trip per person per day

Average # of days taken to issue access permits

Average automobile vehicle miles of travel

Average pavement condition index

Average speed on highway in km/hr

Average time required to evacuate special needs population from affected disaster area

Average time spent commuting per day per person

Journey to work modes

Length of roads network (in km)

Length of roads per 1000 population

Mean travel time to work in minutes

Ratio between average vehicle speed and road utilization

Ratio between volume /capacity in peak periods on major routes

Ratio of annual highway program cost awarded versus annual program cost estimate

Ratio volume to capacity

Road congestion rate

Road miles with inadequate geometrics / total miles

Road quality index

Road standards and proportion of travel done on substandard roads

Total cost per kilometer to preserve roads

Total transit revenue mileage

Safety & Environment

of achieved safety certification and maintaining it for the coming year

# of airport accidents, incidents, events resulting in injury or death

# of bus safety incidents

# of conversion of public transport vehicles to CNG fuel use

# of fatalities in injury accidents

# of injury accidents

# of metric tons of carbon dioxide

# of public transport serious accidents/incidents per 100,000 vehicle km

62. Transportation

of railway victims by type of injury

# of taxi safety incidents

% aircraft emissions above standard

% completion of EHSMS system

% entities with EHSMS certification compared to total # of entities within the transport industry

% of Carbone dioxide emissions

% of implemented compliance safety, security and environment mechanism for the ports sector

% of methane emissions (kt of CO_2 equivalent)

% reduction in # of incidents of oil spills from vessels into the marine environment

% safety and security standards reported on-time

Annual # of railway accidents by type of accident

Annual # of railway accidents involving the transport of dangerous goods

Annual # of railway victims by type of accident

EHSMS certification approval process cycle time (in days)

Reduction in # of reported/detected safety breaches in coastal waters, ports and marine facilities

Total CO_2 produced

Total emissions from the public transport

Transportation Improvement

of established clear interaction mechanisms with relevant stakeholders

# of guidelines for public transport and highways management activities

# of issuance of incremental law updates for the transportation sector

# of miles of bike lanes, routes, and trails

# of neighborhood traffic calming requests received

# of transportation projects completed

# of transportation projects under construction

# of transportation projects under design

% contribution of the transport sector to employment

% contribution of the transport sector to GDP

% of areas achieving concurrency

% of commercial/ industrial developments within 500 meters of public transport systems

% of residential developments within 500 meters of public transport systems

% of residents are satisfied with the completed traffic calming project

% of tourism developments within 500 meters of public transport systems

% of trips undertaken by various modes of transport

Design cost at bid award as a % of contract cost

Total % variance of actual construction costs from the original construction contract

63. Urban Planning

Housing

# of housing units / quarters developed

# of housing units / quarters rehabilitated

# of low cost housing units constructed

# of medium cost housing units constructed

# of new subdivisions approved

# of vacant sites 1 acre or larger

% approved subdivisions by location

% of building permits by location

% of population in unplanned urban settlements who have access to clean and safe water

% of population in unplanned urban settlements who have access to safe means of sanitation

Value of rents accruing to the local authorities from leasing

Neighborhood Zoning

# of neighborhood plans adopted/zoned

# of rounds of golf & crossroads golf courses

% of neighborhood planning participants satisfied with urban planning process

% of resident's positive perceptions of the tidiness of their neighborhoods

Average travel time delay

Supply versus demand per sector

Regulations & Standards

# of best practice urban planning approaches used across government

# of planning forums held

% of new buildings being assessed against standards

% of non-compliant cases enforced

% of urban development public policies aligned across government

Street condition ratings

Sustainable Communities

# of infrastructure zone by Year

# of municipal recreation facilities per 100,000 residents

# of open space and trails

# of parks and recreation facilities

# of retail outlets/mm of habitants

# of total parks and open space

% citizen satisfaction with urban planning for the future

% density comparison of approved subdivision by location

% distribution of social facilities throughout residential areas

% land uses by community planning area (% of acres)

% of green buildings to total new buildings

% of land use allocation

% open space acres

% proximity of parks to residences

63. Urban Planning

% proximity of trails to residences

% residential density by community planning area

% suitability of housing buildings

Attractiveness index

Congestion index

Residential street average pavement rating

Walkability index

United Development

of applied transportation demand management measures

# of awareness campaigns of urban role for key stakeholder groups

# of consolidated master schedules published in the quarter

# of coordination meetings on priority development projects in the quarter

# of master plans reviewed

urban plans completed

% cities plans completed

% of developer confidence in the real estate market

% of development projects inconsistent with urban plan

% of developments monitored per quarter

% of land used for planning and zoning

% of special project teams established within 4-weeks

% of strategic developers and land allocation authorities engaged

% of urban plans completed

Watershed Protection

of watershed development plan reviews conducted

% of creek miles in the inventory maintained for vegetation Control

% of drinking water compliance

% of reviews completed within code

64. Water & Electricity

Alternative Energy

of participants supporting nuclear power activities

% of commercial energy consumed for each dollar of GDP in kilojoules

% of electricity generated from renewable energy sources

% of use of the nuclear reactor

Governmental expenditure on alternative and renewable energy sources as a % of GDP

Ratio of alternative and renewable energy consumption to total energy consumption

Total electricity generated from renewable sources

Electricity Consumption

Total consumption of electricity by households

Total consumption of electricity by industry

Total consumption of electricity by services

Total consumption of electricity by transport activities

64. Water & Electricity

Electricity Cost

% electricity fee increase

Annual residential electric service costs

Average price of electricity versus international average

Citizen satisfaction with the amount pay for electricity

Electricity cost for industrial clients (USD per kWh)

Electricity price for large industrial consumers

Electricity prices by type of user

Total electricity cost for industrial clients

Electricity Supply

of identified pollution problems

# of incidents of interruptions in power provision

# of nuclear power stations

# of required electricity capacity in GW

# of safety incidents per year

% compliance of power with regulations

% contribution of renewable energy to total energy supply

% development of applications

% energy intensity

% implemented ISO corporate governance management 9001, 14000, or 18000

% improved service level in all areas

% increase in future energy supply

% market share of the largest generator in the electricity market

% of community electricity facilities that meets health-based standards

% of decisions reflects the latest system conditions and provides prompt remedial action

% of future energy supply adequately ensured

% of population with access to electricity

% of power transmission system availability

% of renewable energy to total energy capacity

Average duration of interruptions in power provision

Capacity built-up of trained # of users

Demand per capita per year

Electricity consumption Bn kWh/annum

Electricity consumption per capita (kWh)

Electricity production Bn kWh/annum

Electricity production from nuclear sources (% of total)

Satisfaction Index

Supply vs. demand (Power) (unit: MW)

Total electricity generation by hard coal

Total electricity generation by hydroTotal electricity

Total electricity generation by natural gas

Total electricity generation by nuclear

64. Water & Electricity

Total electricity generation by petroleum products

Total electricity generation by wind

Total final energy consumption (million tone oil equivalent)

Total final energy consumption per capita (million tone oil equivalent per capita)

Total imports of electricity

Total indigenous energy production (million tone oil equivalent)

Total indigenous energy production per capita (million tone oil equivalent per capita)

Total supply of electricity

Regulation & Compliance

of accidents per year reported by electric and gas utilities

# of cases filed

# of meetings held to discuss issues between staff and stakeholders in a year

# of surveys and reports issued

% of board members holding positions in national regulatory organizations

% of errata orders issued

% of orders issued on or before statutory deadline

% of peak alert days where load is met by mechanisms in place

% of petitions for approval of new construction processed in a timely manner

% of scheduled inspections of utility facilities completed within a year

Service Improvement

for service irregularities

of areas/power plants for which hydrodynamic and water quality modeling were conducted and updates

# of days from receipt of a complaint to the referral to a utility for response

# of drinking water quality monitoring systems

# of peer-reviewed papers and/or technical papers corresponding to each investigated and applied unique new generation technology

# of peer-reviewed publications and technical reports

# of pending issues

# of projects including initiatives conducted for stakeholders and society

# of research projects with external partners and stakeholders

# of significant consumer concern over a pending proceeding filed with the board

of the governmental entities to be served by nuclear research reactor and its facilities through research and its various applications

of unsuccessful samples

% achieved a return on investment (ROI)

% of annual capital investment projects completed as planned

% of compliance with standards

% of days of the beach season that coastal and lakes beaches open and safe for swimming

64. Water & Electricity

% of electricity operational efficiency

% of enhanced technical capabilities to effectively provide long term needs

% of projects managed efficiently at minimum cost

% of service standards

% of timely and cost effective utilities for developers and industries

% of vouchers processed timely

% progress in the project design and construction scope of work

% quality of water served

% reliability of public worker safety

% staff effectiveness

% transmission system availability

% water distribution system availability

Average resolution time for written complaint fill

Distribution system interruption frequency index

Investment in millions of annual capital investment

Power quality index

System average interruption duration index

Water Cost

% of effectiveness of project spending

% of revenue collection efficiency

% tariff and water fee increase

Average creditor days

Average debtor days

Average monthly water bills single family residential

Average price of water versus international average

Citizen satisfaction % with the amount pay for water services

Cost of regulatory service standards

Cost per property for water

Remuneration and employment costs

Total capital expenditure

Total cost of customer service

Total operating expenditure

Water conservation programs costs per customer per year

Water Management

of fish landings in domestic and foreign ports

# of total gallons of groundwater reserves/availability: fresh Water

# of total gallons of groundwater reserves/availability: saline

# of total gallons of groundwater reserves/availability: brackish

supplied water volume per person

water consumption per capita

% improvement of groundwater reserves/availability: brackish

% improvement of groundwater reserves/availability: fresh water

% improvement of groundwater reserves/availability: saline

% of adopt water conservation ordinance

64. Water & Electricity

% of community water systems that have undergone a sanitary survey within the past three years

% of community water systems that meet all applicable health-based standards

% of community water systems where risk to public health is minimized

% of household with access to basic or higher level of water

% of improve water pumping energy efficiency

% of install a central irrigation control system

% of install high efficiency toilets

% of install low-flow faucets

% of install low-flow shower heads

% of the population served by community water systems that receive drinking water that meets all applicable health-based drinking water standards

% of the population served by community water systems where risk to public health is minimized through source water protection

% of usage of water from non-traditional sources

% of use low maintenance landscaping

% of water quality in term of Nitrogen loading

% reduction of water consumption per day per capita (lit/day/person)

% reduction of water consumption per hector in agricultural zones

% reduction of water consumption per hector in Forestry sector

% Salinity in water

Amount of suspended solids in the drinking water

Annual water abstraction by source and by sector (mio m³/year)

Annual water abstraction by source and by sector per capita (m³/year/capita)

Gallons per day per capita use of ground water

Other sources of water (mio m³/year)

Other sources of water per capita (m³/year/capita)

Per capita daily water consumption

Per capita water abstractions

Renewable water resources (mio m³/year)

Total gross water abstractions

Water consumption per day per capita

Water consumption per hectare in agricultural zones

Water consumption per hectare in forestry sector

Water stress index

Water use balance (mio m³/year)

Water use by supply category and user (mio m³/year)

Water use by supply category per capita (m³/year/capita)

Water Quality

of abandoned wells closed to eliminate potential pathways for contaminants to groundwater

# of active individual certifications for lead based paint activities

64. Water & Electricity

of authorized certification and training programs for lead

# of cities that are on a schedule consistent with national water policy

# of cities that are providing water quality data in a format accessible for storage in data system

# of cities that currently receive funding that have begun implementing monitoring strategies to their water quality

# of cities that have adopted and are implementing their monitoring strategies in keeping with established schedules

# of cities that have adopted approved nutrient criteria into their water quality standards

# of cities that have adopted current pathogen criteria for non-coastal recreational waters

# of cities that have developed and begun to implement a watershed based plan

# of cities that have incorporated into their water quality programs for streams and small rivers

# of cities that provide integrated reports for water assessment

# of cities that within the preceding three year period, submitted new or revised water quality criteria

# of cities using the assessment database to record their assessment decisions

# of cities where the trend in wetland condition has been measured

# of current watershed permits issued

# of grant dollars per pesticide applicator certification

# of inspections to be conducted at treatment, storage or disposal facilities

# of inspections with an approved pretreatment program

# of large and medium public water systems inspected

# of oversight inspections to be conducted

# of permits providing for trading between the discharger and other water pollution sources

# of pesticide agencies meeting water quality commitments

# of pesticide worker safety programs that meet national program commitment

# of private water wells renovated to eliminate potential pathways for contaminants to groundwater

# of storm water permits that are issued and current for construction storm water general permits

# of storm water permits that are issued and current for general and individual permits

# of waste water treatment plants where effluent quality does not meet the current effluent discharge criteria

# of water bodies identified as being impaired that are partially or fully restored

# of water bodies identified as not attaining standards where water quality standards are restored

64. Water & Electricity
# of water segments known to be impaired or threatened that initial restoration planning is complete
# of watershed
water program rebates dispersed
% completion of salinity mapping and monitoring
% improvement in water quality in term of Salinity and Nitrogen loading
% of all public beaches that are monitored
% of beaches where local agencies have put into place water quality monitoring and public notification programs
% of cities water quality standards submissions that are approved
% of citizen satisfaction with drinking water quality
% of citizen satisfaction with lake and stream water quality
% of facilities covered under either an individual or general permit by construction storm water permits
% of facilities covered under either an individual or general permit by industrial storm water permits
% of major dischargers in significant noncompliance at any time during the fiscal year
% of permitted discharges to the lakes or major tributaries that have permit limits
% of private water wells tested in which the homeowner was informed of bacterial contamination
% of private water wells tested in which the homeowner was informed that Nitrate contamination exceeded the maximum contaminant level (MCL)
% of significant industrial users with water pretreatment programs
% of storm water permits that are issued and current for industrial storm water general permits
% of surface water quality in the Collie catchment
% of water bodies identified as not attaining standards where water quality standards are restored

Water Supply

of distribution process documented
# of incidents of interruptions in water provision
# of lab samples processed that support management of water systems
# of liters per capita water use
# of newly installed water points
# of newly installed water points in rural areas
# of newly installed water points in urban areas
# of pipeline maintenance
# of population with sustainable access to improved drinking water sources
# of renewable internal freshwater resources per capita (cubic meters)
# of required water desalination capacity in MGD
# of total abstraction
# of violations of drinking water standards
# of water interruptions

64. Water & Electricity
# of water transportation canals that meets business requirements
# of water transportation main pipes
% compliance of water with regulations
% distribution system water loss
% full functioning of storage facilities
% full functioning of treatment plants
% harnessing development and control
% increase in drinking water sources
% of community water systems that have undergone a sanitary survey within the past three years as required under the rules
% of community water systems that provide drinking water that meet health-based standards
% of population connected to public water supply
% of population with access to safe water (as % of total population)
% of population with access to safe water (as % of total population) in rural areas
% of population with access to safe water (as % of total population) in urban areas
% of population with sustainable access to improved drinking water sources
% of source water areas for community water systems that achieve minimized risk to public health
% of the population served by community water systems that meets all applicable health-based drinking water standards through effective treatment and source water protection
% of the population with sustainable access to an improved water source in urban and rural areas
% of water quality compliance
% of water supply from energy processing facilities
% pollution levels
% supply able to meet demand
% total supply of water with the total demand
% use of water from public water supply by services and private households
% use of water from public water supply by the manufacturing industry
% use of water from self supply by agriculture for irrigation purposes
% use of water from self supply by the manufacturing industry
% use of water from self supply for production and distribution of electricity (including cooling water)
% water transmission system availability
Average duration of interruptions in water provision
Customer satisfaction survey covering water quality, wastewater, drainage and irrigation
Overall % water demand reduction
Peak water demand vs. reserve capacity by water trunk
Score in the annual evaluation of pipeline safety program
Service interruptions per 1,000 service connections

64. Water & Electricity

Supply reliability (outage duration, frequency, and time)

Supply vs. demand (water) (unit:MGPD)

Supply vs. demand: Per capita water abstractions

Supply vs. demand: Per capita water abstractions (Cubic meters)

Total cost of supply

Total drinking water served

Total fresh water abstraction

Total fresh water abstraction per capita

Total non-drinking water served

Total volume of groundwater abstraction

Total volume to surface water abstraction

Total water abstracted by manufacturing industry for cooling

Total water abstracted for agriculture

Total water abstracted for electricity production and distribution for cooling

Total water abstracted for manufacturing industry

Total water abstracted for public water supply

Water consumption in city in liters/day

Water distribution network modeling area coverage index

Water Wells

of drinking water revolving fund projects that have initiated operations

% of community water systems that have undergone a sanitary survey within the past three years

% of community water systems that provide drinking water that meets health standards

% of identified motor vehicle waste disposal wells that are closed

% of salt solution mining wells that maintain mechanical integrity

% of source water areas (both surface and groundwater) for community water systems that achieve minimized risk to public health

% of the population served by community water systems that receive drinking water

% of wells identified in significant violation

% of wells that maintain mechanical integrity

% water level changes in monitoring wells

65. Wildlife

Conservation

of annual student visitations

# of conservation programs developed

# of education hubs up and running

# of members signed up for association

% awareness level of visitors concerning wildlife conservation and education

% of implementation of activities leading to establishment of the association

65. Wildlife

% of required teachers and interpreters trained and hired

% of retail, hospitality and residential developments with wildlife conservation components

Master Plan

% of completion of the master plan phases planning

% of construction of facilities completed that have quality standards

% of facilities having world class management services and standards

Parks Visitors

of accidents which take place within the amenities

% of net profit margin on the sales of the residential units

% of occupancy for hotel facilities

% of residents, visitors and investors with positive perception

Annual # of visitors to the zoo and the wildlife park

Average spend per visit in the zoo and wildlife park

Degree of integration of safety standards into developed amenities

Net cash flow per lettable square meter per annum in the retail facilities

Wildlife Resources

increase of species in ex-situ programs

of acres preserved and protected

# of animal species at zoological parks

# of dollars generated for economy per dollar of funds spent on fisheries management and fishing

# of species of animals at park

% of environmental quality of the swan/canning

Threatened species as % of total species

SECTION C

INTERNATIONAL
1800 Key Performance Indicators

INTERNATIONAL CHAPTERS
(66 to 89)

66. Agriculture & Food

Food & Agriculture Organization - FAOSTAT - (http://faostat.fao.org)

Agricultural production index, 1999-2001=100

Agricultural production per capita index, 1999-2001=100

Area of arable and permanent crops, 1000 hectares

Area, total surface, 1000 hectares

Fish production, metric tons

Food production index, 1999-2001=100

Food production per capita index, 1999-2001=100

Forest area, 1000 hectares

Forested land area as % of land area

Forestry production: roundwood, million cubic meters

Land area, 1000 hectares

Manufacturing production: meat, thousand metric tons

Manufacturing production: paper, paperboard, thousand metric tons

Manufacturing production: sawnwood, thousand cubic meters

Nutrition, dietary energy supply, kcal per person per day

Nutrition, food deficit of undernourished, kcal per capita per day

Nutrition, minimum energy requirement, kcal per capita per day

Nutrition, undernourished as % of total population

Nutrition, undernourished, millions of people

Organization For Economic Co-Operation & Development - (http://stats.oecd.org)

Agricultural production volume

Ammonia and methyl bromide use

Biodiversity - wild species

Biodiversity - ecosystem diversity

Composition of producer support estimate

Consumer support estimate and related indicators by country

EU15: European union of fifteen

Farm management (nutrients, pests, soil, water, biodiversity and organic)

General services support estimate by country

Non-OECD tab I total support estimate - million nat. cur.

Non-OECD tab II MPS and CSE by commodity - million nat. cur.

Nutrients (nitrogen and phosphorus balances)

OECD total support estimate

OECD-FAO agricultural outlook 2008-2017

OECD-FAO agricultural outlook 2009-2018, by commodity

OECD-FAO agricultural outlook 2009-2018, by country

OECD-FAO agricultural outlook 2009-2018, by variable

Pesticides (use and risks)

Producer and consumer support estimates

Producer support estimate and related indicators by country

Soil (water and wind erosion)

Total support estimate by country

66. Agriculture & Food

Water (use and quality)

World Bank - (www.worldbank.org)

Agricultural machinery, tractors per 100 sq. km of arable land

Agriculture, value added (% of GDP)

Arable land (% of land area)

Cereal yield (kg per hectare)

Fertilizer consumption (metric tons)

Food production index (1999-2001 = 100)

Land under cereal production (hectares)

Permanent cropland (% of land area)

World Resources Institute - (http://earthtrends.wri.org)

Agricultural exports

Agricultural imports

Agricultural inputs

Agricultural production

Food and agriculture overview

67. Children

Organization For Economic Co-Operation & Development - (http://stats.oecd.org)

Child well-being

UN Population Division

Child dependency ratio

UN Statistics Division (UNSD) - (http://data.un.org)

% child marriage among women aged 20-24

UNDATA - (http://data.un.org)

Child disability

Child discipline

Child labor

Child marriage

Children orphaned by AIDS

Children orphaned due to all causes

UNICEF - (www.childinfo.org)

Children 1 year old immunized against measles, %

Children under five mortality rate per 1,000 live births

Infant mortality rate

Malaria prevention, use of insecticide-treated bed nets in population <5, %

Malaria treatment, % of population <5 with fever being treated with anti-malarial drugs

World Bank - (www.worldbank.org)

Immunization, measles (% of children ages 12-23 months)

Malnutrition prevalence, weight for age (% of children under 5)

Mortality rate, under-5 (per 1,000)

68. Coastal Ecosystems

World Resources Institute - (http://earthtrends.wri.org)

Aquaculture production by environment: freshwater

Aquaculture production by environment: marine and brackish

Aquaculture production by environment: total

Aquaculture production: aquatic plants

Aquaculture production: crustaceans

Aquaculture production: diadromous fish

Aquaculture production: freshwater fish

Aquaculture production: marine fish

Aquaculture production: molluscs

Capture production by area: inland waters

Capture production by area: marine waters

Capture production by area: total (inland and marine waters)

Capture production: aquatic plants

Capture production: crustaceans

Capture production: diadromous fish

Capture production: freshwater fish

Capture production: marine fish

Capture production: molluscs

Fisheries: decked fishery vessels, number

Fisheries: people employed in fishing and aquaculture, number

Fisheries: population within 100 km of coast

Fishery production totals (aquaculture and capture): inland production

Fishery production totals (aquaculture and capture): major marine
commercial species

Fishery production totals (aquaculture and capture): marine production

Fishery production totals (aquaculture and capture): total for all species

Forest extent: Mangrove forest area

Marine Jurisdictions: claimed exclusive economic zone, area

Marine Jurisdictions: coastline length

Marine Jurisdictions: continental shelf area

Marine Jurisdictions: disputed territorial seas, area

Marine Jurisdictions: exclusive fishing zone, area

Marine Jurisdictions: territorial sea area

Marine Jurisdictions: unclaimed exclusive economic zone, area

Nutrition: annual food supply per capita from fish & fishery products

Nutrition: daily food supply per capita from fish and fishery products

Nutrition: Fish Protein as a % of total protein supply

Nutrition: total food supply from fish & fishery products

Species: fish species, number

Species: fish species, number threatened

Species: mangrove species, number

Species: scleractinia coral genera, number

Species: seagrass species, number

68. Coastal Ecosystems

Trade in fish and fisheries products: exports, quantity

Trade in fish and fisheries products: exports, value

Trade in fish and fisheries products: imports, quantity

Trade in fish and fisheries products: imports, value

69. Culture & Communication

UNESCO Institute for Statistics - (www.uis.unesco.org)

Book production, titles by the Universal Decimal Classification

Cinemas, #

Cinemas, annual attendance, millions

Cinemas, seats - thousands

Newspapers and periodicals, # of titles

Newspapers and periodicals, circulation (thousands)

Newspapers and periodicals, circulation per thousand inhabitants

Radio receivers (thousands)

Radio receivers per thousand inhabitants

Television receivers (thousands)

Television receivers per thousand inhabitants

World Bank - (www.worldbank.org)

Daily newspapers (per 1,000 people)

70. Debt

Economist Intelligence Unit - (http://www.eiu.com)

Bilateral M & LT

BIS banks' liabilities 0-1 year

BIS banks' liabilities 1-2 years

BIS banks' liabilities over 2 years

BIS banks' total liabilities

BIS banks' undisbursed credit commitments

Crossborder liabilities of BIS-reporting banks

Debt-service paid/GDP

Debt-service ratio, due

Debt-service ratio, paid

Effective interest rate (%)

Effective maturity (years)

Export credits

IMF charges

IMF debits

IMF debits & charges

IMF debt

Interest arrears

Interest arrears owed to private creditors

Interest arrears owed to official creditors

70. Debt
Interest due/exports of G&S
Interest on short-term debt
Interest paid/debt service paid
Interest paid/exports of G&S
Interest paid/GDP
International reserves/total debt
M & LT foreign debt service
M & LT foreign debt service by official creditors
M & LT foreign debt service by private creditors
M & LT interest payments to official creditors
M & LT interest payments to private creditors
M & LT owed to official creditors
M & LT owed to private creditors
M & LT principal repayments
M & LT principal repayments to official creditors
M & LT principal repayments to private creditors
Medium & long-term debt
Multilateral M & LT
Net debt
Net debt/exports of G&S
Net debt/GDP
Principal arrears
Principal arrears owed to official creditors
Principal arrears owed to private creditors
Private medium & long term
Public debt
Public debt (% of GDP)
Public medium & long term
Short term
Short-term debt (interest only)
Total debt per head
Total debt/exports of G&S
Total debt/GDP
Total foreign debt
Total foreign debt service, due
Total foreign debt service, paid
Total interest payments, due
Total interest payments, paid
Total M & LT debt4344
Total principal repayments, due
Total principal repayments, paid
Organization For Economic Co-Operation & Development - (http://stats.oecd.org)
Central Government debt

70. Debt

Principal Global Indicators - (www.principalglobalindicators.org)

External debt

Short-term external debt

UNDATA - (http://data.un.org)

Debt service as a % of exports of goods and services

World Bank - (www.worldbank.org)

Debt service as % of exports of goods, services and net income from abroad

Debt service on external debt, long-term (TDS, current US$)

Debt service on external debt, total (TDS, current US$)

Debt service, external long-term interest, US$

Debt service, external long-term principal, US$

Debt service, total external long-term, US$

Debt stocks, total external, US$

Debt stocks, total long-term external, US$

External debt stocks (% of exports of goods, services and income)

External debt stocks (% of GNI)

External debt stocks, long-term (DOD, current US$)

External debt stocks, total (DOD, current US$)

Present value of external debt (current US$)

Short-term debt (% of total external debt)

Total debt service (% of exports of goods, services and income)

Total debt service (% of GNI)

World Economic Outlook - (www.imf.org)

External debt, total

External debt, total debt service

External debt, total debt service, amortization

External debt, total debt service, interest

71. Development & Aid

OECD Development Assistance Database - (www.oecd.org/DAC)

Debt forgiveness, net, as % of official development assistance

Debt relief, net, official development assistance, US$

Landlocked developing countries, ODA received, as % of their GNI

Landlocked developing countries, ODA received, US$

ODA bilateral, % untied

ODA bilateral, untied, US$

ODA provided, bilateral, US$

ODA received, bilateral/multilateral, million US$

ODA received, per capita, US$

ODA to basic social services as % of sector-allocable ODA

ODA to basic social services, US$

ODA to LDCs, net, as % of OECD/DAC donors' GNI

ODA to LDCs, net, US$

ODA, % provided to help build trade capacity

71. Development & Aid
ODA, net, as % of OECD/DAC donors' GNI
ODA, net, US$ million
Small islands ODA received, as % of their GNI
Small islands ODA received, US$

Organization For Economic Co-Operation & Development - (http://stats.oecd.org)

Aggregate aid statistics
Aid Activities
Creditor Reporting System
DAC1 official and private flows
DAC2a ODA disbursements
DAC2b Other official flows
DAC3a ODA commitments
DAC4 private flows
DAC5 official bilateral commitments by sector
DAC7b tying status of bilateral ODA
DACref_reference indicators
DACref_reference total net ODA
DACref_reference total ODF
DACref_reference total official flows
DACref_reference total receipts
HIV_AIDS control by individual CRS aid activity
ODA by Donor
ODA by recipient by country
ODA by recipient by income
ODA by recipient by Region
ODA by sector

UN Development Policy & Analysis Division (DESA)

GDP growth rate, US$
GDP per capita, annual growth rate, 2000 US$

UN HABITAT Millennium Development

Slum population as % of urban (% of households with access to secure tenure)
Slum population in urban areas

UN Operational Activities for Development Database

Development grant expenditure through the UN system by agency, thousand US$

World Bank - (www.worldbank.org)

Aid (% of GNI)
Aid (% of gross capital formation)
Aid (% of imports of goods and services)
Aid per capita (current US$)
Official development assistance and official aid (current US$)

72. Economy

Economist Intelligence Unit - (http://www.eiu.com)

Agriculture (% real change pa)

Agriculture/GDP

Average nominal wage index (LCU, 1996=100)

Average nominal wages (% change pa)

Average real wage index (LCU, 1996=100)

Average real wages (% change pa)

Budget balance

Budget balance (% of GDP)

Budget expenditure

Budget expenditure (% of GDP)

Budget revenue

Budget revenue (% of GDP)

Capital flight

Consumer price index (1996=100; av)

Consumer price index (av)

Consumer price index (end-period)

Consumer prices (% change pa; av)

Consumer prices (% change pa; end-period)

Current-account balance/GDP

Current-transfers balance/GDP

Debt interest payments

Debt interest payments (% of GDP)

Deposit interest rate (%)

Domestic credit growth (%)

Domestic demand (% of GDP)

Domestic demand (% real change pa)

Exchange rate LCU:US$ (av)

Exchange rate LCU:US$ (end-period)

Export deflator (% change; av)

Export deflator (1996=100; av)

Exports of G&S (% of GDP)

Exports of G&S (% real change pa)

External balance, contribution to real GDP growth (% points)

Fixed investment deflator (% change; av)

Fixed investment deflator (1996=100; av)

GDP (% real change pa)

GDP deflator (% change; av)

GDP deflator (1996=100; av)

GDP per head

GDP per head ($ at PPP)

Government consumption (% of GDP)

Government consumption (% real change pa)

Government consumption deflator (% change; av)

72. Economy

Government consumption deflator (1996=100; av)

Government consumption, contribution to real GDP growth (% points)

Gross fixed investment (% of GDP)

Gross fixed investment (% real change pa)

Gross fixed investment, contribution to real GDP growth (% points)

Gross national savings rate (%)

Gross national savings/investment

Growth of real capital stock (%)

Growth of real potential output (%)

Import deflator (% change; av)

Import deflator (1996=100; av)

Imports of G&S (% of GDP)

Imports of G&S (% real change pa)

Income balance/GDP

Industrial production (% change pa)

Industrial production (1996=100; av)

Industry (% real change pa)

Industry/GDP

Inward foreign direct investment/GDP

Inward foreign direct investment/gross fixed investment

Labour productivity growth (%)

Lending interest rate (%)

Manufacturing (% real change pa)

Money market interest rate (%)

Nominal domestic demand

Nominal domestic demand (US$)

Nominal exports of G&S

Nominal exports of G&S (US$)

Nominal GDP

Nominal GDP (US$ at PPP)

Nominal GDP (US$)

Nominal government consumption

Nominal government consumption (US$)

Nominal gross fixed investment

Nominal gross fixed investment (US$)

Nominal imports of G&S

Nominal imports of G&S (US$)

Nominal private consumption

Nominal private consumption (US$)

Nominal stockbuilding

Nominal stockbuilding (US$)

Personal disposable income

Personal disposable income (US$)

Petroleum production (b/d)

72. Economy

Petroleum reserves (barrels)

Primary balance

Primary balance (% of GDP)

Principal repayments due

Private consumption (% of GDP)

Private consumption (% real change pa)

Private consumption deflator (% change; av)

Private consumption deflator (1996=100; av)

Private consumption per head

Private consumption, contribution to real GDP growth (% points)

Real agriculture

Real domestic demand

Real domestic demand (US$ at 1996 prices)

Real effective exchange rate (CPI-based)

Real effective exchange rate (PPI-based)

Real effective exchange rate (ULC-based)

Real exports of G&S

Real exports of G&S (US$ at 1996 prices)

Real GDP

Real GDP (PPP US$ at 1996 prices)

Real GDP (US$ at 1996 prices)

Real GDP at factor cost

Real GDP growth per head (% pa)

Real government consumption

Real government consumption (US$ at 1996 prices)

Real gross fixed investment

Real gross fixed investment (US$ at 1996 prices)

Real imports of G&S

Real imports of G&S (US$ at 1996 prices)

Real industry

Real manufacturing

Real personal disposable income (% change pa)

Real personal disposable income (US$ at 1996 prices)

Real private consumption

Real private consumption (US$ at 1996 prices)

Real services

Real stockbuilding

Rebasing residual (US$ at 1996 prices)

Services (% real change pa)

Services balance/GDP

Services/GDP

Stock of domestic credit

Stock of inward foreign direct investment per head

Stock of inward foreign direct investment/GDP

72. Economy

Stock of money M1

Stock of money M2

Stock of outward foreign direct investment/GDP

Stock of quasi money

Stockbuilding (% of GDP)

Stockbuilding, contribution to real GDP growth (% points)

Total factor productivity growth (%)

Unit labour cost index (US$, 1996=100)

Unit labour costs (% change pa)

IMF International Financial Statistics

BOP: capital account credit, US$

BOP: capital account debit, US$

BOP: current account net, US$

BOP: current transfers credit, US$

BOP: current transfers debit, US$

BOP: exports of goods, f.o.b., US$

BOP: financial account, US$

BOP: imports of goods, f.o.b., US$

BOP: income credit, US$

BOP: income debit, US$

BOP: net errors and omissions, US$

BOP: services credit, US$

BOP: services debit, US$

Consumer prices index, 2000 = 100

Discount rate of central bank, % per annum, end of period

Earnings or wages index, period averages, 2000 = 100

Exchange rate, national currency per US$, end of period

Exchange rate, national currency per US$, period average

Exchange rate, SDR per US$, period average

Exchange rate, US$ per national currency, end of period

Exchange rate, US$ per national currency, period average

Exchange rate, US$ per SDR, period average

Foreign assets, national currency, end of period

Foreign liabilities in national currency, end of period

Government consumption expenditure, national currency

Government finance deficit or surplus, national currency

IMF credits, use of, US$

IMF quota, SDRs, end of period

Income, primary, net payments abroad, national currency, current prices

Industrial share price index, period averages, 2000 = 100

Interest rate, 6-month US deposit London offer

Interest rate, banks prime lending, % per annum, period average

Interest rate, government long-term bond yields, % per annum, period average

72. Economy
Interest rate, money market, period average
Interest rate, SDRs
Interest rate, treasury bills, period average
Investment abroad, direct, US$
Investment, direct, from abroad to reporting economy, n.i.e., US$
Money supply, in national currency
Producer price index, period averages
Reserves, foreign exchange, $US, end of period

Organization For Economic Co-Operation & Development - (http://stats.oecd.org)

2005 PPP benchmark results
Annual national accounts
Annual projections for OECD Countries
Annual trade and payments Projections
Business tendency and consumer opinion indicators
Business tendency and consumer opinion surveys (MEI)
Composite leading indicators
Composite leading indicators (MEI)
Confidence indicators - OECD Standardized
Consumer price Index
Consumer price indices (MEI)
Consumer prices - All Items
Country statistical profiles 2009
Current account % of GDP
Disposable income and net lending - net borrowing
Economic outlook No 86 - November 2009 - Flash file
Financial accounts
Financial accounts - consolidated
Financial accounts - non consolidated
Financial balance sheets - consolidated
Financial balance sheets - non consolidated
GDP per head, US $, constant prices, constant PPPs, reference year 2000
GDP per head, US $, current prices, current PPPs
GDP, total and expenditure Components
GDP, US $, constant prices, constant PPPs, reference year 2000, millions
GDP, US $, current prices, current PPPs, millions
GDP: expenditure approach
GDP: expenditure approach in constant prices (MEI)
GDP: expenditure approach in current prices (MEI)
GDP: expenditure approach, indices
GDP: expenditure approach, national currency
GDP: production approach
GDP: production approach in constant prices (MEI)
GDP: production approach in current prices (MEI)
GDP: production approach, indices

72. Economy

GDP: production approach, national currency

General Government accounts

Government expenditure by function

Gross domestic product

Harmonized unemployment rate

Hourly earnings in Manufacturing

Index of industrial production

Industrial production

International trade in goods

Main aggregates

Main aggregates of general government

Main economic indicators

MEI original release data and revisions

Monetary aggregates - broad money

Monthly economic indicators

National accounts

Net national income per head, US $, constant prices, constant PPPs

Net national income per head, US $, current prices, current PPPs

OECD member countries - GDP expenditure approach

Population and employment by main activity

PPPs and exchange rates

Price indices (MEI)

Prices and price indices

Prices and purchasing power parities

Private consumption (volume)

Producer and other price indices (MEI)

Production in construction

Purchasing power parities (PPP) statistics

Quarterly growth rates of GDP, volume

Quarterly national accounts

Retail trade volume

Volume and price indices- GDP expenditure approach

Year Government Bonds

Zones - GDP expenditure approach

Principal Global Indicators - (www.principalglobalindicators.org)

Base money

Broad money

Business confidence

Central bank assets

Concepts by Country

Consumer confidence

Consumer prices

Current account

Domestic credit (consolidated balance sheet of the banking sector)

72. Economy
Effective exchange rates: nominal
Effective exchange rates: real
Exchange rates
GDP deflator
Government consumption expenditure
Gross domestic product (GDP)
Gross domestic product (GDP) volume
Gross fixed capital formation
Gross official reserves
Household consumption expenditure, including NPISHs
IIP assets
IIP liabilities
International investment position (IIP) - net
Long-term interest rate
Other depository corporations assets
Producer prices
Retail turnover
Share prices
Short-term interest rate

UNDATA - (http://data.un.org)
% of income received by the 20 % of households with highest income
% of income received by the 40 % of households with lowest income
% of population below $1
Average annual rate of inflation
Central government expenditure allocated to defense
GDP per capita average annual growth rate
GNI per capita
Institutional deliveries
ODA inflow
ODA inflow as % of recipient GNI

World Bank - (www.worldbank.org)
Capital formation, gross fixed, national currency, constant prices
Capital formation, gross fixed, national currency, current prices
Capital formation, gross, national currency, constant prices
Capital formation, gross, national currency, current prices
Consumption expenditure, final, national currency, constant prices
Consumption expenditure, final, national currency, current prices
GDP (current US$)
GDP annual rate of growth
GDP at market prices, constant 2000 US$
GDP at market prices, current US$
GDP at market prices, national currency, constant prices
GDP at market prices, national currency, current prices
GDP deflator, national currency

72. Economy
GDP growth (annual %)
GDP in current international dollars
GDP per capita, current international dollars
GDP per capita, PPP (current international $)
GDP, PPP (current international $)
GNI per capita, atlas method (current US$)
GNI per capita, PPP (current international $)
GNI, Atlas method (current US$)
GNI, PPP (current international $)
Government consumption, national currency, constant prices
Government consumption, national currency, current prices
Gross capital formation (current US$)
Inflation, GDP deflator (annual %)
International official net transfers, US$
Investment, foreign direct long-term net in US$
Investment, international portfolio equity, in US$
Purchasing power parities (PPP) for consumption
Purchasing power parities (PPPs), national currency per international dollar
Stocks increase, national currency, constant prices
Stocks increase, national currency, current prices
Value added, national currency, constant prices, by industry groups
Value added, national currency, current prices, by industry groups

World Economic Outlook - (www.imf.org)
Change in reserves
Direct investment, net
Gross domestic product based on purchasing-power-parity (PPP) per capita GDP
Gross domestic product based on purchasing-power-parity (PPP) share of world total
Gross domestic product based on purchasing-power-parity (PPP) valuation of country GDP
Gross domestic product, constant prices
Gross domestic product, current prices
Gross domestic product, deflator
Gross national savings
Inflation, average consumer prices
Inflation, end of period consumer prices
Investment
Official flows, net
Other private financial flows, net
Output gap
Private financial flows, net
Private portfolio flows, net
Three-month London interbank offered rate (LIBOR)

73. Education

Organization For Economic Co-Operation & Development - (http://stats.oecd.org)

Educational personnel
Expenditure by funding source and transaction type
Expenditure by nature and resource category
Foreign / international students enrolled
Graduates by age
Graduates by field of education
New entrants by sex and age
Students aligned to finance and personnel data
Students enrolled by age
Students enrolled by type of institution
Total population by sex and age

UN Statistics Division (UNSD) - (http://data.un.org)

Adult literacy rate
Enrolment in primary education
Enrolment in secondary education
Enrolment in tertiary education
Expected gross intake ratio to last grade of primary
Expected gross primary graduation ratio
Gender parity index for adult literacy rate
Gender parity index for expected gross intake ratio to last grade of primary
Gender parity index for expected gross primary graduation ratio
Gender parity index for gross intake ratio to last grade of primary
Gender parity index for gross primary graduation ratio
Gender parity index for literacy rate of 15-24 year-olds
Gender parity index for primary gross enrolment
Gender parity index for primary net enrolment
Gender parity index for school life expectancy
Gender parity index for secondary gross enrolment
Gender parity index for secondary net enrolment
Gender parity index for tertiary gross enrolment
Gender parity index for transition rate from primary to secondary level
Girls' share of primary enrolment
Girls' share of secondary enrolment
Gross enrolment ratio in primary education
Gross enrolment ratio in secondary education
Gross enrolment ratio in tertiary education
Gross intake ratio to last grade of primary
Gross primary graduation ratio
Literacy rate of 15-24 year-olds
Net enrolment ratio in primary education
Net enrolment ratio in secondary education
School life expectancy, primary to tertiary

73. Education
Transition rate from primary to secondary level
Women's share of teachers in pre-primary education
Women's share of teachers in primary education
Women's share of teachers in secondary education
Women's share of teachers in tertiary education
Women's share of tertiary enrolment
Women's share of tertiary enrolment in agriculture
Women's share of tertiary enrolment in education
Women's share of tertiary enrolment in engineering, manufacturing and construction
Women's share of tertiary enrolment in health and welfare
Women's share of tertiary enrolment in humanities and arts
Women's share of tertiary enrolment in science
Women's share of tertiary enrolment in services
Women's share of tertiary enrolment in social sciences, business and law

UNDATA - (http://data.un.org)

% of pupils starting grade 1 who reach grade 5
Attitudes towards domestic violence
Central government expenditure allocated to education
Net attendance ratio in primary education
Net attendance ratio in secondary education
Net attendance ratio of girls to boys in primary education
Net attendance ratio of girls to boys in secondary education
Net enrolment ratio of girls to boys in primary education
Net enrolment ratio of girls to boys in secondary education
Net enrolment/attendance rate in primary education
Ratio of adult literacy rate of females to males
Ratio of school attendance of orphans to school attendance of non-orphans

UNESCO Institute for Statistics - (www.uis.unesco.org)

Education enrolment at third level by sex and field of study
Education enrolment by level
Education enrolment by level, % girls
Education enrolment ratio, net, primary level, by sex
Education expenditure of government, total, as % of GNI
Education expenditure of government, total, as % of total government
Education, % of pupils starting grade 1 reaching grade 5, by sex
Education, primary completion rate, by sex
Girls to boys ratio, primary level enrolment
Girls to boys ratio, secondary level enrolment
Girls to boys ratio, tertiary level enrolment
Illiteracy rates by sex, aged 15+, %
Illiterate population by sex, aged 15+ (thousands)
Literacy rates, aged 15-24, by sex, %
Women to men parity index, as ratio of literacy rates, aged 15-24

73. Education

World Bank - (www.worldbank.org)

Drop-out rate (%), primary
GPI, gross enrollment ratio in primary
Gross enrollment rate (%), pre-primary, total
Gross enrollment rate (%), tertiary, total
Gross intake rate to grade 1, total
Literacy rate, adult female (% of females ages 15 and above)
Literacy rate, adult male (% of males ages 15 and above)
Net enrollment rate (%), primary level, total
Net enrollment rate (%), secondary, total
Out-of-school children, primary, total
Percentage of repeaters (%), primary
Percentage of repeaters (%), secondary
Primary completion rate, total
Primary completion rate, total (% of relevant age group)
Primary education, teachers (% trained)
Public education expenditure as % of GDP
Pupil-teacher ratio, primary
Pupil-teacher ratio, secondary
Ratio of girls to boys in primary and secondary education (%)
School enrollment, primary (% gross)
School enrollment, primary, female (% net)
School enrollment, primary, male (% net)
Secondary education, teachers (% trained)

World Health Organization (WHO)

Net primary school enrolment ratio female (%)
Net primary school enrolment ratio male (%)

World Resources Institute - (http://earthtrends.wri.org)

Education and literacy
Gender and development
Population and education Overview

74. Energy

International Energy Agency - (www.iea.org)

CO_2 emissions from fuel combustion
CO_2 emissions from fuel combustion (detailed estimates)
Emissions of CO_2, CH_4, N_2O, HFC, PFC and SF_6
Emissions per kWh of electricity and heat output
Energy balances
Extended energy balances
Liquified natural gas exports
Liquified natural gas imports
Natural gas balance
Natural gas balance historical

74. Energy
Natural gas exports
Natural gas exports historical
Natural gas imports
Natural gas imports historical
OECD, electricity and heat generation
OECD, electricity and heat generation - renewables
OECD, electricity exports by destination
OECD, electricity imports by origin
OECD, exports by destination - coal
OECD, imports by origin - coal
OECD, monthly net electricity supply
OECD, net capacity - renewables
OECD, net electrical capacity
OECD, net electricity and heat production by autoproducers
Oil conversion factors (bbl/t)
Oil crude supply (1000 tonnes)
Oil exports (1000 tonnes)
Oil imports (1000 tonnes)
Oil product supply and consumption (1000 tonnes)
Per capita CO2 emissions by sector
RD&D budgets
World, coal supply and consumption
World, electricity/heat supply and consumption
World, renewables balance (Ktoe)
World, renewables supply and consumption

Organization For Economic Co-Operation & Development - (http://stats.oecd.org)

Energy (direct on-farm consumption)

Principal Global Indicators - (www.principalglobalindicators.org)

Oil price

World Bank - (www.worldbank.org)

Energy supply (apparent consumption; Kg oil equivalent) per $1,000

World Economic Outlook - (www.imf.org)

Commodity price Index includes both Fuel and Non-Fuel price Indices

World Resources Institute - (http://earthtrends.wri.org)

Energy consumption by sector

Energy consumption by source

Energy overview

Energy production by source

Fossil fuel reserves, production, and trade

Resource consumption

75. Environment

Organization For Economic Co-Operation & Development - (http://stats.oecd.org)

Estimates of renewable freshwater resources

Freshwater abstractions by major use

Freshwater abstractions by source

Intensity of use of freshwater resources

OECD environmental data - inland waters

OECD environmental data - inland waters by lakes - 2006

Population connected to public waste water treatment plants

Population connected to sewerage

Sewage sludge production and disposal

Water

UN Framework Convention on Climate Change (UNFCCC)

Carbon dioxide (CO2) emissions without land use, land-use change and forestry (LULUCF), in gigagrams (Gg)

Greenhouse gas (GHGs) emissions without land use, land-use change and forestry (LULUCF), in gigagrams (Gg) CO2 equivalent

Hydrofluorocarbons (HFCs) Emissions, in Gigagrams (Gg) CO2 equivalent

Methane (CH4) emissions without land Use, land-use change and forestry (LULUCF), in gigagrams (Gg) CO2 equivalent

Nitrous oxide (N2O) Emissions without land use, land-use change and forestry (LULUCF), in gigagrams (Gg) CO2 equivalent

Perfluorocarbons (PFCs) Emissions, in Gigagrams (Gg) CO2 equivalent

Sulphur hexafluoride (SF6) Emissions, in Gigagrams (Gg) CO2 equivalent

World Bank - (www.worldbank.org)

CO2 emissions (kt)

CO2 emissions (metric tons per capita)

Improved water source, rural (% of rural population with access)

Improved water source, urban (% of urban population with access)

Land area (sq. km)

World Resources Institute - (http://earthtrends.wri.org)

Access to information and technology

Biodiversity Overview

Carbon Dioxide emissions by economic sector

Carbon Dioxide emissions by source

Climate and atmosphere overview

Emissions of common anthropogenic pollutants

Financial Flows

Food and Water

Forestry production and trade

Forests, grasslands, and drylands

Freshwater resources

Global climate trends

Groundwater and Desalinization

Institutions and Governance

75. Environment
Institutions and Governance Overview
Land area classification by ecosystem type
Land use and human settlements
Legal trade in selected wildlife products and CITES status
Multilateral environmental agreements
PAGE ecosystems: area, population, carbon stocks, and protected areas
Protected areas
Species diversity and conservation status
Water resources and fisheries
Watersheds of the World

76. Finance

Organization For Economic Co-Operation & Development - (http://stats.oecd.org)

Bank profitability statistics
Density
Exchange rates (USD monthly averages)
Financial indicators (MEI)
Households' financial and non-financial assets and liabilities
Income Statement and Balance Sheet (New)
Institutional investors' assets
Insurance statistics
Interest rates
Life insurance share
Market share in OECD
Market share of branches/agencies of foreign undertakings in the domestic market
Market share of foreign companies in the domestic market
Monetary aggregates
Penetration
Premiums per employee
Ratio of reinsurance accepted
Relative consumer price indices
Relative unit labor cost (manufacturing) indices
Reserve assets
Retention ratio
Share prices
Total gross premiums

World Bank - (www.worldbank.org)

Interest rate spread (lending rate minus deposit rate, %)
Market capitalization of listed companies (% of GDP)
Market capitalization of listed companies (current US$)

77. Globalization

Organization For Economic Co-Operation & Development - (http://stats.oecd.org)

Activity of multinationals

FDI flows by industry

FDI flows by partner country

FDI positions by industry

FDI positions by partner country

FDI series of BOP and IIP aggregates

Foreign direct investment statistics

Inward activity - Share in national total (manufacturing)

Inward activity Rev 3 by industrial sector (manufacturing)

Inward activity Rev 3 by investing country, total manufacturing

Outward activity - Share in national total (manufacturing)

Outward activity Rev 3 by country of location, total manufacturing

Outward activity Rev 3 by industrial sector (manufacturing)

World Bank - (www.worldbank.org)

Commercial banks and other lending (PPG + PNG) (NFL, current US$)

Foreign direct investment, net inflows (BoP, current US$)

Merchandise trade (% of GDP)

Net financial flows, IBRD (NFL, current US$)

Private capital flows, total (BoP, current US$)

78. Health

Organization For Economic Co-Operation & Development - (http://stats.oecd.org)

Chronic conditions (non-communicable diseases)

Function x financing

Function x provider

Funding x financing

Health care activities

Health care resources

Health expenditure

Health expenditure by financing agent

Health expenditure by provider

Health status (Mortality)

OECD health data 2009 - selected data

Provider x financing

Risk factors

System of health accounts

Total health expenditure by function

UN Statistics Division (UNSD) - (http://data.un.org)

Life expectancy at age x

Life expectancy at birth

Maternal mortality ratio

Prevalence of obesity among adults

Prevalence of underweight children

78. Health

UNDATA - (http://data.un.org)

% of 1 year-old children fully immunized against DPT

% of 1 year-old children fully immunized against Haemophilus influenza type B

% of 1 year-old children fully immunized against Hepatitis B

% of 1 year-old children fully immunized against polio

% of 1 year-old children immunized against DPT1

% of 1 year-old children immunized against measles

% of 1 year-old children immunized against TB

% of births attended by skilled health personnel

% of households consuming iodized salt

% of infants with low birth weight

% of new borns protected against tetanus

% of population in malaria risk areas using effective malaria prevention measures

% of population in malaria risk areas using effective malaria treatment measures

% of population with access to improved sanitation

% of population with sustainable access to an improved water source

% of under-five children sleeping under a mosquito net

% of under-five children with diarrhoea receiving oral rehydration and continued feeding

% of under-five children with suspected pneumonia receiving antibiotics

% of under-five children with suspected pneumonia taken to health provider

Annual # of under-five deaths

Antenatal care coverage

Average annual rate of reduction of under-five mortality rate

Central government expenditure allocated to health

Continued breastfeeding rate

Contraceptive prevalence rate

Crude birth rate

Crude death rate

Exclusive breastfeeding rate

female genital mutilation/cutting

female genital mutilation/cutting of daughters

Lifetime risk of maternal death

Maternal mortality ratio reported

Neonatal mortality rate

Prevalence of stunting

Prevalence of underweight

Prevalence of wasting

Ratio of life expectancy at birth of females to males

Reduction in under-five mortality rate

Routine EPI vaccines financed by government

78. Health
Timely complementary feeding rate
Vitamin A supplementation coverage

World Bank - (www.worldbank.org)

Health expenditure per capita (current US$)
Health expenditure, total (% of GDP)
Hospital beds (per 1,000 people)
Life expectancy at birth, female (years)
Life expectancy at birth, male (years)
Physicians (per 1,000 people)

World Health Organization (WHO) - Disease Mortality

# of confirmed poliomyelitis cases
Adult mortality rate (probability of dying between 15 to 60 years per 1000 population) both sexes
Adult mortality rate (probability of dying between 15 to 60 years per 1000 population) female
Adult mortality rate (probability of dying between 15 to 60 years per 1000 population) male
Age-standardized mortality rate for cancer (per 100,000 population)
Age-standardized mortality rate for cardiovascular diseases (per 100,000 population)
Age-standardized mortality rate for injuries (per 100,000 population)
Age-standardized mortality rate for non-communicable diseases (per 100,000 population)
Deaths among children under five years of age due to diarrhoeal diseases (%)
Deaths among children under five years of age due to injuries (%)
Deaths among children under five years of age due to malaria (%)
Deaths among children under five years of age due to measles (%)
Deaths among children under five years of age due to neonatal causes (%)
Deaths among children under five years of age due to other causes (%)
Deaths among children under five years of age due to pneumonia (%)
Deaths due to HIV/AIDS (per 100 000 population per year)
Deaths due to tuberculosis among HIV-negative people (per 100 000 population)
Deaths due to tuberculosis among HIV-positive people (per 100 000 population)
Healthy life expectancy (HALE) at birth
Incidence of tuberculosis (per 100 000 population per year)
Infant mortality rate (per 1000 live births) both sexes
Infant mortality rate (per 1000 live births) female
Infant mortality rate (per 1000 live births) male
Life expectancy at birth (years) both sexes
Life expectancy at birth (years) female
Life expectancy at birth (years) male
Maternal mortality ratio (per 100,000 live births)

78. Health

Neonatal mortality rate (per 1000 live births)

Prevalence of tuberculosis (per 100,000 population)

Under-5 mortality rate (probability of dying by age 5 per 1000 live births) both sexes

Under-5 mortality rate (probability of dying by age 5 per 1000 live births) female

Under-5 mortality rate (probability of dying by age 5 per 1000 live births) male

Years of life lost to communicable diseases (%)

Years of life lost to injuries (%)

Years of life lost to non-communicable diseases (%)

World Health Organization (WHO) - Healthcare Inequities

Births attended by skilled health personnel (%) highest educational level of mother

Births attended by skilled health personnel (%) highest wealth quintile

Births attended by skilled health personnel (%) lowest educational level of mother

Births attended by skilled health personnel (%) lowest wealth quintile

Births attended by skilled health personnel (%) rural

Births attended by skilled health personnel (%) urban

Births attended by skilled health personnel difference highest lowest educational level of mother

Births attended by skilled health personnel difference highest-lowest wealth quintile

Births attended by skilled health personnel difference urban-rural

Births attended by skilled health personnel ratio highest-lowest educational level of mother

Births attended by skilled health personnel ratio highest-lowest wealth quintile

Births attended by skilled health personnel ratio urban-rural

Measles immunization coverage among one-year-olds (%) highest educational level of mother

Measles immunization coverage among one-year-olds (%) highest wealth quintile

Measles immunization coverage among one-year-olds (%) lowest educational level of mother

Measles immunization coverage among one-year-olds (%) lowest wealth quintile

Measles immunization coverage among one-year-olds (%) rural

Measles immunization coverage among one-year-olds (%) urban

Measles immunization coverage among one-year-olds difference highest-lowest educational level of mother

Measles immunization coverage among one-year-olds difference highest-lowest wealth quintile

78. Health

Measles immunization coverage among one-year-olds difference urban-rural

Measles immunization coverage among one-year-olds ratio highest-lowest educational level of mother

Measles immunization coverage among one-year-olds ratio highest-lowest wealth quintile

Measles immunization coverage among one-year-olds ratio urban-rural

Under-5 mortality rate (probability of dying aged < 5 years per 1000 live births) difference lowest-highest educational level of mother

Under-5 mortality rate (probability of dying aged < 5 years per 1000 live births) difference lowest-highest wealth quintile

Under-5 mortality rate (probability of dying aged < 5 years per 1000 live births) difference rural-urban

Under-5 mortality rate (probability of dying aged < 5 years per 1000 live births) highest educational level of mother

Under-5 mortality rate (probability of dying aged < 5 years per 1000 live births) highest wealth quintile

Under-5 mortality rate (probability of dying aged < 5 years per 1000 live births) lowest educational level of mother

Under-5 mortality rate (probability of dying aged < 5 years per 1000 live births) lowest wealth quintile

Under-5 mortality rate (probability of dying aged < 5 years per 1000 live births) ratio lowest-highest educational level of mother

Under-5 mortality rate (probability of dying aged < 5 years per 1000 live births) ratio lowest-highest wealth quintile

Under-5 mortality rate (probability of dying aged < 5 years per 1000 live births) ratio rural-urban

Under-5 mortality rate (probability of dying aged < 5 years per 1000 live births) rural

Under-5 mortality rate (probability of dying aged < 5 years per 1000 live births) urban

World Health Organization (WHO) - Risk Factors

Children under five years of age overweight for age (%)

Children under five years of age stunted for age (%)

Children under five years of age underweight for age (%)

Newborns with low birth weight (%)

Per capita recorded alcohol consumption (liters of pure alcohol) among adults

Population using solid fuels (%) rural

Population using solid fuels (%) urban

Population with sustainable access to improved drinking water sources (%) rural

Population with sustainable access to improved drinking water sources (%) total

78. Health
Population with sustainable access to improved drinking water sources (%) urban
Population with sustainable access to improved sanitation (%) rural
Population with sustainable access to improved sanitation (%) total
Population with sustainable access to improved sanitation (%) urban
Prevalence of adults (>=15 years) who are obese
Prevalence of condom use by young people (15-24 years) at higher risk sex
Prevalence of current tobacco use among adolescents (13-15 years)
Prevalence of current tobacco use among adults (>=15 years)

World Health Organization (WHO) - Service Coverage

Antenatal care coverage - at least four visits (%)
Antiretroviral therapy coverage among HIV-infected pregnant women for PMTCT (%)
Antiretroviral therapy coverage among people with advanced HIV infections (%)
Births attended by skilled health personnel (%)
Births by caesarean section (%)
Children aged <5 years sleeping under insecticide-treated nets (%)
Children aged <5 years who received any antimalarial treatment for fever (%)
Children aged <5 years with ARI symptoms taken to facility (%)
Children aged <5 years with diarrhoea receiving ORT (%)
Children aged 6-59 months who received vitamin A supplementation (%)
Contraceptive prevalence (%)
Neonates protected at birth against neonatal tetanus (PAB)
One-year-olds immunized with MCV
One-year-olds immunized with three doses of diphtheria tetanus toxoid and pertussis (DTP3)
One-year-olds immunized with three doses of Hepatitis B (HepB3)
One-year-olds immunized with three doses of Hib (Hib3) vaccine
Tuberculosis detection rate under DOTS (%)
Tuberculosis treatment success under DOTS (%)
Women who have had mammography (%)
Women who have had PAP smear (%)

World Health Organization (WHO) - Systems Resources

# of community and traditional health workers
# of dentistry personnel
# of environment and public health workers
# of laboratory health workers
# of nursing and midwifery personnel
# of other health service providers
# of pharmaceutical personnel
# of physicians
Community and traditional health workers density (per 10 000 population) (per 10 000 population)

78. Health
Dentistry personnel density (per 10 000 population)
Environment and public health workers density (per 10 000 population)
External resources for health as % of total expenditure on health
General government expenditure on health as % of total expenditure on health
General government expenditure on health as % of total government expenditure
Hospital beds (per 10 000 population)
Laboratory health workers density (per 10000 population)
Nursing and midwifery personnel density (per 10 000 population)
Other health service providers density (per 10 000 population)
Out-of-pocket expenditure as % of private expenditure on health
Per capita government expenditure on health (PPP int. $)
Per capita government expenditure on health at average exchange rate (US$)
Per capita total expenditure on health (PPP int. $)
Per capita total expenditure on health at average exchange rate (US$)
Pharmaceutical personnel density (per 10000 population)
Physicians density (per 10000 population)
Private expenditure on health as % of total expenditure on health
Private prepaid plans as % of private expenditure on health
Ratio of health management and support workers to health service providers
Ratio of nurses and midwives to physicians
Social security expenditure on health as % of general government expenditure on health
Total expenditure on health as % of gross domestic product

World Resources Institute - (http://earthtrends.wri.org)

Human health
Trends in mortality and life expectancy

79. HIV/AIDS Epidemic

UN Statistics Division (UNSD) - (http://data.un.org)

HIV/AIDS rate among population 15-24 yr
Population 15-24 year-olds who have comprehensive correct knowledge of HIV/AIDS
Population with HIV/AIDS

UNAIDS - (www.unaids.org)

Adults and children with HIV known to be on treatment 12 months after initiation of antiretroviral therapy
AIDS estimated deaths, aged 0-49
AIDS orphans (one or both parents)
AIDS/HIV adult infections prevalence, %

79. HIV/AIDS Epidemic

AIDS/HIV infected persons, adults by sex, 0-14

Condom use, 15-24 year-olds, at last high-risk sex, by sex, %

Donated blood units screened for HIV in a quality-assured manner

Estimated HIV-positive incident TB cases that received treatment for TB and HIV

female and male sex workers reporting the use of a condom with their most recent client

HIV knowledge, 15-24 year-olds who have comprehensive correct knowledge of HIV/AIDS, by sex, %

HIV knowledge, 15-24 year-olds who know healthy-looking person can have HIV, by sex, %

HIV knowledge, 15-24 year-olds who know that a person can protect oneself from HIV infection by consistent condom use, by sex, %

HIV/AIDS prevalence rate for pregnant women 15-24 attending antenatal care in clinics in capital city

Injecting drug users reporting the use of sterile injecting equipment the last time they injected

Most-at-risk populations reached with HIV prevention programs

Orphaned and vulnerable children aged 0-17 whose households received free basic external support in caring for the child

Orphans (both parents) aged 10-14 school attendance rate as % of non-orphans attendance rate, where HIV is 1%+

Schools that provided life skills-based HIV education in the last academic year

Women and men aged 15-49 who received an HIV test in the last 12 months and who know their results

Young women and men aged 15-24 who both correctly identify ways of preventing the sexual transmission of HIV and who reject major misconceptions about HIV transmission

UNDATA - (http://data.un.org)

% of 15-24 year-olds who have comprehensive knowledge of HIV

Adult HIV/AIDS prevalence rate

People living with HIV/AIDS

World Health Organization (WHO) - Disease Mortality

Deaths among children under five years of age due to HIV/AIDS (%)

Prevalence of HIV among adults aged >=15 years (per 100,000 population)

80. Industry & Services

International Civil Aviation Organization (ICAO) - (www.icao.int)

Civil aviation, kilometers flown, millions

Civil aviation, passenger-kilometers, millions

Civil aviation, passengers carried, thousands

Civil aviation, ton-kilometers, millions

Organization For Economic Co-Operation & Development - (http://stats.oecd.org)

All businesses (SSIS)

80. Industry & Services

Business demography

Construction (by size class)

Electricity, gas & water (by size class)

Employer enterprise birth and death rates

Employer enterprise survival rates

Employment creation and destruction

High growth enterprises and Gazelles

Hotels & restaurants (By Size Class)

Manufacturing (by size class)

Mining and quarrying (By Size Class)

Orders

Production

Production and sales (MEI)

Real estate, renting and business activities (by size class)

Sales

SDBS business demography indicators

SDBS structural business statistics

STAN bilateral trade

STAN bilateral trade ed.2006

STAN database for structural analysis ed2005

STAN database for structural analysis ed2008

STAN indicators database

STAN R&D expenditure in Industry (ISIC Rev. 3) - ANBERD ed2009

Structural analysis (STAN) databases

Structural business statistics

Transport, storage & communications (by size class)

Wholesale and retail trade (by size class)

Work started

Principal Global Indicators - (www.principalglobalindicators.org)

Industrial production

UN Statistics Division (UNSD) - (http://data.un.org)

% employers

% own-account workers

World Bank - (www.worldbank.org)

Domestic credit to private sector (% of GDP)

Electricity production (kWh)

Employment in industry (% of total employment)

Foreign direct investment, net inflows (% of GDP)

Gross fixed capital formation, private sector (% of GDP)

Industry, value added (% of GDP)

Industry, value added (annual % growth)

Industry, value added (current US$)

International tourism, number of arrivals

International tourism, number of departures

80. Industry & Services

International tourism, receipts (current US$)

Passenger cars (per 1,000 people)

Stocks traded, total value (% of GDP)

Vehicles (per 1,000 people)

World Tourism Organization (UNWTO)

Tourism expenditures, international, million US$ (UNWTO/SYB51)

Tourism receipts, international, million US$ (UNWTO/SYB51)

Tourist arrivals by region of origin (UNWTO/SYB51)

81. Intellectual Property

Organization For Economic Co-Operation & Development - (http://stats.oecd.org)

Domestic ownership of inventions made abroad

Foreign ownership of domestic inventions

Patents - total and technology domains

Patents by IPC - section A

Patents by IPC - section B

Patents by IPC - section C

Patents by IPC - section D

Patents by IPC - section E

Patents by IPC - section F

Patents by IPC - section G

Patents by IPC - section H

Patents by regions

Patents by technology

Patents by technology or IPC class

Patents statistics

Patents with foreign co-inventors

World Intellectual Property Organization Statistics Database

Patent applications

Patent grants

Patents in force

82. Labor

International Labor Organization (ILO) - (www.ilo.org)

Consumer price index, food, 2000=100 (ILO)

Consumer price index, general, 2000=100 (ILO)

Cost of employing labour, or labour cost

Demand for labour or vacancies

Economic activity rate by sex, 13 age groups, 1980-2020 (ILO estimates/projections)

Economically active population by sex, 13 age groups (ILO estimates/projections)

Employment by sex and industry branch, ISIC 2 (thousands; ILO)

Employment by sex and industry branch, ISIC 3 (thousands; ILO

82. Labor
Extent and characteristics of Labor social security coverage
Hours of work
Income and expenditures of the households where they live
Income from employment of paid and self employed persons during a particular period as well as the earnings of persons in paid employment;
Industry or branch of economic activity of the establishment where they work
Institutional sector (whether corporation, household, public)
Labor occupational injuries and diseases resulting from exposure to risk factors at work
Labor occupations
Labor participation in strikes and lockouts, union participation, collective bargaining and other social dialogue characteristics
Labor status in employment
Labor training experience (lifelong learning)
Unemployment by sex, rates (%) and # (thousands) (ILO/SYB)
Wages in manufacturing (ISIC 2), by sex, national currency (ILO)
Wages in manufacturing (ISIC 3), by sex, national currency (ILO)
Women wage employment in non-agricultural sector as % of total non-agriculture employees (ILO/MDG)
Youth unemployment rate, aged 15-24, by sex, (ILO estimates/MDG)
Youth unemployment, ratio of youth unemployment rate to adult unemployment rate, by sex (ILO est./MDG)
Youth unemployment, share of youth unemployed to total unemployed, %, by sex (ILO estimates/MDG)
Youth unemployment, share of youth unemployed to youth population, %, by sex (ILO estimates/MDG)

Organization For Economic Co-Operation & Development - (http://stats.oecd.org)
ALFS summary tables
Annual labor force statistics
Average annual hours actually worked per worker
Average duration of unemployment
Average usual weekly hours worked on the main job
Breakdown of GDP per capita in its components
Capital Services
Capital services by type of asset
Decile ratios of gross earnings
Discouraged workers
Earnings
Economic short time workers
Employment
Employment by job tenure intervals - average tenure
Employment by job tenure intervals - persons
Employment by permanency of the job
Employment protection

82. Labor
Employment: total & by industry
Exchange rate Adjusted ULC
FTPT employment based on a common definition
FTPT employment based on national definitions
Full-time part-time employment
Harmonized unemployment rates and Levels (HURs)
Hourly earnings (MEI)
Hours worked
Incidence of discouraged workers
Incidence of economic short time workers
Incidence of employment by usual weekly hours worked
Incidence of FTPT employment - common definition
Incidence of FTPT employment - national definitions
Incidence of involuntary part time workers
Incidence of permanent employment
Incidence of unemployment by duration
Involuntary part time workers
Job tenure
Job vacancies
Labor compensation per employee/hour ($US PPP adjusted)
Labor compensation per unit labor input
Labor costs
Labor force statistics
Labor income Share Ratios
Labor market programs
Labor productivity growth
Labor productivity per unit labor input
Labor productivity total economy
Labor statistics (MEI)
LFS by sex and age
LFS by sex and age - composition
LFS by sex and age - indicators
Minimum relative to average wages of full-time workers
Minimum wages at current prices in NCU
Multi-factor productivity
OECD estimates of labor productivity levels
Permanent temporary employment
Population
Productivity levels and GDP per capita
Public expenditure and participant stocks on LMP
Real hourly minimum wages
Real output & total labor cost
Regional labor Market
Regional labor Market NOG

82. Labor
Registered unemployed and job vacancies (MEI)
Registered unemployment rates and levels
Strictness of employment protection - collective dismissals
Strictness of employment protection – overall
Strictness of employment protection – regular employment
Strictness of employment protection – temporary employment
Survey based unemployment rates and levels
Total labor cost & real Output
Trade union
Trade union density
Unemployment by duration
Union members and employees
Unit labor cost - quarterly indicators (MEI)
Unit labor cost Indices
Unit labor costs
Unit labor costs - annual indicators
Usual hours worked by weekly hour bands

Principal Global Indicators - (www.principalglobalindicators.org)

Unemployment rate

UN Statistics Division (UNSD) - (http://data.un.org)

% employed in agriculture

% employed in industry

% employed in services

% employees

% working less than 20 hrs/week

% working more than 40 hrs/week

Employment-to-population ratio

Labor force participation rate

Part-time employment rate

Ratio of youth unemployment rate to adult unemployment rate

Share of women in wage employment in the non-agricultural sector

Share of youth unemployed in total unemployed

Share of youth unemployed in youth population

Unemployment rate

World Bank - (www.worldbank.org)

Employees, agriculture, female (% of female employment)

Employees, agriculture, male (% of male employment)

Labor force with primary education (% of total)

Labor force, female (% of total labor force)

Labor force, total

Population ages 15-64, total

Unemployment, total (% of total labor force)

World Economic Outlook - (www.imf.org)

Employment

82. Labor

Unemployment rate

83. Pensions

Organization For Economic Co-Operation & Development - (http://stats.oecd.org)

Asset allocation

Assets by type of financing vehicle

Autonomous pension funds' assets as a % of GDP

Benefits paid as a % of GDP

Contributions as a % of GDP

DB pension plans' assets as a % of occupational assets

DB pension plans' assets as a % of total assets

DC pension plans' assets as a % of occupational assets

DC pension plans' assets as a % of total assets

Employees' contributions as a % of total contributions

Employers' contributions as a % of total contributions

Geographical distribution

Net income in millions of USD

Non-OECD pension funds' assets as a % of GDP

Occupational pension funds' assets as a % of GDP

Operating expenses as a % of total assets

Pensions at a Glance 2009

Percent change compared to previous year

Personal pension funds' assets as a % of GDP

Public pension reserve funds' assets

Public pension reserve funds statistics

84. Population & Demography

Economist Intelligence Unit - (http://www.eiu.com)

Labour force

Population

Population (% change pa)

Recorded unemployment (%)

Organization For Economic Co-Operation & Development - (http://stats.oecd.org)

Database on immigrants in OECD countries (DIOC)

Demographic statistics

Demographic statistics NOG

Immigrants by citizenship and age

Immigrants by detailed occupation

Immigrants by duration of stay

Immigrants by field of study

Immigrants by labor force status

Immigrants by occupation

Immigrants by sector

Immigrants by sex and age

84. Population & Demography

International Migration database

Large regions (TL2)

Migration statistics

Non official grids

Regional accounts

Small Regions (TL3)

UN Population Division

% aged 0-14 (%)

% aged 0-4 (%)

% aged 15-24 (%)

% aged 15-59 (%)

% aged 15-64 (%)

% aged 5-14 (%)

% aged 60 or over (%)

% aged 65 or over (%)

% aged 80 or over (%)

% of women aged 15-49 (%)

% rural (%)

% urban (%)

Births per year, both sexes combined (thousands)

Crude birth rate (births per 1,000 population)

Crude death rate (deaths per 1,000 population)

Deaths per year, both sexes combined (thousands)

female deaths per year (thousands)

female infant mortality rate (per 1,000 female births)

female mortality under age 5 (per 1,000 female births)

female population (thousands)

Infant mortality rate (infant deaths per 1,000 live births)

Life expectancy at birth, both sexes combined (years)

Life expectancy at birth, females (years)

Life expectancy at birth, males (years)

male deaths per year (thousands)

male infant mortality rate (per 1,000 male births)

male mortality under age 5 (per 1,000 male births)

male population (thousands)

Median age (years)

Mortality under age 5, both sexes combined (per 1,000 births)

Net migration (per year) , both sexes combined (thousands)

Net migration rate (per 1,000 population)

Net reproduction rate (daughters per woman)

Old-age dependency ratio

Population (thousands)

Population aged 0-14 (thousands)

Population aged 0-4 (thousands)

84. Population & Demography

Population aged 15-24 (thousands)
Population aged 15-59 (thousands)
Population aged 15-64 (thousands)
Population aged 5-14 (thousands)
Population aged 60 or over (thousands)
Population aged 65 or over (thousands)
Population aged 80 or over (thousands)
Population change per year (thousands)
Population density (population per sq. km)
Population growth rate (%)
Population sex ratio (males per 100 females)
sex ratio at birth (per 1,000 population)
Total dependency ratio)
Total fertility (children per woman)
Women aged 15-49 (thousands)

UN Statistics Division (UNSD) - (http://data.un.org)

% contributing family workers
% divorced/separated in age group
% ever married or in union among persons aged 15-19
% of births delivered by caesarean section
% of women aged 15-19 who have given birth
% of women who have not given birth by age 40-44
% widowed in age group
Abortion laws by grounds on which abortion is permitted
Abortion rate
Age-specific fertility rate
Antenatal care coverage for at least four visits
Antenatal care coverage for at least one visit
Births attended by skilled health personnel
Condom use at last high-risk sex
Contraceptive prevalence rate - any method
Contraceptive prevalence rate - modern methods
female/male ratio at age x
female/male ratio at birth
female/male ratio of population
female/male ratio of rural population
female/male ratio of urban population
Minimum legal age for marriage without consent
Population
Population by sex and broad age group
Population projections
Rural population
Singulate mean age at marriage
Total fertility rate

84. Population & Demography

Under-five mortality rate
Urban population
Women's share of labor force
Women's share of legislators and managers
Women's share of parliamentary seats in single or lower chamber
Women's share of parliamentary seats in upper house or senate
Women's share of part-time employment
Women's share of population 15+ yr with HIV/AIDS

UNDATA - (http://data.un.org)

% of population urbanized
Annual # of births
Average annual population growth rate
Average annual rate of reduction of total fertility rate
Birth registration
Population size

World Bank - (www.worldbank.org)

Age dependency ratio (% of working-age population)
Fertility rate, total (births per woman)
Life expectancy at birth, total (years)
Mortality rate, infant (per 1,000 live births)
Population density (people per sq. km)
Population in the largest city (% of urban population)
Population, female
Population, female (% of total)
Population, total
Rural population density (rural population per sq. km of arable land)
Urban population
Urban population (% of total)
Urban population growth (annual %)

World Health Organization (WHO)

Adolescent fertility rate (%)
Adult literacy rate (%)
Population % over 60 (%)
Population % under 15 (%)
Population annual growth rate (%)
Population in urban areas (%)
Population median age (years)
Registration coverage of births (%)
Registration coverage of deaths (%)
Total population (in thousands)

World Resources Institute - (http://earthtrends.wri.org)

Demographic indicators
Population and human well-being

85. Poverty

Organization For Economic Co-Operation & Development - (http://stats.oecd.org)

Income distribution - poverty

Income distribution - poverty - country tables

UN Development Program (UNDP)

Human poverty index - selected OECD countries (HPI-2)

Human poverty index (HPI-1)

World Bank - (www.worldbank.org)

GINI index

Income share held by lowest 10%

Income share held by lowest 20%

Poverty gap at national poverty line (%)

Poverty headcount ratio at national poverty line (% of population)

World Health Organization (WHO)

Gross national income per capita (PPP international $)

Population living below the poverty line (% living on < US$1 per day)

World Resources Institute - (http://earthtrends.wri.org)

Income and poverty

86. Public & Market Regulations

Organization For Economic Co-Operation & Development - (http://stats.oecd.org)

Economy-wide regulation

Market regulation

Product market regulation

Professional services

Regulation impact

Regulation in retail trade

Regulation in seven non-manufacturing sectors

Revenue statistics - comparative tables

Sectoral regulation

Taxation

UN Statistics Division (UNSD) - (http://data.un.org)

Parliamentary seats in single or lower chamber

Parliamentary seats in upper house or senate

World Bank - (www.worldbank.org)

Expense (% of GDP)

External debt stocks, long-term public sector (DOD, current US$)

Revenue, excluding grants (% of GDP)

87. Social & Welfare

Organization For Economic Co-Operation & Development - (http://stats.oecd.org)

Composite indicators

Composite indicators copy

Economic status of women

Education

87. Social & Welfare

ELS Pensions

Family Code

Gender, institutions and development database (GID)

Health and fertility

Income distribution - inequality

Income distribution - inequality - country tables

Literacy rates

Other Social Institutions

Political and economic status of women

Political empowerment

School enrolment

Social expenditure - aggregated data

Social expenditure - reference Series

Social indicators TL2

Social institutions (Data)

Social institutions and gender index (SIGI)

Social protection

Tax/benefits

UN Development Program (UNDP)

Gender empowerment measure (GEM)

Gender-related development index (GDI)

Human development index - trends

Human development index (HDI)

World Bank - (www.worldbank.org)

Improved sanitation facilities, rural (% of rural population with access)

Improved sanitation facilities, urban (% of urban population with access)

Proportion of seats held by women in national parliaments (%)

School enrollment, tertiary (% gross)

School enrollment, tertiary, female (% gross)

88. Telecom. & Research

International Telecommunications Union (ITU) - (www.itu.int)

Cellular mobile telephone subscribers

Cellular mobile telephone subscribers per 100 inhabitants

Internet users

Internet users per 100 population

Personal computers

Personal computers per 100 population

Telephone lines and cellular subscribers

Telephone lines and cellular subscribers per 100 population

Telephone main lines in use

Telephone main lines in use per 100 inhabitants

Organization For Economic Co-Operation & Development - (http://stats.oecd.org)

Indicators of international co-operation

88. Telecom. & Research

Innovation indicators

International co-operation in patents

Telecom 2007 by countries

Telecommunications statistics

UNDATA - (http://data.un.org)

Telephone lines

UNESCO Institute for Statistics - (www.uis.unesco.org)

Research and development researchers, by sex

Research and development technicians and equivalent staff, by sex

World Bank - (www.worldbank.org)

Information and communication technology expenditure (% of GDP)

International voice traffic (minutes per person)

Internet users (per 100 people)

Mobile and fixed-line telephone subscribers (per 100 people)

Mobile cellular subscriptions (per 100 people)

Telephone lines (per 100 people)

89. Trade & Balance of Payment

Economist Intelligence Unit - (http://www.eiu.com)

Change in international reserves

Commercial bank loans

Commercial banks' foreign assets

Commercial banks' foreign liabilities

Commercial banks' net foreign assets

Current transfers: balance

Current transfers: credit

Current transfers: debit

Current-account balance

Export market growth (real, %)

Export prices (US$, 1996=100)

Export prices (% change pa; US$)

Export volume of goods (% change pa)

Export volume of goods (1996=100)

Exports of G&S/imports of G&S

Exports of goods/exports of G&S

Financing requirement

Flow of export credits

Foreign-exchange reserves

Gold, national valuation

Goods: exports fob

Goods: imports fob

IMF credit

Import cover (months)

Import prices (% change pa; US$)